10/
99/

W9-ALL-268

Mukiwa

Peter Godwin

Mukiwa

A White Boy in Africa

Harper Perennial
A Division of HarperCollinsPublishers

968.91
God

First published in Great Britain in 1996 by Picador, an imprint of Macmillan General Books.

This book was originally published in the United States in 1996 by The Atlantic Monthly Press. It is here reprinted by arrangement with Grove/Atlantic, Inc.

MUKIWA: A WHITE BOY IN AFRICA. Copyright © 1996 by Peter Godwin. All rights reserved. Printed in the United States of America. No part of this book may be used or reproduced in any manner whatsoever without written permission except in the case of brief quotations embodied in critical articles and reviews. For information address The Atlantic Monthly Press, 841 Broadway, New York, NY 10003.

HarperCollins books may be purchased for educational, business, or sales promotional use. For information please write: Special Markets Department, HarperCollins Publishers, Inc., 10 East 53rd Street, New York, NY 10022.

First HarperPerennial edition published 1997.

Library of Congress Cataloging-in-Publication Data
Godwin, Peter.
    Mukiwa : a white boy in Africa / Peter Godwin. — 1st Perennial ed.
      p. cm.
    Originally published : New York : Atlantic Monthly Press, 1996.
    ISBN 0-06-097723-X
    1. Godwin, Peter. 2. Zimbabwe—Ethnic relations. 3. Zimbabwe—
History—Chimurenga War, 1966–1980—Personal narratives.
    I. Title.
    DT2984.G6A3 1997
    968.91'04—dc21   96-39341

97 98 99 00 01   RRD   10 9 8 7 6 5 4 3 2 1

For my mother and father, with love

Preface

Mukiwa is intended as a memoir rather than an autobiography. The characters who populate these pages are a mixture of actual people and composites. I have changed many of their names and identifying characteristics, not particularly for legal reasons, but to protect them against possible intrusion. In some cases, especially in the war chapters, I have altered quite a lot – people still risk retribution. But all famous people, politicians and other leaders, are accurately identified.

Although *Mukiwa* is a work of nonfiction it is not a work of forensic research. For that you should read *Rhodesians Never Die* – the history book I wrote (with Ian Hancock) on the end of white Rhodesia. In *Mukiwa* I have written as I remember, with all the foibles and imperfections brought on by the passage of time.

This book was both easy and traumatic to write. There are things here which I had very effectively buried under layers of emotional scar tissue. The process of tearing it away was in some cases pleasurable and in others deeply disturbing. But it was always liberating.

I have tried not to be wise after the event but to describe things as they seemed at the time, even where that may have portrayed us unattractively. I have tried not to preach or to politic. I have tried not to be sentimental or censorious.

Above all the book is intended as a tribute to Africa – the home I never knew I had.

Peter Godwin
London, 1996

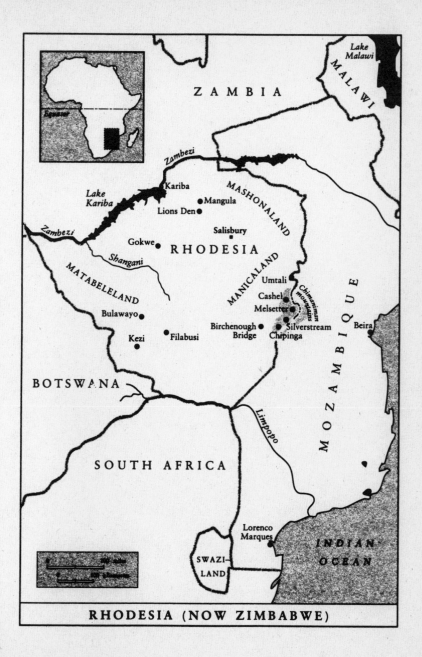

RHODESIA (NOW ZIMBABWE)

Book One

One

I think I first realized something was wrong when our next-door neighbour, oom Piet Oberholzer, was murdered. I must have been about six then. It was still two years before we rebelled against the Queen, and another seven years before the real war would start.

I can remember oom Piet's body lying on the tar road. He was on his back, with the bone handle of a hunting knife sticking out of his chest. Of course I'd seen lots of dead people before, so I wasn't that impressed. In fact I was proud of my familiarity with death. I used to tell other children stories about it, to boost my popularity.

I knew more than other children about dead people because I went with my mother when she dug them up and cut them open. I was allowed to carry her instruments and also to be the Chief Fly Sprayer, which were quite important jobs, especially for a small boy.

My mother was a doctor and she wore a white coat. Although most of the people she operated on were alive, some were dead, and these were the ones I helped with.

Oom Piet was the first body that I'd actually known while it was still alive. In that way it was quite interesting. I didn't know him that well, really. He worked as a shift boss at the factory, and although the Oberholzers lived just down the hill from us, we didn't see much of them. They were a big Afrikaans family with lots of geese and about seven kids who had names like Hennie and Dawie and Hettie.

The Oberholzers were the poorest white people I knew. They had gone bust trying to farm, and the *dominee*, the Dutch Reformed minister, had asked my father to give oom Piet a job, any job. They arrived in Silverstream for the first time in a borrowed pick-up truck. We marvelled at the fact that the whole family and all their possessions could fit into one load. We had taken up a whole Trek Removal's articulated lorry *and* trailer when we arrived.

A year after they arrived in Silverstream, there was great excitement when a bed was delivered by the weekly RMS – the Road Motor Services lorry. Oom Piet told my father proudly that now for the first time everyone in the family would be able to sleep in a bed of their own.

The Oberholzers had an old blue VW Kombi which had the engine at the back instead of the front. They'd been in that old blue Kombi the day oom Piet was murdered.

They were on their way back from a trip to Umtali, oom Piet and his wife and their youngest daughter – when it happened. The reason for their trip wasn't in the newspapers – not the old ones or the new ones – but I know it for a fact. We also went to Umtali that day, and we met them on the way.

'Good morning *meneer* Godwin,' said oom Piet respectfully, to my father.

'Morning OB,' said my father. Only children called him oom Piet. *Oom* was Afrikaans for uncle.

'How was the holiday?' asked my father. They had just returned from their first family holiday ever, and they were still terribly excited.

'Ach it was really *lekker*,' said oom Piet, and he began to describe the holiday in great detail, right down to the meals they had eaten and where they'd filled up with petrol. My father cut him short after day two, or we would never have got to Umtali at all.

'Shopping?' enquired my father, conversationally, to show he wasn't really being rude.

'Ach, not really, *meneer*, we're going to collect our holiday photos from Windsor Studios in town, then we're going to show them to our other kids at school. They've never seen photos of themselves before.'

Mrs Oberholzer proudly held up their cheap plastic instamatic camera.

'It's amazing,' she said in wonder. 'You don't have to focus it or anything. You just point it and press this little red button here. Even I can use it.'

She laughed in a self-deprecating way, and suddenly she lifted the little camera and took a picture of my father and oom Piet leaning against our car. Much later, she sent us that photo, of oom Piet and my father looking startled. Her note said that it was the last picture of oom Piet alive. In spite of the camera manufacturer's boast, the picture is slightly out of focus. When I looked carefully, I could just see myself in the bottom left-hand corner of the photo, peeping through the car window.

The journey from our house at Silverstream to Umtali, which was the capital of the whole of Manicaland, was about a hundred miles long and it took more than three hours because the road was winding and steep in many places. In those days we still had the old white Austin Westminster, the one that Dad reversed over Bingo the dog and killed him when we were setting off to Melsetter church for a wedding. But he hadn't done that yet and Bingo was still alive.

On the day oom Piet was murdered, we also met Sir Hugo on our way to Umtali, where the road goes through his farm just below Skyline Junction. He was burning some fields with his farm boys on the roadside. Sir Hugo Sebright, I was told, was something called an Old Etonian, though he didn't seem that old, even to me. He looked younger than my father and much, much younger than Old Mr Boshof on Lemon Kop. (Jain had trained me to mutter very fast the chant 'You-go-Hugo. You-got-the-shoes-on' whenever we saw Hugo. For some reason we found this hilarious.) Anyway, Sir Hugo was called 'sir' in a different way to Mr Simpson, the headmaster. We kids called Mr Simpson 'sir' on its own. When we talked about him to other people we just called him Mister Simpson. We didn't call him Sir Simpson. And never Sir Jack. It was quite confusing. I fell asleep worrying about it one night, and I decided to ask my father to explain it to me the next morning. But when I woke up I had forgotten all about it.

Anyway, back then, in 1964, Sir Hugo and his wife still lived on their farm in the hills above the Biriwiri valley. Sir Hugo's wife was not an Old Etonian because she was much younger than him. In fact she looked almost the same age as some of my sister's friends, and she had long yellow hair and lots of gold jewellery on her ears and fingers, and her nails were long, and painted red. She was called Lady Sebright. As far as I knew she didn't have a first name.

Sir Hugo leant in at the car window with his signet ring clanking on the glass and he laughed a lot in a snorting sort of way at various things my father was saying. Behind, the gang of farm boys stood resting on their *badzas* and fire beaters, waiting for him to finish. Before we left, he invited us to drop in for sundowners on our way back from Umtali.

It was late afternoon when our Austin finally crunched up the Sebright's gravel drive. I was exhausted from a heady day of traipsing around the clothes racks at Meikles department store with my mother and sister, or following my father through the hardware section, picking out clamps and screws and washers of very particular sizes, all of which he had written down on the back of his Gold Leaf cigarette packet. After a lunchtime treat of a toasted cheese sandwich and Meikles' famous Brown Cow, a drink that consisted of a big blob of vanilla ice cream immersed in a tall glass of Coca-Cola, I had become predictably overexcited and then suddenly deflated.

The Sebright's house wasn't finished yet. It was a big ranch-style place with dark wooden floors and a verandah the length of the front. The garden was still being planted and there was raw red earth everywhere. When we arrived I recognized the Oberholzer's VW Kombi in the drive. They weren't really friends of the Sebrights, but Sir Hugo had bought the farm from them, and I had overheard my parents saying that Sir Hugo still owed some money to oom Piet. Their daughter was asleep in the Kombi so I never saw her.

Soon gin and tonics and whiskies and sodas and sherries and Castle beers were being distributed to the grown ups. Pottery bowls of salted groundnuts still in their dark wine skins and pewter plates of Willards salt 'n' vinegar crisps were handed out. But as I was tired, I collected blair from the car and made for the nearest dog, to have a nap. 'Blair' was a sort of security blanket made of mohair that I insisted on hauling around and was unable to sleep without.

At home my usual manner of going to sleep was to lie by the fire with blair and snuggle up to the dogs. But the Sebright's dog, a skittish Alsatian, became distinctly hostile at the prospect of being used as a pillow by a little boy. I pursued it, trailing my blair, and it grew growly and bared its teeth at me. The less hospitable the dog became, the more fractious and tearful I was until, finally, my mother, having intervened on several occasions, decided it was time to go.

It was a decision that probably saved our lives.

As we swung round the hairpin bends from Tandevel, with the lights of Silverstream twinkling below us at last, a crackling voice began calling us on the radio. We had the radio because my mother was the GMO, the Government Medical Officer, for the whole of the Melsetter district, so she was always on call.

'Blue nine, blue nine, do you read, over?' said the voice on the radio. On the radio they pronounced 'nine' with an 'er' on the end: 'Niner'.

My father stopped the car and fiddled with the knob marked 'squelch' to try and get a better signal. My father knew a lot about radios and even repaired them in his workshop. He unclipped the mike and, pushing down the button, replied: 'This is blue niner, reading you strength three, over.'

Strength three was OK reception, but not great. Strength five was the best, but you usually only got that if you were high up on a hill or very near to the person calling you.

'Blue niner, this is police Melsetter here, police Melsetter. We've had a code five involving serious injury to an EMA. Location two miles west from Skyline Junction on Umtali road at the 95-mile peg. Could you attend soonest? Over.'

Code five was a car accident and EMA was police language for European Male Adult. My father told them how long it would take us to get there. He called it our ETA, our Estimated Time of Arrival. Then he turned the car around and we headed back up the hill, away from the lights of Silverstream. Dad drove faster than usual, not slowing down for nightjars, birds that came out at night and sat in the road because it was warm there. They mostly managed to fly up just before you ran them over, but sometimes they left it too late. We hit a nightjar that night and I went 'urrgh' but no one else said anything. They were all wondering who the EMA would be.

It wasn't far, ten miles perhaps, to the accident, and I was now wide awake with excitement. At Skyline Junction we turned left back down towards Sir Hugo's, and there ahead was a shiny police roadblock sign in the road and, standing next to it, an African constable waving a torch slowly back and forth.

'Ah, Doctor Godwin,' he said in recognition, peering through the window, 'the member-in-charge is expecting you.'

The old blue Kombi wasn't blue anymore. It was mostly a charred blackish colour, and it was parked at an odd angle with its front bumper up against the sheer granite cutting, where the road had been sliced through a hilltop. Across the road was a line of rocks, some of them quite big. They were too high for a car to get over and because of the cutting there was no way round. By the side of the Kombi lay a body with a bloodstained jacket covering its top half. The whole scene was lit up by the headlamps of two police Land Rovers, which gave everything long shadows.

The member-in-charge pulled back the jacket and there was oom Piet. His eyes were open and he looked very surprised. His mouth was also open and there was spit dribbling out of the side of it. His shirt, light blue with little paisley patterns on it, was torn and covered in dark blood and the handle of a knife was sticking out of it. On his feet he wore *veldskoens*, except that one had come off. His sock had a hole and you could see his big toe. It didn't seem real. We had just left oom Piet drinking a Castle lager with froth on the top, picking groundnut skins from his teeth, and now here he was lying on his back in the road with one shoe off.

I made sure I stayed out of the way, standing back from it all, so I wouldn't get sent back to the car. My mother touched the side of oom Piet's neck and nodded to the member-in-charge. They talked for a bit, then she drew oom Piet's eyelids closed and went back to the Austin to collect her things. She returned wearing her white coat and knelt by the body with a clipboard in her hand. I knew this bit well. On the clipboard was a form called a Sudden Death Docket, which had diagrams of the human body, from the front, from the side, from the back. My mother would draw marks with her pen on the diagram to show where the injuries were. Then she would write a COD report. She always had to do this in police cases, where someone had been killed at a beer drink or in a car accident. Only, oom Piet hadn't been killed in a car accident.

Now my mother was pulling the knife out of his chest. She was careful not to wipe any fingerprints off the handle. She passed the knife to the member-in-charge and he measured its blade and put it in a plastic bag. My mother drew a cross on the diagram at the left side of the chest, where the heart was. She wrote down '10 inches'. That was the length of the blade. It was a terrific knife, a proper hunting knife with a knobbly beige handle made of bone and a long curved steel blade which peaked to a crest halfway along and swooped down again to a point. Along the side of the blade, away from the cutting edge, there was a channel gouged out of the steel. This was the blood drain, which was there to help the blade go in and out more easily. I wondered if perhaps I could have the knife after they'd finished with it. But I knew not to ask yet.

The constables lifted the body into the back of a Land Rover and all that was left on the road where it had been was a dark patch, which looked like the oil stain you get where trucks have broken down. Mrs Oberholzer and her littlest daughter, who had also been in the Kombi, had already left. They'd been taken to the nearby Road Camp.

Mrs Oberholzer hadn't yet given a formal statement to the police. She was too upset. But she had told them what happened: the member-in-charge repeated her story to my parents. The Oberholzers had left Sir Hugo's about twenty minutes after us. It was well after dark as they drove up towards Skyline Junction, when they saw the rocks in the road. At first they thought it was a landslide, a common enough event on Manicaland roads. Oom Piet stopped the Kombi and got out to move the rocks, when all of a sudden a group of Africans, who had been hiding by the side of the road, leapt up and attacked him. She thought there were about eight of them. While some struggled with him, others poured petrol on the Kombi and tried to set it on fire.

At the first sign of trouble oom Piet had shouted to his wife to stay in the car and hide their daughter under the seat. So they never really saw the fighting. They heard the Africans shouting and oom Piet swearing at them and sounds of scuffling. The child whimpered under the seat and Mrs Oberholzer told her to hush. She thought they were all going to die. When some of the gang poured petrol on the Kombi, she kept trying to wipe it away before they could light it. Then they started throwing rocks at her. Finally she heard the sound of an engine and saw the beams of headlights sweep across the hillside as a car approached, and the attackers were gone.

I went with my mother to the Road Camp to see Mrs Oberholzer. She was shaking and shivering like a horse trying to get flies off itself. Her thin frock was dirty and torn and she smelt of petrol. She had a nasty gash on her lip and some of her teeth had been knocked out. Her little daughter was whimpering around her legs. Mrs Oberholzer started crying when we came in, and my mother gave her a hug, then examined her cuts and bruises and got her to swallow some tablets.

'I brushed away the petrol, Doctor Helen,' she said, 'and they kept pouring more and trying to light it, you know. And I had to brush it away again.' She made a brushing motion with her arm. 'They wanted to burn us all, you know.' She repeated this over and over like she was mad or something. Finally the ambulance arrived from Chipinga to collect her. My father ordered the African driver out and said he would take his place because it wasn't fair to make him drive back when there might be another ambush.

In those early days before the real war started we didn't call them terrorists yet. We didn't really have a name for them at all. The constables called them *tsotsis*, which in English means 'thugs', I suppose. I had no idea what they were really. I thought they were robbers, African highwaymen perhaps.

The member-in-charge was showing my mother a note, which he'd also put in a plastic bag. Since the body had been moved and the main work was over, I risked edging closer. The note was from the *tsotsis*, and the grown-ups were puzzled by it. No one had heard of anything like it before. I saw it later in the papers, though by then the spelling mistakes had been corrected. The message was written in pencil on a piece of lined paper torn from a school exercise book.

This is the work of the Clocadile Gang, it said. *We will keep on fighting until all white setlars are going and our land is returned. VIVA CHIMURENGA!*

VIVA CHIMURENGA! was heavily underlined.

The member-in-charge shook his head at the note.

'Bunch of bloody ignoramuses, "clocadile" for God's sake. They can't even spell the name of their own gang, and they want to rule the country!'

He shouted over to the huddle of constables. 'Anyone heard of a bunch of *tsotsis* called the "Clocadile Gang"?' He deliberately emphasized the misspelling.

They shook their heads and murmured denials.

None of the Europeans knew what *chimurenga* in the note meant. The member-in-charge turned to his black sergeant.

'What's all this *chimurenga* business, sergeant?'

The sergeant took the note and read it by the light of his torch. He looked uncertain.

'Well, sah, it is the word for the old Shona rebellion in 1896. But I think it can mean any rebellion.' He paused and handed the note back. 'Maybe this is a new rebellion?'

I noticed now that the member-in-charge was also armed. He had a pistol in a blue canvas holster on his belt. The holster flap was fastened with a popper and he kept fiddling with it, opening and closing it, opening and closing. There was much talking on the radio and various police vehicles came and went but it had been decided that it was too dangerous for us to drive home, with the Crocodile Gang still roaming around in the area. We would have to wait for morning.

The African constables had found a rusty 44-gallon drum with holes punctured in its side, left behind by the Roads Department. They built a fire inside it using wood they'd collected in the bush nearby. It was cold now and they stood around the fire watching it crackle and burst into showers of sparks, rubbing their hands together over it and smoking Star cigarettes, cheap non-filters which my father said tasted like camel dung. The wood smoke kept getting in my eyes but it didn't seem to bother them at all. I knew most of them by name, but only their first names, which is what you called them by. Detective Sergeant Solomon was my friend. He was in SB, police for Special Branch, so he didn't have to wear a uniform like the others. Tonight he looked like a giant in a heavy trench coat and a green balaclava helmet pulled down over his head.

Someone had produced a big coil of *boerewors* and Solomon was cooking it on the fire drum. A thermos with sweet tea was being passed round and constables were pouring it into their chipped enamel mugs. When the sausages were ready, I sat with Solomon on the whitewashed wall of the culvert. We ate in silence, waiting for the light. No one slept. My mother kept trying to get me to settle down in the back seat of the Austin but I didn't feel tired any more.

It gets light very quickly in Africa. One minute it's night and then the earth turns a bit more and suddenly it's the morning. And the morning has no memory. This morning was bright and sunny as though nothing had gone wrong the night before.

We heard the sound a long time before we saw anything. A deep throbbing which grew slowly louder. Everyone was scanning the sky and then there they were, two big grey aeroplanes droning along the Biriwiri valley. They were Dakotas. Sometimes they're called DC3s. I knew because I had the Airfix model hanging from my bedroom ceiling. I had all the types of aircraft used by the Royal Rhodesian Air Force: a Hawker Hunter, a Vampire, a Canberra bomber and an Allouette helicopter, which was made in France.

As the planes got closer, the sun's reflection turned their grey fuselages into bright silver and it hurt your eyes to look at them directly. They circled slowly a couple of times and then dozens of soldiers were jumping out, one after the other, in a long line. Soon the sky was filled with white billowing parachutes, each one with a soldier swinging below it. It was a thrilling sight and I watched transfixed. Even Solomon the Special Branch sergeant, who was pretty cool about most things, seemed quite impressed.

The soldiers landed on the slopes below us and we could see them gathering up their parachutes and packing them into their rucksacks. After a few minutes, they fanned out in a long line and set off down the valley to search for the Crocodile Gang.

Willie, the leader of the Crocodile Gang, had been trained in Moscow, the police said, and they didn't seem to be able to find him anywhere. He was an Ndau from our area. His full name was Willie Ndangana, and it turned out that he was the 'blood brother' of Knighty, our cook boy. In those days we called African men 'boys'. We had cook boys and garden boys, however old they might be. African nannies were called girls.

To be 'blood brothers' you both made cuts on your arms or faces and mixed your blood together. After that there was a small ceremony, and then it was as though you were related. (I had become blood brothers with Jeremy Watson who lived at the bottom of the village, even though he was older than me. I still bear the penknife scar today.)

The police phoned my father and warned him that Knighty was related to Willie of the Crocodile Gang. They wanted to arrest Knighty and take him to the police station for questioning, but Dad said no. Knighty had been our cook boy for years and, though he could be quite bad-tempered sometimes, he wasn't a terrorist.

He did get quite cross once when I asked him about his name. I'd just learnt to read and I was questioning him rather pompously about it. I wanted to know if it was spelt Nighty, like the night that follows day, or Nightie, like those my mother and Jain wore to bed, or Knighty, like Knights in armour. I never found out. He just went 'tssk', clicking his tongue against the roof of his mouth, which is one way Ndau people showed you they were annoyed. And he stalked off to the servants' quarters.

He was probably cross because he thought I was making fun

of him, as he couldn't read or write. At the end of each month when Dad paid him he used to sign the wages book, in the column headed 'received', with just a wobbly 'X'.

It is true that Knighty did look very fierce indeed. He had magnificent tribal markings, half a dozen dark purple scars that fanned out like cat's whiskers on either cheek. I greatly coveted his fierce demeanour, and begged to be given tribal scars of my own, but he said I had to wait until I grew up before I could be awarded them.

A few days after the murder, Special Branch came to our house to interview Knighty. It wasn't Detective Sergeant Solomon, but other Special Branch men all the way from Umtali, an African and a European. I wasn't allowed to watch but I asked Knighty about it later. They wanted to know when he had last seen Willie and who his friends were. They questioned him for over an hour. Knighty seemed quite cross about it. He hardly knew Willie, he said. He hadn't really seen much of him since they'd grown up together in Chikakwa, which was part of the Muwushu Native Reserve. Willie had gone to a mission school. Knighty hadn't gone to school.

Willie himself, it emerged, had once worked, under a different name, for my father at one of the Rhodesian Wattle Company estates as a welfare officer. He was known to all the labourers by the *chiLapalapa* title, *lo teacher ka lo football* – the football teacher – because managing the company's soccer team was the welfare officer's main responsibility.

Special Branch had given my father a police 'WANTED' notice offering a reward for Willie. It was published by special gazette, in bold red type. Normally gazettes were in black type, my father explained, but this was an urgent one, sent to all stations and police reserve section leaders. After he had finished with it, he gave it to me. I planned to read it to the servants after supper, but when I practised reading it, the text proved too difficult for me.

Once supper was cleared away, I went round the back of the

house to the Rhodesian boiler, where Knighty and I used to sit on the logs and discuss important matters. It was a big brick fireplace with a 44–gallon drum on a platform above the fire. The fire heated the water in the drum for our baths. You adjusted it by pushing the long wattle logs further in or pulling them back.

The dogs settled down by the warmth and Knighty and Albert and Violet gathered round with their sleeping babies. I showed them the reward notice and they turned it over and studied it intently, and, convinced of its authenticity, handed it back. Then I gave it to Violet, who was the best reader among us. With some difficulty and the occasional stumble, she began to read it aloud by the flicker of the boiler fire.

'At about six-thirty on Saturday, 4th July 1964, at a point nineteen miles from Melsetter, on the Umtali road, Petrus Johannes Andries Oberholzer was murdered, by stoning and stabbing, when attempting to remove a roadblock.

'The undermentioned African is urgently sought by police.'

She held up the photo for all of us to see. It was of a serious-looking black man in a trilby. He was wearing round, wire-framed glasses, a neckerchief and a thick tweed jacket, and he regarded the camera very directly through widely spaced brown eyes.

'William, alias Mutandani, alias Hlebeni (may also use the name of Lovemore), 20910 Chipinga.'

This last was his 'situpa' or identity card number – only Africans had to carry them, we didn't. Then came his description.

'Tribe: Ndau, chief: Musikavanhu, kraal: Mukondo, father: Hlebeni, height: 5ft 7in. to 5ft 9in.; aged twenty-five to twenty-eight years; build: slim to medium: brown complexion; flat nose; broad thick lips; pierced ears and may have small beard. May wear spectacles with ornamental frame on top and open glass at the bottom . . .

'Alleged to have worn the following clothes recently; Grey/

blue trousers; green jersey; white shirt; black leather half-coat, with broken zip fastener; brown pointed suede shoes with five toe protectors on each.'

Then there were some details about his wife, Gladys, and the fact that William had recently returned from Northern Rhodesia, where he had been employed as a carpenter.

'William has a brother,' continued the reward notice, 'African Constable Dumisani, stationed at Salisbury Central, who has been absent without leave since Tuesday, 7th July 1964 . . . He is about twenty-two years of age, height 6ft, weight approximately 190 pounds and may be in possession of a guitar, which he can play.'

Violet handed the reward notice back to me, and we sat in silence for a while, listening to the raucous croaking of the frogs in the stream and the wattle trees rustling in the plantation behind the garden.

'I've never seen a policeman playing a guitar,' I said. 'What kind of tunes would a policeman play?'

No one seemed to know. Albert and Violet got up and he helped her carry her sleeping babies to bed in the servants' quarters at the end of the garden.

Knighty and I stayed while he finished his cigarette. He smoked them right down to the very end, pinching the edge of the paper between the nails of his thumb and forefinger.

'I wonder where Willie is now?' he asked, and blew two streams of smoke out of his nostrils.

'The police think he's run away to Mozambique,' I said.

Knighty flicked his cigarette butt into the boiler and we got up off our logs, pulled them out of the fireplace, and bid one another *a mangwana* – until tomorrow. As we left, the dogs were curling up on the warm ash for the night.

Oom Piet's funeral was held in the Dutch Reformed church in Umtali. My father went ahead to help with the arrangements.

I was allowed to go with him and we gave one of the little Oberholzer boys a lift. Because it was his father's funeral, he was allowed to sit in front, while I was relegated, grumbling, to the back seat. He was about eight and he had been dressed up in a pair of Bata *tackies*, long khaki shorts, a white shirt and a short wide tie, the first time he had worn such a thing. He kept plucking at it until it was all wrinkled and damp. For most of the trip he sat dry-eyed and silent, peering solemnly out of the window just above the sill. On the edge of Chipinga we passed through the bustling African township, with its crowds of blacks waiting in bus queues, shopping at market stalls, and walking along the dusty streets. The Oberholzer boy turned from the window and addressed my father for the first time.

'You know, my uncle shot a *kaffir* once,' he said. 'But it was OK because he had a licence.'

Then he lapsed back into his reverie for the rest of the journey.

In the weeks after the Oberholzer murder they did manage to catch several of the Crocodile Gang. But only the 'locally trained' ones, who were not considered very important. They got one of them the very next day. He had a club foot which dragged along the ground as he walked, making him slow and easy for the soldiers to track. Another one was arrested by the police across the border in Mozambique, and brought back to the Rhodesian side. My father said that the statement had been 'fixed' to give the location of his capture as just on our side of the frontier.

My mother had to go to the High Court in Umtali for the trials of the Crocodile Gang, to give what was called 'sequence of events' evidence, and to tell how oom Piet had been killed, and to show them her Sudden Death Docket. She went on several different occasions and sometimes I went too.

The High Court was just off Main Street, in the centre of the town. It was a large square building with a red tiled roof and green shutters over its tall arched windows. Conveniently, it stood opposite the Cecil Hotel, so European witnesses could sit in the cane chairs on the hotel verandah and have tea until the clerk of court called them over to give evidence.

On my last visit to court, there was a big argument about the age of one of the Crocodile Gang members. My mother explained to me that if he was under eighteen then they couldn't hang him, but if he was over eighteen, they could. Like most Africans he didn't know his exact age, and he didn't have a birth certificate.

His mother, a very thin woman in a long cotton print skirt and a scarf around her head, was called to give evidence. With eyes downcast, she walked slowly up the aisle between the leather-covered benches and climbed up the stairs into the small wooden witness box.

The Indian prosecutor asked her when her son was born.

She spoke quietly in Shona, and the court interpreter translated.

'My son, he is a very good boy. He always sends money home. He never hurt anybody. He—'

'Yes, yes,' interrupted the judge impatiently. 'Will you please confine your remarks to the matter in hand. Just answer the question. When exactly was your son born?'

She apologized and continued.

'Your honour,' the interpreter began. But the woman hadn't called him 'your honour' at all, she had called him *mambo*, which means 'lord' in Shona.

'It was in the year of the bad drought that I gave birth, the year that old Chief Ngorima died. It was also two years after the end of the Gemini rebellion.'

The judge, a white man who was wearing a grey powdered wig and a red robe, looked confused.

'Could you tell the court, what was the Gemini rebellion?' he asked.

'It was the white man's big war overseas,' she replied.

'I believe that when my client says the "Gemini rebellion" she is in fact referring to the Second World War, your honour,' said the defence lawyer, 'the "German" rebellion.'

After the mother there was a schoolteacher, an Assistant District Commissioner, a rural nurse, and more relatives, all giving contradictory stories. His age seemed to vary between fifteen and twenty-three, depending on who you believed.

I looked at the accused. He was sitting in another wooden pen, his hands manacled in front of him. He didn't look particularly worried or frightened, or even that interested. As I looked at him, while the court was trying to decide whether to kill him or not, he began to pick his nose. He did it with great concentration, inserting his left index finger right up to its first joint into his nostril. Because his hands were manacled together, his right hand was also drawn up to his face.

He looked quite young to me – about fifteen. I wondered what it was like to be him.

Some days later the judge decided that there was too much uncertainty about his age to hang him so he was sentenced to life imprisonment instead. But two other gang members were sentenced to death. The Queen of England sent a letter, commanding that they be spared. But by then we were a rebel colony and we didn't listen to the Queen anymore. So they were hanged anyway.

They never caught Willie Ndangana, the ringleader. He came back to the new Zimbabwe as a war hero seventeen years later, after independence brought black rule. Mrs Oberholzer and her children had moved down south long ago. Willie was made Deputy Minister of Para-Military Affairs in the first black government. I remember he wrote an article in the *Herald* newspaper saying that he had been hiding in the culvert that morning when the SAS were searching for him in the Biriwiri valley. The same culvert that Sergeant Solomon and I were sitting on, eating our *boerewors* and drinking sweet tea. The one from which I'd been swinging my legs.

I used to see Willie from time to time, on the TV, cutting the ribbon or pulling the curtain sash at some new government project, or at the opening of parliament. Once I saw him in the flesh. He was sitting in the back of an official black Mercedes which had stopped next to me at a red light on Tongogara Avenue in central Harare.

Whenever I saw him I used to think about the bone handle of the hunting knife sticking out of oom Piet's chest.

Two

Until oom Piet's murder I lived an insular existence at home in Silverstream. My parents both disappeared early each morning, my mother on her rounds of African clinics and small rural hospitals, my father to oversee the factory or travel around the extensive estates, which were a hundred miles long from end to end. They were both fairly remote figures to me. My father was tall and barrel-chested and he had a great walrus moustache. Behind his back, the boys called him *mandebvu*, which means 'beard' in Shona. Sometimes they called me *piccanini mandevu* because I was his son. They seemed to like my father because he was fair and because he seldom shouted, unlike other bosses, who often did. He had tortoiseshell glasses and above them his dark hair was brushed straight back off his forehead. He tried secretly to flatten it with hair cream, which I found in the bathroom cabinet.

My father always wore a safari jacket with matching shorts, long socks and *veldskoens*. He had a farmer's tan: a sunburnt face and a ruddy V down to the collar of his safari suit, brown forearms and brown legs from the bottom of his shorts to the tops of his socks. In between his skin was milky and it reminded me of the plants we kept in the dark at school as an experiment to show how they needed sunlight to grow.

My father was very particular about his safari jackets and they were specially made by a tailor in Umtali to a design that my father drew up on the back of his cigarette packet. The important things were the breast pockets, which had to be subdivided exactly to take a packet of Gold Leafs, a slide rule, a small diary-cum-notebook, two biros and a revolving pencil with 2HB lead in it. It always had to be 2HB lead. Sometimes, before he left for work in the morning I was allowed to load his pockets. I imagined I was arming a fighter plane with its complement of missiles.

My mother had long red hair, so long she could sit on it. Every night after her bath she sat at her dressing table and brushed it with vigorous strokes of her bristle brush until it crackled with static electricity. Then she rubbed cold cream into her pale face. In the morning, after tea, she hid her hair. She would coil it into a tight bun, pack it under a web of hairnet and stab a clutch of French hairpins into it. Then she would put on her 'sensible' shoes and her white coat and be gone.

My days were filled with dogs and servants. There was, of course, Knighty the cook boy, and my nanny, Violet, who became his second, junior, wife. And there was the garden boy, Albert, who came from Mozambique. I don't know any of their surnames. In those days Africans didn't have surnames to us. We knew them just by their Christian names, which were often fairly strange.

Older Africans, whose parents couldn't speak English, tended to have an arbitrary English word as a name. They believed that having a name in the white man's language would attract the white man's power. So they were called by any English word their parents had chanced across: words like Tickie, or Sixpence, Cigarette or Matches were commonly used as names. The next generation of Africans, who were the target of Christian missionaries, tended to have Old Testament names; Jeremiah and Ezekiel, Isaiah and Zephaniah. Baby girls were often called after the emotion felt by the mother at birth – Joy, Happiness, Delight. But, as far as I know, there were no girls called Disappointment, Pain or Exhaustion. Finally Africans began taking ordinary names popular with European settlers. Usually they would retain an African name as well, which only they knew, but after the civil war, the new *chimurenga*, it became fashionable to revert to their African names.

Names were often corrupted by semi-literate District Assistants at the Department of Native Affairs, where births were supposed to be registered. My mother had a medical orderly called Cloud, who should have been Claude but for the slip of a clerk's pen. And on Violet's documents she was called 'Vylit'.

My mother told me later that having Violet all to myself had the same effect as giving a teenager his own car: mobility. We roamed around the countryside at will, going to tea parties with her friends, helping with the harvest, wandering around the market. Violet wore a maid's uniform – a floral dress with a small white apron over it and a little starched nurse-type hat pinned to her tightly plaited hair. As a baby I was strapped on to her wide back, in the pouch of a thin grey blanket, African-style. I can still remember the smell of her. It was a comforting musky smell, a mixture of wood smoke and Lifebuoy soap. She continued to carry me in this way, like a reverse marsupial, on longer journeys to the store or the compound, until I was four or five.

One day Violet became an Apostolic, which was what they called members of the Apostolic Church of Africa. Apostolics were prized as good workers because they didn't drink alcohol. So were Malawians, mind you, because they were migrants who sent most of their money home and didn't waste it on beer, gambling and women. You couldn't really tell if women were Apostolics, there was no outward sign, so my parents didn't know that Violet had joined their ranks. But you could usually tell if men were Apostolics. They shaved their heads and grew long beards, and strolled about with long wooden staves.

Of course, *I* knew as soon as Violet was converted. One Sunday morning she strapped me to her back and walked down the hill, past the factory and the store, turning off the main road and on to a path which skirted around the bottom of the African compound. We crossed the Silverstream river along a log laid from bank to bank. The river, despite its diminutive name, was a full-bodied watercourse and it roiled over rapids beneath us. We paused at the bank for Violet to take her shoes off and make a vigorous sign of the cross, and then she launched us along the log at a brisk teetering walk, her arms outstretched for balance, like a tightrope walker. The trick was not to look down and not to stop mid-stream. It also helped if I sat steady and didn't suddenly crane over one side of the blanket sling to goggle at the river below. Once we were safely on the other side, Violet made another sign of the cross, put her shoes back on and there in a clearing ahead was the Apostolics' meeting place.

We all sat round in a big circle, and in the middle stood a man with a bald head and a long beard. He had a stick with a cross on top of it and he read in Shona from a battered copy of the Old Testament. After each sentence he would pause, and we all shouted out *ehe!* and *ndizvozvo!*, which mean 'yes', and 'it is so'. Then another elder began pounding a tom-tom and we all sang a hymn.

Finally, we all danced around in a circle to the pounding of the drum. I would be jogged up and down on Violet's back, which was a real treat and was known as 'duncing'. Then, sweaty from our exertions, we tackled the river crossing again, and trudged back up the hill, home in time for lunch. This became our regular Sunday outing.

Over the next few years, we Apostolics became more established and more numerous. We built a huge hut the traditional way. Working only on Sundays – we could break the Sabbath because this was Jehovah's business – we nevertheless managed to complete the project in less than two months.

First we cleared a large circle, digging up the ground with *badzas* – traditional hoes. Then we dug a two-foot trench around it. In the trench we planted a circular wall of vertical wattle logs, off-cuts which had been donated by the factory. These we pounded into place, packing the spaces between them with mud. Next, and most tricky, we constructed a large conical frame out of thinner logs and latticed it with a web of saplings, bound together with bark. On one memorable Sunday we hoisted the roof frame on to the walls and lashed it into place.

Meanwhile we had been scything tall elephant grass on the hillside and laying it out to dry in the sun. Even I had been equipped with a small blunt sickle, and my sheaves, though rather puny, were received by the chief thatcher with appreciative formality. We tied the grass into bundles and the thatching began, the bundles being placed in layers from the bottom up. The hut was finally taking shape and it looked magnificent, quite the biggest hut anyone had ever seen.

When the thatching was complete, the congregation were required to bring grass panniers full of fresh cowpats for the floor. As we didn't have a cow, we brought a basket of donkey pats instead and it went in with the rest. The pats were mixed with soil and water to produce a cement-like substance, which was smeared thickly on the ground. It dried to make a floor that was as hard as terracotta.

Now that we had a real church, it was decided that we ought to have proper uniforms. An elder, who in ordinary life was Isaac the chief herd boy on Erasmus estate, had been to Umtali recently and reported that the Apostolics there were wearing a distinctive uniform which they called *gammonts*. The garment consisted of a floor-length red robe with a short, square-necked white smock over it, rather like an altar boy's uniform. The elder had one made up and everyone gathered round after the service to admire it, fingering the hems and pleats and generally examining its construction. Soon all the men had them. The women began to wear long loose red dresses with white collars, and red *dhukus* bound around their heads.

Violet acquired the regulation dress too, although she kept

it rolled up in a plastic carrier bag until we got close to the church hut, and only changed into it behind a boulder near the river. After the service, she changed back into her maid's uniform again. For some reason she had decided that my parents would disapprove of the Apostolics.

'You must not tell the madam or *baas* where we go on Sunday mornings. You understand?'

I must have looked uncertain. She knelt down, held me by the arms and looked me in the eyes.

'It will be our little secret. Between you and me. No one else.'

I loved secrets and readily agreed.

After several more weeks, however, I began to pine for my own *gammont*. I didn't like being left out of the clandestine clothes change at the riverside each Sunday. When I asked Violet if I could have a uniform too, she looked appalled.

Only adults had *gammonts*, she pointed out, and anyway how would we hide it? Disappointed as I was, I reluctantly accepted her objections.

Two Sundays passed. Then the following Monday Violet marched me down to the store just as it should have been closing for the lunch hour.

The store was a cavern of delights. When you entered it from the brightness outside, you could see nothing at first until your eyes adjusted to its gloomy interior. Then, slowly, you could make out the bolts of bright cloth in racks along the wall, and below them rows of tins, cheap canvas shoes, enamel plates and bowls, bars of blue washing soap, bottles of cooking oil. From the ceiling hung bicycle wheels and inner tubes, agricultural implements and kettles and cooking pots. In the back room were big bags of *mealie* meal and flour, sugar and milk powder.

A paraffin fridge bulged with Penny Cools and Lyons Maid ice creams, bottles of Coca-Cola and cream soda. Stuck on the lid was a handwritten notice which said: *Decide what you want*

27

FIRST and then open the fridge LATER. By Order. But no one paid any attention and we would spend hours scrabbling inside it for particular flavours.

On top of the wooden counter was a glass cabinet of sweets: multicoloured jujubes, jelly beans, bulbuls, gobstoppers, little men made of banana-flavoured nougat. Best of all were the sweetie cigarettes – solid white tubes of candy with fiery red tips which came in a mini cigarette packet. I was a four-a-day man.

Joseph the storekeeper let me take as long as I wanted to make up my mind. He went on serving, doing a steady trade in single Star cigarettes and half-loaves of bread. His customers would unknot their handkerchiefs and carefully count out the right coins, which Joseph would ring up on his enormous till, with a balletic flourish.

On the wall behind him was a huge poster of two beaming black women. The message beneath them read: *Ambi skin-lightening cream – for a more beautiful complexion. The one for YOU.* The women in the poster had light caramel faces and were surrounded by admiring African men in tuxedos.

Today Violet bustled me in just as the security doors were closed behind us by MaGlass the tailor, who was usually stationed in the far corner behind an ancient treadle sewing machine. He was known by all as MaGlass because he was one of the very few Africans who wore spectacles. When MaGlass the tailor climbed up his ladder and retrieved two bales of cloth, one white and one red, I guessed what was happening. He brought his tape measure and measured my neck and waist, arm and leg. Each time he moved one of my limbs to measure it, I kept it in place as still as a pipe cleaner. Then he measured out two lengths of cloth on the metal yardstick that was screwed down to the counter, and cut them off the bales.

MaGlass the tailor made some calculations on a piece of paper.

'The cost is nine shillings and sixpence. Six shillings for material, three and six for labour,' he announced.

It hadn't occurred to me that it would cost money. I only had a shilling, which I brought out of my pocket and put tentatively on the counter, but Violet was already counting coins out of her handkerchief. I offered her my shilling.

'No, it doesn't matter. Better you spend on sweeties, I think,' she said and handed it back.

'You come back in two days for fitting,' said MaGlass the tailor.

I could barely contain my excitement.

After one fitting it was ready, a particularly fine *gammont* which MaGlass had embellished with some irregular embroidery around the square neck of the white smock and my name – 'Master Peter' – sewn across the chest.

In time we all had *gammonts* except the growing parade of rookies, who would usually get kitted out within a few weeks of joining. Our success rate was pretty good with these new recruits – the religious cocktail we had concocted was almost irresistible. It was a combination of traditional African animism and selected morsels of Christianity, mostly from the Old Testament.

Isaac the dip boy, who had become the chief elder, was more of a master of ceremonies than a pastor, and he had a natural flair for showmanship. He kept the conventional Bible readings short, and we soon got on to the drumming and dancing.

The drummers positioned themselves around the edge of the great hut – we all had drums, traditional ones made of a hollowed-out log with cowhide stretched over the top and secured with wooden pegs. The biggest were enormous bass drums which were so tall they had to be beaten from a standing position. I had a little canto tom-tom that I beat while sitting cross-legged. Sometimes there were as many as a hundred drums going. It was said that you could hear the beat from the lookout tower on Spitzkop Mountain, which was a good five miles away.

As the rhythm slowly increased, the dancing would grow

more frenetic. Exhausted dancers dropped out to be replaced by new ones, in an ongoing relay. It kept on going, faster and faster, until one of the dancers issued a piercing howl. The drums would stop, and the dancers pulled back to the edge. The one who had howled would usually fall to the floor, writhing and kicking and often frothing at the mouth. He was in the process of becoming possessed by a spirit.

Once possessed, he would quieten down into a trance, eyes unfocused, body limp. He would begin speaking in a voice that was not his own, a voice that really had changed completely. Sometimes he would speak in comprehensible Shona, sometimes in tongues, which only the elders could translate.

The talk would be either in the form of a narrative – usually an obscure Old Testament episode – or in the form of a sermon, urging the congregation to observe certain rules of living. Question and answer sessions occasionally took place, although I noticed that these were usually done during a speaking in tongues, with an elder as interlocutor.

The person in the trance had in effect become a spirit medium, a key player in ancient African animism. The medium was no longer himself, he was now a conduit, usually for a character from the Bible, a prophet, or an apostle – though never Christ himself. Or he became the spirit of a departed ancestor, dispensing wisdom and advice from beyond the great divide.

It was heady stuff.

Spirits could speak through anyone – men, women, even children. I once saw a young girl of eleven or twelve who normally spoke in a high piping voice become possessed and address us in a rich baritone. She held forth in the most detailed way about a smouldering land dispute between two local tribes, going back to its origins in the late eighteenth century. Her discourse was sprinkled with archaic *chiNdau* phrases long passed out of common usage.

One Sunday, when I was a bit older, a most disturbing thing

happened. I had been drumming for half an hour and got up to have a dance. By then we used to dance around a central pole, kicking our feet high and pounding them down in unison on to the baked manure floor so the whole hut shook and the thatch quivered above us. In the middle, next to the pole, was a small fire as it was a bitterly cold winter's morning, the valley outside still contoured in thick *guti*, a drizzly mist. The tempo had become frenetic, and despite the chill we were all lathered in sweat.

The last thing I remember was staring into the flames of the fire and feeling myself slowly being drawn into them.

When I came to, I was lying down by the wall, my head in Violet's lap. She was wiping my forehead with her handkerchief. I felt exhausted, drugged with sleep. My *gammont* was completely sodden, as though I had fallen into the river. Violet was making little comforting noises as she dabbed at my head with her hanky. And she was crying too. Behind her, Isaac the chief elder and other prominent Apostolics were murmuring anxiously to one another.

No one would tell me what had happened. I thought I'd just fainted, but Violet eventually told me I'd been possessed, that I'd talked – in Shona – for about ten minutes. But she wouldn't say who I had become or what I said. No matter how I pleaded and threatened and cajoled, she absolutely refused to elaborate. I had never seen her so stubborn.

I didn't go back to the Apostolics' hut after that. I suddenly felt scared. My *gammont* was left hanging in the back of my wardrobe until my mother discovered it one day, years later, and threw it out.

Whenever I met my old fellow Apostolics on the road or in the plantations, they treated me with a new formality, using the cupped-hand greeting and averting their eyes to avoid meeting mine.

In the years that followed my defection, the Apostolics grew to become one of the biggest churches in southern Africa. They began calling themselves the Zion Christian Church and took to wearing little green ribbons pinned to their chests. Later I saw these had been formalized into tin ZCC badges with a green backing. In the cities and towns at least, they have a more conventional, evangelical approach now. But in the more remote areas, where traditional culture is strongest, Isaac the dip boy or his spiritual successors are still practising their old rites, and remaining in close contact with the wise ones – the ancestors.

Violet's conversion to the Apostolics was not shared by Knighty. He despised them because they didn't drink beer.

Beer loomed large in Knighty's life. Not the Castle or Lion lager in bottles that the whites drank. Nor Chibuku or Rufaro, the thin porridgy African beer made of millet and produced commercially in waxed cartons. Knighty preferred to brew up his own beer. He made it in a 44-gallon drum hidden in the bush at the back of the garden. First he emptied a bag of ground millet into the drum and added some water – rainwater was best. A packet of yeast was sprinkled in. Then, as the mixture slowly fermented, he added various other ingredients to pep it up. Herbs and flowers, cream of tartar seeds from the baobab trees.

Sometimes Knighty used other, less conventional, ingredients. An old car battery gave the beer a delightfully pungent edge, he said. Small rodents were good for body. And he would gratefully receive any snakes that we killed around the garden – boomslangs and green mambas were particularly prevalent.

Knighty had a reputation down in the compound as a master brewer of the old traditional school, and serious drinkers would send their wives up for supplies whenever word reached them that another drum of his special brew had reached maturity. Knighty would ladle the beer out of the vast grimy drum into their large black cooking pots. They would hand over a few coins, or some cobs of maize or heads of cabbage in exchange. Then he would help to hoist the full pots on to the coiled cloth skull pads on their heads, and they would stroll back down to the compound to their thirsty husbands.

Apparently Knighty's brew was staggeringly potent, twice as strong as Chibuku they said. This more than made up for the fact that sometimes it made drinkers violently ill.

Knighty and Violet lived together in one half of the servants' quarters. They called it their *kaya*, which means house. Their *musha*, their real home, was still in the reserve. The other half of the *kaya* was occupied by Albert the Mozambican.

Albert came from a kraal just across the border, about four days' walk, and walking was the only way to get there. He was bald on his head but had a small untidy beard which grew in clumps on his chin and always had grass seeds in it. Albert wore long baggy shorts and his ragged khaki shirt always hung down on the outside. He had bandy legs and bare feet which were as wide as dinner plates and crispy with calluses. He usually chewed a piece of wood and he walked with long strides so I had to jog alongside to keep up with him.

Albert's main job was to do the gardening, which took a lot of energy as the garden was about five acres, although part of that was a paddock for donkeys. It also included a big vegetable garden in which he grew all the vegetables we ate. When my father had a small cement swimming pool built, Albert's responsibilities were extended to keeping that clean too, although this task completely defeated him and the pool eventually became one of the most fecund frog-breeding locations in the whole province. Long slimy strings of frog spawn trailed around your arms and legs whenever you swam in it.

Because Albert's second language was in fact Portuguese, his English was worse than either Violet's or Knighty's, so I ended up learning most of my Shona from him. The language he actually spoke was called *chiNdau*, a dialect of Shona used by the Ndau people who lived in Gazaland, along the eastern border with Mozambique and inside Mozambique itself.

Not many Europeans could speak *chiNdau*, or any of the Shona dialects for that matter. Some priests could, and a few District Commissioners. The rest of the Europeans spoke to Africans in English, talking very loudly and slowly, usually in an African accent. Or they used a bastard language called *kitchen kaffir*, which was supposed to be called *chiLapalapa*.

Kitchen kaffir wasn't really anyone's own language; it was a hybrid, a mixture of English, Afrikaans and Zulu. My father told me it had been invented in the mines so that the white shift bosses could communicate with the various tribes who worked underground. He said that the verbs were Zulu and the nouns were English and the swearwords were Afrikaans.

Albert also taught me how to swear in *chiNdau*. He didn't particularly want to, but I kept pestering him until he agreed. Not even priests or District Commissioners knew how to swear in *chiNdau*. *Mboro* meant cock, *machende* meant balls and *meche* was the word for a fanny. If I got into fights with kids down at the compound I could reel off a string of *chiNdau* swear words that had the adults whooping with astonishment.

One of Albert's lasting memorials was the tree house. It was an ambitious construction at the back of the house, overlooking the red dirt road that led down to the Viljoen's house and on to the Mozambique border. Albert did most of the building, with me as his constant helper.

Knighty the cook boy initially greeted the whole idea with great derision. But as it took shape his scorn was overcome and he became an enthusiastic supporter. He began chipping in with all sorts of ever more extravagant ideas. While Albert and I were up there actually lashing poles together and hammering six-inch nails, Knighty would sit cross-legged at the base of the trunk in his grubby white apron and long white shorts and bare feet, smoking roll-ups, and bossing us around.

Finally he became so enamoured of the project he had

originally insisted would never stay up that he transferred various kitchen activities to his station below the tree. He sat mixing unspecified liquids and beating eggs and sprinkling liberal pinches of seasoning into his bowl, and at intervals shouted up completely unhelpful advice and unworkable ideas with great confidence.

'You put double storey?' he suggested. 'How about we make fireplace?'

Albert and I would exchange a secret look, I would roll my eyes to the sky and Albert would shake his head and we would continue hammering and binding just as before. And Knighty would continue contentedly mixing his potions.

Knighty was, in most regards, an ineffably bad cook. He had only about eight dishes and all these he cooked dismally. Meat rissoles and macaroni cheese used to come around with relentless monotony several times a week. The macaroni was invariably glazed with a cinder crust. The rissoles were always burnt underneath and raw in the middle. But he did have a terrible old wood stove to work with, which had only one temperature and smoked so badly he had to make running forays to move the pans or stir the pots, and retreat coughing and gasping and cursing.

You could adjust the temperature of the stove by the size and type of logs. So from his great log store under the eaves, Knighty would select big or little, split or whole, dry or wet, depending on the recipe. He made a great show of this process but in truth it had little effect on the success of his cooking.

But Knighty did have a couple of real winners that had me growing up believing he was *the* cordon bleu chef of Africa. His home-baked bread was superb. Not content with anything so boring as conventional loaf shapes, Knighty turned first to the farmyard for inspiration. His speciality was 'The Pig'. The central loaf was in the shape of a sow, and along its sides were suckling piglets which could be neatly broken off and eaten as rolls.

Later he went to the wild for his ideas; his final triumph, more of a dough sculpture than a mere loaf, was a crocodile whose scaly back could be dismantled as tiny bread bobbles.

If it was someone's birthday or school holidays had just begun, Knighty would fashion a name on the back of the central animal loaf. As he couldn't read or write, these heroic messages were crafted as ideograms under remote instruction from Violet, who only had standard four herself. They were often massively misspelt, not that anyone cared about that.

Knighty's other culinary masterpiece was the potato bomb, one of the most exciting eating experiences of all time. From the outside it looked like a conventional mound of mashed potato (although inevitably it was littered with little hard bits) but inside was the gravy. I was always allowed to be first in, and the excitement was never knowing quite how far inside the gravy started. Because of the way that Knighty packed down the mashed potato mound, the gravy was stored under pressure and if you weren't extremely careful it could literally burst, splashing hot gravy all over the place to everyone's great amusement.

It became a game between Knighty and me; he would constantly change his construction of the bomb, with dummy compartments and off-centre gravy cores to confuse me.

When the tree house was finally completed, Knighty took to sleeping up there at night, to get relief from the summer heat, or when he had been having words with Violet or the baby's crying got on his nerves. He was often joined by the dogs, who, curious to find out why he was spending so much time up there, eventually managed to climb up the tree. Soon it became a favourite haunt of theirs too, and their habitual sleeping place – a tree kennel. They continued to patronize it long after I'd lost interest and had turned instead to digging an underground bunker.

Three

Our dogs were known as the 'rat pack' and they hunted very effectively in a pack even though they were only terrier-sized. Their talent for scrambling up trees was obviously a great asset when pursuing tree-borne quarry. The father of the clan, Toby, came from the SPCA dogs home in Salisbury. He had the same colouring as the dog on the Toby mug and was a high-spirited animal with an insatiable desire for chasing motorbikes. Unfortunately for Toby, he frequently caught them, and so he was usually afflicted with some burn or other injury. Eventually he lost one of his hind legs to a Honda 125, but he was soon up and about as a tripod. He continued to chase motorbikes, but his resultant loss of speed meant that he seldom caught them after that.

The reputation of the rat pack grew as their hunting prowess improved. They were small but they were many, and they marshalled themselves very effectively. They caught hares and guinea fowl, francolin and mongooses; they even managed to bring down duikers, and young bushbuck. Once they caught an armadillo. It rolled up in an armoured ball and they stayed at it. We heard the hysterical barking from the house and went to investigate.

Ordinary ant bears were rare enough sights, being nocturnal. Their holes, though, were everywhere, with new ones constantly popping up overnight in earth roads and causing broken ankles and broken axles. But their armoured cousin, the armadillo, was even rarer.

I scolded the dogs and chased them away from the rolled-up armadillo so that they knew it was on the prohibited list. Then I scrounged various scraps of food from Knighty to see if I could entice it out of its scales. It finally broke cover at the smell of cabbage. The tip of its long thin nose peeped out, then its dark little eyes darted around and its tongue flicked out to grab the cabbage leaf.

I used to go every day after that with food, always at the same time, and it was always there, waiting for me. It got so bold that as soon as it saw me it would scurry up and snuffle at my leg, making curious little grunting sounds. We even gave it a name, Arnold the Armadillo.

One morning Arnold was no longer there, and I assumed he had moved on to new foraging grounds, as he was bound to do eventually. That afternoon I was up in the tree house with Knighty when a procession of African workers came walking along the road beneath us from the direction of Erasmus estate. They were obviously in very high spirits, singing and laughing. When they got close we saw that they had a dead armadillo slung under a pole carried between two of the men's shoulders. Its legs were tied to the pole and its head lolled underneath. I stopped them to ask where they had found it.

'*Lapa* side,' said one of the men, indicating my armadillo meeting place. 'It was very strange, it came straight up to us without being afraid, and it even tried to bite me, pushing its head on my trousers,' he explained. 'So we killed it. I hit it on the head with *knobkerrie*. One time! Pow!" He swung his *knobkerrie* around in a pantomime of his victorious hunt.

I burst into tears.

'Why?' I screamed down at him. 'Why did you kill him? You can't even eat the meat!'

They were surprised by my anger, but Knighty explained to them that it was my pet.

The *knobkerrie* warrior looked crestfallen.

'I am very sorry, little *baas*, we didn't know it belonged to you. We thought it was a wild one.'

Then they continued on their way, the dead armadillo still swinging on its pole. After they were out of sight, I heard the singing and the laughing start up again.

'They're not sorry at all,' I said bitterly. 'Bastards.'

'You mustn't be cross, *baas* Peter,' said Knighty. 'They killed it because that one brings very good luck, it is very hard to find. If you find one you take it to the witch doctor and you will have good fortune.'

Later my mother was quite sympathetic and even made an unrealistic threat to get action taken because she thought the armadillo might be royal game.

My father sat in his armchair reading a week-old *Rhodesia Herald*.

'It's your own fault for interfering with nature. If you hadn't tried to tame it as a pet, it would never have lost its fear of man and it wouldn't have run up to them like that.'

I hotly denied this. But underneath I knew what he said was true and I was devastated. Arnold had died because of me. I cried myself to sleep that night.

A few weeks later, flicking through an animal book, I saw a picture of an armadillo. Only it wasn't an armadillo, it was a scaly anteater. According to the book, armadillos were native to South America, only scaly anteaters were found in Africa. I hadn't even known Arnold's real species.

Sometimes the dogs' hunting expeditions took several days and ranged deep into the wattle plantations or far across the border. They would come back dusty, covered in blackjacks and brambles and small cuts, their paw pads and snouts raw. But they clearly enjoyed it and it was impossible to stop them.

One day Toby failed to come back from a hunt. The others

trickled in one by one, looking rather confused and ashamed, but no Toby. My parents weren't really that worried. He used to go missing for days at a time, but always turned up in the end. My father said he'd put the word out to all the estates to keep a lookout for Toby.

Violet, meanwhile, was making her own enquires in the compound. Finally she returned to me with some news. Toby, she'd been reliably informed, had been taken by a local witch doctor who was holding him captive on a nearby hill and offering his services as a stud for sixpence a time to anyone with a breeding bitch. According to Violet, Toby's genes were much in demand because of his reputation as a tenacious hunter.

Apparently the witch doctor was doing brisk business.

Violet's informant was very nervous and wouldn't disclose the whereabouts of the witch doctor. Violet was reluctant to get the grown-ups involved. It was generally better not to where witchcraft was concerned. They didn't really understand.

Her informant had agreed to convey a note to the witch doctor.

I got out my new set of Neo-Magics, a rainbow array of broad felt-tipped pens. They were a recent birthday present, made in South Africa, and only to be used for the most important art work. Having illicitly torn a large sheet of paper from my sister's art sketchbook, I set about writing my first threatening letter.

I could speak Shona but I couldn't write it. Violet couldn't either so we decided to write the letter in English. The witch doctor could get an assistant to translate if necessary.

The next problem was how to address him. What was the correct mode of address for a witch doctor? In Shona he was called a *nganga*, but I didn't know how to write that. We could just call him 'Mr Witch Doctor'. But then I got to thinking about the phrase. A witch was usually a woman, wasn't it, and this one was definitely a man.

I phoned my father at the office to ask him what a male

witch was called. He was in the middle of a meeting, but Winfield the weighbridge clerk put me through anyway.

'It's a wizard, of course,' my father replied. 'Now, I'm very busy. I'll talk to you later,' and he hung up.

Choosing a suitably serious black Neo-Magic from the rainbow array, I wrote in capital letters:

DEAR MR WIZARD.

Then we decided to change to red, because red was the colour that made you stop at the traffic light in Umtali's Main Street:

WE KNOW YOU HAVE TAKEN OUR DOG.

I took up the dark blue and continued:

HIS NAME IS TOBY. HE IS NOT YOUR DOG. HE BELONGS TO US.

I wasn't sure what to say next.

'You mustn't be too cheeky to a witch doctor,' warned Violet, 'especially a bad one. Or he might put a spell on you.'

I didn't really believe in all that stuff, and besides, we had to scare him a bit to get Toby back. With a purple Neo, I wrote:

UNLESS YOU RETURN TOBY TO US IN ONE DAY WE WILL TELL THE POLICE IN MELSETTER TO COME AND ARREST YOU AND LOCK YOU IN PRISIN.

I read it back. There was something lacking. So I added ominously, in bright orange:

WE KNOW WHERE YOU ARE.

'If we know where he is, we would go there ourselves,' Violet pointed out. She was right. It was an obvious bluff. I got out the black and crossed out the last line. But no matter how many times I crossed it out, in strokes that went up and down, from side to side and round and round, the neon orange lettering still showed clearly through. There was nothing I could do. So I gave up and finished in green:

FROM THE GODWINS.

I folded the letter and put it in a large white envelope that had been used to send my mother an advertisement for a new contraceptive pill. It still had the logo on the back. '*GYNO-VLAR* – puts *you* in control.'

I crossed out my mother's name and our address and I wrote instead:

TO THE WIZARD, and underlined it.

Then, to make sure there could be no confusion with any other witch doctor, I added in brackets:

(*WHO HAS STOLEN TOBY THE DOG*).

Violet took the letter and passed it on to her informant. Then we waited.

Nothing happened for two days, then on the afternoon of the third I spotted Toby trotting up our avenue of pines. He hopped nimbly over the cattle grid into our garden. He looked in good condition, but clearly exhausted and a bit embarrassed. Suspiciously, he was not at all hungry. He took a few tentative laps at a bowl of water I set down for him, and then curled up and immediately fell into a deep twitching sleep, in which he was clearly dreaming of recent triumphs, whether of the hunt or of the *nganga*'s canine boudoir I did not know.

In the coming months we spotted dozens of puppies bearing Toby markings – black and tan with a small white Superman shield on the chest – around the compound and as far afield as Chipinga. Violet said there were also lots of Toby dogs in the African reserve.

Some denigrated the rat pack, calling them *kaffir* dogs because they resembled the standard African mongrel dogs. We did try other dogs, more fashionable dogs, white man's dogs. But we didn't have much luck with pedigrees. They weren't designed for the bush. They were fragile, impractical, and sometimes downright stupid. The dumbest of all our experiments was a Dalmatian bitch called Sally. Sally was good-natured to the point of imbecility. She had no sense of direction, no idea how to find her way home and no natural ability to survive in the wild.

At about the time we got Sally, there was another of the periodic leopard scares. Though seldom seen, leopards were a real problem in the area. They were considered vermin because they killed sheep and calves and domestic dogs, and in the reserves they picked off goats and the occasional *piccanin*. But they were notoriously difficult to track and shoot because they hunt only at night and live in the safety of the thickest undergrowth during the day. They are lazy hunters, preferring to lie in wait on branches for their quarry to pass below.

It took some time for us to realize that Sally the Dalmatian was responsible for the spate of leopard sightings. Plantation workers glimpsed a black and white spotted animal in the bush, and they didn't tend to stick around for a better look. What else would it be but a leopard?

To stop the panic, my father drew up a poster which had two pictures on it, a Dalmatian and a leopard.

This is a leopard, read the text under the leopard, *it is a member of the cat family, it eats goats and buck and sometimes people. It is dangerous and should not be approached.*

And this is a Dalmatian, it said under the picture of Sally. *It is a member of the dog family, and it is a pet. It is harmless and very friendly. DO NOT CONFUSE THESE TWO.*

My father had the poster duplicated on the office Roneo machine and distributed to the estates. It was pinned up on staff notice boards, in the superintendents' offices and on beer-hall walls.

Sally continued to wander, frequently getting lost, but after the bogus leopard incident, the Africans knew she was a dog and they would always return her. They would wait at the back door while my mother felt in her purse for some coins to reward them for their trouble. Soon this became a weekly event. I only found out years later that Sally's wanderings were not always voluntary. I was passing through Silverstream and Winfield the weighbridge clerk and I were reminiscing.

'And you remember the leopard dog?' he said. 'The one they used to kidnap for money?'

I laughed uncertainly with him.

'For money?'

'Oh, yes. It was a favourite trick. If someone was broke before payday, they would steal your dog and keep it at their hut for a few days. Then they would bring it back to your house saying that they had found it, and collect the reward.'

To combat the real leopard problem, Harry Lovat, the manager of Spitskop, in the hills above the Silverstream valley, kept a pack of hunting dogs. They were known as the leopard pack. They were big and ferocious and they were kept in a pen. Their sole purpose in life was to hunt leopard. We had donated a Dobermann cross to the leopard pack in preference to putting it down, because it kept biting people.

Our dog played a starring role in bringing down what was considered to be the biggest leopard anyone had ever seen, and we all trooped up to Harry Lovat's house for a viewing. The fact that it was the biggest leopard anyone could remember seeing didn't mean a great deal in itself as leopards were so seldom spotted. But no one let this fact diminish the occasion. The beast was proudly displayed on Lovat's verandah, laid out on the red polished-cement floor.

It looked relatively intact and quite peaceful, as though it might have been luxuriously stretched out having an afternoon nap. But Lovat lifted its jaw and showed me where the dog had bitten a chunk out of its throat.

'That's where he's most vulnerable. That's where they've got to nail the bugger if they're to stand any chance of bringing him down,' Lovat explained, to a chorus of protests from the women. They had settled down in cane chairs, and were drinking Tanganda tea and eating flapjacks.

Lovat put his fingers into the leopard's throat and fished out a thick blood vein. I was fascinated.

'This vein here's the jugular,' he said, tugging at it to make sure I'd taken note. 'It's the main blood supply to the leopard's brain. And a good hunting dog knows that if he gets a clear bite at the jugular, then the game's over. Dogs: one, leopard: nil. Hah!'

He sat back on his haunches laughing and holding his bloodied hands out in front of him, and he called to the cook boy to bring him a cloth to wipe them.

'If the pack is hunting well together, then some dogs will harry and divert the leopard while others will wait for the chance to go for the throat. It all depends on this teamwork because, obviously, a dog is no match for a leopard, one to one, especially a bastard this size.'

He gave the animal a kick with the end of his *veldskoen*, and its body quivered like a jelly.

'It's all about teamwork,' he went on, 'like in rugger, say, you've got some players whose job it is to pass the ball along and set up the try for the scorer – well, it's much the same with a leopard pack.'

'How do the dogs communicate with each other?' I wondered.

'Buggered if I know,' shrugged Lovat.

We went over to check on the pack behind the house in their large pen, where they were busily devouring their reward, a great mound of offal and a stack of bones. They looked terrible, badly scratched and mauled and bloody. One had an ear that seemed more off than on. Another's eye was swollen shut.

Lovat didn't seem too concerned.

'I'll get the vet to give them the once-over tomorrow,' he said.

He noticed me looking at one Rhodesian ridgeback that was

lying on its side in the corner. It wasn't eating like the others and it was breathing with great difficulty, in rasping shallow pants. The leopard's claws had sliced a deep gash in its belly. The bleeding had stopped now but you could see where the wound cut through a layer of fat and muscle into the stomach.

'We may have to put him down,' Lovat conceded.

'Dogs: one, leopard: *one*,' I thought, but I didn't say it aloud. I was worried Lovat might think me soft.

Back on the verandah, as so often happened in these country gatherings, tea had made a seamless progression into sundowners, although the sun was still bright above the mountains and the brass ship's clock on the wall showed just after four.

As the grown-ups settled into their second drink, one of the estate's lorries drew up outside and a whole load of Africans piled off, about thirty of them, and approached the verandah. The ordinary dogs, several small mongrels that had been curled up asleep under various tables and chairs, began barking furiously.

'Streuth!' complained Lovat, hauling himself out of creaking rattan. 'What the hell do this lot want?'

The crowd stopped a respectful distance from the house, and a representative, one of the estate's bossboys, Zephaniah his name was, took a few steps forward to address Lovat. He launched into the complicated ritual of a Shona greeting.

'*Manheru*,' he said, clutching an ancient trilby in both hands to his groin.

'*Manheru*,' returned Lovat impatiently. It means good evening in Shona, and you graduate to it from 'good afternoon' once the day is losing heat.

'*Maswera heré*,' said the bossboy, which means 'have you spent a good day?' to which Lovat was supposed to reply, 'I have spent a good day if *you* have spent a good day,' and the bossboy would say, 'I have indeed.' And then Lovat could say, 'Well in that case so have I.'

But Lovat had no time for such drawn-out pleasantries, and he cut the bossboy short.

'Yes, yes. What is it, then? Who are all these people, Zephaniah? What do they want?'

Behind the bossboy the delegation were shuffling their feet and looking down at the lawn. Babies were mewling and small children coughing. A large woman at the front, holding a baby wrapped in a bright floral sheet, was openly weeping.

'We heard that you have killed a leopard,' stated Zephaniah.

'That's right,' said Lovat. He anticipated a protest. 'What about it?'

'We should like to see it,' requested Zephaniah, 'this leopard.'

This was an unusually bold move, a group of black sightseers just dropping in uninvited on the estate manager's house to view the latest curiosity. Lovat was annoyed. But Zephaniah continued:

'This leopard has eaten her first-born child,' he explained, and he pointed to the large woman weeping quietly behind him. Lovat found the manners to look contrite.

'Her boy had eight years of age. The bus was late returning and he was walking home from the bus stop at dark, and then the leopard jumped on him,' said the bossboy. 'And then he died,' he added. 'Now this woman, she must see the leopard which has eaten her child.'

'Why wasn't this death reported to me, Zephaniah?' Lovat admonished. 'You know all deaths are supposed to be reported to the estate manager and noted down in the incident book, even the deaths of children.' He was annoyed at being made to look a sloppy manager in front of my father.

Zephaniah shrugged his shoulders. Lovat sighed and turned to lead the delegation up on to the verandah. They gathered around the beast, making disapproving clucking noises and shaking their heads. Then the dead boy's mother handed her baby to someone and began to emit a piercing keen that developed into a full-throated scream.

'Ayyee! Ayyee!'

She rolled her eyes so that only their whites were visible, and she beat her breast with her fist and babbled hysterically at the prone animal.

The grown-ups were still sitting in the cane chairs, nursing their drinks and observing the scene without comment or intrusion. Every now and then my father would tap some ash from his cigarette into a big glass ashtray glued on to a severed elephant's leg, one of Lovat's hunting trophies.

The bereaved woman shook free of those supporting her and threw herself at the leopard. She kicked it in the stomach several times, then went down on her knees and tried to throttle the animal. She gripped its neck with both hands and began to bash its head on the cement floor. Each time it hit, the head made a dull thud, and the tongue lolled out of the slack jaw – the jaw that had crunched the bones of her first-born child.

The dogs began barking again at the commotion.

'Now that's quite enough,' intervened Lovat, annoyed. 'You'll damage the pelt, going on like that. Up! Come on. Up!'

He motioned to Zephaniah, who prised the woman off the leopard with some difficulty.

The Africans talked briefly among themselves, then Zephaniah came hesitantly forward again.

'We would like to take a part of the leopard,' he said.

'What do you mean? Which part?' asked Lovat suspiciously.

'We would like the heart.'

'Oh, for God's sake,' sighed Lovat. 'This is all your bloody voodoo nonsense again isn't it?'

Without waiting for an answer he asked: 'If I let you take the heart, what'll you do with it?'

Zephaniah looked self-conscious and uncomfortable. 'It is our way,' he said simply.

Lovat briefly canvassed opinion around the verandah.

'Can't do any harm, I suppose,' said Mr Watson.

'It's all a bit gruesome,' said his wife, scringing her nose.

'We ought to find out *exactly* what they'll do with it,' advised my father, ever the stickler for detail. 'It's all tied up with witchcraft. God knows, they might end up killing someone.'

Lovat took the bossboy to one side and they talked for several minutes in low voices. Then Lovat reported back to the verandah.

'Well, they're an odd bunch, these *munts*. Old Zephaniah here, he reckons that according to their custom the mother of the dead boy must now *eat* the leopard's heart to lift the curse that's been put on her family.'

Mrs Watson's nose scringed up even further.

'Zephaniah says the kid was killed by the leopard because of a spell. They're not sure who cast the spell but they've consulted a witch doctor, who said if she eats the heart that will put an end to it.'

Lovat thought for a moment and then came to a decision. 'Well, I've got no use for it,' he said. 'I suppose they might as well have it, if they want it so damn badly. Just so long as they don't muck up my leopard skin.'

With that he bellowed to the cook, who appeared almost immediately around the open door from where he had been surreptitiously observing events. They threw down some hessian sacks on the lawn and dragged the leopard down on to them. The cook disappeared into the kitchen and returned with an armful of knives. Zephaniah, the bereaved woman and the whole delegation gathered in a semi-circle and watched intently as Harry Lovat's cook set about skinning the biggest leopard anyone could remember seeing.

On the verandah Mr Watson had started up a desultory game of darts. My father was busy recharging the drinks.

Harry Lovat's cook boy was one of the best skinners in the business. Rumour had it that he and Lovat used to go on illegal hunting expeditions over the border. I even heard that the cook boy had once been a professional poacher and had been hired by Lovat because of his impressive skinning credentials.

Lovat and the cook boy turned the leopard over onto its back and splayed its legs outwards. Then, with confident movements, the cook boy set about his task. He made an incision at the tip of its chin and cut in deft little strokes all the way along its underbelly, stopping only once to shoo away the mongrels. The knife was superbly sharp and sliced easily through the spotted pelt, the blade's progress marked by little crunching noises.

He kept cutting until he reached its balls. I stifled an embarrassed giggle at them. But without any hesitation the cook cut around the balls. Then he excised them and scooped them up from the animal's groin. He made to throw this morsel to the dogs, but was stopped by a spontaneous outcry from his audience. Lovat, on his hands and knees assisting his cook, looked up in consternation.

'Bloody hell! What is it now?'

Zephaniah spoke briefly to the cook boy, and the cook boy looked amused.

'They want this one,' he said, holding up the leopard's severed genitals. 'They want to use it for *muti*. It is very strong *muti*.'

Muti was Shona for medicine. But it didn't usually mean western medicine, it meant traditional, witch-doctor medicine.

'What the hell will they use it for?' asked Lovat. He was becoming exasperated at their demands.

The cook boy looked abashed.

'Well, what, for Christ's sake?' demanded Lovat.

The cook boy cast a furtive glance up at the white women sitting chatting on the verandah. Then, turning his back to them, he whispered to Lovat. 'It is for . . . It is for . . . for if you cannot have children.'

Lovat looked confused. So the cook boy made a circle with his left thumb and forefinger and thrust his right forefinger rapidly in and out of the circle.

'Jiggi jiggi. It is good for jiggi jiggi, if you eat this one,' he whispered, and cast his eyes down in embarrassment.

It took Lovat a couple of seconds and then he roared with laughter and bellowed up to the verandah.

'Get a load of this. These *munts* now want to take this leopard's wedding tackle and bloody well scoff it as some sort of aphrodisiac or fertility booster. Un-bloody-believable, isn't it?'

There was a general murmur of assent from the verandah.

Lovat addressed the cook and Zephaniah and the whole crowd of Africans.

'You know, when are you *munts* going to get civilized? We send you to school. We teach you to read and write. We vaccinate you against disease. And you still want to eat a leopard's bloody bollocks. I mean, Christ knows . . .'

As he gave his little lecture, they all stared down at the ground, as silent as penitent schoolchildren.

'Sure, give it to them then, if it's so bloody important,' said Lovat with a shrug.

The cook proffered the genitals to his audience and a small riot ensued as they scuffled with each other for possession. A tall elderly man with a grizzled beard emerged the victor. He held his prize aloft in one hand, away from the last few women still jumping futilely to reach it. Once he had established possession, all embarrassment vanished and they began to tease him bawdily about what it would do for his sex drive. The elderly man, unperturbed by the good-natured jibes, carefully wrapped the leopard's genitals in a piece of old newspaper.

Satisfied with their various morsels of the leopard, the crowd hauled themselves back on the truck, pinned back the tailgate, and with a great belch of diesel fumes it clattered away.

In due course the leopard skin was mounted on a backing of green felt and hung at an angle on Harry Lovat's sitting-room wall. He was very proud of it. He told everyone who came to visit that it was the biggest-leopard-that-anyone-had-ever-seen, and no one challenged the claim.

I noticed that, in time, when he was showing it off to women, he dropped the bit about the leopard having eaten a person. The women didn't like that bit, they found it ghoulish, and it detracted from the trophy. With the men, though, it was still a source of pride.

'Come and see my monster,' Lovat would say, drawing them into the sitting room. 'It's a man-eater, you know.'

Not really a man-eater, I thought. More of a small-boy-eater. But I never said it aloud. I was worried Lovat might think me soft.

Four

There is a picture of my first day at school. It is an ambitious photograph that attempts to include not only two children, but also the car and the whole of the house. My father's instinct to catalogue has once again defeated the photographer's art. Although I'm in the middle of the frame, I stand barely half an inch high. The most noticeable thing about my uniform is that everything is vastly too big. The green blazer, with its little lamp of learning on the pocket, complete with rays emanating forth, all but reaches my knees. Only a narrow rim of baggy khaki shorts peeps out at the bottom. A capacious grey felt hat sits at a jaunty angle on the back of my head – there is no sign of hair. My socks have sagged to my ankles, above a pair of Clark's Jack and Jill sandals, which I hated and contrived to lose within a week. And when I look closely, I am standing defiantly in a puddle.

Next to me, and twice my height, is my sister Jain, also on her first day at a new school. She is clearly embarrassed, in a teenager sort of way, clutching the hem of her blazer and looking down. She has good reason to look embarrassed. On her head is the most extraordinary white bowler hat.

To the right in the foreground is the grey Austin Westminster, indented heavily into the soggy driveway, marooned there like an old frigate. And behind us, up a steep slope of lawn, is the house, its verandah dripping with a profusion of crimson bougainvillaea.

My mother ferried me to school each day in her Mini Minor.

It was a fifty-mile round trip along terrible dirt roads, so we had to set off shortly after dawn.

From Silverstream we drove up into the wattle plantations, swinging around hairpin bends with streams tinkling under culverts at every turn. If the wattles were in blossom they were festooned with little yellow pollen balls. When we got to the ridge at Tandevel, we could look back down on Silverstream, just for a moment. The river, the village where the Europeans lived, the factory, with steam rising from the chimneys, and, on the other side of the factory, the African compound. Then we went on through more plantations, thick with pine now. And so dense in some places that the trees formed an arch over the road, so that even on a bright day it was gloomy and cool and damp in there.

These dark places were fairly scary because they were home to *tokaloshes*. A *tokalosh* was a sort of African goblin, a bush imp, a malevolent hobbit.

I'd never seen a *tokalosh* and Violet, who had, gave me a very confused description. She said it looked like a chimpanzee with blazing red eyes and pointed teeth and a little pot belly. Often it had little horns like the devil. But it could change into other forms. *Tokaloshes* spoke Shona and if you came across one it was always very cross because you would have woken it up. Violet used to raise the legs of her bed on to bricks to stop *tokaloshes* from invading her sleep. Apparently *tokaloshes* couldn't reach high beds.

What was even more worrying for me was that both Jain and my mother seemed to believe in *tokaloshes* too. There was a particular glade on the way to school, just on the Melsetter side of Skyline Junction, which they considered a definite *tokalosh* habitat. It had all the requirements: a water source, lots of shade and no human residents nearby. We called it *tokalosh* corner and my mother would always mumble some incantation to placate them as we drove by, especially if it was at prime *tokalosh* time – after dark or early in the morning.

'Oh great *tokalosh*. Spirit of the night,' she would intone in a deep voice full of stentorian formality. 'Do not harm us, for we respect you. Let us pass freely through your territory.'

During this performance I would sit uneasily in the passenger seat, half disbelieving, half nervous.

Once we had passed it without incident, she would always say cheerily, 'Now we'll get home safely. The *tokalosh* has deemed it so.' And I would relax.

Late one night on our way back from Melsetter, the Mini's engine died as we reached the dreaded corner, and we rolled to a stop right at *tokalosh* HQ. We sat in silence. The only sound was the croaking of frogs and the creaking of the umbrella trees in the wind. I was bug-eyed with fear.

'You forgot the *tokalosh* prayer,' I said in a very small, hoarse voice.

My mother seemed rather flustered. She tried the engine again but it showed no signs of life.

'What will the *tokalosh* do to us now,' I asked, tremulously.

'Oh, you don't believe in all that nonsense,' she said irritably. 'The *tokalosh* isn't *real* you know; it's just a legend, a myth to make people respect the bush or something.'

She tried the ignition again. Nothing.

I was indignant.

'But you *said* this is where he lived.'

'Well, if he did exist, if he *does* exist, this is the sort of place he *would* live,' said my mother, trying the engine again.

I looked out at the dark shapes of the umbrella trees.

'Oh great *tokalosh*. Spirit of the night,' I began uncertainly. Then my mother joined in. 'Do not harm us, for we respect you. Let us pass safely through your territory.'

We waited in silence at the end of the prayer. Then she blew on her fingers like a professional darts player and turned the ignition key once more. This time the engine caught. She threw the Mini into gear and we accelerated quickly away in a shower of dust.

'Now we'll get home safely,' I said, imitating my mother's voice, 'the *tokalosh* has deemed it so.'

My mother rolled her eyes. But later she admitted that she had become a bit lax about the *tokaloshes*, and that this was their way of reminding us of their power. And after that her *tokalosh* incantations became more fervent.

Back then, the road from Skyline Junction down to Melsetter was famously bad. It was cut into the steep side of a valley and in the rainy season it was frequently blocked by landslides. It was not unusual to hear small rocks clattering on to the car roof as we drove by. Even when it was nominally open, the road was constantly churned up by huge logging trucks, which created treacherous mud holes that defeated a Land Rover in four-wheel drive, never mind a Mini, even one with specially raised suspension and chains on the wheels. We often got stuck.

But there was a logic to my mother's choice of vehicle. Because the road was so bad, the Roads Department had a permanent depot there, with road gangs in constant attendance. If we got stuck, we would radio in and usually within half an hour the nearest gang would come loping around the corner in their yellow overalls and gumboots.

We would get out of the car, and take my mother's drugs cabinet out of the boot to reduce the weight. Then about eight of the workmen would position themselves around the vehicle and the foreman would count them down. Their backs would stiffen at his shout of 'heave!', and they would lift up the car, carry it over the mud hole and put it down on the other side. If we were on our way back from Melsetter, after school, I was allowed to help lift the car. By then it didn't matter if I was immersed waist deep in mud.

While the men all strained at the vehicle, the sinews in their arms bulging to hold it at knee level, I held it at my shoulder height, often hanging on rather than lifting it up, though I was always sure to huff and pant with the best of them.

Sometimes I was genuinely helpful, I think. Once I made an epic intervention as a human windscreen wiper, when an electrical fault rendered our wipers useless during a heavy downpour. I sat on the bonnet in the warm rain, swishing my arm back and forth over the windscreen like a metronome to clear away the torrent so my mother could squint through at the road ahead.

Finally we would reach the bottom of the Skyline road and the valley opened up and before us was Melsetter. Their settlement was named after a small village in the Orkney Islands, because the area reminded the first white pioneers of their homeland. It was still very much a pioneer village, at the end of the road. Ahead lay the glittering granite and quartz of the Chimanimani mountains, which rose up majestically beyond the village, dominating the view. And beyond that, the most remote, unexplored part of Mozambique.

The district had been opened up for the white man by eight pioneer columns who trekked up from South Africa in the 1890s in ox wagons. There was great rivalry between the Scottish and English treks, which were made up of Moodies and Meikles and Martins, (Moodie's grandfather had been the last laird of the Orcadian Melsetter) and the Boers: Steyns and Nels. At school the two houses into which we were divided for the purpose of competing at sports were called Martin and Steyn, after two of the main treks. I was in Martin, as was my rightful heritage.

Melsetter village was a rambling affair, with only one concession to planning – a wide, grassy central square. In the middle of it was the pioneer memorial, which we visited as part of our history lessons. The memorial was a statue of a wagon pulled by a span of oxen. It was carved from Chimanimani granite and set on a plinth made up of river pebbles from the

Sabi river crossing, one of the main barriers facing the pioneers. Underneath was a plaque which said simply:

Erected in memory of the Pioneers of Gazaland

Next to the inscription was a list of twelve names of people who had died on the treks.

At the top of the square was the Department of Native Affairs headquarters, with the distinctive red corrugated iron roof that all government buildings had. There was always a long queue of Africans outside, waiting for *situpas*. The old police camp was next door. On the other sides of the square were African trading stores, a maize grinding mill, the petrol station, a bakery, the Chimanimani Hotel, a bottle store and Theunessens, the general store presided over by old Ma Theunessen, whose motto was 'If we haven't got it we can order it', as indeed she could. The dusty streets were lined with flamboyant trees that showered down their red flowers in the autumn.

Melsetter school stood alone on a hill top on the other side of the village, a mile and a half away. It was a spartan place, a few low buildings, dormitories, classrooms and the headmaster's green clapboard bungalow. My first challenge there was the classroom door handle. For most of my first year it was beyond my reach and I had to jump up for it, an experience I found deeply humiliating. Sometimes Miss Gloyne, the KG one teacher who had come all the way from Kent to teach us, would open it for me from the inside. I had never seen so many white children all in one place before – there were seventy of us altogether in the school.

To start with school was quite fun. We drew pictures and played with coloured wooden rods called Quizenaire, which were supposed to help us to add and subtract, although we just built towers with them. We life-saved tin plates in the school swimming pool, made paper chains and sang carols. We went for nature study walks and caught insects in jars and pinned them on a board on the classroom wall.

In the end-of-year play I was the small bear in 'Goldilocks and the Three Bears' and had to dance around a big cardboard honey pot and all the parents clapped. On sports day I came second in the egg-and-spoon race and my mother, who was giving out the prizes that year and had a new hat on, gave me a certificate to prove it. Rawdon Ball came first. (He always came first.)

At the end of each school day I would wait on the head-master's verandah for my mother to come up the hill in her Mini and collect me. Often she would be late. All the other day-scholars left, and the older children went to the classrooms for prep. And I just sat on the edge of the wooden verandah swinging my legs and trying to make friends with the diffident cat. Then the bell rang and the older children came out of prep and ran to the refectory for supper. And still my mother hadn't come to collect me.

Mrs Simpson, the headmaster's wife, would come out and suggest that I went and had supper with the older children in the refectory. But I wouldn't go. Eventually my mother would turn up, looking exhausted, still with a stethoscope round her neck and her white coat covered in dust. If it was really late, I would have curled up by then on the Simpsons' sofa and gone to sleep, and they would carry me to the car and lay me down in the back seat with my blair.

After oom Piet's murder my parents decided that this just couldn't carry on – I would have to become a boarder. But I was still under the minimum age for boarding. Mr Simpson wrote a letter to the Ministry of Education in Salisbury, and so did the police member-in-charge and so did my father, explaining why an exception should be made. Thus it was that in KG 2, while I was still six, I became a boarder, and it was all the fault of Willie Ndangana and the Crocodile Gang.

My parents were given a printed list of the things I would

need as a boarder, and we went to Meikles department store in Umtali to buy them. In Meikles' window there was a display of the Beatles: puppets of Paul, John, George and Ringo which turned their heads from side to side, and strummed stiffly at papier-mâché guitars and seemed to sing, although I could see that the singing really came from a loudspeaker buried under some tinsel behind them. I was riveted by this spectacle and stood there, me and a crowd of Africans, all of us singing along lustily to a song which they told me was called '*Can bonni lolo*.'

Later, when I pestered Jain to play it for me on her new radiogram, she insisted it was called 'Can't buy me love now'. But it still sounded like '*Can bonni lolo*' to me.

In Meikles they bought me a black metal trunk and my father stencilled on it in white paint 'PETER GODWIN' in capital letters. Jain gave me special lessons in tying shoelaces, because boarders wore proper shoes, not sandals like the little children.

'You're going to be a big boy now,' said my mother. 'A real grown-up. And we're all very proud of you.'

'Will you come and take me home if I don't like it?' I asked.

'Of course you'll like it. It'll be great fun. You'll have all your friends there. And we'll come and visit you.'

Violet enfolded me into a great damp hug and then turned away to hide her crying. Knighty gave me a firm man-to-man handshake, African-style, alternating up and down. And he slipped a paper bag into my little brown suitcase.

'It is for if you are getting hungry over there,' he said gruffly.

Inside the bag were half a dozen of his best sugar buns, individually wrapped in greaseproof paper, and a note, on brown paper, written in pencil in the tortuous block capitals of a ransom demand. It read: 'Good look *baas* Peter. Love from Knighty.' Violet must have written it out for him.

Albert the garden boy, who never came into the house, waited at the back door to bid his farewell. He presented me with his large penknife, which I had admired on many occasions and which I knew he treasured. I held it in awe, then I shook my head sadly and handed it back.

'I can't take it, Albert. It's your knife. You need it for cutting things here.'

'No, I will get another,' he said, closing my fingers around the knife. 'Take it as a borrowing. You can give it back afterwards.'

We set off in the Austin Westminster and the servants stood in a group, waving. When I looked back from the end of the drive I could see them in the distance, still waving hard. And I knew then that nothing would be the same again.

At Melsetter school they had allocated me a narrow iron bed at the end of a long row of identical beds. It had a thin lumpy mattress and a pillow filled with something called kapok. It had two stiff grey blankets in the summer terms and an extra one in winter. And on the blankets and the sheets, pillowcase and towel, and even on the counterpane, were the letters OHMS, which stood for 'On Her Majesty's Service'. Next to the bed I had my own small metal locker with three shelves. My mother helped me unpack my clothes into neat piles and put them in the locker. Then she sat me on the bed.

'We won't be far away, you know.'

I nodded glumly.

'Now if you have any problems, you just tell the Simpsons and they'll phone us in Silverstream.' She kissed me on the cheek.

'Be a good lad, son,' said my father and boxed me lightly on the shoulder.

Then they got back into the Austin Westminster and drove away.

I wet my bed that night, for the first time since I was a baby. The next morning I told the matron, Mrs Wormald. I tried to do it surreptitiously.

'I'm afraid I've wet my bad, ma'am,' I said in a tiny voice.

But she was rather deaf.

'Speak up, boy!' she said. 'What are you trying to say?'

'I've wet my bed,' I said, only slightly louder.

'You've wet your bed?' she boomed down the dormitory, and the older boys sniggered.

'Well why didn't you tell me you were a wetter?' she asked. 'I would have given you a rubber sheet, saved the mattress a soaking.' She took away my wet bedclothes and returned with a dry set and a cold red rubber sheet.

'Now put your mattress outside to dry in the sun, and when it's dry, make up the bed with this rubber sheet on the bottom.'

After she'd left, some older boys, led by Fatty Slabbert, danced around clutching their balls with both hands and chanting in singsong voices, 'He's a pisser! He's a pisser!'

I started to cry.

'And a blubber! And a blubber!' chanted Fatty Slabbert, and the others joined in.

Later that day, I went to the Simpsons' house. I waited patiently outside while they finished supper, listening for the clatter of the cutlery on plates to stop, and then I knocked on the door.

'What is it, young Godwin?' asked Mr Simpson in a kindly way, smiling at me over his glasses.

'I would like you to phone my parents,' I announced. 'This is their number.' I handed him a folded sheet of paper on which I had carefully written 'Silverstream 303'.

The Simpsons gave me a cup of cocoa and while I drank it on the sofa, where I used to fall asleep, they chatted to me, trying to comfort me. Eventually Mrs Simpson looked at her watch.

'Good gosh, is that the time? It's a little late now to be calling anyone. You'd best go to bed. Let's phone them tomorrow, shall we?'

This routine went on for several days before I finally realized that the Simpsons weren't going to let me call home at all.

That Saturday most of the boarders were taken out for the

day by their parents. But mine never came. I sat alone under the pine trees on a carpet of rusty dry pine needles, disconsolately carving sticks with Albert's knife and nibbling one of Knighty's buns and planning to run away.

Early the next day we had to go to church. We put on our Sunday whites and formed up in a crocodile file and marched down the hill to the Melsetter Anglican church, St George's-in-the-Mountains. My plan was to excuse myself while everyone was in church, run down to the bus depot where the African buses waited, and jump on to the Chipinga Express, which I knew stopped at Silverstream. In my pocket I had all my savings, 7s. 6d, to buy the ticket, and I kept fingering the coins to make sure they were still there.

As we marched down the hill that morning, the sides of the road were bursting with banks of bright blue morning glories. The red-winged loeries called to each other as they hopped from branch to branch, and the smell of pine resin filled the air. For a moment I felt better. I decided to put off my escape until next Sunday.

In church it was Easter, so we sang an Easter hymn with a mournful tune, which made me sad all over again.

> *There is a green hill far away,*
> *Outside the city wall,*
> *Where our dear Lord was crucified.*
> *He died to save us all.*

I was suddenly sure that the hill in the hymn was actually the hill opposite our school, Green Mount, across the valley where old Mrs Randolf lived alone in a scary house with turrets.

It was a grey-green hill, except once a year when it was burnt. Then it was black. After the fire, for a few weeks it was brilliant green with fresh blades of lush new grass. Then it went back to being grey-green again. From school it always looked a desolate, foreboding hill. A heavy, swollen hill with no trees. It was just the sort of hill that Jesus would have been crucified on. Jesus *had* been crucified right here in Melsetter. It all made sense. It was a place where they made people suffer. They'd crucified Jesus, and now they were keeping me prisoner.

On my knees I said a little prayer to the Lord asking him to free me. After all, He had arranged for Jesus to rise from the dead, so getting me home should present Him no problem. But when I opened my eyes, nothing had changed. I trudged back up to school with a heavy heart, not seeing the morning glories nor the loeries and not smelling the pine resin.

My parents came to visit me the following weekend. They took me to the Chimanimani Hotel for tea. I sat sulking in silence in a large armchair by the fire, munching scones.

'The Simpsons wouldn't let me phone you to take me home,' I finally declared.

'Well they did phone us, actually,' said my father. 'But we all decided it was better to give you a couple of weeks to settle in.'

I was astonished at the news that my parents had known I was unhappy yet hadn't come to fetch me.

'Why don't you give it a chance, hmm?' said my mother. 'You'll get used to it in time.'

They chatted for a while to various friends who passed through the hotel lounge, and then it was time to go back.

'I've already given it a chance and I've decided that I don't want to be a boarder at all,' I announced.

But my parents took me back anyway. When we got to school, I refused to get out of the car.

'Come on son. Belt up!' said my father in exasperation.

'We really have no option, Peter,' my mother said as they left. She was blinking back tears. 'You'll soon put all this behind you.'

The next day we had a surprise locker check. I was found to be the principal outlaw. First, Knighty's individually wrapped sugar buns were discovered. There were four left, stale now and covered with ants. I had been rationing myself to one a week to make them last until half term. Then Albert's knife was found hidden rather half-heartedly under my rolled-up balls of socks. Both were confiscated by Mr Simpson in a scene of great opprobrium, and I was sentenced to write 500 lines.

The only bright side of the incident was that it seemed to improve my standing marginally with the older boys. Especially the discovery of the knife, which Mr Simpson mistakenly called a flick knife.

Eventually my life settled into a dreary routine. The days were not too bad because my classmates, who were all day-scholars, were there, and I could pretend that I was a dayboy too, that someone would come and collect me at the end of the day. I was good at class and I usually had my hand up with the correct answer, even when no one else did. At least Miss Gloyne liked me. Then she asked me to stay behind one day after class.

'You're a clever little boy, Peter,' she said. 'But I have to teach all the boys and girls, even the ones who are not so clever. That's what a teacher has to do. Do you understand?'

I didn't understand at all.

Miss Gloyne sighed.

'Well, I can't always come to you for the answers. I have to give the other children a turn, even if I know that you know the right answer.' She handed me some more advanced reading books and said, 'Now run along. See you tomorrow.'

After that Miss Gloyne would often ignore my hand, even if it was the only hand up. Eventually I stopped putting my hand up at all. I just daydreamed out of the window instead.

After classes we had sport and then the day-scholars went home and the boarders had a free period when we went to the Pines, a small pine forest that was part of the school grounds. There we played various games, like hounds and deer. Although we could all name dozens of kinds of antelope, none of us knew what a deer was, really. Fatty Slabbert said it was the animal that pulled Father Christmas's sleigh. The deer got a minute start and had to hide, then the hounds went bounding after them through the bracken, baying at the tops of their voices.

The other game was Pine Cone War. We divided into two teams and blasted each other with cones. The best cones to get were the hard green ones, which went faster and could really hurt your opponents, especially if you could hit them on the head. We used to spend hours collecting and hoarding good cones for coming battles.

After playtime the boarders went back to the classrooms for prep. During prep the last of the sunlight would fade away and Sixpence the lantern boy – he was actually a very old man with a bushy grey moustache – would come around with the Tilly lamps. He filled them up with paraffin and pumped the little brass plunger in the base, lit the gauze mantle and adjusted it with another brass knob. Then, using a long pole with a hook on the end, he would skilfully hoist the lanterns up on to their hooks. The lanterns made a comforting hissing sound and they were soon surrounded by squadrons of moths and flying ants.

When prep was over, we trooped back to the dorm, washed our hands and lined up outside the refectory. Mrs Wormald would come down the line very slowly, holding up a lantern in one hand and a ruler in the other. Each of us had to show her our hands, both sides, and if she found any dirt she would hit the hand with a ruler and send the boy to wash. Girls didn't get hit with a ruler, which wasn't fair.

In the refectory we said grace and then sat on benches at long wooden tables. Tickie was the school cook boy. He was Sixpence's younger brother and had a jolly wheezing laugh and a huge round stomach that tugged at his shirt buttons. For some reason he was called a chef, not a cook boy, and he wore a tall white hat. Tickie cooked meals like toad in the hole and braised liver, steak and kidney pie and Welsh rarebit; and for pudding, tapioca, semolina and baked quinces from the school orchard, all done under the close supervision of Mrs Wormald.

When we had finished our supper we would usually line up at the sickbay for our daily spoonful of malt and cod liver oil, and then read on our beds to the hissing lamps for half an hour until lights out. Mr Simpson would patrol up and down the creaking floors for a bit to make sure there was no talking. When he had gone, I would pull the counterpane over my head and cry myself to sleep. The end of another day. I had perfected the art of silent crying now so no one could catch me.

Paul Withers, the boy in the bed next to me, knew that I cried, but he kindly kept it a secret. Withers became my first boarder friend. But he wasn't much help – he had a crew cut and spoke with a funny accent because he was the son of American missionaries at Biriwiri. Fatty Slabbert and his gang would hop around him chanting, 'kaffir-lover! kaffir-lover!' And they would try to imitate his accent.

On Sundays, after church, we went on 'rambles'. These would take us either to Bridal Veil Falls or up Pork Pie mountain. The waterfall was very tall and thin and ended in a deep plunge pool in which we were allowed to swim, but only in groups of four at a time. The water was icy and there were trout and barbel in there and eels. Odd spider-like animals called daddy-longlegs skimmed across the top of the water. The foliage around the pool was bathed in a constant spray from the falls. It was verdant and cool and covered with moss. Orchids grew on the overhanging trees and vividly coloured kingfishers would sit on the branches peering into the pool and then streak down to snap up shimmering silver tiddlers.

Pork Pie was harder but more fun. It was the mountain that overlooked school hill, and it was supposed to look like a pork pie, though I had examined it from all angles and still couldn't see the likeness. On Pork Pie we would usually see eland, the biggest antelope in Africa. If we all kept quiet and still, they wouldn't run away They'd just stare at us and chew their cud, like cows.

Pork Pie was also good for scorpions, which lived under rocks. While someone distracted the teacher, the rest of us would go around lifting rocks. When we found a scorpion we would taunt it with a stick, provoking it to flick up its arrowed tail and sting the stick. The fact that scorpions were capable of sudden bursts of speed and would sometimes ignore the stick, making instead straight for the hand, made it more fun. Even better was to get two scorpions and make them fight each other. There are over fifty kinds of scorpions. Most could give you a very painful sting. Only two would kill you. But we didn't know which two.

The only other time we ever left school was to go on trips with the YFC, the Young Farmers' Club. As most of the pupils at Melsetter school were the children of farmers, we usually went to their parents' farms. They would explain how coffee or tea or fruit farming worked, or how to run dairy cattle or timber plantations. Most of us knew this anyway, so it was just a good excuse for an outing. Usually the farmer's wife would lay on a lavish cream tea at the end of the day.

In the truck on the way back we would sing camping songs in our piping voices. *My eyes are dim, I cannot see, I have not brought my specs with me*, or *She'll be coming round the mountain when she comes*. And we were all given little YFC badges to wear on the lapels of our blazers.

Every four weeks we would have an exeat weekend, when boarders could go home from Friday after lunch until late Sunday afternoon. The problem with this arrangement was that Friday was fish day. Every Friday lunch Sixpence produced Kariba bream, boiled to a mush in a thin milky sauce.

Kariba bream tastes like mud under the best of circumstances. When Sixpence cooked it to Mrs Wormald's gruesome recipe it was disgusting, and I refused to eat it. As we were not allowed to leave until our plates were empty, I had to sit there over a plate of cold boiled fish, long after everyone else had gone home. My mother would go and have tea with the Simpsons while I sat stubbornly in the refectory, with Mrs Wormald guarding me because she knew Sixpence would gladly have tossed the fish in the bin if we were left unsupervised.

It became a battle of wills.

Sometimes as a concession she would get Sixpence to reheat the bream and put it back in front of me. But I still wouldn't eat it. She would sit there unmoved, her knitting needles clicking. I would sit there staring at my plate and thinking how much I hated her – old Mrs Wormald, everything about her was ugly, even her name, worm-old, old-worm. Her orthopaedic shoes, her fat ankles, the gnarled blue varicose veins that coiled their way up the backs of her legs, her vast boat of a bum and its counterbalancing massive bosom, the wart on her chin with black hairs growing out of it, and her little rheumy, light blue, piggy eyes that stared out from behind thick glasses.

Sixpence would stand, leaning his bulk against the kitchen hatch, wondering at this bizarre contest and at the madness of the *mukiwa*.

Eventually Mrs Wormald would try to do a deal, scooping most of the fish to one side of my plate.

'OK, you eat this little bit here, then you can go. And I'm doing you a big favour, hey?'

When the pile to be eaten got small enough I would fork it into my mouth, pack it into my cheeks with my tongue, mumble my farewell and dash to the lavatory to spit it out.

I found exeat weekends very unsettling. Hardly had I begun to savour the feel of freedom before I was being hustled back to school. It was the one time now that I still cried in public. It was worse in winter, when the school seemed dark and forbidding and isolated, sitting on its lonely hill.

One Sunday, after a particularly lengthy battle with Mrs Wormald the previous Friday, I felt especially sorry for myself.

My parents had brought me back early, before any of the other children, and I sat on my bed, knees drawn up to my chest, crying quietly, alone. Suddenly Mrs Wormald walked briskly into the dormitory, catching me before I could dry up. She looked at me strangely and then walked out again without a word.

A minute later she returned and sat down on the bed next to me.

'Ach, you mustn't cry now *seuntjie*. Growing up is difficult to do. I can remember. I was a child once too, you know. You're a good little boy really, even if you do cause me so much hassle.'

Then from somewhere about her large person she produced a ballpoint pen. It was no ordinary pen, it had four different colours. Depending on which button you depressed it could write in red, black, blue or green. No one else had anything like it. No one had even *seen* anything like it.

'Don't tell the others I gave it to you, hey?' said Mrs Wormald. 'Otherwise they'll all be pestering me for one.' The bed groaned as she leant over and pecked me shyly on the cheek, brushing me lightly with her wart hair. Then, the colour rising in her face, she fled from the dormitory.

My Friday confrontations lost their sting after that. And Kariba bream, though still disgusting, seemed bland enough to swallow without tasting. Besides which, Tickie perfected a way to serve me with a mock fish, made up of fish skin wrapped around mashed potao. As we were allowed to leave the skin, I just had to peel it off and put it to one side of my plate when no one was watching, then eat up the potato and I was free.

'See,' Mrs Wormald would say, regarding my empty plate benignly, 'it's not that bad after all now, is it, hey?'

One morning at school assembly, Mr Simpson told us there was going to be an important announcement on the radio.

It was 11 November 1965. All normal lessons were cancelled and there was an air of great excitement. The whole school gathered together, all seventy of us, in the main block after lunch. The concertina partition between our kindergarten classroom and the classroom next door, which was shared by standard one and two, was opened up, just like it was for school plays. Two standard-five boys carried Mr Simpson's big brown Bakelite wireless over from his house and put it on a desk in the middle of the room. We, the smaller kids, sat cross-legged on the floor beside it. Older kids sat behind us on chairs.

Mr Simpson switched on the radio. It took a few minutes to warm up and then it crackled into life. There was music for a bit and then the announcer came on.

'This is the Rhodesian Broadcasting Corporation,' he said. 'Please stand by for an important message from the prime minister, the honourable Mr Ian Douglas Smith.'

After a pause, Ian Smith began. His voice was easy to recognize because he seemed to speak through his nose and he had a very thick Rhodesian accent. He started by recalling how we Rhodesians had been so loyal to the Queen.

'The people of Rhodesia have demonstrated their loyalty to the Crown and to their kith and kin in the United Kingdom through two world wars, and have been prepared to shed their blood and give of their substance in what they believe to be the mutual interests of freedom-loving people.'

But now, Smith said, all that we had cherished was about to be shattered on some rocks called expediency. He sounded quite cross about it.

At that point I stopped listening because I got into a scrape with Fatty Slabbert, who had flicked an elastic band at the back of my neck. Apparently, while Fatty Slabbert and I were bickering, Ian Smith declared Unilateral Independence, UDI, which meant we were no longer part of the British Empire. He had done it because the Queen wanted us to be ruled by the blacks. Smith said that UDI might be quite hard for us. But that was OK because we were pretty tough:

'The mantle of the pioneers has fallen on our shoulders and we will, I'm sure, be able to face any difficulties which may occur, fortified by the same strength and courage which distinguished our forefathers in days gone by.'

He made it sound as though we were going to be quite important.

'I believe that we are a courageous people and history has cast us in an heroic role.'

I thought that was great, we could all be heroes now. I quite fancied the idea of being a hero.

'We may be a small country, but we are a determined people who have been called upon to play a role of worldwide significance. We Rhodesians have rejected the doctrinaire philosophy of appeasement and surrender.

We have struck a blow for the preservation of justice, civilization and Christianity, and in the spirit of this belief we have this day assumed our sovereign independence.

God bless you all.'

I didn't really know what it all meant, but Mr Simpson and Miss Gloyne seemed very grave and solemn about it.

I'm not sure if anyone tried to explain to us what UDI really meant. Certainly no one said that Rhodesia would be isolated, that there would be economic sanctions against us and a war. That we would have to go into the army, that some of us would be killed, that we would be ambushed and attacked, that our farms would be burnt down and abandoned. No one said that.

But soon after the broadcast things began to change.

At first it was just little things. The men from the Public Works Department, the PWD, arrived in their yellow lorry and fixed anti-grenade screens on to the outside of our dormitory windows.

Then a firebomb was actually thrown into Chipinga school. After that we started practising emergency escape drills. We each had a partner so we could help one another up and out of the windows, which were too high for most of the boys to negotiate on their own.

They started locking the dormitory at night, and if you wanted to go to the lavatory after lights out you had to wake the dorm captain, whose bed was next to the door. He was supposed to unlock it to let you out and lock it again after you returned. But in practice he banned us from nocturnal pissing expeditions and we had to climb on to a locker and piss out of the window instead. You had to aim through the mesh of the grenade screen and if you wobbled it splashed back on you. You could tell where the favourite pissing holes were because the piss slowly dissolved the paint down the wall in those spots, and the flowers in the beds below them shrivelled and died.

There was another drill too, called 'school attack procedure'. It was great fun. We had to pretend that *tsotsis*, who were now called terrorists, or 'terrs' for short, were firing rockets or throwing hand grenades at us. At the teachers' instruction we had to shut down the Tilly lamps and lie under our beds with our hands over our ears. This immediately spawned a new game called 'incoming'. The cry of 'in-come-ing!' by any boy meant that we all had to dive under beds as quickly as possible, and the last one under would be given a 'lamey' – a sharp thump on the arm with the point of a knuckle.

In the Pines, the games began to change too. Hounds and deer and Pine Cone War, instead of being Jerries versus Tommies, or cowboys versus Indians, or even Boers versus Brits, as it had been in the past, were now SAS and the Crocodile Gang, or sometimes, if Fatty Slabbert was organizing it, Rhodies and *kaffirs*.

Of course, everyone wanted to be on the Rhodie SAS side, but because I was little I usually ended up as a *kaffir* and a member of the Crocodile Gang, whether I liked it or not.

Five

The best thing about school was when it stopped. The atmosphere was dizzy with anticipation. We folded our OHMS bedclothes in neat square piles on the ends of our narrow iron beds and packed up our clothes in our black tin trunks. We had a final assembly, after which we threw our hats high into the air and ran whooping and screaming down the pavement to the gravel car park, where parents, or African drivers sent by our parents, would be waiting for us in mud-splattered pick-up trucks, ready to ferry us back to the farms and timber plantations and tea estates.

During the holidays, my mother tried to make up for having sent me away to boarding school so young by letting me come with her on her medical rounds. We went in the Mini, which was like a mobile clinic, equipped with a medical chest built by Francis the carpenter to my father's design. It was a cross between a tool box and a fishing tackle box and it fitted exactly into the boot, opening out in tiers. Inside was a wonderful array of equipment: chrome scalpels with glinting blades, cotton-wool swabs, curved needles and catgut for sutures, and dozens of bottles of pills and tubes of ointments.

We covered hundreds of miles, servicing a network of African clinics and small rural hospitals. All of life was there. And death. It was death that left its image most vividly on me. Death was clearly something special. People reacted to it in dramatic fashion, often screaming and howling when news of it was broken to them. Death could apparently happen to anyone, although obviously it happened mostly to Africans. Whites only tended to die if they were very old. Africans died at any age.

Death didn't seem to worry my mother too much. I suppose she was used to it by now. She sometimes let me come with her to PMs. That's what they were called, postmortems, when the police asked her to cut bodies up to see if there'd been foul play. Our dead bodies were not chilled and odourless like town bodies were. They weren't filed in the drawers of big fridges by men wearing green overalls and white aprons who squeaked about in tennis shoes on cement floors.

Our bodies were often dug up from their graves weeks and weeks after they'd been buried. You could tell how long ago the people had been buried because of the *makonye*, which was Shona for maggot larvae. When Africans buried their dead they got a hollow stick, a length of bamboo or a reed, and placed one end touching the body and the other sticking up out of the grave. They came every day and put some food by the grave, until one day they saw that the *makonye* had come up the bamboo and were wriggling about on top of the grave. Then the family stopped bringing food.

It seemed like a waste of the food, and when I asked my mother why they did it she didn't seem to know. Violet didn't really want to talk about it.

It was only some years later that Father Kennedy the Carmelite told me what grave food was all about.

'Africans practise ancestor worship,' explained Father Kennedy, and we all wrote it down in our exercise books. 'They take food to the graveside because they believe that the spirit of the departed is wandering in a forest, a sort of equivalent to our purgatory, I suppose. And while the spirit is lost, it requires daily sustenance to keep it going.'

Father Kennedy was telling us all this because I had asked, so I put my hand up again to show I was paying attention.

'Yes, Godwin, what is it now?' he sighed. I think he found me a bit tiresome.

'But when the food is still there the next day, don't they realize that the spirit isn't eating it at all?'

'Hmm. That's an interesting point,' Father Kennedy conceded. 'In fact the food is almost invariably eaten by wild animals at night, or by birds, or dogs, thus sustaining at least the myth, if not the spirit.' He chuckled indulgently at his little joke.

I wrote down: 'Spirit food eaten by animals in dark.' And I drew a picture of a grave, and next to it a smiling hyena with a napkin tied round its neck, sitting at a candlelit table piled high with food.

Father Kennedy continued, 'Once the *makonye* appear, the relatives stop bringing the food, because they believe that these grubs represent the spirit, and that it has now successfully navigated its way home.'

Europeans didn't believe in that sort of stuff. We didn't leave food by our graves, only flowers. I wondered whether the spirit of oom Piet was still lost in the spiritual forest, weak from hunger as it tried vainly to find its way back to South Africa, where he had come from originally.

My first PM was in Cashel. We went to the police station, where we met up with a white section officer, two black constables and a black civilian called the complainant. To reach the graves, deep inside Mutambara Tribal Trust Land, we bounced along for hours down a narrow rutted road in a grey police Land Rover which had a spare wheel bolted on to the bonnet and a metal grill over the windscreen.

The bodies to be dissected that day were a mother and her two children. Their father, the civilian man in the other Land Rover, believed they had been murdered. Unfortunately for us he only reported the matter to the police three weeks after they had died, and after he'd completed all the traditional burial rituals.

'Why did he wait so long to tell us if he thought they'd been murdered?' I piped up as we bounced along.

'Well, think about it,' my mother explained patiently. 'This is one of the most remote areas of Cashel. He can't read or write, how can you expect him to know about the finer details of forensic medicine? And anyway, it took him five days to walk to the police station. What was he supposed to do in the mean time, leave the bodies of his nearest and dearest rotting on the floor?'

I couldn't think of an answer. But the section officer, who was driving, seemed to agree with me. He was deeply unenthusiastic about this duty.

'The complainant arrived at night,' he explained. 'There were no Europeans on duty and instead of waiting until the next morning, the bloody charge office sergeant entered the report into the Crime Register and gave it a CR number, so we've got no option but to follow through the investigation. I really am most apologetic, doctor.'

He'd been apologizing for the inconvenience the whole trip.

Finally the road ran out and we drove slowly through the bush, following a footpath, the long grass and shrubs scraping along the bottom of the vehicle. We stopped in a clearing among the msasa trees. The air was hot and the cicadas' screech filled the still afternoon.

In the clearing there were three graves, though they were difficult to make out because they weren't marked by anything. No cross or headstone, not even a little cairn. They were just mounds of fresh earth against the side of a granite boulder, one big one and two smaller ones.

The constables pulled out shovels and picks from the back of the Land Rover, unbuttoned their khaki tunics, wrapped cloths around their mouths and noses, and began digging up the big mound. They dug forcefully at first and then more gently when they thought they were getting close to the body.

My mother put on a white gown with tapes that fastened at the back. On top of the white gown she put on a big red apron made of rubber, just like the rubber wetting sheet I had to put on my bed at school. She tied a white mask over her face and pulled on thick black rubber gloves which reached right up to her elbows.

On the tailgate of the Land Rover she had laid a selection of jars with rubber seals on the lids like the ones you put home-made jam into. There was a big biscuit tin there too, and she was scrabbling around in it for scalpels, forceps and scissors.

The biggest tool of all was so big that it wouldn't fit into the tin and had to be packed separately, bundled into sackcloth. It had long iron handles and looked like a cross between a pair of pliers and garden shears. These were the rib-cutters.

The constables were calling to us through their muffles. They had reached the body. It was folded into a sheet. The SO had set up a wooden trestle table, and he told them to lift the body on to it. Gingerly holding each end of the sheet cocoon, they tried to hoist it out. But the sheet was completely rotten under-neath and the body ripped through it and fell heavily back into the grave.

'Be careful!' snapped the SO. 'You'll damage the evidence.' One of the constables stumbled off into the msasas to vomit. The SO took his place and the body was finally lifted on to the table. A dark cloud of flies hovered over it.

My mother handed me a spray gun. 'Here, this can be your job. You can be my special little assistant.'

I grasped the spray gun, stepped forward proudly, aimed at the flies and began pumping the wooden handle in and out, until most of them had gone. After that I was told to wait back at the Land Rover while my mother got on with the dissection.

The man they called the complainant was a short barefoot

man in torn shorts and a disintegrating T-shirt on which was printed *Things go better with Coca-Cola*. He had come along in the other Land Rover to give us directions, but the SO suggested he stay back from the graves, so he sat with me behind the vehicles while my mother cut up his family.

After a while I asked him what had happened to them.

'I came home late at night,' he said quietly, 'after my wife and children had already eaten their supper. We all went to bed and the next morning I woke up and found them already dead while they were still asleep.'

'How?' I asked. 'How did they die?'

The Coke man lowered his voice still further, so I had to strain to hear. 'It was a spell,' he whispered, 'a spell cast on them by my neighbour, who is a *muroyi*.'

A *muroyi* was an African witch. They didn't have long noses and warts, and they didn't wear silly pointy hats or ride on broomsticks. African witches were much more dangerous than European witches, and they rode around on the backs of hyenas at night.

'He suspect me of stealing his goat,' continued the Coke man, 'so he cast a spell on my family and they died.'

'I see,' I said gravely. Africans often died of spells.

'And I didn't even steal the goat,' he added indignantly as I got up to sneak a closer look at the PM.

My mother was inserting the scalpel at the base of the rib-cage. She sliced downwards and the flesh fell away easily, but there was no blood. The smell was terrible. I'd smelt lots of dead animals before, rotten ones too, but this was different. It was so bad I felt like being sick, and I had to hold my shirt over my nose.

Now my mother picked up the rib-cutters. She had made just enough of an incision so that the bottom blade of the rib-cutters could get a purchase there. Using all her strength she grasped the long handles of the rib-cutters, manoeuvred the blades into position and squeezed them together, grunting with the effort. Nothing happened for a couple of seconds and then there was a loud crunch as the sternum cleaved in two.

She crunched the blades down the ribcage until she reached the bottom. Then she pulled it open like a chicken breast, to reveal all the insides. I belly-crawled forward again to see my mother cutting out various organs with her scalpel. Her forehead was covered with sweat now. As she cut each organ out, she picked it up in a pair of surgical forceps and plopped it into a jar of formaldehyde.

Finally it was over and my mother pressed the ribcage closed, like a pair of double doors. There was no sign of the constables, they had disappeared into the bush. The SO shouted for them, and eventually they stumbled into the clearing looking ill. They reburied the mother and set about digging up the two children, and the whole process was repeated, only this time it was much easier to cut the ribcages open.

One of the children was a little boy about my age, and when they dug him up they found that he had been buried with his favourite toys: a hoop made of a car wheel rim, with a stick to guide it, and a little model bicycle made of copper wire. It was beautifully made, with all the right detail: revolving pedals, mudguards, brake handles, a chain, even a rear-view mirror. The toys were packed in the sheet by his sides, where his hands rested, in case he wanted to play with them while he was lost in the spiritual forest. I wondered how he could see to play with the hoop, though, because he just had empty sockets in his head where his eyes should have been.

'They steal the copper wire from the phone lines, you know,' said the SO, looking at the toy bike. 'That's why the phones are always out of order. It's a bloody nuisance.'

After we'd put the bodies back, the widower approached and looked blankly at the disturbed graves. He said something to one of the constables.

'He wants to know how they were killed and who did this thing,' said the constable.

'Hell, we don't know how they died yet,' explained the SO. 'The specimens have to be sent to the forensic lab in Salisbury to be tested. That'll take weeks and even then we might not be able to tell.'

The constable translated this and the widower spoke up again, quietly insistent.

'He wants to know, if you are not able to tell these things, then why did you dig up his wife and children?'

'I didn't say we definitely wouldn't be able to tell, dammit, I said we weren't sure. He didn't make things any easier for us by delaying so long. And anyway, even if we can establish cause of death, we still won't necessarily know who's responsible.' The SO was getting irritated. 'And constable, you tell him from me that if he tries to take the law into his own hands, and does anything to harm his neighbours, I'll have him arrested so fast his feet won't touch the bloody ground. Goditt?'

It took ten minutes to drive from the graves to the widower's kraal. It was a poor kraal, three little pole-and-dagga huts under ragged thatch that badly needed replacing. Several scrawny chickens foraged in amongst the huts. They were surrounded by a modest field of stunted maize and millet.

My mother nosed around the sleeping and kitchen huts, while the SO wandered over to the granary – a miniature hut raised up on five-foot stilts. This was where Africans stored their *mealie* meal, to protect it from scavenging rodents. He climbed up the crooked home-made ladder and disappeared inside.

'Doctor, I think you'd better see this,' said the SO, emerging fom the granary a few minutes later. He had a large makeshift bucket, a drum with its top cut off. Inside was *mealie* meal. On the drum was a label which read: *Contains arsenic – POISON*

– do not take internally. Do not re-use container. It had a black skull-and-crossbones sign on it.

They called the widower over and asked him about the drum.

'My wife found it at the grinding mill when she went to get our *mealies* ground,' he said, through the constable.

'When?' asked my mother.

'The day before she died,' he said.

'Did you eat any *mealie* meal from here?'

He thought for a moment.

'No. I did not.'

'Mr Mtsoro,' began my mother, consulting her clipboard – it was the first time anyone had addressed him by name all day – 'I think it has been a terrible accident. This drum used to contain arsenic, a very poisonous chemical used to kill weeds. I think your wife put the *mealie* meal inside without first washing out the drum. It only needs a small amount of arsenic mixed in with the *mealie* meal to kill someone.'

Mr Mtsoro looked sceptical.

'I am going to take a sample of the *mealie* meal and have it tested,' said my mother, 'and then we will know for sure.'

The SO gathered a specimen amount in a plastic bag and labelled it. Then he ordered the constables to dispose of the rest. When the widower realized their intention, he was horrified and remonstrated with them.

'We have to throw it out or you may be poisoned and die also,' said the SO firmly, 'and dogs too or goats or chickens.' He ordered the constables to dig a shallow pit and empty the big drum of meal into it. They sprinkled a little petrol on the heaped *mealie* meal and set it alight.

Mr Mtsoro watched as half his season's food slowly burnt away in the thick black smoke. He began to cry silently.

I felt sorry for him and tried to think of something kind to tell him. I walked over to him and patted him awkwardly on the arm.

'Don't worry, Mr Mtsoro,' I said, 'there aren't so many of you to feed now, so you'll still have plenty to eat.'

And he cried even harder.

My mother did lots of postmortems and I began to realize just how many different ways there were to die. You could drown, for example. Drowning was a common cause of death in PMs. Africans were forever falling into rivers, usually on their way back from beer drinks. Few of them could swim even when they were sober.

You had to be careful with deaths by drowning. If drowned bodies had been left for a few days they could turn into 'bloaters' – all swollen up. On the first incision bloaters could spray a fountain of watery blood all over you.

Violet nearly drowned in Silverstream river. We were allowed to swim there, in a deep rock pool between two waterfalls, though we had to be careful to stay well upstream of the bottom waterfall. As far as we knew no one had ever seen a crocodile this far up, either. There were *leguaans* here, water iguanas which looked like mini-crocodiles, but they didn't eat people. Sometimes there were water snakes too.

Violet was supposed to be looking after me while I swam in the rock pool but it was such a hot day that she stripped to her underwear and jumped in too. Then she remembered she couldn't swim. Her head bobbed up a couple of times, and she panicked, uttered a single piercing scream and disappeared coughing beneath the water again.

I swam over to her and, remembering my life-saving lessons from school, I manoeuvred her into the correct position to life-save her. But she was much, much heavier than a tin plate, which was the only thing I'd actually life-saved before. Her head kept going under the water and her eyes started rolling around so I could only see their whites.

We started to drift slowly down towards the waterfall, and

I could hear it roaring close by. We were both going to get sucked over the edge, I thought. Violet was getting heavier and I felt weaker, but I still held on to her and tried to life-save her. Then suddenly Jain was there, and together we managed to drag Violet to the river bank and haul her out. I lay on my back on the bank, breathing hard, while next to me Violet vomited up water.

It was amazing how much water she vomited up.

Postmortems could even be quite funny, although of course it was very bad manners to laugh at them. I did laugh once, though, at a man who had hanged himself from a msasa tree because his wife no longer loved him. He worked at the factory and had been missing for several days when it was reported to my father that some men hunting in the bush had seen him hanging there.

My father reported it to the police and they asked him to send the body in to the station. So we drove out to retrieve it, taking one of the hunters for directions.

We climbed up a little *kopje*, and there, near the top, was the man, hanging from a msasa tree. His neck was tied to a branch by a piece of bark plaited into a rope. There was a strong breeze ahead of a thunder storm, and the body swayed in the wind, almost as if it were still alive. And it slowly rotated one way and then the other, as the rope twisted and untwisted against the branch.

'Hmm, well there's nothing for it, I suppose,' said my father, and he called me over. From his pocket he took his Swiss Army knife that I was usually not allowed even to touch.

'You're the tree climber in the family,' he said. 'Climb up the tree and cut the rope.'

He considered several different bits of the knife, including a little saw and some pliers – folding them back into the wide red handle in turn.

'You can use this blade,' he said finally, indicating the biggest of all the blades. 'But don't open it until you get up there.'

I shinned up the tree easily and out along the branch, and got myself in position over the rope. From up above, the dead man's body looked somehow different. He had a bald patch on the crown of his head and his chin was resting on his chest, making him look as though he was in mourning.

'OK, you ready?' I called down.

'Yes, yes. Get on with it,' said my father, and I began hacking away at the bark rope. It was surprisingly brittle, and tough to cut, and I had to have a rest halfway through. Finally there was a ripping sound and the body plunged to the ground below. He hit the ground feet first, and then collapsed forward on to his face, with his knees tucked in under his chest and his bottom in the air. And as soon as he fell, he began to fart. It was a loud, foul-smelling fart that went on and on as if he were farting the life out of himself.

I was still at the age when I instinctively found farts amusing, and I began to titter, up on my branch.

'Have some respect!' my father hissed.

I noticed him glancing at his watch. Later he told me that the fart had lasted for over five minutes, which we both agreed was probably the longest fart in the world.

Of course, most of my mother's patients were still alive. At the African clinic on the edge of Melsetter there were hundreds of them. They lined up from early in the morning, sitting in a ragged queue that often meandered all the way down to the main road, more than eight hundred yards away. The Africans were very patient and it was an orderly queue, with no shoving or jostling for position. Just the sounds of coughing and hawking and chattering, of children crying and mothers murmuring to their babies as they breast-fed them.

The patients flocked in from the surrounding tribal lands, and they brought their own provisions with them in bundles balanced on their heads; maize cobs, sweet potatoes, mangos and bananas. And for those that hadn't, a flourishing market had grown up around the clinic's permanent queue.

The clinic itself was a small ramshackle building, easily overwhelmed by the swell of humanity that swarmed there to audition their various ailments. It consisted of two *rondavels* joined together and each topped by a conical roof of galvanized tin that gave off noises as loud as gunshots as it expanded in the sun, and again when it cooled in the late afternoon.

Every time the roof cracked, the purple-headed lizards that sunned themselves on it got a terrible fright. They scuttled desperately down the walls and slithered off into the bush. A few minutes later they returned and the whole routine would begin again. They never seemed to learn.

Janet, the nurse, lived in another double *rondavel* next door with her husband and two children. She would deal with the routine cases and keep the complicated or serious ones back for my mother to look at. Even the very serious cases would take their places patiently in the queue.

Once, when my mother was busy inside the clinic, I was playing outside with Janet's children, and I was astonished to see a man towards the end of the queue with a barbed fishing arrow straight through his head. He was sitting cross-legged, messily eating a mango with great gusto. The point of the arrow stuck out of one temple, its tail into the other.

Janet hadn't noticed him because she'd been swamped in her office processing other cases. No one else had thought to bring him to her attention. In fact no one else in the queue showed any great interest in this man who appeared to have an arrow lodged right through his brain.

I went up to say hello and he went through the whole Shona greeting rigmarole, without appearing to be in any pain.

'May I have a look?' I asked politely, as though I might have been seeking permission to inspect a piece of handiwork. He was happy to oblige and bowed his head to my level so I could examine its resident arrow. I fingered the arrowhead gingerly; the tip itself wasn't that impressive, it was very narrow, like a flattened nail, but sharp too. The impressive feature was the fearsome rows of barbs down either side of the shaft, that disappeared into a surprisingly small wound in the side of his skull.

'It is to stop the fish from escaping away,' he explained. And he launched into a learned account of the finer points of arrow fishing, which I found fascinating.

'So how did the arrow end up through your head,' I asked finally, when there was a lull in the conversation.

'It was my friend,' he said. 'My friend slipped on the mud when he was aiming the arrow.' He cocked his head to one side and laughed as though it were a minor inconvenience.

'Doesn't it hurt?' I enquired.

'No. When it first went in, it felt like a bee stinging me. But once it was inside my head, it didn't hurt too much. And my wife gave me aspirin for making headache better.' He gave his wife, who was sitting next to him, an appreciative pat and she grinned.

'Come with me,' I said. 'You should be a priority case.'

I led him to the clinic door, and called to my mother through the bead curtain that was supposed to keep the flies out of the examining room.

'Mu-um. There's a patient here that I think you should see.'

'I'm busy,' she said. 'Anyway Janet's already picked out the acute cases.'

'I think you'll want to see this chap,' I said confidently, nodding reassuringly at my companion.

I was eventually allowed to bring him in after she'd finished with her previous patient. We were delayed while I disentangled the fly beads that had got caught up on his arrow. Then we made our triumphant entrance.

My mother had her head down, writing out case notes on a filing card.

'Meet Mr Arrow Head,' I introduced.

Janet gasped and my mother looked up.

'Good God!' she spluttered.

Mr Arrow Head looked gratified that he was of such interest, and he smiled cordially as he accepted the chair Janet proffered him.

Since I had scouted him out, I was allowed to stay for the examination. They dabbed disinfectant on the entrance and exit holes, and they injected him with antibiotics and anti-tetanus serum. Then my mother shone her special torch into the pupils of his eyes, and did various other tests to check his reactions.

Finally she took hold of the tail end of the arrow and joggled it very tentatively. Mr Arrow Head gave a sharp intake of breath.

'Sore?' asked my mother, unnecessarily. He nodded vigorously and his arrow rotated with each nod.

'I'm afraid there's nothing more we can do for you here,' she explained to him. 'We'll order you an ambulance to take you to Umtali, and there they will x-ray you and see what to do next.'

Mr Arrow Head seemed disappointed that she wasn't going to pull the arrow out there and then.

'Will I be all right?' he asked, sounding fearful for the first time.

'Of course you will be,' said my mother. 'They've got all the latest equipment in Umtali, and I'm sure they'll take very good care of you there.'

Mr Arrow Head seemed very grateful for this reassurance, and insisted on shaking everyone's hand before leaving to sit outside on the grass once more with his wife, waiting for the ambulance to collect him.

'Remarkable!' said my mother to Janet, after he'd left.

'Absolutely extraordinary. The arrow's gone directly through his frontal lobe without any apparent ill effect on his neurological activity. Incredible.'

A few weeks later I was playing Indians in our garden before breakfast. Albert the Mozambican had helped me pitch my wigwam on the front lawn, and I was parading around barefoot on the dewy grass in a home-made cloak and a feathered headdress, armed with my bow. I reached into my quiver for another arrow to shoot at the old gum tree when I suddenly remembered Mr Arrow Head.

Over breakfast I asked my mother what had happened to him. She continued to crunch loudly at her burnt toast, behind her newspaper, and then said through the crumbs, 'He died, of course. He never had a chance. It was a complete fluke that he lived as long as he did.'

'Well, I wish you'd told me at the time,' I grumbled.

Her newspaper came down.

'What is it now?' she asked, exasperated.

'Nothing. It's just that if you'd told me then, I would have said goodbye to him properly.'

I got down from the table and mooched around outside for a bit. Then I fired off a couple more arrows at the old gum tree, in memory of Mr Arrow Head.

One of them was a bull's eye.

Some of the women who came to see my mother in the early days were insistently vague about their ailments. It began with one young woman who refused to give any useful medical details to Janet, the nurse, and preferred to face relegation to the back of the queue. Eventually she made it to the examination room, having revealed only a general headache and non-specific pains. She threaded her way through the gaudy fly-bead curtains and saw Janet at my mother's side.

'I will not be needing a translator,' she said, fiddling with her hands on her lap. 'I can speak to doctor myself.'

'But nurse Janet is my assistant, not just a translator,' said my mother huffily. They couldn't start taking this sort of strop from patients.

The patient sat in pointed silence. My mother broke first. She caught Janet's eye and nodded her to the door. Janet departed, sniffing with indignation. I was sitting just outside the bead curtain, pretending to be absorbed with my colouring-in book.

My mother consulted the unhelpfully brief case card.

'Now what seems to be the problem, Mercy?' she asked when they were alone. 'Remember that anything you say to me is confidential. It is a secret. No one else will know.'

The woman hesitated again, and then seemed to come to a decision.

'Doctor, I am not yet twenty-four years of age and I have six children. My husband has no job and we have no money.'

It sounded like a punt for charity, not an altogether unknown tactic. But the young woman continued:

'Doctor, children is now enough. No more. You must give me *muti* for to stop more babies.'

This was the early sixties and modern contraception was almost unheard of in rural African communities.

'I have read about birth control. In a magazine. From town,' said Mercy. Then, expecting to have her word doubted, she continued, 'I went to school until standard eight. I wanted to train to be a nurse or a teacher, but my father was poor and he had only enough money for school fees for my brothers. So he married me to another for *lobola*.'

Lobola was the Shona bride price and was a widely accepted custom. Among ordinary folk it usually amounted to a few head of cattle and goats, and sometimes cash too. Cash was paid on a sort of instalment plan. A down payment followed by regular premiums until the full amount was reached.

'I have had a child every year since I was married,' said Mercy. 'Now I want no more.'

My mother outlined the contraceptive possibilities. The condom, the diaphragm, the inter-uterine device—

But Mercy interrupted.

'It has to be something that my husband will never find out about. If he discovers that I have done this contra . . .'

'Contraception,' coaxed my mother.

'If he finds out, then he can divorce me, according to our custom.'

My mother talked to Mercy for a long time. Then and on subsequent occasions. She learnt a lot from Mercy. She learnt that if an African woman fails to conceive within the first two years of marriage, this is grounds for divorce. She learnt that in some cases if a woman bears only a small number of children, one or two, then this too can justify the husband returning her to her father, as a poor breeder. She learnt that many African women, educated for the first generation now, no longer wanted the tyranny of a dozen children, especially when ten were likely to survive, unlike the old days when they were lucky if two or three made it to adulthood.

'The pill?' suggested my mother. 'You could use that without him noticing. Where could you hide it?'

'In the tea tin,' replied Mercy confidently. 'African men will never ever go to the tea tin. That is only a woman's job.'

And so my mother began her family planning advice service. Mercy evidently had a lot of friends, and within weeks dozens of women were turning up at the clinic with 'non-specific ailments' – 'NSA', as Janet now noted it down on the cards in their code. Word got around that Janet too could be trusted, and she soon took over family planning services.

In time Mercy broke cover and went on a family planning course in Umtali. She came back as a qualified 'educator' and was given charge of a mobile family planning clinic that traversed the Tribal Trust Lands in a converted Land Rover. Their announced function was to check on the health of new mothers and young children, but surreptitiously they also doled out contraceptives to those women who wanted them. Even today, in many huts throughout the eastern highlands and further afield, you will find a little something extra at the bottom of the tea tin.

Years later I heard that Mercy was killed in the war. She had chosen to ignore warnings from the guerrillas to stop her family planning services. Contraception, the guerrillas said, was a white man's conspiracy to reduce the black population. By carrying it out, Mercy was the white man's stooge.

The guerrillas pointed out that at the same time as the government was encouraging black people to have fewer children, they were also trying to encourage more white people to immigrate to Rhodesia. The government even had a special settler campaign where all the whites in the country were asked to write letters to ten of their friends abroad, telling them what a pleasant life Europeans could have in Rhodesia. The government would pay for them to come and would find them jobs.

In reply the guerrillas launched their own 'have a baby for Zimbabwe' campaign, and told Africans that the more children they had the sooner the country would be theirs.

Mercy, by then a grandmother, scoffed at the politicization of family planning and not long after her Land Rover detonated a land mine. Her legs were blown off and she died before they could get her to hospital. Her driver and some passengers who had hitched a lift were killed too. It didn't get much publicity, though. By then black civilians were being killed by land mines every day.

When the Africans did finally inherit the country in 1980, one of the first acts of the new government was to ban the

Family Planning Association, as a racist organization. The ban lasted less than a year. It was overturned after a mutinous horde of African women threatened to march on parliament and roast the politicians – most of them men – alive.

Now family planning trucks are once again traversing the countryside, tendering choice to women who have so little of it in their lives.

Easily the single biggest life-saving aspect of my mother's practice was her vaccination programme. It was a long haul, though, to get it going. To start with the witch doctors were totally opposed to it. A vaccination might initiate rural Africans into western medicine and help to break down their fear of it. And for every patient who went west for medical treatment there would be one fewer for the *ngangas*.

The witch doctors put out the most hair-raising rumours about the dreadful things that would happen to people who were vaccinated. They would be rendered infertile, they would go mad, they would die a lingering, mouth-frothing death.

Eventually the Internal Affairs Department, and even the police, had to intervene, bullying the witch doctors into sullen submission by threatening to imprison them if they continued peddling these lurid warnings.

There was, in general, an ambiguous relationship between my mother and the local witch doctors. She took them extremely seriously, refusing to dismiss them as quacks, like my father and most other Europeans did. For my mother respected the power that the *ngangas* had over their believers.

The Shona believed that all illnesses had a reason, a cause that could only be found in the spirit world. So though my mother could usually treat the symptoms of an illness, the witch doctor still had to be consulted to divine the cause. Eventually she struck up an accommodation with certain 'enlightened' witch doctors, and she would even refer to them patients in whom she could find no medical symptoms. In return many witch doctors began referring their patients to my mother and then sharing credit for the cure.

My mother also became increasingly influenced by the obvious power of witchcraft. She was not above fighting fire with fire, developing her own spells to help convince patients that they would now get better as long as they continued to take their prescribed medicine as well.

By the time I was old enough to accompany my mother on her rounds, the witch doctors' opposition to vaccinations was on the decline. Grand tours to inoculate people against smallpox, diphtheria, tuberculosis and polio had become part of our dry-season routine, and there is no doubt they saved thousands of lives. The same lives that the guerrillas would later claim we were trying to snuff out with hard-sell contraception.

I can remember one tour which took us high up into the mountains on the Mozambique border. It must have been in the mid-1960s and the war between the Portuguese and their black anti-colonial guerrillas was well underway. Large tracts of Mozambique were already without any real administration.

We had sent word out ahead that we would be carrying out the vaccinations, and when we arrived there were already thousands of tribespeople gathered – almost all of them Ndau from across the border. We weren't really supposed to vaccinate Mozambicans, but my mother felt that it made good sense, to prevent disease spreading across to our side, because so many of the Ndau moved freely back and forth.

I was allowed to help with the polio vaccine for the children. I carried the tray of sugar lumps and behind me came a health assistant with a bottle of polio vaccine. He would squeeze a drop of the bright pink vaccine into each lump and place one on every tongue. Then I'd call for 'tongues out' and march down the line checking that they'd swallowed.

My biggest problem was to prevent the children from coming around again to get a second sugar lump.

Six

Some diseases were more interesting than others. The most interesting of all was leprosy. If you got leprosy, bits of your body fell off. Only black people got leprosy.

Fatty Slabbert told leper jokes at school, but he'd never seen a leper in real life. In real life the first sign that you had leprosy was when you felt numb in your end bits, your fingers and toes or the tip of your nose. My mother would check patients for burns on their hands. Often lepers would burn their fingers in the cooking fire in the early stages because they couldn't feel the heat.

The first leper I ever diagnosed was Jacob Number Ten from the factory, although no one believed me at the time. Jacob Number Ten was a boiler stoker and he was called Number Ten to distinguish him from another Jacob. Number Ten was his clocking-in number.

I had gone to work with my father that day. My father had a big office with a window that looked out over a lawn with sprinklers on it. Inside, there was a row of tall grey filing cabinets and a sloping desk on which to look at technical drawings and plans and maps of the estates. On the wall was a calendar from 'SKF – *The world's leading ball bearing manufacturers.*'

My father sat behind a wide mahogany desk. Most of it was covered by wire baskets piled high with manila folders. There was a huge piston from a bulldozer that he used as an ashtray. And there was a roladex office diary, with a new page for every day and Sundays in red. When I went to work with my father he let me move the diary forward to the next day, carefully lifting the previous day's page over the metal hoops on to the pile of days gone by.

If I agreed to be quiet I was sometimes allowed to settle in the corner at the angled drawing table, where I was provided with crayons and paper. I would doodle away contentedly with my tongue stuck out of the corner of my mouth in concentration, interrupting my father only to present him with completed art works.

From time to time Old Zuma the tea boy would shuffle in, bearing a tray of tea arranged carefully on little crocheted doilies. Old Zuma had permanently trembling hands, from what was probably early Parkinson's disease, and try as he did to hold the tray steady, much of the tea slopped over into the saucers. But he was a tribal headman and had immense authority over the workers, often being brought in to settle disputes. So there was no thought of getting rid of him.

Old Zuma had somehow found me a chipped china mug with a picture of elephants around it, each one using its trunk to hold on to the tail of the one in front of it. He would serve my father first and then, approaching with almost unbearable slowness, set the elephant mug carefully down on the window ledge above my table, usually splattering tea on my drawings. He would smile a wide, toothless smile, and say in Shona, 'I have brought you your elephants.'

He always said that. Then he would shuffle slowly away with the empty tea tray.

It was just after morning tea that Winfield the weighbridge boy knocked on my father's door. He was so agitated that the biro he kept lodged snugly in his hair fell on to the floor – the only time I ever saw it fall.

'Jacob Number Ten is on fire,' said Winfield, on his hands and knees as he searched for his fallen biro under the desk. 'Come quickly.'

He and my father dashed out of the door and down the corridor, pushing past Old Zuma. I trotted along behind, grateful for the excitement. I imagined that Jacob Number Ten would look like the burning bush in my illustrated Bible, permanently on fire but never burning up. A bit like the blue brandy flames that played over Christmas pudding.

We soon reached the clinic. It was a prefab – a white tunnel of corrugated asbestos. Cuthbert the orderly was away and Jacob Number Ten sat by himself on the patients' bench in the deserted clinic. He held his hands gingerly in front of him. From his elbows down they were red and gooey and skinless. They smelt like roast pork. Winfield blanched and fled, leaving my father alone with Jacob Number Ten. The burns really were horrific but Jacob Number Ten was astonishingly stoical.

'I am very sorry for the trouble, *baas* Godwin,' he said as my father yanked open drawers and cupboards, collecting dressings and bandages, scissors and ointment.

Jacob Number Ten threw open his bloody, roasted arms in a gesture of apology. 'I was stoking the big boiler as usual,' he explained. 'I was using the iron stoking rod to push down the ashes before throwing in more firewood, and then I looked down and saw that my arms were on fire.'

'Is that sore?' asked my father, as he gently dabbed the wounds.

'No, it's OK,' said Jacob bravely, giving me a friendly wink. He appeared to have complete control over pain.

'How long have you been a stoker, now, Jacob?' asked my father.

'Ah, more than ten years,' he said.

'Ever hurt yourself before?'

'No, never.' Then he thought for a moment. 'Well, just recently, in the last few months, some small burns on my fingers from going too close to the fire. But small only.'

My father continued to dress the wounds and Jacob never

winced or showed any sign of discomfort. My father was full of admiration.

'Well, Jacob, I'll say one thing for you. You're a much braver man than I am,' he said, looking over his handiwork. 'Now I'll get a truck to take you to Chipinga hospital.'

'Did you burn your nose as well, Jacob?' I asked as we were leaving. I had noticed a dark patch on the end of his nose.

Jacob laughed. 'No, just my arms.'

We walked back to the office and soon I was back at the drawing table while my father read through a pile of letters. I was drawing a picture of Jacob Number Ten. He was throwing an enormous load of firewood into a huge furnace. His arms were engulfed in flames but he was smiling. I drew a speech bubble coming from his mouth. 'I feel fine,' it said. I took it over to my father.

'Yes, very nice,' he said in a distracted way.

'Dad?'

'Mm?'

'Maybe Jacob Number Ten is brave because he's numb on his end bits. Maybe he's got leprosy?'

'I doubt it,' said my Father and sent me back to my corner.

Old Zuma came shuffling back in with his doily-covered tin tray to pick up the empties. I began working on a cameo of him in the corner of my Jacob Number Ten sketch.

Two days later my mother examined Jacob and diagnosed him as an early leper. We were in the sitting room and the eight o'clock news had just finished. I was freshly bathed and attired in my brushed-cotton pyjamas, the ones with the ladybird motif. I had just 'settled' on the sofa under my blair with two dogs at my feet. My parents sometimes let me do that instead of going to bed on my own. The noises outside my bedroom window frightened me – everything seemed so much louder in the dark – the chirping and the croaking, the branch that scraped on the grenade screen, and especially the big African owl which hooted aggressively at me from that corner of the garden.

I was supposed to be asleep but when she told my father that Jacob Number Ten had leprosy I leapt up from under the blair.

'I told you! I told you!' I chanted, jumping up and down on the sofa. But my father claimed he had no recollection of my earlier diagnosis.

'Wet' leprosy was becoming rare, even by the mid-sixties. Most cases were picked up in tribespeople who had come from very remote areas across the border in Mozambique. The Provincial Medical Office employed leper scouts to spot lepers as they came over and to weed them out. Cuthbert, the rather officious medical orderly at Silverstream, who had once worked at Ngomahuru leper asylum, also conducted his own freelance operation. He would board buses that stopped in Silverstream and vet the passengers. He hauled off any lepers he detected and handed them over to the leper scouts to be taken to Umtali.

Most of our lepers ended up at Biriwiri rural hospital, which was also a tuberculosis sanatorium. Biriwiri didn't really look like a hospital. It had a central clinic with a treatment room, a pharmacy and a food store, and all around it were little huts in which the patients lived, often with their families. There were usually several hundred patients and together with their families they made up a colony of over a thousand people.

The colony was presided over by Eric Mutara. Eric had a surname because he was a male nurse and had been away to train at nursing school. As well as a white coat, Eric also had a stethoscope just like my mother's, though his was older and the plastic disc on the end, the bit that you put against the patient's chest, was badly chipped. Eric let me listen through the stethoscope to the breathing of the TB patients. You could tell the really sick ones because their chests bubbled like our aquarium when they breathed. They also coughed a lot and spat gobs of thick green phlegm on to the ground. No matter how much they spat up, there was always more of it left in their chests.

Lepers and TB patients and general patients all mixed together quite happily at Biriwiri. No one was scared of the lepers, because they were 'dry' cases and no longer contagious. Some of the older ones were quite badly disfigured, but even these were not shunned.

The king of the lepers was an old man called Joachim who came from Mozambique. He was also the most dramatically disfigured. He had no fingers left, his arms ended at the pads of his palms. His nostrils had dropped off too. Most of his lips were gone, so that his teeth were permanently bared in a grinning rictus. Joachim spoke with a strange lisp because of his ravaged lips, and at first he was quite difficult to understand. In the side of his head were holes where his ears used to be; the ear lobes had long since gone.

When I first met Joachim he had given me a dispassionate conducted tour of his body, pointing out each deformity and explaining precisely how it affected him. He sometimes wore a bandanna over his nose holes, because without nostrils he found he was breathing in dust and other wind-borne particles. He had been this way for years and was extremely agile on his wooden crutches, which were smooth with age and darkened by sweat.

'How do you pee, if you can't hold your *mboro*?' I had once asked him, and he roared with laughter.

'I just lean back and make sure the wind is behind me,' he said.

Most of the time we would sit on the ground outside the treatment room and play *tsoro*, a traditional Shona game that was a cross between drafts and mahjong. You played it by moving stones along rows of holes in the ground. Joachim was a grand master at *tsoro*. He would deftly move the pebbles from hole to hole by pinching them between his stumps. When we played, a fair crowd of patients would gather round, advising each of us on tactics and breaking into spontaneous little war dances upon victory. He would routinely let me win every second game.

The lepers were better dressed than the other patients because of a bequest of money that had been left by a white farmer 'to be spent on suitable clothing for lepers'. Twice a year the RMS would deliver another order of clothes for them. They were always the same – dresses, skirts, blouses, shirts, trousers, shorts, even hats – all made of tough, light blue denim. And the hems were all trimmed with rose-bud-patterned braid. You could tell the clusters of lepers from far away by their uniform.

With food and accommodation provided, the patients lived fairly indolent lives. They spent much of the time sitting on the banks of the Biriwiri river washing their clothes, fishing or just lounging and chatting. Eric Mutara made sure that the clinic itself was kept neat and well ordered. It was surrounded by a high fence to keep the goats out, and within the fence there were flowerbeds of cacti and money trees. They were the only things he could get to grow in the dry heat down here below the escarpment.

From time to time the Provincial Medical Department would carry out snap inspections concentrated on the hygiene at Biriwiri, as they did at all their hospitals. These inspections concentrated on the kitchens and the toilets. The toilets at Biriwiri were immaculate, and my mother always complemented Eric on this fact. What she didn't know was that if you went outside the fence of the hospital grounds you encountered a terrible smell. For this was where the patients came to relieve themselves. Eric kept the toilets locked to make sure they stayed clean to pass inspection.

White people didn't get such interesting diseases as Africans. They sometimes got ill, and even died, but this was rare. Down the hill from the African clinic in Melsetter was the European clinic. It was in one wing of a smart three-bedroom bungalow that was supposed to be the house of the Government Medical Officer, my mother. We didn't stay there because we lived in Silverstream, but my mother held clinics here for whites three times a week.

There wasn't a queue of patients like the one at the African clinic. Just one or two Europeans sitting in the waiting room paging through old copies of *Illustrated Life Rhodesia, Scope* and *Fair Lady*. On the waiting-room table was even a vase of plastic flowers. They were a mixed bunch of flowers, and the rose looked the most realistic. From a distance it looked just like the real thing. It was only when you got really close that you could see it had 'made in Taiwan' stamped on its stalk.

Often in the rainy season, when some areas were cut off by road, sick Europeans would ring up to be diagnosed over the telephone. If they were really ill, I learnt, they usually had one of four diseases. Meningitis was easy to spot because the patient would suffer from a stiff neck and vomiting. But the other three – malaria, typhoid and tick fever – could present confusingly similar symptoms. And all of them could easily be mistaken for flu in the early stages. When she wasn't sure which of the three it was, my mother called it PUO – pyrexia of unknown origin – to make it sound medical and more impressive.

With PUO, my mother would use what she called the blunderbuss therapy, to be safe. A patient undergoing blunderbuss therapy had to take an anti-malarial, an antibiotic, and an analgesic all at the same time. It was a fairly potent cocktail but at least it meant that they wouldn't die.

When whites did die they tended to die in car accidents or because of old age. Old Mr Boshof died of old age and I watched him do it. He had been getting ready to die for a long time, my mother said. He was so old he had been on the pioneer trek as a child, coming up in an ox wagon all the way from the Transvaal. It was indeed a beautiful farm they had carved out of the bush at Lemon Kop, with orchards of apples and lemons and avocado pears and big-eyed Jersey cows in the meadow. In the stables there were small woolly lambs that I was allowed to feed with milk from a baby's bottle.

We visited the Boshof's farm many times before the night old Mr Boshof decided to die. It was just him and his daughter-in-law living there. His son had been killed in the First World War, fighting in German East Africa. There were no grandchildren.

The Boshofs did have a dog, though, a young bull terrier called Porridge. Porridge was completely blind. An African cobra had spat in his eyes when he was a puppy. He trotted around the house, bumping into the furniture and tumbling down the steps. You would think that, being unable to see, he would be fearful and suspicious. But Porridge wasn't like that at all. He was a friendly dog and if you called to him he would turn his head to one side, cock his ears, then bound over to be petted. Usually he failed to stop in time and butted you in the balls.

The cobra that had blinded Porridge lived under the front doorstep. Every time we arrived, the old man's daughter-in-law, 'young Mrs Boshof' as she was known, although she was almost seventy herself, would say: 'Be careful now, young Peter, there's a very big cobra that lives under the front doorstep. It blinded our Porridge, you know.'

Every time without fail she said this.

Naturally, I was terrified of going into the house. I would find a variety of excuses to remain outside.

Finally, when I had gathered up my courage, I would pace out a fifty-yard run-up. I liked to imagine I was a rugger player getting ready to boot a conversion over the crossbar. As the crowd quietened in anticipation, I would rise up on tiptoe, point confidently at the imaginary posts and sprint off towards the doorsteps, leaping up them in one bound, and crashing through the screen door onto the hall rug, which slid along the polished floor and deposited me against the far wall, breathless but triumphant.

There were a number of false alarms before old Mr Boshof eventually died: several nights which my mother had passed at his bedside only to have the old man awake the next morning, bashful at still being alive and apologetic for the inconvenience he'd caused.

'Next time I really will die,' he assured her. 'No more wasted journeys for you, doctor, I promise.'

The Boshofs had bought the coffin already. The old man had chosen it out of a catalogue from Doves Morgan the undertakers in Salisbury – 'for all your funeral requirements'. It was sitting on the workbench in the garage, just waiting there for old Mr Boshof to die. I made the cook boy, Regis, show it to me, although he was nervous about it.

The coffin was constructed of dark wood, mahogany I think, like my father's desk. It had three ornate brass handles on each side. While Regis kept watch, I climbed up on to the workbench and lay down inside the coffin to see what it would feel like when you died. It smelt of sawdust and varnish and glue. I got Regis to put the lid on. It was completely dark inside and quite peaceful. I crossed my arms over my chest like dead people do. Soon this would be old Mr Boshof's new home, I thought.

'OK, Regis,' I called. 'You can let me out now.' But there was no reply.

'Regis? Regis!' I pushed up at the lid, but it was a snug fit and it wouldn't budge. Swallowing back my panic I punched up at the lid with both my fists together. It came flying off and clattered noisily onto the cement of the garage floor. As it did so I heard a scream of alarm. It was my mother, who had come looking for me. Regis had obviously fled.

'Good God!' said my mother, regaining her composure. 'You'll frighten *me* to death. What on earth are you doing in Mr Boshof's coffin? Get out this second before they find you in there.' She held me by the ear and marched me out of the garage.

Later that night old Mr Boshof finally kept his promise to die. I was curious to see how death actually happened. I'd been there afterwards often enough, but never during the event itself. I had so many questions. Was death sore? Would he groan and call out? Would he tremble and shake? What would his last words be? Would there be a death rattle?

I took up position on a threadbare chaise longue in the corridor. From here I had a good view through the half-open door of old Mr Boshof's bedroom. He was dressed in a blue-striped nightshirt, propped up on a bank of white pillows, in a narrow bed. There was an extravagant arrangement of freshly cut flowers on his bedside table, next to a clutter of medicine bottles. Young Mrs Boshof sat at his bedside, holding his hand and murmuring endearments to him. Porridge was stretched out on the bedroom rug, snoring contentedly.

Old Mr Boshof had his eyes open. They surveyed the room groggily under the heavy hoods of their lids. I didn't know him very well. He was normally a fierce-looking man, with a soaring hooked nose over a clipped white moustache and thin lips. His eyes were blue, but now they were a washed out, tired blue. He breathed with a gurgling wheeze. He was suffering from something called emphysema, my mother said. From time to time he burst into a violent coughing fit that left him pale and shaken. A big blue vein throbbed ominously on his freckled temple.

Early in the morning, at about three, my mother checked his pulse again and drew young Mrs Boshof discreetly out of the room.

'He could go literally at any minute. You should get through the farewells before he gets any weaker and loses consciousness.'

Young Mrs Boshof called Regis, who had been waiting in

the kitchen. 'The old man is ready to leave now. You can say goodbye,' she said. 'But don't be too long.'

Regis walked uncertainly into the bedroom. He started fiddling with the bedclothes and tidying up the bedside table, as though he'd just come to do the chores. Young Mrs Boshof urged him forward and the old man caught sight of him for the first time and lifted his hand feebly towards him. Regis clasped the hand.

'I will pray to your ancestors to welcome you on the other side,' he said.

'Never mind about that,' said the old man. 'Make me a pipe, Regis.'

Regis picked up the old meerschaum pipe from the table and began packing it expertly from the old leather tobacco pouch. When it was done he handed it to the old man and stood by with a lit match. But old Mr Boshof didn't have the breath to start it.

'You do it for me,' he said. He was asking a black servant to suck the same pipe as him.

I sat up on the chaise longue – this was astonishing. Regis was pretty astonished too. He turned to young Mrs Boshof, but she nodded. He put the match to the pipe bowl, pursed his large aubergine lips around the stem and sucked. When it was glowing he handed the pipe over to the old man, who drew feebly on it before launching into another racking cough.

'You're a good boy, Regis,' said the old man between coughs. 'The young madam will look after you now. I have made sure.'

Regis clasped his hand once more and then fled from the room.

Young Mrs Boshof returned to her position at the old man's bedside. He was beginning to cough again and she gently extracted the pipe from the bony claw of his hand. The narrow iron bed squeaked and shook as he coughed. When it finally stopped he looked exhausted.

'Porridge,' he said quietly, and young Mrs Boshof scooped

the surprised dog up from the rug and deposited him at the top of the bed. The old man patted him gently and Porridge licked his face a couple of times. Then young Mrs Boshof lifted the dog back on to the floor.

The old man was trying to speak again and young Mrs Boshof put her ear to his mouth. He murmured something and then blinked rapidly several times. His eyes got a faraway look in them. Was he dead yet? No, he breathed in again and gave a big sigh. His body trembled briefly and then he was still. His eyes were still open but I knew he must be dead because young Mrs Boshof began wailing. My mother put one arm over her shoulders to comfort her. With the other she drew the blanket over the old man's face.

When young Mrs Boshof went off to wash up I infiltrated the bedroom and had a closer look at the dead man. I lifted the blanket from his face. His forehead still shone with sweat but he had definitely stopped breathing.

'What were his last words?' I asked my mother.

'Remind the boys to spread compost on the top field,' she said.

So much for famous last words, I thought. I imagined it etched into a granite headstone in Gothic script. Not really the stuff of epitaphs.

My father and Regis collected the coffin from the garage and brought it into the old man's bedroom, where they propped it between two chairs. They lifted him out of bed and loaded him into the coffin. One of his arms hung over the edge as though he was waving goodbye. My father put it back inside. He and Regis manoeuvred the lid into position and he got out his new ratchet screwdriver and screwed in every other screw. I was allowed to do the rest. He and Regis watched in silence as I worked. I had to concentrate on making sure I didn't cross-thread the screws. I thought to myself, here I am, screwing down the lid on old man Boshof's coffin and he'll never come out again.

My mother was on the phone, organizing the funeral with Exchange. Exchange was Mrs Roberts. To get through to her you wound the telephone handle continuously for about twenty seconds. Mrs Roberts knew everything that happened in the district. She functioned like a communal answering service. Often if you rang someone, Mrs Roberts would pop up on the line instead, telling you that they were out, where they'd gone and when they'd be back.

Mrs Roberts was also a terrible gossip and listened in on people's conversations. Mrs Watson had caught her out once. During a telephone conversation with someone else, she mentioned that Mrs Roberts listened in. Mrs Roberts spluttered an indignant denial before she could stop herself.

In order to announce old Mr Boshof's death, and his funeral arrangements, all my mother had to do was to tell Exchange and she would tell the whole district in the course of the day. It was our early information highway.

It was a hot wet summer that year and the body was unembalmed, so the funeral was held the next day. Both the service and the burial were held on the farm at Lemon Kop. All morning it had rained, a steady soaking rain, slowly draining the towering cumulus clouds that had been building up for days. But the weather put off no one: Old Mr Boshof, being one of the last pioneers, was held in high regard. The cars and pickups churned their way down the muddy red farm road. From the house you could hear their engines revving as their wheels lost traction and they had to tow one another out of mud holes.

An advance party of Afrikaner men in identical black suits and white shirts had been toiling at the burial site, digging the grave with shovels and *badzas* in the rain. They had taken their jackets off, but their trousers were sodden and their white shirts stuck opaquely to their flesh as they dug on in silence. This was black man's work, but the Afrikaner men had chased away the farm labourers.

'Why can't you do the digging?' I asked the bossboy.

'The *mabhunu*, they are funny about their graves,' he said, shaking his head. *Mabhunu* was their name for Afrikaners. 'They don't like black man to dig their graves. It has to be their own people. Otherwise they cannot reach heaven.'

'Hmph. That's stupid,' I said, feeling embarrassed that the helpful bossboy had been chased away by the *mabhunu*. But the bossboy seemed to accept it without rancour.

'No. We are just the same. If I die, it must be people of my own tribe who dig the grave. Otherwise it will confuse my ancestors.'

I remembered at Biriwiri there had nearly been a riot when patients refused to dig graves for patients of other tribes who died there. They said it would bring them bad luck to dig the graves of other tribes. Eventually my mother had got the Roads Department to send a work gang. They had been told they were digging drainage ditches.

It was still raining when the funeral procession set off from the house on the two-mile journey to the family grave site. The coffin was loaded on the back of a Land Rover, sticking out into the wet on the open tailgate. A column of cars trailed slowly behind it. As we arrived, the rain stopped and the sun suddenly cut through the billowing edges of the cloud, casting shafts of silvery light upon the scene, like the ascension of Christ in my illustrated Bible. Maybe old Mr Boshof's soul was being sucked directly up the sunbeams into heaven, I thought, *mabhunu* heaven where he might meet oom Piet Oberholzer.

There were already four graves on the hillside: old Mr Boshof's father and mother, his brother and uncle. They all had a grand view across the valley, over the wattle plantations and down the escarpment, to range upon range of distant blue mountains stretching away into Mozambique.

The ladies of the district trooped out to deposit their wreaths next to the open grave. The wreaths were works of great skill, intricately woven into chicken-wire bases: arum lilies and nasturtiums, delicate red flame lilies – the national flower – and white roses. There was great competition over the wreaths, and the women squatted down to read the soggy notes and to compare the arrangements attached to them. My mother had set aside a special section of our garden and devoted it to growing wreath flowers.

It was an impressive turnout – over a hundred Europeans, the men awkward in their mothballed suits, the women clutching wide-brimmed hats onto their heads in the tugging breeze. Behind the phalanx of whites, hanging back a good ten yards, were the black farm workers and their families. They were dressed in ragged formality: ancient jackets and trousers torn at the knees for the men, wraparound cloth *kikoyis*, woollen bobble hats and plastic shoes for the women.

The Dutch Reformed *dominee* had come all the way from Chipinga. He stood ankle deep in the mud in a simple white cassock, peering at us through small round glasses. It was a strange gathering but not really an unhappy one: old Mr Boshof had been old and ready to die. The *dominee* called it 'a blessed released from earthly bonds'. No more worrying about the compost for old Mr Boshof.

The *dominee* handed out some roneoed hymn sheets and we tried to sing some hymns, but we weren't very good at it. Most people just mumbled the words, apart from Mrs Bezedenhout, who claimed to have been an opera singer in Pretoria before she met Jack and came farming in Rhodesia. Her strident soprano pierced the air and caused a colony of crows in a nearby tree to flap off, cawing in alarm.

The six Afrikaner men in dark suits, the *mabhunu* grave-diggers, lugged the coffin out of the Land Rover and brought it over to the fresh grave. They threaded three ropes underneath it and held it over the hole ready to lower it in.

'From dust to dust,' said the *dominee*.

The pallbearers were sliding in the mud and having great difficulty keeping the coffin balanced. One of them lost his footing, slipped onto his bottom, recovered and then lost it completely. He disappeared up to his waist into the grave, but managed to stop himself falling all the way in and was hauled up by his companion. But the coffin was now at a sharp angle, it was in danger of prematurely toppling in itself. There was a gasp from the congregation and several men rushed forward to help recover it. This was turning into one of the most exciting funerals I'd ever been to.

Finally the coffin was successfully lowered and young Mrs Boshof threw the first clod on to it. The *mabhunu* got their shovels and covered it over with the mound of mud and we all got in our cars and drove back down to the farmhouse for the best part of the ceremony – the wake.

The sitting room was decked out with flowers and throbbed with a feast of snacks. Young Mrs Boshof had spent the whole day baking with Regis, and most guests had also brought snacks with them. Treacle tarts, sponge cakes, cheese scones, miniature sausage rolls, samoosas, *koeksisters* (a plaited sweet pastry), chicken legs, vol-au-vents, meat balls, curried eggs, cheesecakes, macadamia nuts and game *biltong* pieces.

For drink, young Mrs Boshof had gone into her late father-in-law's cellar and brought up bottles of his best *mampoer,* a sweet Afrikaner schnapps. It came in various flavours: *naartjie,* peach, and marula berry. I tried it and it was very strong. Soon the party was steaming. The level of noise rose to a din as dozens of conversations competed.

Porridge meandered around the room nudging people, and each time he butted someone they would feed him whatever was in their hand. After an hour or so he was bloated from his mixture of rich snacks and vomited noisily on the corner of the old Persian rug, but no one was cross with him.

As the rain stayed away, the party spread out on to the lawn, with people constantly moving in and out of the house. In all the excitement I had completely forgotten to be frightened of the cobra under the front doorstep, and I went in and out of the door without my usual run-up. Then suddenly a piercing soprano scream rang out. Porridge began barking wildly and butted his way through the crowd to the door. Mrs Bezedenhout was standing at the step, now speechless, and in front of her, coiled and poised to spring, was the cobra. It was very long, of a glistening oily green colour and had a flared hood. It had obviously been disturbed by the party.

'Stay absolutely still and put your hands over your eyes,' said one of the *wabhunu* gravediggers. 'If you move or try to run, it will strike.'

Mrs Bezedenhout looked about to faint. The gravedigger was armed with his shovel now, and he began to circle behind the cobra. He was measuring the weight of the shovel in his hands, preparing to run in and take a swing at the snake, when Porridge came skidding down the stairs, barking.

What happened next was all so quick it had to be pieced together afterwards: the cobra was distracted by Porridge, its old foe. Mrs Bezedenhout regained her voice and screamed again. The snake appeared to launch itself at the dog, but as it did so the gravedigger launched himself at the snake. Then the snake seemed to be in two different places. Its head and about six inches of its neck was on the step at Porridge's paws, and the rest of its body was on the grass near Mrs Bezedenhout. And that was how the Boshof's cobra was killed.

The *mabhunu* gravedigger was plied with more *mampoer* and toasted for his quick wits. The cobra – both pieces – was hung over the lamp hook above the front door to stop Porridge from eating it. And the party resumed with even greater fervour. The *mampoer* was getting to people now, and several were starting to stagger. Young Mrs Boshof had definitely had too many. Someone put on an Afrikaans folk record and she started to dance unsteadily, and soon lots of people joined in.

It was like a country and western square dance and adults were trying to pair me up with an irritating little girl from school, so I escaped and slid into the kitchen to chat with Regis. He was standing, straight-backed, over the chopping board.

'Hi, Regis! Good funeral, hey? See they finally killed the cobra?' I sallied.

But he kept his back to me. Hesitantly I moved around him. As he sliced tomatoes on the cutting board, he was crying. His old face was crumpled in grief. Big tears rolled down his cheeks and splashed on to his grubby white apron. He seemed to be the only person who was still sad at old Mr Boshof's death.

I fled back to the party.

Seven

My father, *mandebvu*, was king of the factory, which was the headquarters for all the estates. The bark from all the wattle trees was processed at the factory. Trees were stripped in the plantations and the bark was tied into big bundles and ferried there on a fleet of old trucks. They were Thames Traders with snub bonnets, and they were all painted in the company's colours of Bermuda Blue and Sunshine Yellow. The cutters clung on to the top of the precarious piles of bark on the back of the trucks. They looked like rustic pirates, barefoot and usually shirtless, with bright bandannas wrapped around their heads and *pangas* through their waistbands. The cutters were very high-spirited, always whistling at passing women and moving everywhere at a run. They were phenomenally fit and lean from constant exercise. All of them were young. You couldn't keep up once you were out of your thirties.

The trucks stopped at the weighbridge and Winfield the weighbridge clerk noted down their weight in a ledger, using the biro he kept lodged in his hair. He sat on a high wooden stool and wore a safari suit like my father's, though Winfield's had long trousers and my father wore long flappy shorts. Winfield explained to me that he knew how much the trucks weighed empty, so if he subtracted this amount from the weight of the full trucks on the weighbridge, this equalled the weight of the wattle bark. It was the difference between gross and net, he told me, but I didn't really understand it.

Once the bark went into the factory it was minced into little pieces and boiled in great vats called autoclaves. Then it was passed through evaporators and vacuum pans for eight hours and came out the other end as thick treacle, which was poured into sacks where it set hard like toffee. This was called tannin. I never saw what happened to the tannin after that. Big trucks took it away to Umtali. My father said it was used to treat leather for shoes. The wood from the wattle trees was very hard and it was used to make telephone poles, props for mine shafts, and rafters. First, though, they had to dunk it in creosote so the white ants couldn't eat it.

For three months every winter the factory converted to sugar. The trucks trundled in weighed down with sugar cane, which was grown on the lower estates down the mountain near Chipinga, where it was hotter. After a complicated process of boiling and crystallizing and spinning, raw brown sugar and molasses finally came out at the other end. My father was very proud of the fact that his was the only factory in the world that made sugar by pure diffusion. I didn't really know what that meant, but I boasted about it at school.

At the beginning of the sugar season the Mauritians Louis and Gervase, the pan boilers, arrived to work the vacuum pans. They were Indian and they spoke French and they always brought us the same present: a lamp made out of a big pink cowrie shell. We had dozens of them at home.

During the sugar season, the factory came alive with bees. They weren't interested in stinging you though, as long as you didn't actually sit on one or swallow one, as workers occasionally did. There was also a seasonal invasion of cane rats, which scuttled among the piles of cane. Some of them were as big as small dogs. The workers spent hours hunting them with catapults or sling shots, or trying to swat them with the backs of shovels. Whenever they killed cane rats, they kebabed them on a sharp stick and roasted them over a fire.

The factory had its own workshops, which were run by Charlie Bikkers. My father said he was probably the finest fitter and turner in the country – a real craftsman. He could make absolutely anything at all on his lathe. He was very tall and stooped and thin, wincingly shy and monosyllabic. He made me a splendid sheath knife for Christmas and I was allowed to watch him do it.

First he took an old industrial hacksaw blade and slowly sculpted it into a knife shape. Then he locked a bar of brass, called a chuck, into his lathe vice, and turned it into a hand guard. He adjusted the lathe chisel so it scraped at the rotating bar, scooping off thin coils of brass. It was cooled by a thin jet of lathe milk, called suds. He made the knife handle out of perspex, and the real triumph was my name, which he had somehow written in the middle of the perspex so no one could scratch it off.

Because Charlie Bikkers didn't really talk, I had to do the talking for both of us. While he frowned over his lathe I chatted away brightly. I don't think anyone had ever talked to Charlie Bikkers for this long. He seemed to quite enjoy it. From time to time he would look up briefly and say, 'Is it, hey?' and then swoop back down to his beloved machine.

Charlie Bikkers's finest accomplishment, even more impressive than my perspex-handled knife, was the fire engines. First there was Gunga Din, which was actually a big red water bowser. My father let me name it after the water carrier in Kipling's poem. The name was painted on the door and also on the side of the tank. Then there was Jumbo, which was fitted with a proper brass London Fire Service fire pump and had a control panel crowded with various dials and switches, like aircraft instruments. My father said it could pump 1000 gallons in five minutes, and suck water out of a river at 150 gallons a minute. And finally there was Scorpion, which was based on a Land Rover. All the forest companies – Gwendingwe, Tilbury, the British South Africa Company, the Forestry Commission and us – had their own fire engines. My father said that there were more fire engines in Melsetter district than in the whole of Salisbury.

Fire was our biggest enemy. Everything possible was done to prevent it. There were signs everywhere entreating people not to start fires and threatening them with huge fines if they did. Rewards were offered to those who informed on arsonists. The signs had a picture of a Bambi-like buck, wet eyes big with alarm as it was enveloped by tall red flames. And they had a clock whose hand told you if the fire risk was low, moderate or high – green, amber or red.

To slow the spread of fires, the plantations themselves were divided into blocs by wide firebreaks, which were kept free of all vegetation. All the plantations had watch towers which peered out over the forest roof. The one on the top of Cecilton, the highest of all, had a permanent lookout man with a radio, even in the wet season when the fire risk was low.

When a fire did break out the watchman struck the *simbi* in the compound to raise the alarm. The *simbi* was a big piece of metal that hung on a tall wooden frame. When the watchman whacked it with an old wheel jack it sent a loud clanging right across the valley and all the workers knew to report for fire duty. There were similar *simbi* on all fifteen estates, and when the alarm was raised we could muster 3000 men for fire duty, 200 from each estate.

The sound of the *simbi* was a terrifying one. But it was also secretly very exciting. The truth was, fires were great fun. We would all load into the trucks with our fire beaters, which were big square flaps of rubber fixed to the end of a pole. Then we would set off in a long convoy behind the fire engines. It wasn't a very fast convoy – Scorpion always led, then Jumbo and finally Gunga Din, which had a top speed of less than forty – but it was still impressive. It felt like we were going off to war, which in a way we were. The fire engines even had home-made sirens – Charlie Bikkers had wired up the hooters so they gave a double blast every few seconds.

In the back of the trucks the boys sang Shangaan hunting songs to keep their spirits up. They weren't really Shangaans themselves, they were Ndau, but the Shangaans had better hunting songs. I learnt the words and sang along. They would break into four-part harmony, quite naturally, without anyone conducting them. It was a thrilling sound – scary and comforting at the same time. It made me glad they were on my side. Sometimes they would sing hymns in the back of the trucks on the way to the fire. Their favourite hymn was the one where Jesus urges the fishermen to become his disciples:

> *I will make you fishers of men,*
> *fishers of men*
> *fishers of men.*
> *I will make you fishers of men*
> *If you fol-low me.*

And they also sang a round in English:

> *One man went to mow, went to mow a meadow.*

During the song the mowing party got bigger and bigger. I didn't know what it meant and evidently neither did they, but we all sang it at the top of our voices. My voice, the only unbroken one there, rang out high above the rest.

October was the worst time of year for fires. By then the winter, our dry season, was coming to an end and the forest had seen almost no rain for five months. The trees were crinkly dry, the outer branches faded in the heat. The *moto makuru*, the 'big fire', the one the boys still talk about today, started in late October. It didn't start the usual way, from a cigarette end, or the ember of a cooking fire, or the sunlight magnified through an old bottle, or even from lightning. It was started deliberately by the *tsotsis*, like the ones who killed oom Piet Oberholzer.

We didn't know that at the time, though. At the time we thought it was an accident.

Cecilton lookout raised the alarm late one Friday afternoon. I heard him on the radio, the one by my father's armchair in the sitting room. His voice was high and excited. He had forgotten all his radio procedure and was mixing up Shona and English and *chiLapalapa*. The factory hooter had just whistled and main shift was knocking off when the *simbi* was sounded. The Silverstream valley was roofed in smoke from the cooking fires of supper. But instead of going home to their families, the boys clambered on to the trucks.

They weren't to come home until the next day.

I was allowed to go to fires, so long as I stayed out of the way, near Gunga Din. And I had been to quite a few. But this one was special. It was already gigantic when we arrived, a cavern of flame that soared ten storeys into the sky and blotted out the stars. A wall of intense heat blew off it and it was impossible to get anywhere near. The noise, too, was tremendous. Above the background roar, there were constant crashes as trees collapsed.

Hundreds of birds wheeled about, calling in alarm at their destroyed nests and their lost young. And a barrage of wild animals came bowling out of the fire towards us, crazed with a fear more ancient than their fear of man. In just a few minutes I saw kudu, bushbuck and waterbuck, antbear and duiker. They weren't looking for trouble but if you were unlucky enough to get between them and freedom, the males would run you through in panic. Civets and hyenas, mongooses and jackal came leaping and scurrying out of the flames. And a great shout went up as a leopard yowled right through a group of beaters.

But it was the snakes that really got to the beaters. As they worked, they constantly scanned the ground at their feet. These forests were home to two of the most poisonous snakes in Africa: the puff adder, fat and sluggish, which waits for you to stand on it and then finds a tremendous lick of speed to whip round and bite your ankle; and the one that frightened us most, the uncontested champion of the poison snakes, the gaboon viper, a rare snake found exclusively in these forests. A bite from one of those speckled monsters and you were beyond help. There were pythons too, slithering out of the undergrowth, but though they were as thick as a beater's bicep, they scared no one. We all knew that they were only squeezers, not biters.

I stayed obediently by Gunga Din with Harry Lovat as he directed operations. He was still dividing the beaters into fire groups when a great cry went up. They were all looking up at the tops of the trees.

'Oh my God! That's all we need,' said Harry Lovat.

He had just seen what the beaters were looking at. It was turning into a crown fire – the worst kind of all. Just the tops of the trees were burning, and the fire was jumping quickly from tree top to tree top, while the forest floor was initially unaffected. We had no chance of actually fighting a crown fire like this, only of containing it. Harry Lovat gave the bossboys orders to back-burn. The beaters began clearing makeshift firebreaks and then lighting fires which they directed back at the main fire. It was a risky strategy, especially on a night like tonight when the wind kept changing.

We fought that fire through the night and in the early morning at about 3 o'clock – the time, my mother said, when the human spirit is at its lowest – it finally defeated us. Undeterred by the back-burning, the fire had leapt forward until finally the beaters found themselves forced back to the main firebreak. We were going to have to sacrifice this whole bloc – a thousand acres of prime wattle, only one season away from harvest.

The beaters regrouped on the far edge of the firebreak, resting exhausted on their beating poles. The break itself was a hundred yards wide and had been freshly watered from Gunga Din and the other fire engines. There was nothing to do now but wait.

The fire raged right up to the edge of the firebreak. It spat great showers of sparks down on to the break and the beaters ran to flatten them. The heat caused whirlwinds which suddenly spiralled up out of the flames, whirling embers high into the air. As its lateral progress was halted, the crown fire descended from the tree tops to consume what was below and the heat grew even more intense.

Then, even as the first glimmer of dawn began to compete with the fierce glow of the fire, the most appalling sight greeted us. Several hundred yards down the firebreak from where we had all gathered, a fireball shot up into the sky like some festive firework. It seemed to float in a lazy parabola, arcing brilliantly through the dark and landing in the next bloc of forest behind us. A great groan went up from the beaters and there was a general surge towards the area. But it was already too late. The fire had established a bridgehead on the adjacent bloc and was leaping fast from tree top to tree top again.

Harry Lovat was sitting on the footplate of Gunga Din. He hadn't even bothered to go forward to the new outbreak. He knew it was hopeless. Another thousand acres gone. He stood up and punched Gunga Din's red tank. Then he turned to his bossboy.

'Make sure you do a head count before you change shifts. I'll walk back.' And he trudged off down the firebreak, a lonely figure with stooped shoulders, silhouetted against the burning forest. As he disappeared into the faint glimmer of dawn he emitted an enraged bellow that rolled back up to us.

'Faaark! Fuck! Fuck! Fuck! Fuck!'

And then he was gone.

There was no singing in the trucks on the way back to Silverstream, no Shangaan hunting songs, no 'Fishers of Men' or 'Mowers of Meadows'. The beaters sat in rows, sweaty and soot-stained and utterly dispirited. As the convoy strained up the last hill into Silverstream village we had a wide view back over the scene. Where there had been a profusion of olive-green wattle leaves and yellow mimosa flowers, now there was a black scar across the mountains. A terrible, charred scar.

*

Wattle and sugar weren't the only products of the Rhodesian Wattle Company. We were also cattle ranchers. We ran Aberdeen Angus and Herefords for beef and a dairy herd of Guernseys. The best cattle, though, were the Afrikanders, a local breed that was very hardy and resistant to disease. They had big humps on their backs and great folded dewlaps which wobbled under their throats. Unlike the Aberdeen Angus and the Hereford, which were fussy eaters, Afrikanders would eat pretty much anything, so you could herd them all over the place to graze.

During the school holidays, Jeremy Watson and I helped to herd the Afrikanders. Herding was good fun because you got to ride horses and stay away from home for days at a time, and to carry guns. At first I only had a pellet gun. But Jeremy had a .410 shotgun because he was older than me, and the chief herd boy, Isaac, had an old, scarred .303 rifle. It stayed permanently in its scabbard, which was attached to his saddle. It wasn't loaded and I suspect he didn't know how to use it. It was there simply as a totem of his status.

Sometimes we stayed out herding for a week at a time. We rode our horses 'farm style', holding the reins with one hand. This left the other hand free to crack the *sjambok*, an Afrikaans whip made out of cow hide. In a roll behind my saddle I had a groundsheet and a blanket and some dry socks and a couple of fresh T-shirts and underpants. Jeremy and I pretended we were cowboys, like the ones in the bioscope. The herd boys were loyal Apaches who fought with us in our epic struggle against 'the bandits'.

Herding was most fun when people were watching you, when you could show off. In reality, your bum hurt from hours in the saddle and your legs chafed against the stirrup leather and at night the ground was hard to sleep on. Horse races and rock-throwing competitions helped to liven things up a bit. Branding was quite fun, although I didn't like the smell of burnt hide.

At dipping time we indulged in our own method of fencing:

we duelled with electric cattle prodders, which we tied on to
sticks. A prodder looked like an electric torch but instead of a
light bulb at the end, it had a pair of spring-loaded prongs.
When you poked an animal or a person with the prongs, they
got a 10,000-volt shock. It was a jolt sufficient to make an
Afrikander bull leap into a dip, and certainly enough to make
a small boy airborne.

Despite these various distractions, herding would have been
quite boring except for the eccentric behaviour of Isaac, the
chief herd boy. I had known Isaac ever since I could remember,
because he was an elder of Violet's Apostolics. When not quot-
ing the Old Testament, Isaac spouted Shona proverbs and fables
and cautionary tales. They weren't like the English fairy tales
I'd read, which were fairly obvious and easy to understand.
Shona ones were oblique and puzzling. Often they were
deliciously rude and frenziedly violent. The tales themselves
sometimes took hours to recount, with all sorts of irrelevant
diversions and asides. They usually involved animals which had
human characteristics. Mr Baboon and Mr Hare were two of
the most common adversaries.

'One day many, many years ago, Mr Baboon and Mr Hare
decided to sew up their bottoms so that once they had eaten
enough food, they would never feel hungry again,' Isaac would
begin.

Fair enough, I thought. Jeremy also accepted this preliminary
presumption without a flicker.

'*Dzefunde* – Go on,' we said, because that's what the audience has do to after every sentence in a Shona folk tale.

'Mr Hare sewed up Mr Baboon's bottom very tightly. But Mr
Baboon sewed up Mr Hare's bottom only loosely.'

'*Dzefunde.*'

'One morning Mr Baboon chanced upon a field full of
delicious pumpkins and he ate and he ate until he could eat
no more, completely forgetting that his bottom was sewn up.
Because he was stuffed with pumpkin and could not empty his

bowels, he fell over in a dead faint. The woman who owned the field then arrived and, seeing Mr Baboon lying on the ground, took him for dead. She loaded him into her basket, and carried him home.'

'*Dzefunde.*'

' "Look what I've found us to eat," she said proudly to her husband. And he immediately set about skinning Mr Baboon. He started with the bottom, and the first thrust of his knife cut the stitches and released a great mound of dung all over the husband. But he couldn't get away because his hand had stuck fast up Mr Baboon's bottom.'

'How did that happen?' I asked Isaac. 'How did his hand get stuck up there?'

'Well, because Mr Baboon contracted his anus muscle.'

'Oh, OK. *Dzefunde.*'

'Mr Baboon ran off into the bush, dragging the man behind him, through the thorns and over the rocks. The wife, who thought only that her husband was reluctant to let Mr Baboon escape, shouted "Please my dear, let him go!" '

Isaac did the wife's part in a high falsetto and we both laughed.

'*Dzefunde.*'

'The husband shouted back angrily, "I would if I could, but I'm stuck! Why were you so stupid to think this was a dead baboon?"

'However hard he struggled, he could not free his hand from Mr Baboon's bottom, and eventually the thorns and the rocks killed him.'

'*Dzefunde.*'

'When Mr Baboon met Mr Hare they chopped the man's head off and hung it on a branch, leaving the body nearby. The wife came searching for her husband, and she saw his head from a distance and said in relief, "Oh, there you are at last. I'm so glad that you're safe. But why are you smiling?"

'When she got closer she saw it was his severed head, and

that his broken body lay nearby. And she lamented her decision to bring home Mr Baboon in the first place.'

'*Dzefunde*,' we chanted.

Isaac shook his head. 'That is the end.'

'What does it mean?' I asked.

'Mean? It means nothing. It is a story, that's all,' said Isaac.

We thought about it for some time as we rode along.

'Perhaps,' Jeremy suggested, practically, 'the moral is: always check that an animal is really dead before you pick it up.'

'How about: Stitching up your bum is not such a good idea?' I offered.

'Or: never put your hand up a baboon's arse,' chortled Jeremy.

But Isaac maintained a gnomic silence as always. He would never explain his stories.

Isaac was also a fund of wise sayings, many of which were equally mystifying to us. He would insinuate these proverbs into our most mundane conversations.

'I wish I were taller,' I would be saying to Jeremy, and Isaac would solemnly announce: 'The clever cripple supports himself against a wall when dancing.' This, we decided, meant it was unwise to reveal one's faults.

Or I'd be moaning about my sister and he would observe: 'If an idiot is your relative, you still applaud his dancing.'

'Blood is thicker than water?' wondered Jeremy.

When I was silent for a long time, Isaac rode up next to me and said: 'To think secretly is like the journey of a dog.' And when I refused to complain about being saddle-sore until I had raw weals down the insides of both thighs, Isaac was unimpressed by my fortitude and said simply: 'A child who does not cry will die on its mother's back.'

I absorbed many of Isaac's sayings, even without fully understanding them. And I was forever spouting them myself.

'The animal that has mud on its hooves is assumed to have

been to the water hole,' I said to Harry Lovat, one day, trying to explain guilt by association.

'Bah! Isaac's been filling your little head with half-baked *munt* philosophy,' he replied.

I irritated my family to distraction with the sayings. My father called them 'The Sayings of Chairman Isaac', like 'The Sayings of Chairman Mao'.

If I'd been bickering with my sister and she was about to leave the house, I would say sonorously, 'Be on good terms with those you leave, because it is night where you are going.' And she would grudgingly make her peace with me before she left.

When Fatty Slabbert was bullying me at school again, I narrowed my eyes menacingly and said: 'The axe forgets, but not the tree.'

'What you talking about?' he asked suspiciously.

'It's a Shona curse,' I said dramatically. 'It means a wronged person remembers long after the one who has wronged him has forgotten.' He seemed to lay off me a bit after that.

Isaac also had a whole litany of complicated rules. He wouldn't let you do all sorts of quite ordinary things. If you sat down on a path, you were in danger of developing boils on your bottom. If you knocked down unripe wild fruit from a tree, a lion might eat you. If you talked in a forest, you would get lost for ever. If you wandered about after dark, you would be beaten by witches or evil spirits of the night. If you imitated certain birds, like the 'go-away' bird, then your clothes would catch fire. If you wore red when it was raining, you would be struck by lightning and if you spat at a person, he would become a leper.

There were also various rules about the fire. If you jumped over it or pissed on it, you would catch bilharzia. If you sat with your back to the fire, you would be turned into a *muroyi* – a witch – and if you warmed your feet at the flames, you would trip over while walking.

Isaac showed us all the unusual things you could eat in the bush. You could eat grasshoppers and locusts, for instance. First you broke off their heads and scraped out their innards, then you threaded them on to a stick and smoked them over the fire. They didn't taste bad actually, as long as you could forget what they really were.

Flying ants were better. Isaac ate them raw, after pulling their wings off. But they were more tasty if you fried them in oil. So were caterpillars. You could eat snakes as long as you cut off the head and about the first three inches of the neck where the poison sacs are located. Lizards too, Isaac liked to eat, and frogs, but never toads because they were poisonous.

It was Isaac who told me why we were called *mukiwa*. He picked a wild fig and held it up. It was a pale pinkish colour. 'It is called *Mukiwa*,' he said. 'Same colour like you.'

Isaac's real enthusiasm was for honey. We would herd the cattle miles out of our way in pursuit of it. Sometimes we were lucky enough to encounter honey-guide birds, which lead humans to beehives. They would fly on to a tree nearby and make an excited chattering call until they had attracted your attention. Then they would fly in short hops, always waiting until you had caught up before they moved on. Finally they would guide you right to the hive.

Isaac would smoke the bees out by lighting a fire at the foot of the tree and putting green leaves on the flames. Once the bees had gone he would scoop out the honeycomb for us to eat. He was always sure to leave a generous portion for the honey-guide. I was amazed that honey-guides knew that taking humans to beehives would mean that they would get honey too. And it wasn't only humans, they also guided honey badgers.

The honey-guide was our friend but the 'go-away' bird was a nuisance. Its real name was the grey lourie and it was a big grey bird with a prominent crest. It was known as the 'go-away' bird because of its call, 'kweh-h-h!'or 'go-way-y-y!' It made the call loudly every time it was disturbed, and if you were hunting it would fly from tree to tree ahead of you warning all the animals to 'go away!' as humans were approaching. It was the hunters' least favourite bird and they were often tempted to shoot it. I hated the 'go-away' bird. I felt it was taunting me personally, telling me I didn't belong there. But Isaac's greatest warning was reserved for the 'go-away' bird. If you dared shoot one, all was lost: great disaster would befall you and your entire family.

I had already learnt that there were certain animals you could shoot with a pellet gun and others you definitely should not. Toppies, called black-eyed bulbuls in our bird bible, *Roberts' Birds of Southern Africa*, were fine to shoot because they ate fruit and were vermin. So were fiscal shrikes, which were called butcher birds because they killed other birds. But you were not supposed to shoot honey birds or weaver birds or any hawks or eagles. And most certainly not owls.

One of my first actions, when I was given my new air rifle, had been to shoot the owl in the avocado tree outside my bedroom window, the one that tormented me at night. I tied my torch to the underside of the rifle barrel, and when the owl hooted, I loaded the rifle with a pellet, knelt on the bed and poked the end of the barrel through the grenade screen. Then I switched the torch on and pointed the barrel at the tree. I swept the torch beam over the branches until it settled on the two enormous owl eyes. I aimed between them and fired, remembering to squeeze and not pull the trigger, just as my father had taught me. There was a strangled croak, a rustle of leaves and a thud. Hah! The reign of terror was over.

The next morning I retrieved the dead owl from under the avocado tree and took it down to Ron Barton, the chemist at the factory laboratory. Ron Barton was Scottish and he had ginger hair. He was a fanatical ornithologist and I felt sure he would be interested in this fine specimen of an African owl. He might even stuff it and put it in a glass display case, as he did with some birds.

Half of his lab was an amateur natural history museum. It was littered with jars of formaldehyde containing various small animals. The animals in the jars were all unusual in some way. Mostly they were deformed. A calf foetus with two heads. A baby chick with three feet. An albino crocodile foetus. Ron Barton was also a snake expert and he could milk the venom from the fangs of a snake, to use as anti-snakebite serum.

I found him leaning over a beaker, concentrating on draining a pipette. I held up the scary old owl by its scaly feet.

'Look what I've brought you,' I said proudly. It was the first thing bigger than a toppie that I'd bagged. He looked up from his pipette.

'*Bubo capensis* – the Cape eagle owl,' he said professionally. 'How did it die?'

'It didn't die,' I beamed, 'I *shot* it!'

'You what?' He leapt up from the lab bench and strode over to me. 'Do you realize you have just eliminated an extremely rare bird? This owl is so rare it's royal game, you little idiot. You've shot royal game – a protected species – and that's a crime. You could be sent to jail! You *should* be sent to jail!'

This was not the reaction I'd been expecting. Hunting was clearly going to be more complicated than I'd anticipated.

'But it was deliberately scaring me,' I said defensively. 'It hooted at me during the night and gave me nightmares.' I cupped my hands around my mouth and tried to imitate the frightening owl call.

'Ta-*wit* ta-*wooo*.'

'That's not what it sounds like at all,' said Ron Barton, momentarily distracted. '*Bubo capensis* goes: "*Hu*-hu-hu, *Hu*-hu-hu."'

'Ta-*wit*, Ta-*wooo*,' I repeated.

We exchanged a few more rival owl calls across the lab bench, and then Ron Barton collected himself.

'You little vandal. Wait till your father hears about this!' He grabbed me firmly by the arm and shoved me out of the lab and across the courtyard to my father's office. There he told my father the whole story while I sat on the big wooden chair staring at the floor.

At the end of his fulmination my father said, 'OK, Ron, I'll deal with the little *skelm*.'

Ron Barton harumphed at me and stormed out of the room.

I was clearly so humiliated that my father never punished me. He just gave me a list of six birds I could shoot and told me never to shoot at anything else.

Eight

Most of the time, life in Silverstream was quite lonely for a white boy. In the whole of the Silverstream area, there were probably no more than fifty white families. The main focus of socializing – in fact, about the only focus of socializing for the Europeans – was the Silverstream Club. It had tennis courts and a playground, and a rough cricket oval, a dam in which you could swim or fish, a pub, and a small hall where they showed the bioscope once a week and put on the children's Christmas play and fancy-dress competitions.

The film choice was relentlessly populist: Carry Ons, James Bonds, the evil Fu Manchus. The children would sit on the floor and behind us, the grown-ups in rows on hard-backed chairs, and behind them, craning through the service hatch, the black club staff and their families.

Every year, Father Christmas would arrive at the club by a different form of transportation. He came in a red Land Rover trellised with tinsel; he came on Jumbo the fire engine, which had been decorated with false snow; he came on a sledge made of wattle logs wrapped in red crêpe paper and pulled by Mr Watson's horse, Flicka; he came on a litter, carried by African labourers dressed as Santa's elves with conical red hats and green felt waistcoats; he came on Flicka, again – this time the horse was disguised as a reindeer with a red nose and false antlers. One year Father Christmas even came in an Allouette helicopter of the Rhodesian Air Force, which happened to be on exercise in the area. It put him down on the cricket oval, amidst a shower of grass and dust, while the black club staff hid under the table in alarm.

On Sundays in winter, for a treat, we used to escape the misty coolness of the highlands by driving down the escarpment into the heat of the Sabi river valley. The road that wound round the mountains, south towards Chipinga, was a feat of engineering which really impressed my father. This stretch of road had been built by Italian internees and prisoners of war. At its highest point, where you had a magnificent view south over the rounded hills of Chipinga and north over the more rugged terrain of Silverstream, the Italians had built a little roadside shrine, next to a bridge called the Ponte Italia. The shrine had a plaster statue of the virgin Mary and, etched into the concrete, a picture of a wheelbarrow and the date of completion: September 1943.

The Italian POWs couldn't have been that badly treated, said my father, because thousands of them had stayed on in Rhodesia after the war and even brought their families out to join them. Enzo Morelli at school was Italian. His father spoke with a funny accent. When I teased Enzo that his father fought with the Jerries on the wrong side in the war, and had been an enemy POW, he went all red in the face and started to cry.

As a punishment for teasing Enzo, Miss Gloyne made me apologize to his father. At end of term prizegiving I had to go up to him and say: 'Thanks very much Mr Morelli for building the Chipinga road during the war. It's a very fine road and we use it all the time.' I shook his hand and he looked a bit confused. I later discovered he'd only emigrated in 1960.

From the Ponte Italia shrine the road wound down to the Willemses' house, which was designed to look like a pioneer's ox wagon, complete with two huge concrete wagon wheels at either end. Jain said it was kitsch, but I thought it was great and I wished we lived in a house that looked like something else. Not a wagon, but a plane maybe, or, even better, a ship.

The Willemses were of pioneer stock, and below their wagon house was a trekkers' graveyard, where old man Moodie himself was buried. It was called Moodie's Rest and it was a national monument, and had a metal plaque outside it saying that if you defaced it you would be sent to jail.

Outside Moodie's Rest the road divided into two. The left fork was a proper tar road that went up to Chipinga, but we took the right fork, a strip road that descended rapidly into the Sabi valley. We passed through the vast Tanganda tea estates, where nearly all the country's tea came from, and then soon we went over a cattle grid and into the Mutema Tribal Trust Land. There was no grass in the tribal reserve, only stony red ground and thorn trees and thousands of goats.

The roadside here was dotted with Africans trying to hawk fruit to passersby. They would stand on the very edge of the road with their hands outstretched, proffering mangos and *kaffir* oranges, which were also called snot apples, and cream-of-tartar pods. They smiled dazzling smiles and tried to encourage you to stop and buy. And at the last second, just when you thought the car would hit them, they would step out of the way. Through the back window I watched their disappointed faces disappear from view in a swirl of red dust.

Behind each hawker there was an optimistic little pyramid of fresh supplies. Some had fashioned rough signs on torn pieces of cardboard advertising their wares. But the signs didn't last long because the goats came and ate the cardboard.

The strip road was dangerous to drive on. It was made of two narrow ribbons of bumpy concrete, and when you encountered oncoming traffic, each vehicle had to pull off so that only the right-hand wheels were on a strip and the left side skidded along the gravel. It was quite easy to lose control when coming off the strip, because the gravel on either side was usually pitted and eroded.

In the back of the car, Jain and I competed to be first to spot a baobab tree. Baobabs only grew down in the Lowveld. They were bulbous, elephantine trees, ugly and grey, not very high but of enormous girth with a soft pithy wood. The Shona called the baobab the 'upside-down tree', because its branches looked more like roots than branches. Naturally Isaac the chief herd boy had a long complicated legend about how the baobab had come to be upside down.

My father said that the baobab was the oldest tree in the world, unchanged since prehistoric times. Some of the trees were known to be over a thousand years old – growing here, in Rhodesia, during the middle ages. Imagine that. Cream-of-tartar was the fruit of the baobab, and it hung off the tree in furry pods which looked like green maracas. The seeds inside were covered with a white flesh that tasted like bitter peppermint when you sucked them. Baobabs flowered just once a year, a big white flower that stank of rotting meat and died after only twenty-four hours. No one knew for sure how the flower was pollinated, but my father said that the latest theory was that it was done by bats, at night. Isaac said that if you picked the baobab flower there would be drought for ten years.

The other contest Jain and I had in the back of the car was to be first to see the bridge over the Sabi river. Birchenough Bridge was not just another bridge, it was a soaring silver suspension bridge that appeared above the Lowveld scrub like a shimmering mirage, an apparition from a different, more modern world. Jeremy and I spent hours examining it, its web of cables, struts, bolts and arches. We agreed it was easily the most impressive structure we had ever seen, more impressive even than the new factory at Silverstream.

My father knew all about the bridge. When it was built, in 1937, he said, it was the highest bridge of its type in Africa, and the third largest suspension bridge in the whole world – 1000 feet long. We were thrilled by this information. The third largest bridge in the world, and it was *ours*. The bridge was an exact replica of the Sydney Harbour bridge, and was designed by the same man. It was called Birchenough Bridge after Sir

Henry Birchenough, who was the president of the British South Africa Company at the time. He and his wife were even buried in the bridge, inside its eastern gatehouse. There was a plaque on the wall to prove it:

> *Within these walls repose the ashes of*
> *Sir Henry Birchenough and of Mabel, his wife.*
> *They wished to be laid to rest in the country they*
> *had served among the people they had loved.*
> *Rhodesia will hold them forever in*
> *fond and grateful memory.*

Underneath, it added:

> *E'en in our ashes live their wonted fires.* AD *1937.*

'What does that mean?' I asked my mother.

She thought for a while, and repeated it several times aloud. Then she began reciting:

> *On some fond breast the parting soul relies,*
> *Some pious drops the closing eye requires;*
> *E'en from the tomb the voice of Nature cries,*
> *E'en in our ashes live their wonted fires.*

'By Thomas Gray, from "Elegy Written in a Country Churchyard",' added my father.

'It means that those who die need to be missed by those who remain behind. They mustn't be forgotten, just because they're dead,' said my mother.

'I suppose that's why they had themselves buried in the bridge,' I said.

On the far side of the bridge was the Birchenough Hotel, where we would meet up with the Watsons and other Silverstream families for a curry and rice lunch. It was run by Doc

Crighton, who had once been a vet. His wife cooked the best curry outside Assam, said Mr Watson, and he knew because he was brought up on a hill station in Assam.

We sat at a long table on the verandah and all the space was taken up with platters of popadoms and bowls of diced onions, tomatoes, bananas, chopped macadamia nuts and grated coconut specially imported from Mozambique. There were also mounds of various exotic spices, including saffron, which my father said was even more valuable than gold, ounce for ounce.

After lunch Jeremy and I would walk down to the river. Usually we went barefoot, but if we were shouted at we had to put on flip-flops because of the Matabele thorns. These thorns were up to three inches long and enamel hard. They could go right through the sole of a *veldskoen*, never mind a flip-flop. They were called flip-flops because that was the sound that they made as they flopped up against your heel. The Africans called them *pata patas*, because that was the sound they heard. Jeremy and I once did a test. We walked along listening to the sound and saying 'pata, pata', and then 'flip, flop', to see which was the more realistic. *Pata pata* won, and from that day on that's what we called them. A lot of Shona words were like that, simply the sound of the thing they described. A cow was a *mhou*, like 'moo'. A motorbike was a *mudhudhudhu*. If you said it fast you could see why: 'Mudhudhudhudhu,' just like the sound of the engine.

In the days of the treks, the Sabi river had been the greatest barrier facing the pioneers. In the dry season it dwindled to a trickle, but in the wet season it was a mile across in places. There was also quicksand on its banks which sucked in the ox wagons.

There were still many dangers lurking in the Sabi. Crocodiles, for instance. They basked in the sun during the day and could easily be mistaken for sandbanks. Or they floated around looking like logs. They would wait at the edge and prey on goats or calves which came down to the river to drink. The bigger crocodiles would go for humans who came to bathe or wash their clothes in the river.

More dangerous than crocodiles, though, were hippos. They wallowed in the deeper pools in the day, but at night they came out to forage along the banks. Although crocodiles *seemed* more frightening, hippos killed more people. In fact hippos killed more people than any other wild animal in Africa. In the day they attacked fishermen in canoes. And at night, when the hippos went on shore, they got irritated by cooking fires and attacked people who were sitting by them. They had bad eyesight and if they were disturbed on shore they would run blindly down the path and trample anything in their way. My mother often had to treat people who had been attacked by hippos.

If you survived the Matabele thorns and the crocodiles and the hippos, then you could still fall victim to bilharzia. It was a disease you caught by swimming in Lowveld rivers. Bilharzia was carried by the parasitic larvae on water snails. The larvae burrowed through your skin into your bladder where they grew into worms and hatched more larvae. Bilharzia made you very tired and if it wasn't treated it could eventually make you piss blood and die.

Sometimes I grew weary with the worry of it all. All the things out there that were waiting to harm me. I longed to live in a safer place, a place where there weren't so many dangers to spoil my fun, where I could bathe in quiet, bilharzia-free rivers without being sucked over waterfalls, or fearing for crocodiles and hippos; where I could wander in soft thornless meadows with no leopard or lion to scare the horses. A place where there were no scorpions or lethal snakes, or rabid jackals to bite me, or mosquitos to infect me with cerebral malaria, or tsetse flies to give me sleeping sickness. A place free of the *tokalosh*, and the *muroyi* – the evil African witch; a place where there were no *tsotsis* setting fire to the forests or killing Europeans for the *chimurenga*.

From the books I'd read, and the pictures I'd seen, and the films I'd watched, I thought maybe that place was England, a gentle deciduous place where man had tamed nature and moulded it to do his bidding.

My parents had both come from England, although they didn't talk about it much. On my mother's passport it said she had been born in a place called Weymouth. She told me that her father was a chaplain in the Royal Navy, but he had died when she was a little girl. She was also in the Royal Navy, in the war. She had been a Wren, a woman sailor. But she didn't go to sea, she stayed on the shore and sent messages to the ships. She had even been bombed by the Germans and had a small jagged scar on her finger to prove it. My father was in the war as well but he didn't want to talk about it. In fact he didn't really want to talk about the past at all. They both said it was much better over here in Africa now. That England was small and grey and wet and full. And that people there spent all their time standing up in trains, trying to get to work.

'Anyway, Peter,' said my mother, taking me on her lap, 'You're a *pukka* African. The first Godwin to be born out here.'

This was true. Jain was already four when she arrived in Africa.

'You're actually a Pom, you know,' I taunted her, and she pinched me and called me a rock spider, which was a derogatory name for Afrikaners. But at least real rock spiders had lots of relatives in Africa. Uncles and aunts, cousins and grandparents, who came to visit and gave them presents. Black people all had plenty of relatives too, and they were never lonely. It made me sad that we had no relatives around. My mother had an elder sister called Honor but she lived in England and we had never seen her. My father's relatives had been killed in the war.

We did have one relative in Africa, of course – Great-Aunt Diana, who lived in Bloemfontein, Down South. My mother had plied me with glamorous stories about her. She told me that Great-Aunt Diana was 'a real character'. And to prove just how much of a character she was, my mother revealed that Diana had been the first woman in southern Africa to ride a motorbike with a sidecar. I was hugely impressed by this obscure feat.

Diana was also a talented pianist and an accomplished horse-woman. Her surname was Rose, which was also my mother's maiden name. She came to South Africa after the Anglo-Boer War when there was a big English community in Bloemfontein. My mother said she was fleeing a disastrous love affair. She died a spinster, although it was not through want of pursuit by eligible bachelors, my mother added emphatically.

I met Great-Aunt Diana three times in all. Twice alive, and once dead. On my first visit she was still a music teacher at the Eunice School, Bloemfontein's Anglican cathedral school for girls. I don't remember much about her from that first visit; a tall old woman with a very straight back. A long face with fine features and clear green eyes and grey hair pulled back into a severe bun. I do recall that she took us on a curious tour of the city sights. Prominent among these was a memorial to the 26,000 Afrikaner women and children who had died in British camps during the Boer War. The monument was called the *Vrouemonument*, the National Women's Memorial. On it there was an Afrikaans inscription:

Aan onze heldinnen en liewe kinderen
– Uw wil Geschiede.

'What does it mean?' I asked Great-Aunt Diana. But she had no idea. Fifty years in the Free State and she still couldn't speak a word of Afrikaans. She beckoned at a group of Afrikaner tourists – pilgrims they were, really – and demanded that the inscription be translated. A middle-aged woman in widow's black volunteered.

'I'm not really sure of the English,' the widow said politely, 'but I think it means, "Dedicated to the women heroes, the heroines I mean, and to the beloved little ones, the children. Thy will be done." '

'Thy will be done?' asked Great-Aunt Diana. 'Whose will be done?'

'Thy will be done. You know, like in the Lord's prayer,' said the Afrikaner widow. 'Thy kingdom come, Thy will be done, on earth as it is in heaven.'

I wandered over to an information board, which said that 20,000 of the 26,000 who died were under sixteen years old. The information board called the camps concentration camps.

'Hmm. I thought Hitler invented concentration camps,' I said.

'And so he did,' said Diana curtly. 'These were nothing like the death camps of the Nazis, these were simply internment camps where the families of Boer guerrillas were sent as an alternative to starving to death on their burnt-down farms. They were sent to these camps for humane reasons. They were refugees.'

'Who burnt down their farms?' I asked.

'Well, we did,' she conceded. 'But only because the menfolk were out fighting us while their women supplied them from the farms.'

'With respect, *mevrou*,' said the widow, 'that was not the case. My own grandmother died in the camps, so I should know. She was a prisoner there and the conditions were terrible. *Terrible*. One in five of the prisoners died.'

'How did they die?' I asked the widow.

'Measles. Diphtheria. Terrible epidemics. They just swept through the camps. Conditions there were very unsanitary. Squalid.'

But Great-Aunt Diana wasn't taking this. 'Oh, for God's sake, *everybody* was dying of disease in the Boer War. We lost far more soldiers to disease than in battle. And so did you.'

Great-Aunt Diana's lecture on Boer exaggeration had drawn an audience of some fifty Afrikaners, and my mother was clearly anxious that we were about to be lynched for preaching heresy on this sacred site. But Diana was in full flow.

'And another thing. We established schools in the camps. Many Afrikaner children were educated there for the very first time.'

The widow and her attendant phalanx of pilgrims were muttering mutinously in Afrikaans now and my father shepherded us back to the car, out of harm's way. As we departed, Diana was still lobbing debating points back over her shoulder at the Afrikaners.

'And anyway, if we'd left you on the *veld*,' she concluded, 'you would have been at the mercy of marauding natives from Basutuland.' She slammed the car door and we drove off, before a second Anglo-Boer war erupted.

The second time I visited Great-Aunt Diana she was bedridden, having finally been immobilized by a fall from her horse at the age of about seventy-five. She was living in an old people's home called the House of St Paul and run by Irish nuns. It was just outside Bloemfontein in a little town called Reitz, ironically named after a famous Boer general. Although she was no longer mobile, she was still alert. She took my hand in hers and tried to talk to me in a clear, weak voice. But I wasn't listening. I had just seen snow for the first time in my life and wasn't in much of a mood for old people with bony hands and parchment skin. Eventually my father sent me outside to play and I was soon absorbed breaking the ice on the birdbath. I hadn't seen ice on a birdbath before either.

That was the last time I saw her alive. The next time I saw her, she was in the mortuary. We had come down to Bloemfontein to bury her. It was a big town so bodies were kept in special fridges there. The mortuary man, an old Afrikaner with a squint so severe it made my eyes water, pulled out a drawer from the filing cabinet and folded back the sheet so my mother could see if it really was Great-Aunt Diana's face and not someone else's.

I stood on tiptoe and peered into the drawer. Great-Aunt Diana looked asleep and she didn't smell bad at all. Maybe she wasn't really dead, I thought, but just tired – I knew that old people needed frequent rests. And, most suspiciously, there were no maggots on Great-Aunt Diana. When I asked my mother about this, the mortuary man got quite cross.

'There's no maggots in here, *seuntjie*,' he said. 'I run a hygienic mortuary.'

My father tried to make a joke of it, but the mortuary man was an Afrikaner and he hadn't been drinking beer and Afrikaners didn't laugh much unless they'd been drinking beer.

Great-Aunt Diana's funeral was a remarkably grand affair held at the Anglican cathedral of St Andrew and St Michael in the centre of Bloemfontein. As the hearse came slowly down St George's Street it was escorted by outriders from the South African Police on huge, gleaming chrome motorcycles. The cathedral was full, and most of the mourners were Afrikaners. By the time of her death, Great-Aunt Diana was one of only a handful of English-speakers left in Bloemfontein. The heyday of English society in the Free State was a sepia memory in the city's museum. But despite her petulant refusal to learn Afrikaans, she was very popular with her Afrikaner neighbours, many of whom regularly visited her, when they had to speak English for the only time in their lives.

After the burial I went with my mother to sort through Diana's effects. There wasn't much. A few faded photos, mementos, books, sheet music. And then my mother came across a little box tied with a dainty pink bow. Inside were dozens of love letters. They were from the man over whom she had fled England. He was already married to someone else. The letters spanned more than thirty years. They had clearly been read and reread, folded over and over until they were torn along the creases. My mother read the first few in tears. Then she put them all back into the box without reading on.

When we got home to Silverstream, we burnt the love letters in the boiler behind the house, the one where Knighty went for his after-supper cigarette, where Violet had read the Crocodile Gang 'WANTED' poster. In a little ceremony, my mother declared that Diana would have liked the love letters to go with her. We all sat on the logs while she tossed them, one by one, into the tall flames that licked up the firebricks and into the chimney to heat the water for our baths.

'To think,' said my mother dreamily, 'a love so strong it survives a thirty-year separation.'

Nine

It was Jain's idea to move me to a new school. At the end of term she came home from her girls-only convent, Marymount, and announced that it was opening up a brother school next door. She had put my name down for it. My parents just sort of accepted it – after six years at Melsetter I was still unsettled there. My mother was now busy with our little sister, Georgina, born when I was ten. So at the beginning of standard five, when I was about eleven, I moved even further away from home, to Carmel College in Umtali.

I remember the car journey to my first term – I sat silently in the back with butterflies in my stomach, drinking in every detail of the drive as though I might never return. Past Lemon Kop where old man Boshof was buried. Past the spot where oom Piet Oberholzer had been killed. Past Sir Hugo's farm. Past Biriwiri hospital and the lepers. Over the extraodinary curved bridge across the Umvumvumvu river, named after the hippos, the *mvu*. Through the Mutambara tribal reserve, where we had to slow down for cows and goats on the road, and where we had done the postmortem on Mr Mtsoro's poisoned family. Past the township of Sakubva, on the edge of Umtali, where the blacks lived in rows and rows of identical little box houses. And eventually we reached the sign which said, *You are now entering Umtali, capital of Manicaland. This city welcomes careful drivers.*

My father was an extremely careful driver because it was the first major trip we had made in our new car. It was Citroën DS

21, a truly amazing vehicle, very advanced for its time, packed with novel features. My father had showed me around it before we left, explaining all its technological wizardry. It didn't have ordinary leaf springs like other cars, it had special hydraulic suspension that gave it a spongy-smooth ride. The suspension was self-correcting so that even if the car lost a wheel it could continue on the other three. It had a sleek, sloping, futuristic shape, a bit like a shark. Its headlights, which were inside little glass cages, actually swivelled when you turned the steering wheel so that you could see round corners. It had special brakes that also worked on hydraulic fluid, and instead of a normal brake pedal there was a mushroom-shaped valve. When you stepped on it, the brakes engaged with a soft sigh.

Most impressive of all, and most practical for us, was the fact that you could raise the suspension up to three different levels, depending on conditions. The highest one gave you ample clearance for rough roads. When not in use, the car sat low on the ground, and when you started the engine, the whole car slowly reared up like a hovercraft.

At the end of the tour my father said, 'It's called a DS because that sounds like *déesse*, which means goddess in French. That's what she is, the goddess of motor cars.' He gave her another reverential buff with his chamois leather.

But not even the *déesse* could distract me. I felt like I was being conducted to prison to begin a sentence. The fact that everyone was being artificially nice to me only made it worse. When we arrived my mother helped me unpack my new school uniform from my new, bigger tin trunk. This time my blazer was blue and the pocket badge was a star-studded shield, out of which thrust a fist clutching a sword. My mother smuggled my beddy zebby, a small bedraggled zebra, into my bed, even though I was too old for it really. Then they were gone. Their new Citroën swept away down the long avenue, into the gloom of early evening, its headlights swivelled round the corner and were lost in the twinkling lights of the town.

My new school was run by Carmelite priests and monks who wore long brown cassocks. They had come all the way from Ireland to teach us. The school was only for boys but some of the boys were Asian and Coloured, though there were no actual blacks. I learnt Latin for the first time and went to Catholic church a lot. Father Kennedy was the rector, he was the one who knew a lot about Shona customs. He had run an African mission at Chisumbanje in the Sabi valley. But it was Father Mathias who taught me, mostly. He was quite young for a priest, and although he did have a receding hairline, he was quite fit and coached football.

We used to go over to Marymount to use their pool and their tennis courts, and to visit our sisters. We sang in the Marymount Glee Club and Mother Magdalena taught me to play the guitar. Marymount was far grander and older than us. It had extensive landscaped gardens and red clay tiles on the roof. There were two types of nuns at Marymount, the American nuns, who you called 'Mother', like Mother de Lourdes and the principal, Mother Richards, and the 'kitchen nuns', who were Portuguese and were called 'Sister'. The American nuns were quite modern, and after my first year they stopped wearing habits and changed into ordinary dresses, although they kept small veils on the backs of their heads as a reminder that they were still brides of Christ.

Marymount and Carmel were dominated by Cross Kopje, a sharp conical hill with a great crucifix on the summit in memory of all the black soldiers, the *askaris*, killed in the First World War. I hadn't known that black men went to fight in the war, but apparently they had been killed in great numbers. Father Ignatius told us that they weren't allowed to carry guns, because we didn't trust them and were scared they might mutiny and turn the guns on us. It was, after all, only twenty years after the African rebellion in Rhodesia – the first *chimurenga*. So the *askaris* were just used to dig and carry stuff. But that didn't stop them getting killed.

On Sundays we climbed up Cross Kopje with packed lunches. We sat on the warm sloping rock at the top, eating our sandwiches and our oranges. We looked out over the town and the mountains beyond it, and through the valleys down to Mozambique. I thought of African soldiers leaving the tribal reserves and going all the way to North Africa or to England or Italy or even Germany, eventually. *I* hadn't even been to those places, and *I* was a European. I wondered what they thought of it, so far away from the bush; the cities and the snow and the sea and all the *wakiwa* – the white men – killing each other.

I was still homesick at Carmel. It was a small school and it was only for boys, most of whom were day-scholars. All of the Asian and Coloured boys went home in the afternoon. The boarders were mostly white Zambians – Zamboons we called them. They were a rough lot whose fathers were on contract at mines on the Zambian Copper Belt. Most of them came from England or South Africa originally, but they were professional expatriates.

I had my first serious fight with a Zambian, although it wasn't my idea. There was a standing arrangement that if you fell out with another boy you could challenge him to a fight behind the water tank. The fights happened on Friday after lunch and there was even a proper timetable. They took place on a square patch of concrete, called the arena, and all the boarders gathered around. The dayboys had all gone home by then. There were no rules except that you couldn't use weapons. So once you had been frisked the fight began.

One Tuesday Chris Partridge came up to me and said, "See you behind the water tank on Friday." He was in a class above me and I hardly even knew him. I tried to find out what the problem was, to see if we couldn't resolve it. But Ernie van

Reenen, an older boy, was hovering behind him, encouraging him.

'If you're not there we'll come and hunt you down wherever you are, you little shit,' van Reenen said.

Everyone was scared of van Reenen. He was one of the oldest boys in the school and he had so many freckles on his face that they joined into one. He was tall and wiry and he was a bully.

For three days I couldn't eat. Partridge wasn't much bigger than I was but I didn't have the stomach for a fight, especially with someone I had no grudge against. I tried again to talk him out of it, but he just mocked me.

The appointed time arrived, and I trudged up to the water tank with a heavy heart. One or two boys had encouraged me privately but they were all too scared to support me in public. Partridge was limbering up, shadow-boxing with van Reenen, his coach. He looked fit and athletic and co-ordinated. Shit, I was going to get my head kicked in. And for nothing. I fought back my tears and did some half-hearted shadow-boxing on my own. Then when we were ushered into the square, I addressed the crowd.

'I don't want a scrap. I've got no beef with Partridge. I refuse to fight.'

Van Reenen and his gang started to chant 'Fight! Fight! Fight!', faster and faster.

I turned around to appeal to other boys, when suddenly a punch caught me under the eye, and I started to bleed.

A great cheer went up from van Reenen's bunch.

'First blood! First blood! First blood!'

I stood there, foolishly gesturing that this was ridiculous, when Partridge landed a mouth shot, splitting my lip. Van Reenen's camp were all cheering again.

After I was struck a third time, on the nose, I had just had enough of the whole thing and went in like a windmill, fists flailing wildly. All I can remember was a look first of uncertainty and then of fear, in Partridge's eyes. I can't remember how I hit him or where, but after ten minutes of trading blows, I saw his shoulders sag in defeat. We were both exhausted, staggering like drunks. I turned to the crowd to appeal for an end to it. But van Reenen would have none of that, he kept egging Partridge on, and Partridge launched charge after ragged charge at me.

Mustering my last reserves of strength I gave him an uppercut to the stomach. He gagged and fell to the ground. I fell on top of him, forcing him face down on to the concrete. I can remember the scene so clearly, the way the afternoon light fell on the water tank, the rows of boys sitting in the dust under the msasa trees, the blood in my eyes and the taste of it in my mouth. I was shouting at Partridge.

'Give up! Give up!'

And he mumbled into the concrete, 'Never.'

I was sitting on his back, holding his hair in one fist and twisting his arm behind his back with the other. I was desperate for it to end. Every time he refused to surrender, I smashed his head down against the concrete. Finally they pulled us apart. I staggered to my feet and wiped the blood off my face with my shirt-tails. But Partridge wouldn't get up. His forehead was bloody and his head lolled around, falling back on to his chest every time they tried to revive him. They dunked him in water and slapped his face, but he wouldn't come round.

'This is all your fucking fault, van Reenen!' I screamed. He suddenly looked panicked himself. We all agreed on a cover story that Partridge had fallen out of a tree, trying to pick muzhanje berries.

Then we carried him to sickbay. The matron looked appalled and rushed him to hospital in her little Morris Minor. We'd never seen her drive so fast.

When they'd gone, I washed and changed and ducked into the little chapel. I knelt and prayed for forgiveness for killing Partridge, for he was clearly dying. The crucifix hanging on the wall above the altar was a particularly gory one. Christ sagged heavily on his cross, blood glistening on his forehead from his crown of thorns and on the nail-holes in his hands and feet. The spear wound in his side gaped open to reveal dull ivory ribs within. His eyes were closed and his chin slumped forward on to his chest, just like Partridge.

I rattled off a dozen Hail Marys and a few Our Fathers and an approximate Credo for good measure. Then I fled the accusatory image of Christ on the cross and went for a slow walk around the playing fields to contemplate my more immediate temporal fate.

I wondered if I would be arrested and put on trial for murder like the Crocodile Gang, in the High Court opposite the Cecil Hotel? I remembered the trial of the youngest Crocodile Gang member; the way they argued back and forth about whether he was eighteen. At least I had a birth certificate which proved my age, so I was safe from being hanged. But he was still sent to prison for life. Maybe I would meet the Crocodile Gang in prison. I wondered how to find a lawyer to defend me. I didn't know any lawyers. Maybe I could get a letter from the Queen ordering them to let me off.

More immediately, I worried about what to tell Father Mathias when he asked me why we had been fighting. Silence, I decided. I would just stay silent. A dignified but implacable silence.

In the event, when I was called in by Mathias my resolve lasted all of five minutes before the whole story came tumbling out. I was so miserable with guilt and drained of aggression. I sat there in his office, my right eye swollen closed, my split lip throbbing, feeling sorry for myself. Yet I was the culprit, not the victim.

'Young Partridge is a very sick boy. He has a fractured skull,' Mathias said to me, pacing up and down his study, his cassocks swishing. 'Honestly, fighting is one thing, but this was really over the top. What did you think you were doing smashing his head on the concrete?'

I stared dumbly at the floor.

'What was the fight about anyway?' he asked.

'Nothing.'

'You must have been fighting about something?'

'No. It was van Reenen's idea that we had to fight. He organized it. I tried to get out of it. But they wouldn't let me.'

'So if van Reenen tells you to jump off a bridge, you'd do that too, would you?'

I shut up then. There seemed no point in trying to explain how complete the bully's hold could be.

Partridge made a full recovery in time but I suffered a package of punishments that seemed to drag on for months, long after he was back frolicking on the football field. I was gated and made to stay late after class. My sister was brought over from Marymount to have 'a talk' with me, but I was sullen and uncommunicative.

My fight with Partridge was the last water-tank fight, the tradition stopped after that. But whenever I walked past the arena, usually to buy cigarettes at the trading store behind the school, I felt again that lurching sick feeling in my stomach, and again I tasted blood in my mouth.

Carmel College, it soon became apparent, was an ill-starred venture. It was in the wrong place at the wrong time. Economic sanctions against Rhodesia were beginning to bite, and the Carmelites could no longer get money from Ireland. The school itself was located only a few hundred yards from the Mozambique border, and the war in Mozambique was hotting up. Sometimes we could hear the faint chatter of small-arms fire in the middle of the night, floating up on the breeze from the other side. I would pull the blankets up over my head and wish it was all over. But the war in Mozambique was not going well for the Portuguese. They were losing huge areas of the country to their black Communist guerrillas.

It was a pity about the war in Mozambique, because we had been going on holiday there every year since I could remember. As we didn't have a sea of our own, we used theirs. The Portuguese people themselves were quite strange. Although they were Europeans, they couldn't speak English. In fact some of the boys at school called them *sea-kaffirs*, or Porks, and treated them as though they weren't entirely white. They *were* unusual for whites because quite a few of them couldn't read or write and did jobs that Africans did in Rhodesia. They operated the lifts and drove taxis and buses, which were black men's jobs, really.

Mozambique seemed very exotic to me. It seemed like abroad. They kept their wine in round flagons encased in raffia nets. They doused their food in a hot sauce called *peri peri* which made your lips burn long after you'd finished eating. Their buildings were different too, because they often forgot to finish them. They just left them as rough concrete skeletons with bits of metal rods sticking out. Their roads were very bumpy, and their drains smelt awful.

But the Portuguese were our friends. They still let us buy petrol from them, even after the rest of the world imposed economic sanctions against us. When the Rhodesians drove down to Beira lots of them put stickers on the back windows of their cars which said: *OBRIGADO MOZAMBIQUE* – thank you Mozambique.

Mostly we went on holiday to Beira, which was a town on the coast only three hours' drive from Umtali. We stayed at the Estoril Hotel, or in chalets behind the beach. In Beira there were trampolines on the beach and a funfair and a harbour with big ships that you could watch.

One day my father took me on an outing to the airport because I hadn't seen airliners before. We sat on the balcony overlooking the runway and my father had a Manica beer, and I had a 7Up. We were waiting for a plane from the Mozambique airline DETA to take off, and it was getting dark. But there was a technical problem. The man with the ping-pong bats who directs the plane into the right position for take off couldn't get the lights in his ping-pong bats to work.

We watched as a growing crowd of technicians and airline officials fiddled with the paddles, while the plane sat on the runway. Eventually he jumped on to his motorbike and rode off into town. The aeroplane still sat on the runway with all the passengers inside. He returned half an hour later with new batteries and loaded them into his ping-pong bats, and finally directed the plane into position. My father was laughing at it all.

Later at the Oceana restaurant, over *peri peri* crayfish and prawns and bottles of *vinho verde*, he told the story to the Hayters and the Watsons.

'Just imagine,' he said, 'a plane is delayed forty-five minutes on the runway so an airport worker can go to town for four torch batteries. I tell you something, the Portuguese will never win their war here.'

The Oceana restaurant was right on the beach. It was so close to the sea that when the tide was in the water from the waves sprayed on to the windows. You could swim in the Indian ocean, though the waves got very big and the undertow could drag you out to sea. There were jellyfish and Portuguese men-o-war, which could sting you, and occasionally there were sharks.

When we got tired of swimming, or too sunburnt, we visited Mrs Trinidade's zoo, a private zoo on the edge of town. Mrs Trinidade, the owner, was a big fat woman, a Coloured, we would have called her. But down here as long as they took Portuguese names and promised to speak only Portuguese, they were allowed to pretend they were Portuguese, that they were European. They were called *asimilados*, black whites really.

Mrs Trinidade's zoo was a great novelty to us, because back home in Rhodesia we only had game reserves – zoos were illegal. Mrs Trinidade's zoo had an old lion that liked to lick your ice cream, a bored-looking leopard and even a tiger, I think. There were two crocodiles that lay half-submerged in a tank of fetid water and only seemed to move when Mrs Trinidade brought them hens to eat. She also had a colony of chattering monkeys which lived up a fenced-in tree and snatched the sunglasses off your face if you stood too close.

Some years we took our holidays on board ship, sailing up the Mozambique coast almost as far north as Tanzania and down south to Cape Town. We usually went on English ships from the City Lines, like *The City of Exeter*, but after sanctions they didn't want to take us any more. So we tried a Portuguese ship, the SS *Mozambique*. We drove down to the Mozambique capital, LM – Lorenco Marques – to get aboard.

It was my first time in LM, but I knew all about it, because that's where LM Radio came from. It was a pop station broadcast principally to South Africa. But we used to listen to it on our pocket transistors at school after lights out, under our blankets. We listened through little earpieces and the reception was a bit crackly, especially when there were thunderstorms around, but we didn't mind, it made the whole experience more deliciously clandestine. I imagined I was listening to the Voice of the Resistance in the war. In fact it played a steady stream of mainstream pop, interspersed with commercials for South African cigarettes and alcohol.

LM was much bigger than Beira and it had a whole nest of skyscrapers in the centre. As we approached the city it looked like the pictures I'd seen of New York. But when we got closer, it was quite shabby and people hung their washing out of the windows of the skyscrapers. We stayed for several nights in a very posh hotel called the Polana, a graceful colonial building overlooking the sea. Inside, it had high ceilings with ornate cornicing and chandeliers. The waiters, who opened the doors for you, wore starched white uniforms with gold braid on their epaulettes. They brought you *peri peri* cashew nuts on little silver saucers, to accompany your drinks. The drinks themselves had monogrammed swizzle sticks in them, the first time I had ever seen such sophistication. Even the fluffy white towels had the hotel's monogram and crest.

My father said that the hotel had a long and distinguished history. During the Second World War, in which Portugal and its colonies were neutral, the writer Malcolm Muggeridge was based in the Polana as a spy for British Intelligence, MI6. His German and Italian counterparts also took up residence in the Polana. The level of spying and sabotage was absurdly petty, said my father. One night Muggeridge had tiptoed down the hotel corridor and mixed up all the shoes of the German and Italian spies. On another evening, peeping through a chink in the curtains of his German rival's room, he was greatly excited to discover that the German wore a hairnet in bed, and rushed off to file a report on this valuable intelligence.

Finally, said my father, Muggeridge was so despairing at the futility of it all, that he decided to commit suicide by drowning himself in the ocean. He set off at low tide, and waded out for a quarter of a mile with the sea still only up to his waist. Bored at having to wade for so long, and irritated that he couldn't think of the French words for 'I am drowning myself', he finally returned to the Polana in time for breakfast.

These stories added enormously to the romance of the Polana, and I used to walk down the long, high corridors imagining mismatched German and Italian shoes outside the bedroom doors, and spies in hairnets, with monocles and duelling scars. I found out from my father what the French was for 'I am drowning myself'. And I began to follow a bizarre ritual whenever I swam off the beach in front of the Polana: I would run into the waves yelling, '*Je me noie! Je me noie!*' Apart from the word for goddess, *déesse*, from our Citroën, they were the first French words I ever learnt. But in my version '*Je me noie!*' was soon corrupted to 'German ahoy!'

*

At last the SS *Mozambique* arrived from Lisbon and was ready for boarding. We watched as our car was swung high above the dock by a giant old crane, and then lowered into the hold. On board we were shown to our cabins. I shared a cabin with my sister, Jain, and my parents were next door. The cabins were small and panelled with blond wood, each with a single porthole. Everything was bolted down, my father explained, so that it wouldn't fly around in a storm.

The SS *Mozambique* wasn't as clean as the English ships we'd been on. And when they had a lifeboat drill the hawsers on some boats were rusted solid. After half an hour hitting them with hammers the crew just gave up. My father noticed that the radar on top of the mast wasn't going round and round, like it should have been, and he mentioned this to the captain after dinner. The captain, an elderly man with flowing white hair, got into a real snit.

'We don't need radar here. The channel is very deep and clear. There are no other vessels here of any size like us, and I have been doing this route now for thirty-five years, thank you.'

'Pompous bastard,' my father said under his breath as the captain flounced off, but he let the matter rest. Later, after we got back home, we read in the newspaper that the SS *Mozambique* had collided with another boat in the Tagus estuary, coming in to Lisbon. Everyone had been evacuated off the SS *Mozambique*. It was damaged beyond repair and had to be scrapped. My father folded the paper up and grunted with satisfaction.

The route of the SS *Mozambique* took us north along the coast as far as Porto Amelia. We hugged the shoreline and stopped at every port along the way to unload things. Every time the ship stopped we were allowed to get off and look around.

After a few days we stopped at Mozambique Island. It was about a mile from the mainland and at low tide you could walk between the two. My mother told me that Mozambique Island was the first landfall made by Europeans on the African continent. Bartholomew Diaz had landed here almost five hundred years ago. I worked out that meant that Europeans had been in Africa since the Middle Ages, since before America was invented even.

The buildings on Mozambique Island were the oldest buildings I had ever seen, except for Great Zimbabwe of course, but that was a ruin. Here there were great stone churches with huge, delicately carved wooden doors, a crenellated fort in which a Portuguese garrison had been based for hundreds of years, and narrow cobbled streets just like the ones I'd seen in pictures of European towns.

The top two decks of the SS *Mozambique* had ordinary passengers like us, but the bottom decks were packed with thousands of army conscripts form Portugal who were on their way to war for the first time. None of them had been to Africa before. They were pale young men in olive fatigues, with cropped blue-black hair and sad brown eyes. Few of them were over eighteen years old. And they were scared. You could feel the fear radiating up from the steerage deck. Every morning their warrant officers would drill them on deck, but the boys didn't seem to be able to march in step or keep in line. The warrant officers shouted at them and made them cry.

At night they sang very sad songs in Portuguese, accompanied by guitars. Lieutenant Soares, who was one of the ship's engineers, told me the songs were called *fado* and they were all about love and death. They had a favourite *fado* song which they sang every night after supper. It was about homesickness. Lt Soares translated it for me.

> *Look gentlemen,*
> *At this Lisbon of days gone by,*

Of the Crusades, the Esperas,
And of the Royal Bullfights;
Of the Festas, of age-old Processions,
Of street-cries in the morning,
That are no more.

The conscripts were not allowed to mix with paying passengers, and the gate between their deck and ours was kept locked. But you could talk to them through the fence. Some of them could speak English and I used to go down to the fence to chat to them.

'Pedro! Pedro!' they called out when they saw me coming down. 'Tell us about Africa. Tell us about the bush.'

They were completely ignorant about Africa.

'We are scared of lions,' they said. 'Back home they told us that we will get eaten by lions in Africa.'

'A lion will hardly ever attack you unless you provoke it or threaten its cubs,' I lectured importantly, relishing the unusual experience of a raptly attentive adult audience. They looked relieved at this information. 'Anyway, you'll have guns. Phou! phou!' I pantomimed the shooting of a lion. 'Shoot the bloody thing!' They laughed uncertainly.

'You *do* have guns, don't you?' I asked.

'Yes, of course,' they said. Then one added, 'But so far they have not given us any bullets.'

'It is in case of accidents,' another hastily explained.

I tried to tell them about other dangers they might face in Africa, and the precautions to take. I told them not to swim in rivers or they would catch bilharzia. They had never heard of it. I told them always to check their boots for scorpions and spiders before putting them on, to look carefully where they walked in case they stood on a puff adder, how to apply a tourniquet if they were bitten. I told them that if a cobra spat in their eyes, they should wash them out with water or milk or even with piss, to prevent blindness. I told them how crocodiles sometimes looked like driftwood, that hippos were unpredictable, that they should take their anti-malarials religiously, and that the best way to get rid of a leech was to burn it off with a cigarette. I told them not to pet African dogs because some of them had rabies.

But instead of reassuring them, my informal round-up of how to counter the dangers of the African bush left the conscripts looking terrified.

That evening I was standing at the railings on the top deck with my father. We watched the frothy wake trailing away behind us into the setting sun, and the dolphins leaping out of the sea by the side of the ship. A breeze ruffled my hair – it was a warm breeze unlike any I had ever felt, warm like the air from my sister's hair dryer. The coast, a tangled green bank of mangrove and palm trees, was only a couple of miles to port.

'You know, Dad, I think you're right about the war here in Mozambique,' I said. 'There's no way these blokes can win a war. They're terrified of wild animals, never mind the terrorists.'

My father sighed and nodded in agreement.

'God know what's going to happen here,' he said.

It was the first time I'd seen him really worried about the political situation. He drew heavily on his cigarette and began to tell me a story about a visit made by Rhodesian officers to the Portuguese military commander of Tete, one of the provinces in Mozambique. When they went into his headquarters tent, the Rhodesians discovered that he was using a Shell road map as his main operational map. The Shell maps were given out free in Rhodesia with every five gallons of petrol you bought. They were small-scale tourist maps decorated with bright pictures of wild animals and waterfalls and ancient ruins. The successors of the famous Portuguese navigators Vasco da Gama and Bartholomew Diaz were conducting a counter-insurgency war from a petrol-station freebie. My father shook his head in disbelief at it all.

The next morning Lt Soares told me that the Major in charge

of the conscripts was furious with me and had complained to him that I had been terrifying the soldiers.

'Some of them want to jump over the side and swim for the Algarve,' Lt Soares laughed. 'They want to mutiny, to desert from the army.'

After that I was banned from going anywhere near the steerage deck. But I still listened every night to their *fado*, and I felt sorry for them, so far away from home and so afraid, about to go into war on a tourist map. At Porto Amelia, they all got off. They filed down the gangplank with their kitbags on their shoulders. They were wearing their black berets with the little ribbons down the back.

'*Adeus! Boa sorte!*' I called down to them. It meant goodbye and good luck and Lt Soares had taught me how to say it. They all waved back and gave jaunty thumbs-up signs. Then they were loaded on to big green army trucks on the quayside and driven away.

Ten

Back at Carmel College, Father Kennedy called a special assembly to break the news to us that efforts to save the school had failed. It would close down at the end of the year. We were standing in lines in the open-air concourse beneath the classrooms, and the summer rains had just started. It was difficult to hear what he was saying – a huge storm was in progress with driving rain blowing in through the open sides of the concourse and wetting us. But Father Kennedy didn't seem to notice. He was all choked up and looked like he was going to cry. There were long pauses in his speech, when he seemed to have forgotten what to say next, or even where he was. We stood there, on the puddled cement floor, damp and uncharacteristically quiet, wondering what would happen to us now. Father Kennedy announced that the school had been bought by the army, who were going to turn it into a barracks.

At the end of the term, our parents came to collect us for the last time. I said goodbye to my friends, and we promised to stay in touch with each other. But we were scattered to schools all over the country, and most of us never wrote or met again.

I sat in the back of the Citroën as we drove away, and I actually felt sad that I would never come back. I felt sad that Father Kennedy's dream had collapsed after less than five years. I took a last look at the school and tried to imagine it as a barracks – soldiers parading on the sports fields, camouflage troop carriers parked in rows, sentry boxes and sandbags and radio masts, and barbed-wire fences around it all. I wondered what would happen to the little chapel with its stained-glass windows and its gory crucifix.

The priests themselves were also scattered. Father Kennedy went back to his beloved mission station at Chisumbanje on the banks of the Sabi river. Some of the other priests went to live with Bishop Lamont at the bishopric next to Marymount. And when Bishop Lamont was expelled from the country a short while later, accused of 'assisting terrorists', they went with him back to Ireland. Father Galvin came to live at the Carmelite seminary near Skyline Junction, just past the spot where oom Piet Oberholzer had been murdered.

The seminary was called St Charles Lwanga, after Africa's first saint, a Ugandan martyr who was burnt at the stake by the tribal chiefs for refusing to renounce Jesus, or at least that's what Father McLoughlan told me. I never quite knew when he was joking, though. Father McLoughlan joked most of the time, and he swore, something I'd never heard a priest do before. Not *really* profane words, but 'damn' and 'hell' and 'bastard' – still quite impressive for a priest, I thought. And he drank whiskey. It was very good whiskey, my father said, Irish whiskey that you could no longer get in Rhodesia because of sanctions.

I think it was because of his whiskey that we went to church at St Charles Lwanga, even though my parents weren't Catholics. Father McLoughlan kept the service very short, and he even cracked jokes in his sermon. Afterwards the congregation gathered for pre-lunch snacks and drinks in the priest's house, where Father McLoughlan was prepared to share his Irish whiskey with a few select whiskey aficionados.

He would sidle up to my father and say, 'Spiritual fortification, my son?', even though my father was the same age as him.

And my father would always reply, 'Amen to that, Father,' and Father Mac would hand him a double Bushmills.

Sir Hugo Sebright also came to St Charles Lwanga on some

Sundays, although he usually skipped the service itself and turned up only for the whiskey afterwards. Sir Hugo and Father McLoughlan were allies in a spiritual range war against the Reverend Merritt, an American Methodist who ran the mission down the hill in Biriwiri.

The Revd Merritt and Father Mac were as different as two members of the same faith could possibly be. While Father Mac was a libertarian connoisseur of fine malt, Revd Merritt was a fundamentalist and a vehement teetotaller and wore a little badge on his lapel to prove it. The two of them were locked in a bitter battle for the souls of the local Africans.

It was a strange struggle, played out for the most part on the football pitch. The church with the stronger football team tended to attract the lion's share of religious recruits, as the locals seemed to believe that the winning side had stronger divine backup. But St Charles Lwanga had suffered a long run of humiliating defeats on the field and Father Mac was con- vinced that Revd Merritt had unfairly imported soccer talent from outside the district to reinforce his spiritual hold.

Sir Hugo's farm adjoined the Methodist mission and he dis- liked the Revd Merritt because residents from the mission tres- passed on his land to graze their goats and at harvest time they stole the occasional *mealie*. Revd Merritt and Sir Hugo had heated rows about it. Sir Hugo was also infuriated to discover that the Revd Merritt had come over on to his farm, without permission, to proselytize among his farm workers. He had warned the reverend that the next time he found any of the Methodist mission lot on his land, he would shoot them. Sir Hugo had a beautiful old twelve-bore Purdey shotgun with ornate engraving on the barrels. He called it his Merritt gun. One day during after-service drinks, Father Mac even blessed the Merritt gun – as a joke I think. But then you never knew for sure with Father Mac.

Father Mac's dead now. He was ambushed in his car by guerrillas, not far from where oom Piet had been killed. He was shot several times in the back, chest and groin and very badly wounded. The two African nuns with him in the car jumped out and berated the guerrillas at the tops of their voices, saying they should be ashamed of themselves for shooting a priest. In the face of such righteous ire, the guerrillas slunk away instead of finishing him off. But Father Mac never really recovered. He was taken back to Ireland and died there.

That holiday, after Carmel closed, my parents had some even more unsettling news for me. They had decided that we should move away from the eastern highlands altogether, to a place called Mangula, where my father had a new job running a copper mine. Mangula was on the other side of the country, more than five hundred miles away, on the edge of the Zambezi valley. My father broke the news to us at supper, round the table. Jain didn't seem to mind much, she was about to leave school for Teachers' Training College in Bulawayo. My little sister, Georgina, didn't really understand what it would involve. Only I seemed upset.

'What's wrong with here? Why do we have to move?' I asked crossly. To my annoyance, I found myself in tears. My father explained to me that the Rhodesian Wattle Company had been bought by a big multinational company called Lonrho, and that he didn't like the way they did business, or their plans for the estates. He'd been offered a very good job at Mangula, where he had worked once already, many years ago. Mangula would be closer to my new school in Salisbury, he said, and it wouldn't be so lonely, because it was a much bigger place than Silverstream.

'And you can get television in Mangula,' promised my mother. It was her strongest enticement so far – at fourteen I'd never seen television in my life.

But I remained unconvinced.

'What will happen to Knighty and Violet? Will they come with us?' I asked.

'No, they can't,' said my father. 'Mangula's too far away from their families, and it's a different tribe down there. Don't worry, I've found them good jobs with other families here.'

After Christmas, as a farewell ritual, we went on one final expedition up the Chimanimani mountains. It was something we had done each year ever since I could remember. As a little boy, I used to be carried most of the way up by Violet. She had all my clothes and my blair and beddy zebby in a pillowcase slung over her shoulder. On the pillowcase she had embroidered the words 'Love makes the world go round', and underneath some hearts and noughts and crosses for hugs and kisses. We used to head for the Hut, a shelter half a day's walk from the bottom. From there we would go on expeditions to Martin's Falls, Southern Lake, Peza and Binga peaks and Red cave.

We parked the Citroën at Dead Cow Gulch, the Department of Parks and Wildlife base in the foothills. The mountains loomed massively above us. Glittering and mysterious as always, they never failed to excite me.

I set off immediately, ahead of the others, feeling the need to be alone. I knew my way well enough. Up Long Gully, scampering over lichen-blotched granite boulders, steeper and steeper. Chimanimani: in *chiNdau*, the name meant 'a pass too narrow to turn round in'. And soon the path did narrow so much that at times I had to walk sideways to squeeze through. This pass was part of the ancient slave trail from the interior out to the Mozambique coast. I thought of all the thousands of slaves that must have trudged over these mountains, shackled together by logs attached to collars around their necks; wrenched from their homes and destined for a miserable life of captive toil. And now I was being wrenched from my home too.

Up here I felt like the last human being on earth. The range was sixty miles long and thirty wide, and there were no roads or human habitation anywhere within it. Rock dassies scurried between the boulders, and in the distance a baboon sentinel barked a low mastiff bark to warn his troop of my approach. His bark hung in the air, echoing between the outcrops. I rested on the flat of a rock, lying back on its comforting warmth. High above me, eagles were lazily riding a thermal, adjusting their wing tips minutely as they wheeled. From time to time one would fold its wings and drop like a missile on to a dassie. Way below the timber forests rolled away into the hazy blue distance, punctuated here and there by tea and coffee plantations. I got up and strode on up the trail, higher and higher.

Soon the terrain opened out on to a steep slope covered with a fine sandy loam, beach white, from which rose cedar and yellowwood trees. Their branches were draped with vines, and delicate orchids clung to them too. Klipspringers, disturbed at their grazing, bounced away from me in dainty bounds. Then another barrier of granite and I was above the tree line. Only ferns, the odd protea and aloe survived up here. It was a strange vista, called the Mountains of the Moon, a barren landscape dotted with craggy rock formations, whipped by a cool wind, the south-east monsoon that swept unhindered across the flood plains of Mozambique before coming up abruptly against the formidable 8000-foot barrier of the Chimanimanis.

As I strode through the Mountains of the Moon the sun suddenly retreated, and a roiling mist swirled between the outcrops, whistling through the jagged rocks. Storms brewed with little warning up here, when the rain-bearing monsoon was forced up and chilled by the mountains. I had been following one of several vague paths, taking my bearing from a soaring peak called Dragon's Tooth. But Dragon's Tooth had now disappeared into the cloud. The mist was becoming more viscous and soon it condensed into violent bursts of rain that stung cold against my cheek. My stride slowed to a trudge, and I pondered waiting for the rest of the party to catch up. But

I decided to carry on, across this plain, to the shelter of the next range.

I could hear the rumble of distant thunder as I walked, my head bowed against the downpour. There was a dazzling flash of lightning, and a sound like a whip crack, and the air crackled light blue around me. My heart kicked at my ribs and a blast of thunder crashed down, and rumbled away to the peaks and back and away again and back, becoming slowly fainter. A small herd of klipspringer bounded past in the rain, bleating in terror.

Maybe I would be killed by lightning, I thought. Lots of people were struck by lightning in Rhodesia – although they were mostly Africans, it was true. My mother quite often treated the victims. At school we learnt that more people were killed by lightning in Rhodesia than in any other country in the world, except perhaps Uganda, but they no longer kept records there, since Idi Amin took over. Maybe this was God's way of ensuring that I would never leave the Eastern Highlands. I couldn't think of anywhere I would rather die than on top of the Chimanimanis. Maybe this was fate.

I adjusted the small rucksack on my back, straightened my shoulders and walked out confidently into the frenzied electrical storm. The shafts of forked lightning followed one another almost continuously, each volley of thunder merged into the next. But I didn't care any more. I wasn't even scared. I squelched along, with my face lifted to the storm, no longer sure where the path was. And I found I was humming a Shangaan hunting song, one of the borrowed hunting songs that the Silverstream beaters sang to keep their spirits up, on their way to tackle a forest fire.

It was to be my last time up there for twenty years. Soon after we came down the mountains the Portuguese left Mozambique and guerrillas began using it as a base from which to infiltrate into Rhodesia. In a loop of history, the old slave route across the Chimanimani was used in reverse by people who proclaimed they were fighting against their own enslavement at home.

The mountains were too long and wide and remote to be effectively patrolled by the Rhodesian army; whole battalions would have been swallowed up with ease. So the commanders decided to turn the Chimanimanis into a lethal barrier by seeding them with anti-personnel mines. The whole range was transformed into a vast minefield. In the valleys below, in the fortified homesteads on the timber estates and the coffee plantations, they would hear loud booms rolling down from the mountains from time to time. Not thunder, but explosions, as klip-springers, baboons, sable, eland and blue duiker set off mines and blew themselves to pieces. And for almost ten years humans never ventured there at all.

At the end of those school holidays my parents took me to Umtali station and put me on the overnight sleeper train to Salisbury and my new school. I'd never been on a train. My compartment had room for four people, but I was alone in it. I stood at the window and waved to my parents on the platform. My mother held up my little sister to the window for a 'lucky touch' and then the train lurched off.

It was just getting dark as the locomotive strained to climb out of the Umtali valley, around Christmas Pass, and we slowed to walking pace. *Piccanins* from the farm compounds ran along-side, whooping and waving. Knighty had made me a packed supper and loaded it carefully into an old shoe box, but I wasn't really hungry so I leant out of the window to hand down the food. The *piccanins* leapt up to grab it: an orange, a Fray Bentos sandwich on one of Knighty's crocodile rolls, a boiled egg and a slice of fruitcake.

When I'd disposed of it all, one of the boys jumped up and threw something into my compartment. It was a little toy zebra, like beddy zebby, but intricately carved from wood and stained with black stripes. I kept it as my new good luck charm for my new school, a talisman against unhappiness.

After a while an African steward brought me some starched linen bedding, which he unrolled on my bunk. I sat on the bunk below staring out of the window and wondering what my life would be like. It was dark outside. Really dark in the way that African nights are, without the sodium glow of cities or towns to compete with the stars. I couldn't see anything at all out there. Only the words 'Rhodesian Railways', delicately etched into the window glass, and my own reflection staring dolefully back at me.

Finally I brushed my teeth in the stainless-steel basin, got undressed and went to bed. I lay awake listening to the rhythmic clatter of wheel on track, worrying about my new school. The train had to stop at every single station and depot, no matter how small, to pick up milk urns and postbags. Just as the rhythm lulled me through doze towards sleep, the train would lurch to another juddering halt, until dawn broke and I arrived, red-eyed and nervous, at the capital.

My first abiding memory of St George's was the great brooding castle that dominates the college. A russet granite tower complete with a full set of crenellations, it stands on top of Gun Hill, with a commanding view over Salisbury.

'The whole white population of Salisbury gathered here for protection during the Shona rebellion,' Dimitri Paphos told me as we stood on top of it. 'They mounted a Maxim gun up here in the tower and mowed down the *muntu* warriors, row after row, as they charged up the hill.'

We were up there in the turret raising the school flag for Candlemas day. I looked down over the city; you could hardly tell it was a city from up here. From up here a green and mauve canopy of jacaranda covered all but the city centre, where a cluster of high-rise blocks poked through. Paphos had finished tying the cleat in the flag rope and was now firing an imaginary Maxim gun.

'Uh-uh-uh! Uh-uh-uh! Uh-uh-uh!' He turned the handle to rotate the multiple barrels of his killing machine.

I looked down at the long sweeping driveway up to the castle and imagined it soaked in the blood of a thousand Shona warriors, whose restless spirits must still wander the school grounds at night.

Paphos was busy reloading his Maxim gun to keep up his body count. His father was a Greek greengrocer who had immigrated after the Second World War, like most suburban Rhodesians.

'Just like the Shangani patrol, outnumbered a hundred to one by the *munts* but this time we won. Hah!' he said, and raked his fire in great notional arcs across the school grounds. The Shangani patrol was a famous battle in 1893 in which a thirty-four-man patrol of police troopers led by Major Allan Wilson had been surrounded and eventually wiped out by a far bigger force of Matabele warriors.

Dimitri Paphos began singing the ballad of Shangani patrol:

> *His troopers they were loyal,*
> *His troopers they were young.*
> *They followed Allan Wilson,*
> *Till the setting of the sun.*

Then he recited the chorus for me and insisted I join in. He was a hefty boy, the only one in the class to shave, and I was hoping he might be my friend. So we stood at attention, looking over the battlements and together we sang the rousing chorus:

> *Up the wild Shangani!*
> *And down the other side.*

171

Up the wild Shangani!
Where Allan Wilson died.

Above us the flag was now flapping in the breeze. The school crest on the flag, which was also on the pockets of our scarlet blazers, was a complex heraldic playground which we had to learn off by heart. The two rampant wolves holding a black cauldron came from the name St Ignatius of Loyola. In old Spanish, the *loy* of Loyola meant wolf and *olla* meant cauldron. For some reason the wolves were impishly waggling their tongues at one another. St Ignatius was the patron saint of the Society of Jesus, the Jesuits, who ran St George's. The Jesuits, or the Jays as we called them, were Catholic priests like the Carmelites, only stricter. Paphos told me that the Jays were the Pope's commandos, His Holiness's SAS. They certainly made the Carmelites look benign and avuncular.

The roses above the wolves on the crest represented Rhodesia, because *rhodon*, the Greek for rose, was the closest they could get to Rhodes. The red cross between the roses was the cross of St George, patron saint of the school. And the victory of the knight St George over the evil dragon was represented by the crown and the sword plunged between the dragon's wings, which topped the crest. Underneath it a scroll bore the words *ex fide fiducia* – from faith comes confidence. This was the college's second stab at a motto. The first – St George for merrie England – had to be dropped after the Queen wrote a letter complaining that it was a royal motto for her own, exclusive, use.

After several verses of the ballad of the Shangani patrol, in which Allan Wilson's patrol is slowly but unavoidably annihilated, our singing session ended. Paphos was sweating from the effort of it. He leant on the battlements to catch his breath.

'Never walk around under the castle when the moon is full,' he suddenly warned. 'Father Stanley comes up here with a rifle, a .22 Hornet, and takes pot shots at wild cats.' He drew a bead on a small boy slouching up the drive, and squeezed off a couple of rounds from a pretend .22 rifle. 'You could get caught in the crossfire. Stanley's a crazy old fucker.'

Paphos cleared his throat. 'Hands out of pockets!' he bellowed down, and then ducked behind the battlements. Below us the startled form-one boy jerked his hands out of his blazer pockets and scanned the sky in bewilderment.

I thanked Paphos for the advice and he led the way back down the spiral stone staircase. Every time we passed an alcove window the light fell on the dense peppery stubble covering his cheeks. It was the envy of the other boys in our class. Not all of us even had hair on our balls yet. But we suspected that Paphos had been *born* with hair on his. It was Paphos who showed us pornography for the first time – a postcard-size picture of a plump Portuguese woman, photographed from behind, kneeling on a red plastic bench. She had nothing on at all except a pair of white high-heeled shoes.

We all crowded round to examine her. A fearsome beard of pubic hair grew in dense profusion all the way up the inside of her thighs and right up the crack of her bum, some tendrils even probing up to explore the dimples in the small of her back.

Most of us found it rather frightening.

'It's not natural,' said George Leddy, peering at her pubes through his round gold-rimmed glasses with all the concentration of a ticket inspector.

On the back of the photo it said her name was Maria. I looked at her again. She had swollen blue-veined breasts that hung heavily beneath her. The network of veins reminded me of rivers on an Ordnance Survey map. Dark brown nipples brushed against her hairy forearms and almost reached the bench.

Maria's pair of watermelons made Katie Frost's little under-ripe plums look like a different part of the body altogether.

Katie Frost was a girl at home who wanted to be chased, but not to be caught. Which was OK with me really, because I wasn't sure what I'd do with her if I caught her. I was allowed to kiss her and to feel her small hard breasts through her shirt. But that was all. She just hugged me and kissed me back, always with her eyes closed. I kept mine open, that's how I could see hers were shut. We used to meet secretly down by Silverstream river. In public, we normally ignored each other. A few weeks earlier, before I left for St George's for the first time, she had given my balls a painful tweak, as a special favour.

I knew all about sex, how it was done, and how it made babies. But before Maria, the most graphic things I'd ever seen were my mother's medical books. Gray's *Anatomy* was a huge blue book which catalogued the parts of the body in minute detail. It made the woman's sexual bits look immensely complicated. And all the bits seemed to have Latin names.

Common Diseases of the Skin, by A. C. Roxburgh, I found *really* disturbing because it contained gory close-up photos of all the terrible diseases you could get from actually going 'all the way'. The various stigmata of sexual intercourse were truly horrific: boils and pustules, seeping abscesses and crusty warts, bulbous lesions, infiltrated abrasions, ganglions and cysts, nodules and polyps, chancroids seeping serum, and chancres oozing yellow slough. Frankly it was quite a relief that Katie Frost didn't want to go any further.

I regarded Maria again. There was nothing like her in my mother's medical books. The women who posed in Gray's *Anatomy* and *Common Diseases of the Skin* by A. C. Roxburgh, either had their heads chopped off by the camera or had black bars across their eyes so you couldn't recognize them. But not Maria. You could certainly see *all* of her. Her hand reached back to peel apart her fleshy bumcheeks. I noticed her fingernails were bitten down to the quick, the cuticles in shreds. You could just make out the look on her face, in profile, half-hidden behind a curtain of black hair. It was a bored look.

My attempts to fit in at St George's – lustily singing the ballad of the Shangani patrol with Dimitri Paphos, enthusiastically examining Maria's nether regions, smoking non-filters behind the bike sheds without coughing, hurling myself around on the sports field, affecting a nonchalance in class, tattooing myself with a needle and fountain pen – all these were only partially successful. I was always to remain a new boy at St George's because I had only arrived at the beginning of form three. Most of the other boys had been together up through the prep school, Hartmann House, since they were about eight years old. They might as well have been brothers.

St George's was the second oldest school in the country, founded in the 1890s. This was as old as European tradition got in Rhodesia. This was our history. And being such a recent history, the school jealously guarded it and kept an obsessive observance of tradition.

My first problem was learning all the peculiar college traditions. Most of them were absurd. Each year had certain privileges, particular walls they could sit on, stairs they could use, items of clothing they could wear. Seniors could wear straw boaters, slip-on shoes and long charcoal trousers on Sundays. Juniors had to wear shorts and grey felt hats and lace-ups. And we had to learn off by heart the names of the rugby first fifteen, the cricket first eleven, the prefects, and college colours.

Seniors had the right to stop us at any time and demand a word-perfect rendition of these lists. It was supposed to engender college spirit. The team lists were posted on the notice board each week and we gathered round to write them down and memorize them. Every morning, on our way to class, we had to walk past the seniors on the 'island', a concrete traffic island on which it was their vaunted right to perch. This was the danger zone, when we could be picked on to recite the names. For my first few weeks I managed to sneak past, then one Monday I was nabbed.

'Oi, you!'

I continued to walk, head down.

'You!' The voice had risen an octave in outrage. I walked on. Then I felt my collar being yanked back, and found myself staring at Hardy, a sixth-former with mutton-chop sideburns and an acne-pocked face who had made it his personal mission to subjugate all juniors.

'I'm talking to you! Ignore me again, and I'll break your arm, you little wanker.' He twisted my arm painfully behind my back to show he meant it.

'Right, first eleven.'

I stood to attention, took a deep breath and began. 'Abrey, Beesley, Coppinger, Dell, Furnell, Hunt, Money, O'Dwyer, Pechey . . . Pechey.'

'You've said Pechey already, you little prick. Write the whole team out five hundred times and—'

'Rogan and Stonier,' I remembered.

'Too late. Bring the lines to the senior common room tomorrow morning after breakfast. What's your name?'

'Godwin, sir.'

In the classroom that evening during studies I began writing out my lines surreptitiously, under cover of some textbooks. We sat in long rows on fixed-bench seats at sloping Dickensian desks with redundant china inkwells still in place in the right-hand corner, and the names of previous generations carved into the desk lids. My homework lay on one side. I had more important things to do, topping up my levels of school spirit. At the head of each page I wrote the letters AMDG: *Ad Majorem Deum Gloria*, which meant 'to the greater glory of God'. We had to put that at the top of all our work. I wondered how a list of the first fifteen was contributing to the Almighty's glory.

I failed to complete my lines that night. After lights out I had to wait for half an hour while Father Ross walked up and down the dorm thumbing his rosary, the leather of his sandals squeaking with every step. The lights of the school drive reflected in his bifocal spectacles and on the smooth dome of his bald head. Only when he'd muttered his last Hail Mary and departed for his cell-like room could I get to work under a tent of bedclothes, writing my lines by torchlight. But I soon fell asleep.

The next morning I offered up my incomplete set and I was duly ordered to report for 'feds'. The word itself – feds – made me tingle hotly in trepidation. Feds were administered with a ferula, an ancient whalebone in the shape of an elongated and flattened shoehorn and covered in a leather sheath. You held out your hands and were whacked with the ferula. It burnt like fire but left no marks.

Father Stanley was on ferula duty that morning.

'*Salve*,' he said solemnly.

'*Salve*, Father,' I replied – it was another of the traditions that we greeted teachers in Latin.

He read my fed note.

'Nine ferulas for failing to recite college teams.'

I held out my hand, palm up, and he steadied it with his left hand while waggling the ferula deftly in his right hand, to limber up.

'Now you understand why you're being punished, don't you?' he asked.

Thwack!

The first fed came down. I instinctively tried to pull my hand back, but he held it firmly by the wrist.

'No, Father,' I said, my eyes already squinched shut in anticipation of the next blow.

Thwack!

'For failing to know the names of the first eleven.'

Thwack!

'And why is it necessary to know the names of the first eleven?'

'I have no idea, Father.'

Thwack!

'Because it is a tradition, and we value tradition here, don't we?

Thwack!

'Tradition doesn't happen by accident, boy, it is the distillation of all that is best in our past, the accumulated wisdom of those who have gone before us.'

Thwack!

'Without tradition we would be condemned to repeat old mistakes. Tradition ensures stability in society.'

Thwack!

'Tradition is the way that the past speaks to the present. Tradition is our anchor in stormy seas.'

Thwack!

'Tradition is bigger than you and me.'

There were many traditions like ferulas and lists which had remained largely unchanged since the founding of the college in 1896. St George's had been modelled on Stoneyhurst, a Jesuit College in England, but unlike the original model, which had been infected by the changing values of the times, St George's had remained perfectly preserved, suspended in the cultural aspic of colonial Rhodesia. So much so that in the early 1980s, when Stoneyhurst despaired of the drug-taking, declining academic standards and general laxity that had gripped the school, they called for the rector of St George's to come over and restore some of the discipline of the old version.

The Jesuits were enthusiastic about two things in particular: religion and sport, which was unsurprising I suppose, given that they were the Lord's SAS. Sport and chapel were both compulsory, and our school day contained great helpings of both. Hindus and Muslims were excused from chapel, but the rest of us went on frequent religious manoeuvres.

Our day often started with a cross-country run, followed by breakfast in the refectory, where we sat at long wooden tables under the beady eye of a huge stuffed bateleur eagle shot by a Jesuit eighty years before. After breakfast, there were matins. When classes finished at 3 o'clock there was sport, five days a week, and matches on Saturday. In the late afternoon, following sport, there was benediction. The main school mass was on Sunday morning, and there were regular times each day for confession.

Religious Doctrine classes took place several times a week. Actually RD wasn't as boring as it sounded. I found that the Jesuits quite liked to argue about things, because that was what they were trained to do. We used to argue with Father Jolson for hours about faith and God, and natural disasters and free will. Father Alfred Jolson was an American Jesuit, a great furry bear of a man, who thought all the traditions and rules of the college were silly.

'Call me Al,' he said to us. But Father Al was as informal as we dared.

I was quite good at RD, and Father Al once asked me if I thought I might have a vocation to the priesthood. I thought about it for about five seconds and then declined politely. There were some things I still wanted to try with Katie Frost, the frightening portents of my mother's medical books notwithstanding.

St George's was desperate for boys to have vocations, but the sad reality was that very few did. A special roll of honour of Old Georgians who had joined the priesthood hung in the small remembrance chapel. There were only four names on it, and one of those, Ronald Kemp, had to be painted over later, when he finally lost the unequal struggle with his libido. His vocation foundered on the rock of Miss Harmsworth the drama teacher.

There was one way, however, in which St George's rigid conservatism had been punctured. The college admitted black boys, one of the very few schools in the country to do so. There were two types of black pupils: scholarship boys, who had been selected as the brightest boys at the Jesuit mission stations, and rich blacks, whose parents paid fees like everyone else.

The rich boys were unlike any other blacks I had encountered. They didn't want to discuss African things. They wanted to be like whites. They spoke English without much of an African accent. They didn't want to talk Shona, except to each other, as a private language. Most of them came from Highfield, which was the wealthiest of the African townships in Salisbury. But although they lived in town they were all boarders.

I had never lived in such close quarters with blacks of my own age before. They were just like us really. In our vast dormitory where narrow beds were sandwiched together, with only iron lockers to separate them, Sipho Mpofu had the bed next to mine. He was a rich black whose father owned a big fleet of buses. Most of Rhodesia's successful black businessmen ran buses or supermarkets. Every morning, just after dawn, Augustus and I and the rest of the dorm would stumble off, half asleep, to the shower block to take our showers in long lines. The prefect on duty was armed with a wet towel and if we overstayed our time he would flick our arses with the end of the towel. Then we marched back to the dorm to change into uniform.

Mpofu did have one or two strange habits. He used to rub Vaseline all over his body every day after his shower, and he backcombed his hair with a special wide-toothed comb. Back at Melsetter school Fatty Slabbert always used to say, '*Kaffirs* pong because they don't wash. That's why we can't live with them.'

But Mpofu didn't smell bad. He smelt of Vaseline. I discussed this with him one day when we were changing for a cross-country run.

'We're just as clean as you are,' he said. 'It's just that for poorer people without running water, it's difficult to wash. Anyway, the smell that they say blacks have, that's just the smell of wood smoke from cooking on open fires.' I realized he was right. The smell of Africans that I recognized so well from my childhood was nothing more than wood smoke.

My sister's school, Marymount, also had blacks. She said that they had special classes for the mission girls, before the first term of each new year. They had lessons on table manners, dress code, etiquette and, most important, a class called personal hygiene.

'Why do they have to have a class on personal hygiene?' I asked Jain.

'Because they're used to toilets with footpads where you don't sit down on the loo, you squat down on your haunches over the hole. Then when they come to Marymount for the first time, instead of sitting on the loos they climb up and put their feet on the seats, and squat on top of the toilet, like they're used to doing.'

At the time I'd laughed at the thought of black girls perched on top of the toilets and the nuns having to show them the right way to take a crap.

I asked Mpofu if it was true that Africans preferred to squat. He agreed that it was.

'It's more hygienic,' he said. 'Think about it. You put your bum down on the same seat as someone else. He may have a dirty bum. You don't know what germs you might catch from him. Huh?'

After that, whenever I went to the lavatory, I would always vigorously wipe the seat with paper before sitting down.

In a school of about seven hundred, there were fewer than a hundred blacks and another hundred or so Asians. The government said that under the Education Act we weren't allowed to have more than 6 per cent blacks, but the rector continued to ignore the law. He threatened to close down the college if the government tried to enforce the limit, and the government backed off.

There were other problems caused by our blacks. They weren't allowed to play sport on the playing fields of government schools. So St George's teams with blacks in them could never play away games. Some schools, like Bothashof, the only Afrikaans medium school in Salisbury, refused to play against our blacks at all.

Racial tensions were worsened when one of our black rugby players landed a tackle on a boy from Prince Edward school and put him in a coma. It was a hard tackle but it was low and clean. The referee never even penalized it. But rumours began to circulate that Prince Edward boys had sworn to exact revenge on St George's for the injury. And for ages after that we only went to town in groups, for fear of attack. Even after hospital tests showed that the injured boy had suffered from a congenital brain condition since birth.

St George's was a bizarre cocktail of moralities: racial enlightenment within a system of extreme conservatism. Father Stanley would promptly stop a rugby match and lead his team off the field because the father of one of the rival team kept barracking from the sideline, 'Nail the *kaffir*! Nail the *kaffir*!' Then Stanley would beat the '*kaffir*' concerned the very next day for a minor infringement of some arcane tradition.

The arcane tradition that was probably most central to the fabric of college life was fagging, the system inherited from English public schools where senior boys are allocated junior boys as servants. We called them skivvies, and they were based on batmen in the army. In my first year I had to skivvy for Peter Chingoka, a black prefect in the Upper Sixth – the first black prefect. Every day I had to clean his shoes, make and turn back his bed, tidy his room, whiten his cricket pads and rub linseed oil into his cricket bat.

Chingoka was strict, but a decent enough bloke – softly spoken and reasonable. Comparing notes with other skivvies, I realized I had an easy time of it. It was only by reading his letters that I discovered his father was a sub-inspector in the police, the highest rank a black could be.

Each morning while Chingoka was off taking his shower, I was required to lay out his fresh uniform carefully on his bed. I had to knot his tie in a double Windsor and leave it in a loose noose, so that he could just slip it on and tighten it, saving him the trouble of having to tie it himself. It was a strange experience for me, ministering to a black boy in the way that black servants ministered to me.

At the time the *Rhodesia Herald*, which I read each evening on the lectern in the junior common room, was full of reports of the war. It had just started again in earnest in the northeast of the country. There had been a new guerrilla offensive, the biggest so far, and white farmsteads were regularly being attacked. In the paper Ian Smith, the prime minister, said that white Rhodesia would never give in to black rule, that the blacks were not ready for power, that we whites would fight to maintain civilized western standards. I thought about it all while I polished Peter Chingoka's shoes, and knotted his tie, and smoothed out his bed sheets.

Here I was, a white boy, skivvying for a black in a country that was embarking on a civil war to prevent black rule. I must be the only white servant of a black man in the whole damn country, I thought. And I felt oddly special.

Eleven

I never said goodbye to Knighty and Violet, or to Albert. My parents moved house when I was away at St George's, so at the end of term, instead of heading east back up to the Chimanimanis, I found myself going west, over the Great Dyke range and down towards the Zambezi valley, to our new home at Mangula.

I told myself that I would return to Silverstream and seek them out to make a proper farewell. But life moved on and I never did. My parents heard later that Knighty and Violet hadn't stuck at their new jobs; Knighty was too old to adjust to the foibles of another white family and he retreated with Violet back to tribal lands, back to his little plot of *mealies* and his sixteen goats and seven cows, animals he had told me about so often I felt I knew them personally. Back to his home kraal in Chikukwa, soon to be engulfed by the war. I don't even know if he and Violet are still alive.

Albert was supposed to be joining us in Mangula. Before he did, he went on a fortnight's leave to his home across the border in Mozambique. He had left on the bus, weighed down with provisions for his family that were unobtainable over there; pots and pans, bicycle tyres, new shoes and T-shirts for the children, *badzas* to till the fields, axe heads, metal buckets and bags of sugar. But he failed to return. My father grumbled like mad about how unreliable Albert was, and we had to employ a temporary garden boy, who naturally did everything wrong. Then, after three months, a letter arrived from Albert. It was in a grubby and much-handled envelope, stained with sweat and dust. Inside was a single sheet of cheap lined paper, written on in blotchy biro. Albert must have dictated it to someone else, as he couldn't write himself.

Dear Baas Godwin,

I am very sorry I am not at work. But I am not possible to cross the border any more. They have put barbid wire fence and bombs in the ground there now and the sojas are stopping me. They take away my travel documents and not give them back. When I ask they beat me. So now I cannot come back any more. Things is very bad over here. Many many people is killed. I am very sorry again. I hope your new garden is good there in Mangula and everything is growing nicely. (Please remember to plant the amaryllis bulbs before the rains start.) Tell the madam and Peter and Jain and Georgina – hello from Albert.

I am, sir, Yours faithfully,

Albert your garden boy

We never saw him again.

At the time I reckoned that Albert was lucky never to have made it to Mangula. The place was a tip. It was a company-owned town, self-contained and completely isolated. Even the promise of television proved false. It was on the outer edge of the reception area and in spite of the 100 foot aerial masts that peppered the town, all you could make out, however hard you peered, was a fuzzy shadow image, which soon gave you a headache.

Altitude was the crucial factor in Mangula for more than just TV aerial masts. You could determine people's status by altitude alone. At the very bottom of the town was the African compound: lowest were the black hostels, the single quarters for migrant workers; up a bit were the small concrete houses for the families of ordinary workers; and, a little higher still, the slightly larger houses of clerks and bossboys and skilled workers. Across the tar road, the European houses began. There were about four basic designs of European house. Miners and artisans lived in smaller houses along the avenues at the bottom of the slope, and as you ascended, so the houses and gardens grew in size. The miners called the top of the broad incline Snobs' Hill. We lived on the crest of Snobs' Hill in a large rambling house with wide rolling lawns, bougainvillaea hedges and a long view that went on almost as far as the Zambezi escarpment.

I had the use of the guest cottage, behind the house on the side of reservoir kopje. It was completely private, with its own bedroom and bathroom and hall. Jain had first choice but she preferred to be in the main house, the guest cottage was too scary. It *was* quite scary. The security situation was rapidly deteriorating. There had been guerrilla attacks on farms just across the Hunyani river, and the Zambezi valley was one of their main incursion routes. My father had to spend more and more time away on police reserve call-ups.

In the cottage I slept with two guns. Under the bed was my .22 Brno, a beautiful rifle made of cobalt-blue steel, with a carved wooden stock, given to me by my father for my thirteenth birthday. And under the pillow I had one of my father's .38s, a stubby little revolver, ugly but very effective at close quarters, as I knew from firing it on the shooting range, at the cardboard cut-out targets of snarling oriental soldiers. At night I lay naked on my bed with my guns, all the windows and the door wide open against the heat, only the insect screens down. I listened to the mournful calls of the nightjars and to the cicadas' shrill chirping. Every time the cicadas stopped chirping, I held my breath and felt for the pistol. Until finally I drifted into an uneasy sleep.

In the morning it all looked benign and safe again, the sprinklers softly puffing over the lawns, the sunbirds fluttering over the honeysuckle, the fragrant frangipani trees covered in dew, and I would lock the weapons into the gun cabinet for another day.

Life in Mangula revolved around the mine club. There were squash and tennis courts, a bowling green, a rugger field and a swimming pool with diving boards. It was at the swimming pool, under the moulting thatch of a gazebo, that I assiduously courted Ilse Badenhorst, the daughter of an Afrikaner miner. Katie Frost from Silverstream, with her little plum breasts, was soon forgotten in favour of Ilse, with her high blonde ponytail and her pale blue eyes. I was permitted to baste her limbs in suntan oil and buy her Cokes and packets of Chicken Flings and Corn Curls from the pool tuck shop. Once a week I was granted the honour of escorting her to the bioscope at the club hall, where we held hands chastely during the show. She called me *bokkie*, which means sweetheart in Afrikaans.

Under the influence of Ilse I became a fervent admirer of the Afrikaners. After all, they were *real* white Africans. That's what Afrikaner meant, it was simply the Afrikaans word for African. They seemed more secure than us, more settled. I began to wish that I was an Afrikaner with a solid identity and I even started spelling my name the Afrikaans way – Pieter.

Finally Ilse announced that her father, Tienus Badenhorst, would like to meet me. This was getting serious. I boned up on my rudimentary Afrikaans in preparation, and after much indecision I dressed in long trousers, a long-sleeved white school shirt and a tie with small elephants on it, the only non-school tie I had. I wet my unruly hair, rubbed a blob of my father's Brylcreem into it and brushed it back off my forehead, like he did with his hair. Then I presented myself to my mother and sisters for inspection. Jain straightened my tie, removed a fleck of lint from my shirt, then pronounced me 'very handsome', and off I cycled down the hill to the Badenhorsts' house.

As I arrived, Ilse's two raucous young brothers were playing barefoot in the yard. They howled with laughter.

'Have you come for church, hey?' they mocked. 'What happened to your hair, man?'

I was rescued by Ilse, who was wearing jeans and a fluffy pink jersey with sequined appliqué. She ushered me into the sitting room, where her father was sprawled on a brown plastic sofa. Tienus Badenhorst shook my hand and greeted me in bad English. I replied in worse Afrikaans. The two boys, their faces pressed up against the fly-screened window, were sniggering loudly, and Ilse tried to shoo them away. She served me instant coffee in a floral china cup, and Marie biscuits carefully arranged on a saucer. Tienus drank a Lion lager from the bottle. He was wearing baggy shorts, and old T-shirt and dog-chewed slippers.

We attempted desultory conversation for a few minutes and then an embarrassing silence descended.

'I'm just going to put the radio on,' said Tienus, after several minutes of the silence. 'Northern Transvaal is playing the Orange Free State in the Curry Cup.'

The radio went on and any attempt at conversation ended. I sat straight-backed, looking around the room. Across the fireplace, there was a bright copper fireguard featuring a sable antelope. The walls were bare but for a lurid print of some rampant wild horses with wind-blown manes, set against a stormy background. There were no books around except for a coffee-table book on African wildlife. Then Ilse showed me her room. It was decorated with posters of pop stars. A fluorescent lime-green gonk and several Cabbage Patch dolls lolled on the bed.

We returned to the sitting room and I excused myself, saying I'd better get home. Tienus shook hands absent-mindedly without getting up. Outside, Ilse had little tears in the corners of her eyes.

'I think he liked you,' she said, bravely.

'Yes, I think he did,' I lied. 'And I really liked him.'

We didn't last for long, after that. As her body rapidly ripened, Ilse caught the eye of older boys – working, wage-earning men, even. She soon moved on and I went back to spelling my name the normal way.

For the adults the focal area of the mine club was the two bars. One was bright and carpeted, and the miners could take their wives there. The other, a gloomy flagstoned place, was for hard drinking, and no women ventured inside. When the white miners came off shift many of them headed straight for this bar, where they got swiftly drunk on Lion beer and cane spirit chasers. Thy often fell to noisy brawling, using fists and bottles and ashtrays and anything that came to hand. The fighting was furious, but brief, and they usually hugged and made up afterwards and admired each other's wounds.

I would stand on an upturned beer crate at the window together with the bar waiters and my new friend, Patrick Pittaway, watching the fight. When it was all over the waiters went back in to clean the glass up off the floor. Sometimes one of the brawlers would be Tienus Badenhorst, and I watched in horror as he launched himself across the bar, roaring in a drunken rage, and I wondered what it would be like for Ilse and her brothers when he finally staggered home.

The club was for whites only. The blacks had their own recreation centre at the compound: a football stadium and a beer hall. I used to sneak down there to listen to the bands play *simanje-manje* music in the beer hall. I was the only white person there, but soon they just accepted my presence, and the band even let me play guitar with them.

There was a legion of resident hookers at the beer hall too. They were called 'runners' and they seemed to be ranked by size. The fatter they were, the more expensive. Africans found fat women attractive, so we Europeans believed, because to be fat meant you were wealthy and ate well. To them it meant status. Fatty Slabbert used to say that black women had 'Bantu bums'. He said it was a scientific fact that black women stored fat on their bums, not on their hips as white women did. *He* could talk, he had a pretty generous backside himself.

The Mangula hookers sat on the beer-hall stools, their vast haunches flopping over the seats, their wide feet squeezed into cheap stilettos. And they wore dark wigs and heavy eye make-up, rouged their cheeks and painted their lips magenta. They smoked menthol cigarettes and, as the black miners passed by, they called to them and teased them and cadged drinks off them.

The black miners also got fearsomely drunk when they came off shift, and they also brawled. But their brawls were bigger and they often used knives. Fatal stabbings were quite common. Usually they fought over women. Then there would be revenge attacks by the dead man's comrades, and these quickly developed into tribal battles. But no one ever attacked me. They just bought me the occasional beer and let me enjoy the music.

I never told my parents that I was hanging around the compound, but later I found that they knew all about it, because the welfare officer had kept my father informed. It turned out he didn't mind after all.

At fifteen, in order for me to get work experience and save up to buy a second-hand motorbike, my father arranged for me to work at the mine in my school holidays. I reported to the mine stores and was issued with a regulation hard hat, a yellow one – white ones were reserved for senior grades – two pairs of blue overalls and a pair of black boots with metal toecaps. Then I joined the long line of black workers trudging in for the morning shift. The whites came by car, but my father gave me a lift only as far as the main office, where he worked.

I had been given a job in the mine heavy plant, where all the trucks and heavy mining machines were serviced and repaired.

It was about the dirtiest place on the whole mine. Everything was coated in grease and mud and slurry. Heavy plant was presided over by an immensely large Pole called Radetski, who had jumped ship fifteen years before. He had a wild zapata moustache and a distended belly that strained at the worn fabric of his overalls. He was clearly a very skilled mechanic, and a strict disciplinarian. If anybody questioned his authority he would roll up his sleeves and take up a boxing stance and demand to settle matters there and then. No one ever took up the challenge.

Quite often we had to go underground to repair the scoop trams, huge excavators that scooped up the copper ore from the rock face. I remember the first time I went down, climbing into the big cage at the top of the shaft with Radetski and about a dozen black miners. The bellboy unlocked the bell and yanked it, then he pulled the gate shut and, after a warning bell, the cage hurtled downwards. The wet rock of the shaft flew past, inches from my nose, and my stomach seemed to be caught in my throat. As daylight disappeared above I fought back a feeling of suffocation. Most of the black miners around me were dozing on their feet.

One of them murmured in Shona: 'Well, at least the mine shaft must be safe today, if the *baas*'s son is allowed to come down with us,' and they all laughed, even the ones who had been dozing.

'What's so bladdy funny?' demanded Radetski. He suspected they were laughing at him.

'Nothing, sah,' replied the one who had cracked the joke. 'We are just talking.'

'Ja, well don't.'

It was often quite tense underground. So many men from different races and tribes working so close together in the heat and the noise. But the Rhodesian mines weren't as bad as the ones Down South. Down there on the Rand, my father told me, they had to frisk the black miners for weapons before they went underground, because they took their faction fights down with them, the Zulus and the Xhosas and the Sothos. And even while they were drilling away at the rock face they could be attacked by a member of a rival tribe with a machete or a knife. Many of the white mine captains down on the Rand carried pistols underground, my father said. I tried to imagine being down here when you were in danger of being ambushed by your shift mates. The prospect of ordinary mining accidents underground was bad enough without the shafts being turned into a battle zone.

Because of my father's position, Radetski treated me well. Others under him were not so lucky. The mechanics' assistants – who were all blacks and were known as 'spanner boys' – had to put up with a stream of racial joshing and taunting. Most of them had been working there for years and just ignored it. They seemed not to hear it any more. But one young assistant, Elijah, who was new, got extremely rattled by it. I soon got quite friendly with Elijah, who was doing O levels by correspondence and had ambitions.

'You can take the *kaffir* out of the bush, but you can't take the bush out of the *kaffir*,' Radetski would say, whenever one of the workers had failed to understand something or had made a mistake. Or he would shake his head in despair and say simply 'AWA,' which, he said, meant 'Africa Wins Again'.

He would lecture the other European mechanics on the nature of the black man. 'I'm not a racist but . . .' he would always begin his philosophizing. 'You know your black man, he cares only about three things in life: food, fucking and beer. He's not really interested in work.'

I was tapping out a gasket nearby and did my best to ignore him, but he was a difficult man to ignore.

'Hey, Clever, *buya lo* two-inch bolts!' he shouted across the workshop.

Clever was a quiet man of about fifty. He was the senior

spanner boy, and worked as Radetski's personal assistant. He came over looking apologetic.

'I'm sorry, *baas*, we run out of two-inchers. They all finished.'

Radetski emerged from under the bonnet of a tipper truck. 'For fuck's sake, Clever, *how* many times must I tell you.' Radetski's wide face was livid with irritation, and he grabbed Clever by the ear like a naughty schoolboy. 'Don't-wait-until-things-run-out-before-you-report-it! Warn-me-when-stocks-are-low-so-I-can-order-more!' With each word he tweaked Clever's ear. 'You know, sometimes you're a bloody waste a rations, Clever,' he sighed.

'Yes, *baas*. Sorry *baas*,' replied Clever and retreated.

Radetski turned to me in exasperation. 'You see what I mean. Your *munt* has no bloody foresight at all. They have no initiative and they don't know how to plan ahead. Personally, I blame the African climate. We Europeans, in the summer we had to collect food in order to survive the cold winter or we died. Simple as that. Out here there is no bloody winter, they just picked fruit off the trees. It's an evil . . . an evil-lutionary thing, you know.'

I concentrated closely on tapping out my gasket.

Shortly Radetski's face lightened. 'So d'ya hear the one where Van goes drinking with his crocodile?' he asked.

He was always telling jokes, his preferred comic vehicle being the Van der Merwe joke, the southern African equivalent of the Seamus, or Rastas, or Hymie joke.

I was now on my back on a trolley underneath a scoop tram with Elijah and I pretended not to hear.

Radetski kicked the trolley. 'Well, have you?'

'Nah, not really,' I said in what I hoped was a bored, discouraging voice.

He was now slurping a mug of tea and unwrapping a sandwich.

'Ol' Van takes his pet crocodile to the pub,' began Radetski anyway, 'and he says, "Barman, a beer for me and a Matabele for my croc." The barman gives Van a beer and goes over to the freezer and pulls out a dead Matabele, which he throws over the bar to the croc. The croc gobbles up the Matabele stiff and Van downs the beer.

' "Same again," says Van. And so it goes on until he's had four beers and the croc's had four Matabeles.

'When Van orders a fifth round, the barman says: "Hell, I'm really sorry Van, we've run out of Matabeles for the croc. But I've got some *lekker* pygmies here."

'And Van replies, "Hell no, once he starts on shorts, I'll never get him out of here!" '

Radetski exploded with mirth, spluttering a mouthful of tea and egg sandwich across the greasy floor. I was about to laugh too at the absurdity of it, but Elijah caught my eye and I stayed silent. Radetski looked expectantly at me.

'What's wrong? Don't you see? Beers – Matabeles. Shorts – pygmies. Geddit?' he asked.

'Yes I get it,' I said quietly, and carried on working.

When I emerged from underneath the vehicle, Radetski strolled over with a monkey wrench.

'You know your problem?' he said, pointing at me with the wrench. 'You're a bladdy snob,' and he walked away.

Some time later I made the mistake of trying to strike back with a Van der Merwe joke of my own.

'Have you heard the one about Van's car prang?' I asked, to everyone's surprise. Elijah regarded me coolly, and Radetski looked rather pleased at this apparent olive branch.

'Van's pissed out of his brain, weaving wildly across the road in his old Chevy,' I began. 'He smashes into a black man walking along the side of the road, and the black is sent flying some yards away. But Van carries on and after a while he smashes into a *second* black pedestrian, who comes crashing through the windscreen. But Van still carries on and after a while he smashes into a *third* black man, this one on a bicycle, and the bike is badly mangled. Anyway, the cases come to court a month later: the first black is convicted of leaving the scene of an accident; the second of breaking and entering; and the third is convicted of riding an unroadworthy bike.'

Radetski observed me suspiciously, and then to my consternation, his face lit up and he roared with laughter and walked off, chortling still. Elijah just looked at me and shook his head.

'It's a satirical joke,' I said defensively. 'It's supposed to show how South African law is unjust to blacks.'

But Elijah was unconvinced.

'Underneath, you are just the same like him,' he said bitterly, nodding at Radetski's back.

I felt hard done by and resentful. I'd been trying to stick up for Elijah and now he'd gone off in a huff. You just couldn't win, really. I felt resigned to the fact that there really wasn't much room in the middle in Africa – all sides ended up despising you.

As I was leaving the workshop that evening, Clever fell in step with me. 'Don't worry about Radetski,' he said.

'Well, I don't know how you stand for it,' I sympathized, trying to re-establish my credentials as a friend of the black man.

'Underneath he is OK,' Clever continued. 'He just want to talk like the big *baas*. But really he is OK in his heart. You know he even lends us spanner boys money when we run out. And he never charge us interest. None of the other *baases* lend us money.'

It was into the conservative confines of Mangula that my English cousin Oliver arrived. My aunt Honor wrote from England to say that he would be driving down from Nairobi, one of five cities around the world in which he was studying comparative racism, for a Ph.D. Jain and Georgina and I had never seen a relative before, apart from our immediate family and Great-Aunt Diana. We were pretty excited.

Then we received another letter from Honor to say that Oliver was bringing his girlfriend with him, a *black* girlfriend called Lydia Lively *and* her four-year-old son. Lydia Lively, wrote Honor, was a black American civil rights activist and feminist campaigner.

This was pretty exciting news, and just what Mangula needed, I thought, to really shake it up. My father got into quite a flap. According to the law, under the Land Apportionment Act, Lydia Lively wasn't even supposed to stay with us in a white residential area. My mother became convinced that Honor, who made no secret of voting Labour, was sending out Lydia Lively to test us. So my father had a word with the police member-in-charge, a friend of his, and explained the ticklish situation. The member-in-charge was happy to turn a blind eye, Lydia Lively was only staying a few weeks after all, but he warned us not to parade her about too blatantly, or the miners might complain.

Eventually Oliver rolled up in a hand-painted psychedelic VW Beetle, which wheezed and rattled up the drive. The engine stopped and in the silence there was a crash as the exhaust fell off. The door opened and cousin Oliver emerged. He was about six-foot-four and wore nothing but a crimson loincloth and an ash-blond Afro. I peered into the car but could see no sign of Lydia Lively or the kid.

'Where's your girlfriend, then, Oliver?' I enquired.

'Oh, we had a big bust-up in Zambia, and she left. She just couldn't handle being on the road. So, it's just me,' he shrugged apologetically.

My parents visibly relaxed at this news, and my mother rolled her eyes heavenward in thanks. I was quite disappointed really. I had been looking forward to the notoriety. I had even hatched a plan to stir things up by making anonymous calls to the police to complain about ourselves.

Still, cousin Ollie was good fun. We took him into Salisbury, my father and I, to show him around. As a special concession to town, he put on a misshapen tie-dyed T-shirt over his crimson loincloth, though he remained shoeless. My father walked alongside in his olive safari suit and *veldskoens*, patiently explaining the workings of white rule in Rhodesia, while the people of Salisbury, white and black, stared openly at the apparition of cousin Ollie. We even took him to Parliament, but the white policeman at the door took one look at Ollie and snorted with laughter.

'There's no way you're coming in here,' he said. 'Pa-lease! You break so many of the dress regulations I don't know where to start even,' and he called over his colleague to view the freak.

So we sat on a bench outside parliament while my father explained the constitution, and the fact that there were some black MPs, but only sixteen of them out of a total of sixty-six. And that the blacks had a separate voters' roll to whites. He explained how our brand of racism was more subtle than apartheid Down South, but probably just as effective. My father had just joined a new political party that was trying to reform the constitution, but most whites were still in the thrall of the prime minister, Ian Smith.

At the time I thought Oliver was pretty strange, really eccentric, with his loincloth and Afro and everything. But in his eyes I saw that he thought we were the odd ones. And for the first time I got a glimpse of how we appeared to the outside, of just how far we had strayed from our mother culture and mutated into this quite separate people. And I realized that was why my parents would never really consider going home to England, because England wasn't home any more, even to them.

Our main escape from the constriction of Mangula was Lake Kariba, a couple of hours west. Patrick Pittaway's parents had a cottage at Charara, a fishing camp on the lake's edge. We would get a lift with a mine truck as far as the railhead at Lion's Den, and then hitchhike from there. We wound towards the Zambezi valley and could feel it getting hotter and hotter, until we turned off at Makuti and into the Kariba safari area. The road down the escarpment followed the old elephant trail, and our progress was punctuated by fresh steaming green mounds of elephant dung.

The lake itself was vast, 2000 square miles. It was said to be the second biggest man-made lake in the world, after the Aswan dam on the Nile, in Egypt. Kariba was so big, the water stretched over the horizon, just like the sea. But the curved wall itself, spanning a narrow gorge, looked inappropriately slim. It had been built by Italians, just like the road from Silverstream to Chipinga, although these Italians weren't prisoners of war. During construction three of the Italians and fourteen African workers had fallen into the wet concrete of the wall and were entombed inside it. Patrick and I used to peer over the edge and try to work out where they were.

The local Tonga tribe, who had to be shifted out of the way when the dam was built, said the accident was the revenge of *Nyaminyami*, their river god. They still believed that he would strike down the wall one day and return the river to its natural state. The few Tonga left in Kariba town were reduced to selling carvings of *Nyaminyami* to the tourists. In their carvings they always portrayed the river god as a coiled snake with bared fangs. But to make him sell better they attached him to the top of a walking stick. I felt sorry for *Nyaminyami*, once a powerful god, respected and feared by the Tonga, now reduced to a decoration on top of a tourist souvenir.

When the dam was built, there had been a much bigger fuss made over moving the wild animals than over moving the people. As the area flooded and hilltops became islands, special teams of volunteers collected the stranded animals and transported them to safety. It was called Operation Noah, and everyone came and made documentary films about it, which were forever being shown at school.

Along the dam wall, down by the water's edge, was a string

of hotels; the Cutty Sark, the Caribbea Bay, the Kariba Breezes, the Lake View Inn and others. They proudly called this the Rhodesian Riviera, and lots of people came here for their holidays, especially when we could no longer go to Mozambique, after the Portuguese had left. But Patrick and I preferred to stay up at the fishing camp, where we had the use of his father's boat.

Boating on Kariba was quite difficult because you had to avoid the Kariba weed which floated around in great spongy green carpets, just waiting to wrap itself around your propeller, and also the petrified trees which protruded from the water, grey and ghostly and leafless.

We used to take the boat across to Sanyati Gorge on the other side of the lake and fish for tiger fish. Tigers had gold and black stripes and big piranha-type teeth and, pound for pound, they were the liveliest fighting fish in the world. You couldn't eat them or anything, it was just the fun of fighting them in. Tigers just never gave up, tugging and jumping and diving.

Sometimes near Sanyati, if we were lucky, we would see the elephants crossing the water to get from an island to the mainland. They could walk along even in the deep, with just the tips of their trunks poking out above the water like snorkels.

Kariba could be quite dangerous, which added to the fun of it. Storms blew up out of nowhere, and sometimes there were dramatic waterspouts out over the lake. You could swim in the middle, where the risk of bilharzia was less. But you were sharing the water with crocodiles and hippos and water snakes. Near Charara there was even a crocodile farm where they bred the things to make into handbags and belts and shoes. By law they could only farm the crocodiles if they released 2 per cent of them back into the lake to keep up stocks. We used to go out with the crocodile farm boats and help chuck the little crocs over the side into the lake. Even at this young age, when they were only four feet long from snout to tail, they would be trying to bite you. They could easily take your finger off.

At night Patrick and I would sit around the fire, grilling Kariba bream over the flames and looking out at the twinkling lights of the kapenta rigs. Each rig was a floating pontoon with a big winch over one end. The fishermen dropped a net from the winch and hung a bright light above it, which attracted the kapenta, tiny sardine-like fish. When a big enough shoal had gathered, the fishermen killed the light and the fish dived down in alarm, straight into the net. A lot of the Tonga had gone to work on the kapenta rigs, but it was a hard, lonely job. They slept on the rigs at day, in temperatures of up to 50 degrees, and worked all night, for weeks at a time.

I wondered what *Nyaminyami* made of it all, the pride of his Tonga men spending their lives incarcerated on steel platforms, tricking little fish into a net. Still, it was a beautiful sight, a galaxy of twinkling lights bobbing on the swell of this vast man-made ocean.

Going back to St George's didn't seem so bad, after Mangula. I even began to look forward to it. I can remember feeling almost happy on the first day of term, at the Ascensio Scholarum in the Beit Hall, when Father Brewer, the first prefect, read out the College rules.

The Beit Hall, a cavernous neoclassical hulk, was the setting of many of our triumphs and disasters. We sat our exams there, and school plays were put on there. I performed there in French, as Polignac, a mad Parisian jockey, in the school play directed by Mrs Harmsworth before she lured Ronald Kemp away from his vows. School dances with the girls from the Dominican Convent were also held in the Beit Hall. Only form four and above could attend and we went to great lengths to decorate the hall, draping nets from wall to wall to lower the ceiling, and generally trying to make it more cosy.

In truth the convent dances were fraught affairs of ritual awkwardness. The girls sat on benches along one side. They were dressed in ankle-length patterned frocks, usually long-sleeved. We sat twenty-five yards away, along the other side, in our school uniforms. The floor between us was patrolled by squads of priests and nuns. Father Stanley even had a whistle around his neck, and if he saw any hanky panky on the dance floor he would blow his whistle, like a referee spotting a penalty.

I had been looking forward tremendously to my first school dance. Ilse Badenhorst and I had just finished and I was desperate for another girlfriend. Also, I considered myself a pretty good dancer. My sister Jain had taught me well, jiving with me on the verandah at home to her Beatles and Sonny and Cher records. And I had been to dances at the mine club too.

The police dance band struck up and I checked out the line of convent girls sitting opposite. After some discussion with my friends, I finally picked out my target. She was sweet-looking, with short, soft, chestnut hair and a quick smile, but not *too* pretty. If they were *too* pretty they were more likely to snub you. After a final consultation with my bench mates, I took a deep breath and launched myself on the lonely walk across the floor. My target appeared to be in deep conversation with her friends, but I went ahead anyway.

'Would'yaliketadance?' I gulped.

She took her time, looking me up and down before deciding. 'No,' she said, and carried on with her conversation, while her friends giggled at my discomfort. Not even 'no, thank you'. I mean, what did they come here for if they didn't want to dance? Why not bloody well stay at the convent?

I fled blindly back across no-man's-land, humiliated and angry, and stumbled into Father Stanley, patrolling vigilantly as ever. 'Better luck on your next foray,' he said kindly, as though I'd just failed to score a try.

There was no next foray. After a short time Michael Moore, a gormless boy with thick glasses that magnified his eyes, approached the same girl, and she leapt to her feet straight away, and they danced for hours.

I turned to my friends.

'Tell me, honestly. Do you think Moore is better looking than me? Go on, be honest. I don't mind.'

They chorused their opinions.

'Nah. He's a dork.'

'And he's got spots.'

'He's got flat feet too.'

But Moore certainly had *something* going for him. I sat there fuming at the fickle nature of girls.

I'm sure it was partly in response to the fiasco of that convent dance that I joined the shunt hunt, something I had previously disdained to do. St George's was surrounded on three sides by the National Botanical Gardens, which at night became a favourite spot for courting couples to make out in their cars. You could usually tell who was at it by the way the car shook. This was called shunting, and our night-time patrols to seek it out were called shunt hunts.

Only senior boys were allowed on the shunt hunt. We would dress in dark clothes, black balaclavas and trainers and, equipped with powerful hunting torches, we crept out of our cubicles, leaving home-made dummies behind in our beds.

A hunt of about five boys was the optimum size, not too big to be cumbersome, yet big enough to defend ourselves from enraged lovers. We sneaked up to our chosen car and peered in at the occupants. We could hear them groaning and moaning and sighing but, disappointingly, we couldn't usually see very much in the gloom. So at a given signal we all jumped up and switched on our hunting torches, dazzling the lovers. There was shouting and squealing, and wobbling pink bums and breasts caught in the beams as the lovers hastily covered up. Then we swiftly melted back into the foliage of the botanical gardens.

*

On Sundays after mass, boarders were allowed out with their parents or relatives for the day. But my parents lived too far away, and they hardly ever came into Salisbury. So I took up rowing instead, because the regattas were always on a Sunday. Bill Jacques was the rowing master, and he was pretty entertaining, for a teacher. He was from Northern Ireland and taught us English and Latin. Jacques had a beaky red nose which he was for ever blowing, and a scathing manner in the classroom, with no patience at all for the thicker boys. After an early spat, when I had mistakenly judged it amusing that in Shakespearean English a jaques meant a lavatory, we got on rather well.

Every Sunday we piled into the open back of his battered Land Rover and he drove us off to the Mazoe Dam, about half an hour out of town. It was a small lake set in lush bush surrounded by low hills. They had built a graceful granite boathouse there, and grass terraces sloping gently down to the lakeside, for the spectators to lounge on and eat their picnic lunches. After the rains the waters lapped at the edge of the boathouse, but in drought we had to shoulder the boats five hundred yards down to the jetty.

I started off as a cox but within the space of a year I grew so quickly I moved into the first eight. It was punishing stuff, rowing in that kind of heat, and afterwards everyone repaired to the bar. We weren't allowed to drink alcohol, but Bill Jaques had an awesome capacity. Occasionally, if he'd had too many, one of us would have to drive the Land Rover back to school.

In time, Mazoe found itself overtaken by the war, and rowing became a dangerous sport. Bill Jaques kept a rusty old revolver on the dashboard of the Land Rover and loose bullets lay about everywhere, on the floor and under seats, and they rolled from side to side whenever we hurtled round a bend. We assembled with the rest of the oarsmen on the outskirts of Salisbury before setting off in a convoy for Mazoe. Other oarsmen had weapons too, and they all took turns standing guard at the boathouse. After I left school the boat club was ambushed, I heard. The head of the 2000-metre course, which was situated on the far side of the dam, came under fire from guerrillas. No one was hurt in the attack, but it resulted in one of the fastest starts ever recorded at Mazoe, so they say.

The other way to get out was to do social work with the school sodality society. I used to go to Nazareth House and visit an ancient priest, Father Brennan, who was ninety-something. He was more or less blind, so I had to read to him. He would sit in his wheelchair sucking his pipe through bent, mossy old teeth and nodding away. Occasionally he gently corrected my pronunciation.

I thought it would be a real pain, reading to the old monk for hours, but he had some pretty interesting books, actually, and I began looking forward to my visits. Then I started reading my set books to him, and he had terrific ideas about what was really going on in *King Lear*, *Antigone*, *Middlemarch*, *Absalom and Achitophel* and *The Canterbury Tales*, ideas that none of my teachers had really mentioned. When I incorporated them into my essays, they thought I was being pretty original and made me read them out to the class. And of course I never told anyone where I got them from. I felt a bit guilty about it and one day I told him what I'd been doing, and instead of being cross he sucked on his pipe some more and looked terribly pleased.

'I'm just teasing the ideas out of you,' he said. 'I'm just getting you to ask the right questions.'

Father Brennan also coached me in chess and bridge. He was a demon at both. In a funny sort of way, he reminded me of Great-Aunt Diana, who would have been about the same age. I felt that I'd made up for not listening to her by listening to him. When he died, I was really annoyed.

I transferred my sodality work from Nazareth House to St Peter's after that. St Peter's was a Catholic school for black boys in Mbare, a Salisbury township. I used to teach them English. The real problem was that they were being taught English by African teachers who themselves had thick accents, and so the kids could end up speaking almost unintelligibly.

I felt really shamed by those kids. At St George's a lot of us were complacent and lazy, and had to be threatened and beaten and cajoled into doing any work at all. These St Peter's kids were absolutely voracious for learning. I remember walking into the classroom for the first time. Fifty kids at shared desks rose to their feet and sang out a greeting. Fifty hands straining to volunteer for any reading. Fifty faces rapt in complete concentration when I read to them. Fifty sets of homework in before time. In the two years I taught there, the only discipline problem I had was trying to keep their enthusiasm within manageable bounds.

As well as teaching them grammar and pronunciation, I tried to encourage them to question and debate among themselves. When I first brought up political topics for discussion, they looked embarrassed and became uncharacteristically reticent. On the blackboard I had written, 'Do you think that Rhodesia should have majority rule?'

Eventually one boy raised his hand. 'No! I! Do! Not!' he sang out and then sat down.

'Why not?'

He looked a bit uncomfortable, and then replied, 'Because the tribes will keel each udder.'

'*Kill* each *other*,' I corrected.

'Because the tribes will *kill* each *other*,' he repeated.

'Do you really think that? Or are you just saying that because you think that's what I want to hear, because I'm a *mukiwa*?'

They all laughed, and another boy said, 'We always used to keel each udder before the white man came. The Matabele would come up and steal our cows and keel us, and we had to hide in caves.'

'*Kill* each *other*,' I corrected again. 'Say after me class: *Kill* each *other*.'

'*Kill* each *other*! *Kill* each *other*! *Kill* each *other*! *Kill* each *other*! They chanted.

And at that moment I noticed the astonished headmaster standing at the open door.

As the time for me to leave school drew closer it was clear that the war was getting pretty serious. Conscription had gone up again, from nine months to a year, and several St George's alumni had already been killed. Their names were announced in chapel, and sometimes their funerals were held there. The coffin would stand in front of the altar, a frightening reminder of our own youthful mortality. It would be smothered in flowers: arum lilies, roses and flame lilies. The dead boy's mother and sisters and girlfriend, all dressed in black, would sit in the front pews and weep. They would lean on red-eyed brothers and fathers. Behind them we would stand tall and bellow out the college songs extra loud for their benefit. The more we sang these songs, *Ex Fide Fiducia* and *St George*, the more I became aware that they were dripping with the metaphors of war, all of which now assumed a worryingly real aspect.

> *Arm! Arm, for the struggle approaches!*
> *Prepare for the combat of life.*
> *St George be our watchword in battle,*
> *St George be our strength in the strife.*

Struggle, combat, battle, strife. It suddenly seemed literal.

> *Great Saint George our patron hear us,*
> *In the conflict be thou nigh,*
> *Help us in our daily battle,*
> *Where each one must live or die.*

Conflict, battle, live or die.

For the first time, really, I began to think about death. Not the death of others, not the death of oom Piet, or Great-Aunt Diana, or Mr Arrow Head, or the corpses my mother used to cut up, or old Mr Boshof, or even Father Brennan. But my own death.

On the television in the senior common room the news often began with a security force communiqué. We looked up from our snooker table, our bridge fours and our chess games as the news reader adopted a specially solemn tone to say, 'Combined Operations Headquarters regret to announce the deaths in action of . . .' and a list of names would follow. And at the end, the news reader would look up from the communiqué, fix the camera with an expression of restrained sympathy, and say, 'The chief of combined operations has sent his personal condolences to the next of kin,' as though that would make up for everything.

Often those killed were known to at least some of us. After all, there were less than a quarter of a million whites in the whole country.

By now my whole class had received their call-up papers. All the whites, that is. The blacks didn't have to do military service, and we envied them. But there was no tension over it. After all, many wealthy and middle-class blacks were regarded as sell-outs by the guerrillas, and they were just as worried about the war as anyone else. It was only much later that I discovered that, on leaving school, my friend Sipho Mpofu crossed the border and joined the guerrillas.

We white boys had all been required to register with the ministry of manpower at the age of sixteen. And after that we couldn't even leave the country without a special permit. Our real grievance was that the rules had just been changed to abolish all deferments for university. Until then, if you had a university place, your military service was automatically deferred until you had completed your degree. Many who went to university outside the country never returned. But now the manpower shortage was so critical they insisted that all white school-leavers went directly into the security forces.

I remember discussing the matter with my parents, at home in Mangula. They didn't support Smith and his Rhodesia Front Party, unlike most whites. My parents supported the Rhodesia Party. The Rhodesia Party advocated a negotiated transition of power, so it never got anywhere in elections – less than 5 per cent of whites voted for it. But on the one occasion I brought up the possibility of doing a runner, my parents thought it dishonourable for me to try to skip the country.

'The way I see it, Pete,' said my father, 'we've been kept safe all these years by other people's sons, yet when it comes to our turn you scarper. It's not really on, is it? In any case, you'll only be holding the line while the politicians negotiate. We have to keep the war under control while they hammer out a settlement. We can't let the future of the country be dictated on the battlefield.'

In many ways my mother took a tougher line than my father. 'You'll be serving for blacks as well as whites, just keeping people safe and, anyway, it'll do you good,' she said. 'It'll stand you in good stead in later life.'

I was very conscious of the fact that each of them had spent five years in the services during the Second World War. But they were lucky, theirs had been a simple war to fight. A moral war. A just war. The right war. This war seemed messier and more complicated. I thought about it that night as I lay on the bed in the cottage, with my revolver under my pillow, listening to the nightjars. It was true that Ian Smith had already conceded that there would be black rule, so I wouldn't be fighting for his Rhodesia Front. And I wouldn't do anything I disagreed with or was ashamed of.

At school we discussed our limited options. If we did nothing, we would automatically end up in the basic army intake, and take our chances. Or we could apply to the police or Internal

Affairs, which had both just started taking national servicemen. Internal Affairs, which used to be called Native Affairs, was considered a bit soft. The police seemed a better bet. You did more interesting work, not just patrolling around the border and guarding things. The police had much higher entrance qualifications than the army, but if you made it you got the rank of patrol officer. And you got better pay.

When the time came, I felt almost sad to bid farewell to St George's. In the end I'd been a prefect myself, with a skivvy of my own. I found myself dormitory prefect for form three, living in Peter Chingoka's old room. Form three were the worst age, full of energy, disrespectful of authority, not yet worried about O-level exams. I tried to be firm and reasonable at the same time. I ignored the silly rules and enforced the practical ones, and we got on fine. To my great surprise, when I left they presented me with a copper tankard, engraved simply with the words. 'To Pete – from Form III'. I was quite moved.

Book Two

Twelve

The training camp for white police officers, Morris Depot, was in the Avenues, round the corner from the president's residence, not far from St George's. I'd been there once from school, to Camp Hospital to have my police medical. Some boys at school had heard that the tests would include one where the nurse scooped up your balls in a cold metal spoon and then asked you to cough, to see if they retracted properly. This was apparently an important test to see if you were man enough. Man enough for what, I wondered uneasily as I reported to Camp Hospital. The matron was sternly middle-aged, with grey wings to her hair, and an unembarrassable air.

'Take your shoes and shirt off,' she said, when it was finally my turn. 'Oh, and loosen your trousers.'

I unbuckled my belt warily and she approached me, brandishing a sort of spoon. Here goes, I thought, and unzipped my flies for the testicle spoon.

'Stick your tongue out and say "ah",' she said, and brought the spatula not to my crotch, but up to my mouth.

There was a battery of tests after that. She weighed me and measured me, x-rayed me, checked my eyesight and my lung capacity, took urine and blood samples, and made sure I didn't have flat feet.

Soon I was lying back on the hard surgery bed, where an elderly doctor felt my spleen, prodded my liver, tapped my ribcage, and listened to my heart with his stethoscope. He was shining his torch into my eyes, and pulling the lids down and

213

peering in at my eyeballs, when suddenly he slid his cold hand down my loosened waistband. I let out an involuntary squawk.

'It's all right, relax,' he soothed, and pressed his fingers above and slightly to the side of my balls. 'Now cough.'

'Uhuh, uhuh,' I coughed, rather pathetically.

'No, boy, cough properly,' he insisted irritably. I coughed again, and he removed his hand and ticked something on his clipboard.

'What's it for?' I asked.

'To check for your proneness to hernia, boy. We can't have you in the Force if your guts are going to be popping out now, can we?'

To get into the police, you had to be at least 5ft 9in., 140 pounds and have good eyesight, a driving licence, and at least six O levels. In our year, though, they raised the academic requirement to three A levels, because of the large number of candidates. You also had to pass an interview. Finally, I got an acceptance letter ordering me to report to Morris Depot and informing me of my regimental number. Quite a few of the applicants from St George's got 'regret to inform you' letters, so the five of us who had been accepted felt pretty chuffed, fancying ourselves as an elite.

With the acceptance letter came a little booklet on the origins and traditions of the British South Africa Police. The BSAP, said the booklet, was the country's senior service, raised in 1889 to protect the first pioneer column trekking up from South Africa. Originally it had been called the British South Africa Company Police, after Cecil Rhodes' company. It was a paramilitary force organized, like most British colonial forces, as an *askari* regiment, African ranks under European officers.

The booklet included a picture of the regimental crest, a lion rampant with an *assegai*, an African hunting spear, lodged in its chest, destined for all time to be preserved in the throes of fatality. In the scroll beneath the staggering lion, below a few more *assegais* and a discarded Matabele shield, appeared the words '*pro rege, pro lege, pro patria*' – for king, for law, for country. When we had rebelled against the Queen more than ten years before, the crown had been removed from the top of the crest, but the motto stayed the same, continuing to proclaim our loyalty to the rejected monarch.

We arrived at Morris Depot one Monday morning, and stood about apprehensively in twos and threes, swapping training horror stories. We were rather a scruffy bunch. Several of the intake had come from university and wore their hair at shoulder length. Suddenly the instructors were upon us, shouting and screaming. We were lined up in order of our regimental numbers, divided into squads, arranged according to height and marched off to the Portuguese barbers, who speedily sheared us with electric clippers and were to do so once a week for the rest of training.

The instructors marched us to another room, where we were photographed for our identity cards. I've still got that photograph. In it I'm holding a small blackboard with my regimental number chalked on it, like a convict. My hair is so short my ears seem pale and enormous, sticking nakedly out of my head. My taste in clothes is gruesome. I'm wearing a wide tie made out of some sort of crêpe material, and knotted in a huge triangular Windsor knot; a checked shirt with rounded collar tips and a treasured tweed hound's-tooth jacket given to me by cousin Ollie and so old it has great irregular lumps in the shoulder pads. The shaven-headed conscript that stares out of the photograph looks all of fifteen. In fact I had just celebrated my eighteenth birthday.

After haircuts and photos, we were herded on to the parade ground and given an introductory address by Depot Chief Inspector Trangmar. He told us we were the highest-qualified bunch of recruits they'd ever had in Depot, and that we weren't to try any 'smart Alec' nonsense. They would have to grind us down, he said, in order to build us up again with the right instincts and reactions – the instincts and reactions of police officers. He told us that we were privileged to be in the force, and that anyone who didn't make the grade would be busted down to the rank of an ordinary troopie in the army and start their time from the beginning again, in boot camp.

We shambled over to the stores, a giant warehouse full of the paraphernalia of policing. Indian tailors measured us and fitted us with baratheas, our dress uniforms. They chalked them up for alterations and removed them again. When we got them a week later they all fitted perfectly. We queued up to be issued with our full kit: mahogany baton; hat, soft, blue; peaked cap; badges; torch; batteries; rifle-cleaning kit; mess tins; blue canvas anklets and blue canvas stable belts; bedding; blue lanyard, gym kit; riot blues; green shirts and green issue underwear; and something called a 'husiff', which was a mending kit, actually spelled 'housewife'. We loaded it all into our huge kitbags and then we were made to double back to barracks in squads.

We spent the rest of that first day modelling our various outfits, to be shown exactly how we had to wear them. Caps had to have space for exactly three fingers between peak and eyebrow. Hats, soft, blue, had to be starched so that they looked like lampshades. The toecaps of drill boots to be 'boned' by smoothing over them with a heated teaspoon. Naturally, leather and brass had to shine.

In many ways it was just like boarding school. There were all sorts of petty rules that had no particular point to them. Beds had to be made up into bed packs each morning, a sandwich of folded bedclothes squared up with rigid right-angled corners. So we boxed them with pieces of plywood or cardboard and most of us slept in sleeping bags on the floor under the bed, leaving the bed packs pristine, because there wasn't time to make them up in the morning. It was illegal to do this, and if you were caught during a night spot check there was hell to pay. Lockers had to be loaded in strict sequence.

Every few days we would dismantle the brass runners from the windows, lay them out on newspapers on the floor and polish them until they gleamed. The instructors inspected everything. No detail was too small to escape their attention; they even unscrewed the light bulbs to see whether the brass on the base of the bulb had been polished. They put on white gloves and ran their fingers along the ridges under the bed and the springs. However much you cleaned and polished, they always found something. You couldn't win, and you weren't supposed to.

For the first few weeks the depot routine was exhausting. We had little sleep; after lights out at 10 p.m. we would stay up polishing and cleaning by torch light. We'd be up at 4 a.m. the next day to polish and prepare. At six we'd parade in gym kit and go for a cross-country run. Then shower, breakfast and on to main morning parade at eight. We would inspect each other's uniforms: seams had to be straight and on trousers it was imperative they be unbroken, so we all walked stiff-legged to Hard Square for morning parade. The roll-caller, a recruit himself, would be lifted by the arms by two of his mates on to the chair, so as not to break his crease climbing up.

An instructor would move slowly down the ranks inspecting us in meticulous detail. If a tiny thread on a button showed, he would unravel it until the button came off, then bellow, 'Man undressed on parade!' and the orderly at his side would note it down in his book. Or the instructor would rub a wad of cotton wool over your face, and if any of the lint came off on your stubble, it would be: 'Man unshaven on parade!' The slightest speck of food on your clothes was 'Food all over uniform!' In each case you were charged and put 'behind the guard'.

Being put behind the guard was like being gated at school. You had to parade behind the guard commander every half-hour in the evenings and at weekends. Or sometimes you had to shovel horse shit in the stables or weed the flowerbeds at Police General Headquarters, next to the president's residence.

Once, when the whole of Three Squad was sent on weeding duties, we planted marijuana seeds outside the Commissioner's window. Whenever we marched past, we inspected their progress. They came up looking just like marigolds at first and, tended lovingly by the gardeners, they grew vigorously. Eventually an inspector from the drugs squad recognized them and there was a big stink about it. Number Three Squad was suspected but we maintained a unified silence and nothing was ever proved.

After morning inspection, Depot Chief Inspector Trangmar would deliver some daft lecture, usually about an aspect of camp protocol. One morning I remember he even gave us a lecture on self-abuse. One hundred and twenty men stood to attention on the parade square while DCI Trangmar addressed us. 'It has been brought to my attention that certain recruits have been masturbating in their beds at night.' – I remember he pronounced it mars – like the planet Mars-turbating – 'This practice will cease henceforth,' he ordered.

Most of the drill instructors, known as drill pigs, had come across from British regiments, the Royal Marines in particular. Number Three Squad's drill pig was Section Officer Crabb. He'd never been near the Royal Marines, he was a career policeman and before that had dabbled in insurance. Crabb was a huge red man: a balding red head above a red bulbous face with a ginger moustache, red knuckles on his plate-size hands and red knees on his ginger-fuzzed legs. And on the few occasions he took off his mirrored aviator sunglasses, red-veined eyes. Initially he had a murderous temperament and blared abuse more or less constantly. He was a devotee of the theory of collective punishment: penalties for the lapse of the individual were visited upon the entire squad. We called him Pops Crabb behind his back. I think it was in an effort to puncture his image as a professional hard bastard.

One of Pops Crabb's first acts was to belt me on the head with his brass-topped swagger stick, because I muttered something when I was supposed to be silent. It hurt like hell but I was determined not to let him see that, so I stayed rigidly to attention until a line of blood trickled below my cap line, down my temple and on to my chin. I made no attempt to wipe it, and by the time he came back down the line there was an impressive stream of blood dripping down my face. Pops regarded the blood. For the first time he seemed slightly unnerved. 'What's the matter with your head, man?'

'Nothing, *sir*,' I shouted, as we were required to do whenever addressing the instructor.

'Then you won't be needing to attend camp hospital then, *will you*?' he screamed.

'No, *sir*,' I shouted.

For the first few weeks Pops Crabb drilled us and ran us relentlessly. The rains were heavy that year and we always seemed to be running through mud, at first in our gym kit and later in battledress with packs of bricks on our backs. We ran around the perimeter of Morris Depot, and out over the soggy *vlei* past the Tomlinson Depot, where the black constables were trained, and round the edge of Salisbury Central Prison, whose tall guard towers were visible from our barracks and appeared to be the bastions of our own incarceration.

Prisoners – or bandits, as they were known – came up to Morris Depot in groups from the Central Prison, herded by a warder with an ancient Greener shotgun, which had a Martini Henry drop-action breech-block, and took one round at a time. The bandits wore coarse white shirts and baggy shorts with horizontal stripes, and they sat under the trees weeding very slowly. They were mostly lifers imprisoned for murder, wizened old men who seemed utterly unthreatening. They stopped their murmured conversations and looked up with mild interest as the *mukiwa* recruits panted past again in the heat, and I envied them their gentle lounging under the flamboyant trees.

In those first weeks the only time we ever got off base was when we were marched down North Avenue to the Andrew Fleming hospital to donate blood – a regular date. We stood to attention in front of the Blood Transfusion Centre and were called up in groups of four to be bled. Then we were given a mug of sweet tea by the young nurses and marched back again, a pint of blood the poorer.

Despite the off-take of blood, Pops Crabb marched us straight over to the assault course. He was obsessed with the assault course, and he made us do it again and again to get our times down. It was a standard military assault course: swinging on ropes across water, vaulting over ten-foot walls, balancing along logs, pulling yourself across a long jungle gym, crawling through tyres and under barbed wire and down concrete pipes, and shinning up ropes.

The worst feature on the assault course was an edifice called Jacob's Ladder. It was a giant ladder made of black creosoted wattle logs and which loomed some fifty feet into the air. When you stood on one rung you could only just reach the next with your outstretched hands. It would have been bad enough had Jacob's Ladder been vertical, but it wasn't. It sloped back at about 25 degrees. If you fell, you were likely to break a limb or even your back. Recruits were forever freezing in fear on Jacob's Ladder. Pops Crabb would lumber up and scream at the terrified recruit, his spittle-spraying mouth inches away from the man's face. Naturally this only unnerved the frozen man further. It got even worse when we had to start doing the course with packs and rifles.

Later, the reason for Pops Crabb's obsession with the assault course became clear when we were pitted against other squads in time trials: the instructors bet on the results.

Pops Crabb also taught us unarmed combat, an art at which he thought himself notably talented. After we had mastered all the basic holds and parries, Pops progressed to the more advanced moves, most of which involved a *coup de grâce* in which the opponent sustained crushed balls or gouged eyes or, in one immensely complicated move, both. He was also a devotee of the nose bite, as an opportunistic, free-style move.

'Not just a bladdy snot suck, mind you,' he advised. 'Don't

nibble it, sink your fangs in and bite the fucking thing right off if you get the chance.'

In the course of these unarmed combat lessons, Pops Crabb regaled us with tales of his derring-do in the Flying Squad and gave us the benefits of his mistakes, very rare occurrences he assured us.

'Like the time we got called to a disturbance at the Queen's Hotel.' Queens was a rather seedy place, patronized mostly by Coloureds. 'The goffel whores and pimps and drunks were all kicking the shit out of each other, so I waded in to sort them out, and I was doing OK when one hooker took off her shoe and hit me on the head with the high heel. I just went down, and they would have killed me if the constables hadn't climbed in and pulled me out.'

Crabb removed his cap and bent down to reveal his balding, dandruff-flecked head. And, sure enough, there on the top of it was a surprisingly large indentation about half an inch deep.

'So let that be a lesson to you all,' he continued, replacing his cap. 'Don't wade in. Let them fuck each other up first, then arrest anything that doesn't move.'

I gradually lost all sense of what was beyond our walls. Which is as it was supposed to be. We all lost weight through the punishing physical regime, but the mess food was surprisingly good, and after a month or so we began to build up our weight again, although its distribution was different. I looked in the mirror each morning when I shaved and saw my face changing shape, becoming more angular.

After a few weeks of intensive physical training we began classes in law and police work, radio procedure, African language and customs, and first aid. We were taken to the Black Museum, a chamber of horrors above the ballistics HQ, where there was a display of gory photographs of crimes of violence. Some were from famous cases, others were there to show how particular weapons killed.

'EMA shot by .45 revolver from six feet. Entry left temple.'

SO Ellis read the caption. 'See, the entry wound is relatively small, but look at the right temple. It isn't there is it?' he chuckled. Indeed the whole of the right side of the EMA's head was missing.

We were shown the many and varied ways you could be killed, and how to distinguish between them. There was also a rogues' gallery of notorious murderers, and a collection of bloodcurdling knives and *pangas*, accompanied by photos of those they had been used upon. Cloven heads, severed arms, crushed torsos, all were studied with a detached scientific curiosity.

Finally, we were issued with weapons: an FN 7.62mm rifle and a P1 9mm pistol each. Initially we were given no ammunition, and SO Ellis concentrated on training us to drill with a rifle. He was very particular about firearms terminology. If you mistakenly referred to your rifle as a gun, you found yourself doubling around the parade ground with your rifle in one hand above your head at the high port, and your other hand clutching your balls. As you ran you had to shout: '*This* is my rifle, *this* is my gun, *this* is for fighting, *this* is for fun.' On 'rifle' and 'fighting' you had to brandish your weapon in the air, and on 'gun' and 'fun', you had to squeeze your crotch.

Once we'd got the hang of rifle drill, we were passed on to our musketry instructor, Section Officer Pike, who would teach us how to use the things. SO Pike was a tall, dark, taciturn man with a turned-down moustache that made him look permanently melancholy. In marked contrast to the bellowing SO Crabb, Pike spoke so quietly we had to strain to hear him.

The first thing SO Pike wished to teach us was the complicated choreography of riot control. For this we marched about in ridiculous Second World War helmets. They were white, with 'POLICE' stencilled on them in blue. We were armed with round perforated aluminium shields and our eighteen-inch mahogany batons. SO Pike taught us how to split a crowd using a Greek tortoise, where the front line hold their shields vertically and the next line hold theirs above their heads. And as we manoeuvred around, instructors hurled what they called 'brickbats' at us, wooden bricks.

We were shown a wonderfully dated training film on riot control. In the film, the inspector i/c riot squad addresses the rebellious crowd through a megaphone. 'If you do not disperse we will fire upon you,' he warns in a clipped colonial accent. But instead of dispersing, the crowd, in reality black constables dressed in civilian clothes, advances and starts taunting the police. One man in a red shirt produces a huge *panga* and waves it about, boasting that he will chop up the officers into little pieces. The crowd of off-duty constables then breaks into an energetic war dance. At which point the inspector decides enough is enough and delivers an order to his police marksman, who is armed with an antique Greener shotgun.

'Man in the red shirt, one round, fire!' A shot rings out and the man in the red shirt falls dramatically, clutching his heart and performing an enthusiastic death rattle in the best traditions of the amateur actor.

A generation of policemen were introduced to riot control by that old film and it used to be said, quite seriously, that you should never wear a red shirt if you were thinking of being anywhere near a riot in Rhodesia. Some of the policemen were so conditioned by the training film that they were likely to follow it literally and shoot at 'the man in the red shirt'.

In fact, there were several stages to the ritual of riot control: warning to disperse, tear gas, firing over their heads, taking out their ringleaders, finally escalating to the order to 'fire freely'. But SO Pike had a few extra riot control stages of his own that weren't in the police manual.

'Riots are bladdy frightening things. Those *munts* will kill you if they catch you. Pull you apart, limb from limb, with their bare hands,' he warned. He picked up a stubby mahogany baton and wound the leather strap tightly around his hand.

'Use it like this to stab upwards into their stomach with the end of the baton.' He jerked the baton like a bayonet towards a recruit's stomach. 'At the very least this will wind them. But aim below their heart, on their left side, just under the ribcage – if you're lucky, this should burst their spleen.'

Then he lifted the sole of a recruit's drill boot, 'Your riot boots here, they've got metal heels and metal-studded soles. Most of these rioters have got flimsy shoes or even no shoes at all, so stomp down hard on their feet and break their instep. Their heads will automatically come down, and what you must do is keep your shield low and forward so that the jaw hits it on the way down. If it misses, bring the edge of your shield down sharply on to the top of their heads.'

We all leapt around practising raking shins and batoning spleens and crushing feet and smashing shields on to heads.

'As a last resort,' continued Section Officer Pike, 'instead of hanging your handcuffs on your belt, hold them in one hand, with the metal cuff around your knuckles like a knuckleduster. That way, when you clout someone, they won't come back for more.'

We practised wearing our steel handcuffs as knuckledusters, and shadow-punching imaginary rioters.

'And just remember,' warned SO Pike again, 'they catch you, they lay their hands on you – they tear you apart. No bullshit. We'll have to come afterwards and pick up the little pieces of you to put in the body bag.'

Tear gas was the main riot controller, of course, and we practised for hours with it. To initiate us, SO 'Pussy' Smith, so called because he addressed all recruits as 'puss', marched us past the rifle range to the horse paddock. He had a tear gas canister which, he told us, he intended to let off among us. We would then have to march in squads through the tear gas without breaking rank.

'Anyone who breaks rank will be on a charge for the next month,' said SO Pussy Smith and he pulled the pin and threw the canister on the ground. We waited. Nothing happened. In the row behind me someone tittered.

'Who was that?' shouted SO Pussy Smith. Everyone stayed at attention, eyes front.

'*Who was that?*' he screamed.

Nothing.

He unsheathed his bayonet, ran over to the tear-gas canister and stabbed it repeatedly until it poured smoke. Then he kicked it into the middle of our squad.

'No one move a fucking muscle, or I'll have you,' he shouted, holding his bayonet threateningly. We stood rigidly to attention, eyes squinched shut. The tear gas started to sting wherever their was moisture, under my arms, my crotch, my lips, around my eyes. After what seemed like an age, several recruits broke ranks. They ran bellowing over to the horse troughs and threw themselves into the water. The rest of us scattered too, coughing and retching, our eyes streaming.

As well as the tear-gas canister, which you lobbed into a crowd like a grenade, there was also the tear-gas cartridge, which you fired from a flare gun. SO Pitt had some extra-curricular tips on the use of these too.

'Always keep a couple of real distress flares about your person in this situation,' he advised. 'And if things are getting really hairy, and you're cornered, instead of firing a tear-gas cartridge into the crowd, load up with a flare, and shoot it into a rioter's stomach from as short a range as possible. Whereupon you will observe that he bursts into flames – pink or yellow, or red, depending on the colour flare you've used. This, you will find, serves as a mighty distraction for his colleagues, and buys you valuable time to effect your retreat.'

SO Pike also taught us the correct procedure for arresting a so-called 'Section One suspect'. Section One crimes were crimes of violence, life-threatening crimes. If you were attempting to arrest a suspected Section One offender, and he was attempting to escape, you had to shout, 'I am a police officer. Stop! Stop!

Stop!' And if he didn't stop, then you could shoot him. By law you had to shout 'stop' three times. SO Pike gave us lessons in speed shouting 'I'mpliceoffcer. Stostostop!' all in one gulp. He reckoned you could shoot legally in less than two seconds.

We learnt to dismantle and reassemble our rifles, faster and faster, eventually while blindfolded. We shot thousands of rounds at the range, standing, kneeling, lying. And we learnt to shoot accurately when we were out of breath, after doing the assault course or a run. And every time we fired our weapons we stripped them down completely and cleaned them, oiled them and buffed them until they gleamed.

At weekends we were put on riot standby. We would sit around in barracks in our riot gear with our helmets, shields and batons at hand, waiting for the call. The big grey riot trucks were parked behind the guardhouse, their engines started and run every few hours to make sure they were ready to take us wherever we were needed. We longed to be called out, just to alleviate the tedium. On one occasion we were scrambled into a 'scene' in Mbare township that looked as though it might escalate. I remember sitting in the back of the truck, looking through the grille at the passersby and regarding them all as potential rioters.

In the event, the trouble fizzled out, and we debussed to stretch our legs and have a smoke break before going back to Depot. We were bitterly disappointed that we had missed out on a chance for some action. I took off my helmet and leant against the truck drinking a Coke. A group of black youngsters detached themselves from the main crowd, strolled over to us and looked on curiously. One of them, dressed in a misshapen red T-shirt, approached me hesitantly.

'Good afternoon, sah. It is Bornwell,' he said.

I looked at him blankly.

'Do you not remember me, sah? From St Peter's School.'

Bornwell, Bornwell. I tried to remember.

Suddenly he called out, '*Kill* each *other*! *Kill* each *other*!' and he gave a high-pitched giggle.

'Oh yes,' I recalled, 'that Bornwell.'

Several recruits had turned to listen to this unlikely exchange.

'Did you not receive our letters?' asked Bornwell.

The riot squad commander was ordering us back into the trucks, we'd been given the all clear.

'Ah, yes, thank you,' I said to Bornwell. I had indeed received a bunch of forty-five letters from my old class at St Peter's, but with training and everything I hadn't got around to replying yet.

'Please will you write to us, sah,' said Bornwell, and he stood there in his red shirt, solemnly waving me off in the riot truck.

Man in the red shirt, I thought as we drove away, *one round, fire!*

'Stop the vehicle!' I shouted and I banged on the cab wall.

We lurched to a stop. The squad commander peered back through the grille, 'What is it?'

'I've forgotten something, sir,' I said. 'I won't be a minute.' I jumped down from the truck and jogged over to Bornwell.

'Bornwell, do me a favour. Next time you join one of these crowds, don't wear a red shirt, OK?'

'Why not, sah?'

'Just don't, please, it'll be much safer for you. OK?' I insisted.

'OK, sah. Thank you, sah. Bye bye,' and he shook my hand formally.

I climbed back into the truck and we drove away.

'Fraternizing with the enemy, Godwin,' someone joked in the truck as we bounced along back to Depot. I stared through the grille at the township passing by and realized just how much the training was getting to us. How it did that to you. Turned you into a fighting machine and set you loose on people who were writing letters to you. My shoulders slumped and I sighed a ragged sigh and with it I felt the fight drain out of me.

*

Back at Depot, our relationship with our squad instructor, Pops Crabb, was beginning to change subtly. Initially he had been scathing about us, because we were the A-level intake.

'Think you're fucking intellectuals, do you?' he'd taunt, and then he would mince about, because 'only pooftahs have A levels'. He once singled me out for some minuscule misdemeanour. 'You, Godwin, you fancy yourself as a bit of a brainbox, don't you?' he sneered. 'I suppose you think that "ammo" is a fucking Latin conjunction.'

'A conjugation, *sir*!' I corrected before I could stop myself. I was clearly in the grip of temporary insanity. Crabb's moustache bristled and his face swelled with a dark fury. The throbbing vein in his florid forehead twitched towards a thrombosis we much anticipated.

'You fucking A-level intake, every one a bladdy Einstein, hey. Well, as far as I'm concerned A level stands for Arsehole level!' he boomed, and put the whole squad behind the guard for another week. From then on I determined never to show a flicker of anything that might be misinterpreted as intelligence.

A few weeks later, he was questioning us about the Force's traditions.

'*Pro lege, pro rege, pro patria*, that's what our motto says we're here to protect, now what does it mean, eh?' He walked slowly down the ranks. 'Hendrix! *Pro lege*?'

Hendrix came to attention. 'For law, *sir*!' he shouted.

'Good.' Pops Crabb walked on. 'Godwin, *pro rege*?'

Once again, I found myself unaccountably playing the jester. '*Pro rege*, um *pro rege* . . .' I pretended to ponder deeply, remembering the last time I admitted to any knowledge of Latin. 'Pro reggae, for music, *sir*! It's the tradition of the BSAP band, *sir*!'

I heard an intake of breath around me as the rest of the squad braced themselves for another eruption, but Pops Crabb just looked down and shook his head to hide a smile.

'Arsehole,' he said mildly, and moved on.

The truth was, he was becoming almost proud of us, although he would never say as much. We had won him a lot of money by winning the assault course time trials. And then there was the tug-of-war against the African constables from Support Unit, a police commando unit based just outside Salisbury. Their tuggers were vastly bigger than us, but by good co-ordination and teamwork we actually beat them. We'd never seen Pops Crabb so pleased. He marched us over to the camp pub, a gloomy place called the Left, Right Inn, with bare walls and government-issue hard-backed chairs. Pops ordered us inside and bought us each a bomber of Lion, a big two-pint bottle.

On one occasion Pops Crabb was drilling us on Hard Square when Inspector Lambourne, the equitation instructor, rode past with another horseman, a tubby potato-shaped man with bushy white mutton-chop sideburns and a handlebar moustache. He rode with clear trepidation, with the reins held high, and his legs wide, away from the horse's side. With each stride he looked as though he was about to slide off his mount.

'Quick!' hissed Crabb. 'It's Jimmy Edwards.'

'Who's Jimmy Edwards?' I asked Hendrix next to me.

'Some third-rate British comedian well past his sell-by date,' replied Hendrix out of the side of his mouth. It was true, Rhodesia was the last venue for a coterie of desperate 'international stars' at the twilight of their careers, who came over, in defiance of the international boycott against us, to entertain the troops and boost morale. Having to treat the likes of Jimmy Edwards as an honoured VIP only made me feel our isolation more keenly.

Pops brought us smartly to attention and made us salute him.

'This is humiliating,' I whispered to Hendrix. 'GIs in Vietnam got Marilyn Monroe, and we here get fucking Toad of Toad Hall.'

Jimmy Edwards nodded to us as he trotted by, and gave us

a limp-handed civilian salute in return, as though he were inspecting us.

'Very good. Ah, carry on, chaps,' he said tentatively, as though he were some colonel in a Carry On film. And Pops, quivering with pride, stood us at ease.

There was another breakthrough in our relationship with Pops Crabb, at the end of one of our first shooting practices. Once we'd cleaned our rifles, we had to store them in racks in the armoury before going back to barracks. The armoury had a very narrow door, so instead of all squashing in to rack our weapons individually, we formed a human chain and passed them along. It seemed the obvious thing to do, but Pops was deeply impressed.

'You know,' he said thoughtfully, 'I've been doing this job for nearly six years now, and I've never seen recruits do that on their own before. I've always had to show them how.'

After six weeks we were given our first weekend pass. We were marched down to Camp Hospital and issued with condoms. They were called French Lace, and they were stored in a chalky white powder. We filled them with water, and discovered that, despite the thickness of the rubber, one in ten leaked.

When we were dismissed I wandered out of Depot in a daze, and made my way home. My parents had just moved into Salisbury from Mangula. My father had a new job as engineer in charge of government transport, and my mother was working as a Government Medical Officer rotating between the casualty and emergency wards of Andrew Fleming Hospital, Salisbury's main white hospital, Harare Hospital, for blacks, and Princess Margaret Hospital, which was reserved for Asians and colour-eds. They lived in a house with a swimming pool in the northern suburbs.

The outside world looked different, softer and gentler. It seemed luxurious. People were polite to each other, they talked in soft voices and thanked each other. And there were women. *Women*. I realized how starved I was of their company. Anne, my current girlfriend, had promised to write to me in barracks, but her once passionate letters had become worryingly less steamy, and less frequent. As soon as I got home, I phoned her to plan our weekend. Two precious days had to be used wisely. She sounded distracted on the phone, as though someone else was there.

'I'll come round now, ' I suggested enthusiastically. 'No, no,' she averred, too quickly, and put me off until the next day.

Just then my mother came in the door, back from the hospital. 'Oh, this arrived for you,' she said. It was a letter in Anne's small neat hand. I retired to my room to read it. The letter was a pro forma 'Dear John'. It might as well have been written by the manual. Great timing, I thought, and immediately embarked on a drunken weekend of nightclub-hopping.

Hendrix and Hobley and I and a few other recruits trawled through Club Tomorrow, the disco at the Park Lane Hotel, Barney's, and various clubs with pretentious French names: Le Coq D'Or, Le Matelot and La Bohème. I couldn't remember much of it by the time we reported back to barracks on Sunday afternoon. There always seemed to be more men than women, and the women all seemed to be taken. Because we were so hyped up from training we got into a succession of brawls, mostly with members of other units. But we were pulled apart by colleagues and busy bouncers before we could put into practice all the crotch-kicking and eye-gouging techniques we had been learning. Mostly we were too drunk to inflict much damage.

Monday morning found us back on parade, red-eyed and hung-over. DCI Trangmar delivered a homily on maturity, or our lack of it. Several recruits had been hospitalized over the weekend. Others had gone AWOL, he told us. He suspected this might be a record for a weekend pass. Obviously, he thundered, our training was not thorough enough. He had ordered the instructors to make up for this deficiency. After our brief weekend of freedom, the atmosphere was like doom as we set off on our five-miler.

But the attitude to us changed noticeably, after that first six weeks. We were treated less like imbeciles. There was still an awful lot to learn. More and more of it had to do with soldiering than police work. The force, which had always been a paramilitary one, was becoming more military than ever as the country slid further into civil war. We used to listen to the news on Hobley's rough plywood radio. He'd made the cabinet in woodwork at school. Relations with the new black government in Mozambique had deteriorated. Finally, one morning it was announced that Mozambique's president, Samora Machel, had declared 'a state of war' with Rhodesia. A great cheer went up in the barracks at the news. Now we would be able to go over and *stonk* the terrs on their home ground. The gloves would be off. I remember feeling a sense of unease – we now had hostile countries on three sides – but I kept it to myself.

The military side of our training was SO Pike's job. He gathered us together at the start of our COIN course. COIN for *co*unter-*in*surgency, he explained. He apologized that our intake would have to cut down on equitation, but we needed more time for musketry and COIN. There was a real shooting war out there, he told us, and he intended to make sure we were well equipped to fight and survive it. Our lives would depend on this, so we might as well listen up, said SO Pike quietly. We did.

That day we were issued with bayonets for the first time. They locked in underneath the barrels of our rifles, long sharp blades with an indented blood channel. We were marched over to a field near the assault course where the bandits had erected a line of straw-filled dummies on posts in the ground.

'You, Godwin. Show us how it's done. Fix bayonet and charge the enemy,' ordered Pike.

I clipped on the bayonet, jogged over to the dummy and impaled it – pretty thoroughly, I thought.

'Nah, nah, nah. Not like that, you pansy. It's not foreplay,' said Pike. 'Like this, for Chrissakes.' He grabbed the rifle from me and, emitting an enraged roar, he sprinted to the dummy and thrust the bayonet into its stomach, twisted the blade up and around and yanked it out. 'Up and under, up and under. You must go in under the ribcage and up into the guts, then twist the blade and pull.'

From then on we bayoneted dummies on a pretty regular basis, roaring and cursing as we did so. And the elderly black murderers, the prison bandits, sat under the trees looking on with mild amusement as we shredded their handiwork.

The weeks went by and we became proficient at map reading and orienteering, night marches, laying ambushes, basic tracking and bushcraft, dozens of different bush-patrol formations and attack skirmishes, and anti-land-mine techniques. And we went on a more advanced medics course where we learnt how to set up a drip and treat for shock. They taught us that the most effective way to staunch a gunshot wound was to insert a tampon in it, because a tampon is designed to expand on contact with blood and to absorb it. So we always carried tampons in our medical kits.

Our final COIN exercise was a live operation at Gokwe, a remote area of bush that was a wildlife safari area, adjacent to Kariba. For two weeks we were to cover long distances through the bush, following routes marked on the map and living on light rations. We were trucked down to an old District Commissioner's camp in Gokwe and divided into groups of a dozen, each accompanied by an instructor, whose function was to observe and assess us. He was only to intervene in a crisis. Our instructor was SO Pike. We were issued with two magazines of ammunition each, also only to be used in case of emergency, and off we went.

Meteorological records show that in those two weeks Gokwe had its heaviest rains for nearly twenty-five years. They started almost as soon as we set off into the bush. Vast cumulus clouds towered into the late afternoon sky as the sun slunk away, not to be seen again for a fortnight. Our route differed from the other five squads: we were the only ones to go north of the Umniati river. We crossed it late that afternoon, wading through with our rifles lifted at arm's length above the swirling river. We camped that night on the banks of the river under our little canvas ponchos, rigged up as bivouacs. After cooking our ration-pack suppers on little gas burners we went straight to bed. Operational rules applied: no open fires, no loud noise, no rubbish left, and continuous sentry guard.

I lay with my head resting on my pack, listening to the thunder rumbling around the sky, and waiting for my sentry duty. At 2 a.m. Hendrix shook me and I got up to take over the guard. The night was tar black, with only the flicker of lightning to lift it. A few minutes later the downpour began. Soon there were curses from around the camp as bivouacs began leaking, and by morning we sat, bedraggled and sopping, waiting for a sun that never came.

That morning we climbed over the Nyamapudzi mountains and into one of the most inaccessible spots in the country – nobody lived for a hundred miles around. At midday our routine radio communications with the operational HQ at the Gokwe base camp failed to get through, even though Hendrix climbed a tree with the aerial. The mountains were blocking transmission.

We had to cover between thirty and forty miles a day, depending on the terrain. There was no road or path, so we navigated our way through virgin bush by hill features, contours and streams. It rained and rained, making the terrain more difficult to slog through. But we were determined to make our schedule, and we trudged on, day after day, through a soggy landscape filled with buffalo and elephant and antelope.

On the sixth day we were supposed to loop round and begin the journey back by a different route. We camped at the top of a *kopje*. I was on radio duty that day and everyone gathered around the set while I tried to call HQ at the fixed time. After fifteen minutes I was about to give up to save the batteries when a thin metallic voice finally broke through the static. It was barely intelligible.

'Return our location soonest,' it said, then we lost it. 'Operation cancelled, repeat: cancelled.' It faded again. 'Bandits your location, repeat: bandits your loc., sighted four days ago. Group of sixty, six zero, sixty, heading south-east from Omay Tango Tango Lima.' Then, maddeningly, the voice went for good. Omay TTL was a Tribal Trust Land between us and Kariba.

SO Pike had smuggled an extra carton of ammunition along and he broke it open and divided it up between us. We doubled the guard and chose concealed sites to camp in at night. And still it rained and still the bivvies leaked. I kept a rudimentary diary in my little green police notebook with the dying BSAP lion on the cover. It was mundane stuff mostly. On the third night I noted that a snake 'query, boomslang' had slithered across my legs that night while I lay shivering in the wet. On the second to last night, I made a note that it was Hendrix's nineteenth birthday. We arrived at the Umniati river that afternoon to find it had burst its banks and was impossible to cross. We decided to camp there for the night.

Hendrix had brought three birthday cigars, which he had wrapped, individually, in forces-issue French Lace condoms. He carefully unbound them and sliced off the tips with his bayonet. We sat together in the downpour on the banks of the swollen river and puffed our stale cigars, Hendrix, Hobley and I. It was luxurious. SO Pike had relented and allowed us to build a huge bonfire on the river bank. We sat up chatting late into the night, with our rifles across our knees, huddled by the leaping flames that could be seen for miles around, not caring if the guerrillas attacked us.

For the first time the taciturn SO Pike relaxed a bit, even rubbing his legs and admitting ruefully, 'My pins are sore.'

By the flames of our Gokwe fire SO Pike told us what we all suspected. That the war we were about to enter was much more intensive than was being publicly admitted, and that it was probably unwinnable.

'I feel sorry for you *ouens*,' he said, carving away at a stick with his bayonet. 'You don't know what you're going into. The shit is really hitting the fan. That's why we've been so tough on you. We save lives here, you know, by making it hard for you.'

It was the most SO Pike had ever said to us conversationally. 'I wonder how many of you will be zapped,' he mused.

I relit my stale cigar and sucked on it some more. Above us the stars had come out for the first time in over a week. 'Halleluia! The rain's finally stopped. Happy birthday, Hendrix,' I said, and we turned in for the night.

The next morning we formed a human chain and forded the Umniati river. When we finally reached the base camp, everyone had gone back to Salisbury, except a driver and a radio operator and a stick of black police reserve guards. The exercise had been cancelled on the second day, because of the danger posed by the arrival of real guerrillas in the area. We eventually arrived back at Depot, the lost squad, our camouflage battledress fashionably faded by the constant rain.

Then, quite suddenly one day, we found ourselves doing our end of course tests, and practising for our passing-out parade. Inspector Lambourne, Jimmy Edwards's friend, had measured out Green Square with his pacemaker, a pair of giant wooden dividers with brass spikes at the ends and a brass hinge. He had pegged small white discs to the ground where the squads had to wheel and come to attention. For the parade itself we dressed in our baratheas and burnished our rifles. The squad instructors wore Sam Brownes across their chests, jodhpurs and riding boots with jingling spurs, and they drilled with swords. The BSAP band was in its formal dark blues, and the bass drummer was wrapped in a leopard-skin cloak. We had learnt to take our pace from the sight of his drumbeat because its sound was delayed by the distance.

On the day itself a flock of foreign reporters and cameramen came to cover the event. My parents had also come. My father, ever inquisitive, wandered over to ask one of the reporters why they were there.

'We're doing a story on the end of white Rhodesia, you know, the country falling apart, and the war being lost,' said the reporter, dismissively. 'We've got to use this footage 'cos we can't get in to film security forces in the operation areas at the moment.'

'I see,' said my father, and thanked him politely, but the reporter had already moved on.

During the parade the photographers and cameramen climbed over the red rope cordon and scuttled between the squads, filming and snapping and getting in our way. The instructor in front of us, while saluting, brought the pommel of his sword down hard on to the head of a photographer who was taking a low-angle shot at his side. The photographer howled in pain and retreated.

My father also took some photos, although he stayed on the grandstand with the other parents. He took one as we marched past the Minister of Justice, Hilary Squires, in his dark suit and little homburg hat.

Pops Crabb bellowed: 'Eyiss, *right*!' and we snapped our heads round to look at the minister. He was a slight man, towered over by the senior officers who flanked him. We came to attention in front of Squires and he began his speech. He told us that we should be very proud of ourselves, that we were now members of the best counter-insurgency force in the world.

At the time we actually believed it.

Afterwards there were tea and buns in the marquee. Pops Crabb was shaking hands with members of Three Squad. He looked almost sad to see us go. I went up to him and shook his hand too.

'Bye then, sir,' I said. 'So, we survived.'

'Ja, well you make sure you carry on surviving, hey,' said Pops. He punched me lightly on the shoulder and turned away.

Thirteen

I have no idea why I was posted to Matabeleland. On my preference form I requested Mashonaland or Manicaland. In the box reserved for 'reasons', I wrote 'good spoken Shona'. So they posted me to southern Matabeleland, where no one at all spoke Shona. Matabeleland was part of Operation Tangent. Virtually the whole country was divided into operational areas by then. It had started with Operation Hurricane in the North East, where the big incursion occurred in late 1972, then it had spread to Operation Repulse, in Manicaland, Grapple in the Midlands, Tangent, and even Salops, to cover greater Salisbury.

I got the overnight train to Bulawayo with a dozen or so of my fellow conscripts, and once there we reported to Stopps Camp, police headquarters for Matabeleland. The Personnel inspector called us together into a bare room and announced our postings. I was going to somewhere called Filabusi, which was so remote I hadn't even heard of it. The inspector sniffed and shook his head, 'You'll have fun there, son,' he said. 'Don't count on retaining your sanity.'

Filabusi was located at the base of a low spine of hills. They were strange hills, granite polyps that had thrust their way out of the earth's crust in some violent Neolithic eruption. But in these hills there was gold, and the area was pocked with small gold mines.

The village itself was tiny. There was the police station, of course, a modern building, sheltering incongruously behind a wall of breeze blocks, which was actually there to shield against rocket attacks. To one side was an old colonial house with a steep red roof and screened-in verandah, that now served as the patrol officers' mess. At the back of the station, behind a high hedge, were the African police lines, rows of small brick houses for the black constables and sergeants and their families. The whole complex was dominated by a huge radio mast that was kept aloft by a taut web of cables.

Inside the station were offices, an armoury, and a cell block where suspects were locked up. You came in through the charge office, which was small and invariably packed with Africans. Black charge office sergeants did constant battle with the stream of humanity, and the din would rise in a crescendo until one of the sergeants would roar for quiet. Everyone was mixed together in there, complainants waiting to report crimes, suspects waiting to give warned-and-cautioned statements, people with minor injuries, witnesses to crimes, sometimes the odd goat or dog, when they were exhibits. Whores and drunks, schoolchildren and pastors, murderers and headmen, rapists and poachers and thieves. All mixed together in the little sweltering charge office and overflowed onto the scrappy lawn outside, in spite of the gardener's remonstrations.

Although the disputes sometimes flared up again in the charge office and the constables had to come out from behind the protection of their wooden counter to break them up, the people who waited there had remarkable patience. It was not unknown for them to wait several days before being attended to.

Filabusi was the end of the road, literally. It was situated just off the main road from Bulawayo to Fort Victoria. They had built a narrow tar spur five miles from the main road to the village, and there the tar stopped. The area we covered was thousands of square miles, although it fell into two quite distinct districts. Everything south of the station was white land, vast ranches and small mines. And to the north of us was all black tribal reserve.

One or two of the mining concessions that littered the southern sector were viable, but most were the stuff of broken dreams, from which the old prospectors burrowed out modest amounts of gold. The miners would gather at the pub at Fred Mine, a mile out of the village, to drink away their sorrows. I was taken there by my three fellow patrol officers on my first evening.

Fred Mine had long since closed and its little club nestled within the ramparts of overgrown mine dumps, terraces of yellow soil gouged from the earth in the pursuit of gold. It was really only a bar and two tennis courts. And parked outside were the battered pick-up trucks of the old prospectors. Inside, at the bar, the prospectors slowly marinaded in the bile of their own disappointment. It was a godforsaken place, but the only public place for whites to drink in fifty miles.

I'd only had time to dump my stuff and receive a perfunctory briefing from the member-in-charge, Inspector Buxton. The first job he wanted me to carry out, he said, was to do a round of all the working gold mines and advise them on extra security precautions.

'You've learnt all about homestead security at Depot, haven't you?' he enquired.

'Yes, sir.'

'I'll give you a sergeant who knows the area well. It'll be a good way for you to get acquainted with the geography.'

That evening I mentioned my first assignment to the others at the bar.

'Christ, that's a dangerous job to be starting with,' said PO Moffat, a large jovial man who was also the mess chairman. 'Some of those miners are completely bushwhacked, they shoot at vehicles which come on to their concessions.'

'Yeah, and watch out for the wives,' said PO Kruger knowingly. 'They're bloody piranhas.'

'Especially Ma Whitlock,' agreed PO Moffat, 'she'll have your stable belt round your boots while you're still shaking hands. But don't be tempted, her husband's a fucking psychopath. He tends to shoot anyone who looks at her.'

I dismissed it as so much bar talk, and we made our way back to the mess. I had been allocated a little *rondavel* behind the main building. It had an iron bed, a mosquito net hanging from a hook in the rafters, an upturned crate as a bedside table and an old cupboard. I unpacked my kitbag and fell into bed.

Sergeant Ncube and I spent the next day driving around the mines. They tended to have grand names like Epoch or Vanguard, or patriotic ones, like True Blue, and Royal Family and even Teutonic. At each of the mines I gave the same little lecture on homestead security: to erect fences, grenade screens, floodlights and sandbags and clear the bush for 500 yards around the house.

When we finally arrived at Eldorado mine, late in the afternoon, I was exhausted, and had completely forgotten the bar talk of the night before. Ma Whitlock met me at the homestead door. She was a reasonably attractive woman in her early forties, ancient by my adolescent reckoning. Her husband was underground, she said, and invited me in. We went slowly through the various rooms, talking about the security of the house, until we reached the bedroom. I remember standing there telling her about anti-grenade screens and rocket walls. She was standing close behind me. Very close. I was aware of her breath, hot and pepperminty on my neck. Outside I could see her husband directing some labourers. He had a large pistol in a holster on his hip. I continued to blather on about security precautions. Ma Whitlock inched even closer and I felt the sharp cones of her bra nudge up against my back.

'Mmm, go on,' she urged. 'It's *so* interesting. You certainly know your stuff.' And she rubbed the tips of her breasts gently against my back, up and down, up and down. I edged forward and had just convinced myself I was imagining it, when a hand – long, vividly red-varnished claws, followed by fingers with rings on every one – snaked between my legs and gave my crotch a little strum. Suddenly there was the squeak of shoes on the polished red floor and her husband was in the room.

'Patrol Officer Godwin is just telling me all about our lax security, dear,' she said, smoothly unhanding me, and peering intently at the windowsill.

'Hmph,' he said, and shook hands with me. He was a short, wide man, bald with a ruddy face. I took him through the security precautions drill and then he excused himself. 'I've just got to go and check a few things in the shaft, my wife'll make you tea. I'll join you later.' And he squeaked away over the red cement floor back to his little mine, pistol flapping at his hip.

Ma Whitlock seemed contrite after the interruption. 'You've no idea how the bloody boredom gets to you here,' she complained over tea. 'I sit here and feel my whole youth just draining away into the bush. I go to Bulawayo whenever I can but Jack keeps a tight hold on the money, so I always come back.'

She stared out of the window as the headgear rattled into action and the wheels spun, unwinding the hoist cage back into the ground. 'You know sometimes I hope the bloody cable snaps, or that the whole damn shaft collapses, so I can claim on the insurance and just walk away. Isn't that terrible?'

I sat there, wordless, sipping my tea.

'And I work on Jack to leave – to take us away from this, this damn isolation. And just as I'm really getting through to him, just as he's wavering, he hits another little pocket of ore, or the gold price goes up again and shores up all his dreams of making it big. It's a disease, you know, gold-mining, like gambling. It's a disease that's infected my whole miserable bloody life.' And to my embarrassment she began go cry.

'Why don't you leave if you hate it so much?' I asked.

She dabbed at her mascara with a damp tissue.

'Leave? Where would I go? And with what? I'm the wrong side of forty and I've got no money of my own. No, Jack's got me trapped here in the bush.'

Ma Whitlock picked glumly at her red talons. They seemed

hopelessly inappropriate and sad out here. All her finery did, her thick make-up and her glittering costume jewellery, her appliqué jumper and her high heels.

'I suppose I should be grateful, really,' she sighed. 'At least Jack hasn't got a black mistress. A lot of miners do, you know. Can you believe it?' She lowered her voice to a disgusted hiss. 'They sleep with *kaffir nannies*.'

I finished my tea and said goodbye to her. And as I put the truck into gear, Jack Whitlock strolled over from the shaft. He leant in at the vehicle window. 'I should have warned you about my wife,' he said quietly, his eyes fixed on mine. 'She gets a bit lonely out here at the mine.'

'No, no. She was very well behaved,' I protested, blushing.

'Of course she was,' he said, giving me a knowing look, and waving me off. 'Of course she was.'

The next day was Saturday. I woke up early to the sound of the door crashing open, and in my confusion I thought we were under attack. I sat bolt upright in my bed with my pistol pointed at the door as an elderly black man shouldered it open. He flung a mug of coffee, half-empty by now, on to my bedside crate, cast a withering glance at the pistol pointing at him and said reproachfully, 'Door sticks. Don't close.'

'Who are you?' I asked.

'I am Moses the batman,' he said. 'You pay half my wages.' And he departed, leaving behind him a whiff of alcohol.

I stumbled off to shower and shave and when I returned Moses had laid out my full uniform on the bed, all starched and polished; even my underwear and socks were neatly arrayed. This was certainly better than Depot.

Being the junior PO, I had been rotaed on as duty officer for my first weekend. The duty wasn't so bad. You just had to stay on station in case of emergency, and every now and then you wandered over to the charge office and made sure they were coping. All the other white officers were off station. The member-in-charge and his family had gone to Bulawayo, and the POs had gone hunting on one of the ranches.

On Sunday morning I was sitting in the mess reading a book and drinking another of Moses's execrable cups of coffee, when the phone rang.

It was Shumba, a new constable about my age who, like me, had drawn the weekend shift. 'We have report of a car accident on the main road, sah,' he said.

'Is it bad?'

'No, sah, it is minor one only.'

We got directions and Shumba and I set out in a Land Rover. I chucked in a first aid kit, just in case, and some reflective POLICE road signs to divert traffic, if need be. We drove for thirty minutes along tar that shimmered with heat. Just when I assumed they'd thought better of it and driven away, we came over a rise and there in front of us was a juggernaut jack-knifed on the verge of the road. We parked nearby and walked over to the truck. I climbed up into the cab. *Simanje-manje* music was blaring from the radio. The keys were still in the ignition but there was no one about. I switched the radio off and climbed down.

'He has run away,' observed Shumba. It was quite standard in Africa that professional drivers ran away after accidents.

At that moment we heard a faint groan around the other side of the vehicle. We went around and there lodged underneath the truck was a terribly mangled car. I had to get down on my hands and knees to see inside. The two people in the front seats were clearly dead already, massively crushed. They were flattened in an impossibly small space and I could barely make out their sex or age. In the back was a little girl, about four, trapped. She bore no outward sign of injury. Her eyes were closed but as I reached for her wrist to feel her pulse, they flickered open.

'Hello. You've been a long time,' she said in a small voice. 'My name's Melanie. We've had a car crash.'

'We've come to get you out, Melanie. Everything's going to be all right now,' I assured her. I had no idea how we were going to free her from the vehicle. Nothing in my training had prepared me for this.

'Look, I've cut my leg,' said Melanie proudly, and she pulled up her skirt to show a big gash in her thigh. I ripped open the small dressing from the first aid kit and bound the wound as best I could. Then Shumba called me to the other window. That side was crushed even further down, the car roof less than three feet from the ground. There was a young woman there, bleeding badly from a cut on her shoulder. I broke away the jagged shards of glass from the window and reached inside to see if she was alive. Her pulse was strong but she was unconscious. We had run out of bandages already – the last person to use the first aid kit had forgotten to restock it – so I began to tear big strips off my uniform shirt with which to staunch her wound.

Constable Shumba and I began working at the car body. We prised at it with a crowbar, a jack, a hammer and our bare hands to try to free them.

'Is terrible. Is terrible,' Shumba kept muttering to himself, as we worked, and from time to time he wiped his eyes fiercely with the back of his hand.

While we jemmied and hacked out way into the car, I tried to chat to Melanie, the little girl, to calm myself as much as her. We talked about where they were going on holiday, to Lake Kyle, with her grandparents, now dead in the front. She explained to me the complicated plot of a Barbar the Elephant book that her mother had been reading to her when they'd crashed. I could see the bloodstained book on the floor by her feet. Every now and then she'd get tearful again and ask why her mother wouldn't wake up, and I would reach in and give her little hand a squeeze. Finally, our breath rasping with effort, we wrenched off the back door.

The little girl came scampering out first. Then, very carefully, I reached over to lift out her mother.

As I touched her, she opened her eyes, and slowly focused them on me.

'You will make sure Mel gets home safely, won't you?' she asked quietly.

'Yes, of course I will, don't worry about a thing.'

'Thank you so much for all your help,' she said, and closed her eyes once more. Constable Shumba and I began to lift her out as carefully as we could. But as I moved her head a terrible thing happened. Her whole skull began to distort. It was obviously shattered and the only thing keeping it together was her scalp.

'Stop! stop!' I shouted to Shumba, and I laid her head gently back on the seat rest. I took her pulse again, but it was gone now. Melanie was calling from outside. 'Mummy. Mummy?'

I took her by the hand and led her to the Land Rover. Leaving Shumba behind to guard the bodies I drove Melanie to the village, to the schoolteachers' house. One of the teachers came to the door, looking horrified.

'What on earth happened to you?' she said.

To me? I looked down at myself. I was covered in blood. Some was theirs and some was from cuts and nicks on my arms and hands from wrenching at the wreckage of the car. My uniform was in shreds, I had ripped away most of my shirt for bandages. I handed Melanie to her and went to borrow cutting equipment from one of the mines, to free the bodies.

Much later, using a chain saw and a bolt cutter, we finally peeled the wreckage open and hauled the bodies out. I eased Melanie's mother out very gingerly, as though she might still be alive, and laid her gently down on a blanket in the back of the Land Rover, and drove her to the mortuary at the rural district hospital.

*

On Monday, when Doc du Preez had returned from his golf tournament, he rang and asked me to attend the postmortem. I arrived at the mortuary just as he was about to begin.

'Righty-ho. Let's get on with it,' he said cheerfully, and he began noting down her external injuries. 'Your mother's a GMO I hear, so you're probably well used to this sort of thing,' he said, as he wrote. I nodded. 'Well thank God for that. I'm sick of patrol officers throwing up in my mortuary.'

He put down his clipboard and, picking up a pair of scissors, snipped them rapidly. He reminded me of a concert pianist limbering up with scales before a big performance.

Melanie's mother was lying peacefully on her back. She was a remarkably good-looking woman of about twenty-five. Doc du Preez began snipping his way down her clothes. But I suddenly felt ill at the prospect of seeing her cut up – I'd never seen a white person cut up before. I turned to leave.

'Where do you think you're going?' said Doc du Preez without looking up. 'I need a police witness.'

He manoeuvred her body to remove the strips of clothing. Her head lolled and distorted again, her shattered skull moving inside the bag of her scalp. I felt another wave of nausea and moved away to dry retch. When I turned back the doctor was regarding me over his half-moon spectacles with dry amusement.

'Pretty girl, eh?' he said, and bent over the corpse again to begin the incisions of his postmortem.

'Busy weekend, I hear. Bit of a baptism of fire,' said Inspector Buxton jovially when he called me into his office later that Monday.

'Yes, sir, it was a bit disturbing.'

'Well, never mind,' he continued briskly. There was neither sympathy nor praise on offer here. 'Listen, I want you to concentrate on the Tribal Trust Lands. We've rather neglected them of late, and were getting all sorts of dark rumblings from the Special Branch detective constables on plainclothes duty in there. So I want you to consider yourself in charge of Ground Coverage, i/c GC. Spend as much time as you can down there, get to know the kraal heads, find out what's going on. I want a white man in there.' He pushed his chair back and stood up to stretch, the interview clearly over. 'PO Moffat will go down with you for an initial patrol, to familiarize you. Then you're on your own.'

PO Moffat was extremely annoyed at having to venture into the African reserves, something he usually avoided. As a senior, two-bar PO he normally supervised investigations, did a little public prosecuting and played a little golf.

'You drive, I'm knackered,' he said and heaved his considerable bulk into the passenger seat, where he promptly fell asleep. A couple of constables hopped into the back and we set off. I turned left out of the station and across the low narrow bridge over the Insiza river, past Marvel general store, Filabusi's only shop, where I stopped briefly to buy supplies. It had a low ceiling and chipped lino floors across which rat-sized cockroaches scuttled. Because it was so far from Bulawayo, Marvel prices were pretty steep.

After Marvel store the dirt road began, a savagely corrugated road that shook the Land Rover half to pieces and covered us all in a layer of fine white dust. I had to battle with the steering wheel as it juddered in my hands. The trick was to go fast enough to plane from the crest of one corrugation to the crest of the next without lurching down into the trough. Soon my arms ached from wrestling with the wheel.

It was bare, arid country on either side, chewed to the quick by goats. The only greenery was the thorn bushes and the very tops of the mopani trees. As the morning wore on, the temperature soared. Old colonial hands are fond of saying that it's not the heat that gets to you in Africa, it's the humidity. They couldn't have summered in southern Matabeleland. It's a dry baking heat that grows with the day until it radiates back off the ground at you. It is a heat that stuns, that can sap all energy and resolve by eleven in the morning.

I drove for several hours, until we came to a long low cement causeway where the road crossed the Insiza river again. I eased the vehicle down on to the causeway and stopped so we could stretch our legs and take a piss. The river had evaporated down to a few stagnant pools, in which a gaggle of *piccanins* frolicked, sharing the precious water with their goats and cows. I looked down to them and gave them a tentative wave in greeting. They whooped and waved back, yelling: '*Mukiwa! Mukiwa!*' We'd been here for a hundred years. But not many of us came into the TTLs. The odd government vet, the lands adviser and, on special occasions, the District Commissioner. A few missionaries, but they didn't really count. And now me.

PO Moffat woke up briefly to catch the end of my wave. 'What you doing?' he grunted.

'Being friendly to the natives,' I replied.

'Don't waste your time.' He looked down at the scene. 'They're just kids, anyway.'

'Today's kids, tomorrow's *mujibas*, next week's terrs,' I said. *Mujibas* were local kids used by the guerrillas as their eyes and ears to keep them informed about the movement of the security forces.

'What the fuck's that supposed to mean? Some new bullshit they teach you in Depot these days?' asked PO Moffat.

'No, I'm just working on the theory that it's more difficult to kill someone who's been pleasant to you than it is to kill someone who's ignored you or been a bastard. I mean it stands to reason, doesn't it?'

'Jesus, you've got a lot to learn,' said PO Moffat contemptuously. 'The only thing these fuckers understand is this,' and he clenched his fist. 'These are Matabele, they're a martial race at heart, they despise weakness. They drove the Shona off this land by brute force. And that's what they respect. So that's what we've got to show them. The minute they think we're soft, we're lost.'

I thought about this for a few minutes then drew breath to argue otherwise, but when I looked up at PO Moffat, he had dropped off again, a series of surplus chins conveniently cushioning his jaw against his chest.

PO Moffat was no political scientist, but he was a pretty good policeman. He understood the importance of minimal policing, of interfering only where we really had to, in order to maintain stability. In Rhodesia in those days we had two parallel legal systems. There was the white man's law as legislated in parliament and dispensed in the courts by judges. And then there was traditional tribal law, by which chiefs dealt with disputes in the African reserves.

It was tricky navigating your way through it all as a policeman. There could be more to a report of abduction, rape or stock theft than one initially realized. Often it was really a dispute about *lobola*, bride price. If the parents opposed the marriage, the young couple would elope, and the girl's parents would report her abduction. The charges would only be dropped once they had received a satisfactory bride price from the boy's parents. If a girl became pregnant without *lobola* being sorted out, her parents might prefer a rape charge. And in some cases if the *lobola* wasn't paid they would help themselves to cattle from the boy's family, which would be reported to us as stock theft.

All these matters should have been sorted out by the chiefs or the headmen, but they were often reluctant to make unpopular decisions, and the cases ended up with us. I was loath to press charges, preferring instead to hold informal arbitrations at my Ground Coverage base in Avoca, deep inside the Godlwayo reserve. One of my constables would translate and advise.

I must have cut a faintly ludicrous figure, an adolescent sitting in judgement at my little camp table, in the shade of a fever tree, my papers all weighed down with smooth rounded river pebbles against the dust devils. I rather fancied myself as some old-style colonial administrator. I would speak to the sides separately and then to the girl on her own, to find out if this was a love match. It usually was. The constable and I would then propose a compromise, which they would invariably refuse. Then I would heave a weary sigh and grimly open my CR (Crime Report) book.

'You know that once I give you a CR number, this matter will then be a reported crime, and you will have to go to Gwanda or even to Bulawayo to a white man's court. I will have to arrest this boy and he will be gone for months, and if he is found guilty your daughter will have no husband, because he will be in jail. Do you understand?'

Yes, they would say, they understood.

'As soon as this pen starts writing, it is out of my hands . . .' And I would slowly bring my ballpoint down to the CR form. And just before it reached the paper, I'd say, 'Let's have a short break, and fill out the details in a few minutes.' And when we reconvened they had nearly always come to an agreement.

I got to know those TTLs so well. I even felt comfortable there. I could drive down a track and recognize almost everyone I saw. My base at Avoca was originally a District Commissioner's camp, a small thatched house situated on the edge of a little dam. I had poached Moses the batman away from PO Moffat, and he now accompanied me on patrol. He liked patrols because he received an away-from-station allowance on top of his normal pay. I would sit on the verandah examining maps and writing up reports in the light of a hissing Tilly lamp, listening to the screeching cicadas, the lowing of the last cows to be watered, and the tinkling of their bells as they receded slowly into the distance.

Moses would be clattering around in the kitchen, and he would eventually emerge with an enamel plate of *sadza* and some meat, usually goat, sometimes chicken, and occasionally beef, if there had been a fresh slaughter nearby.

'Scoff, *baas*.' Moses would always say, and crash the plate down on the table. A few minutes later, while I was still eating, an enamel mug of black coffee would arrive in similar manner. Moses would then depart into the night whistling tunelessly, off to drink beer at the grandly named Avoca Business Centre.

In reality the Business Centre was a collection of one or two stores, a small clinic, a primary school and a petrol station with hand pumps. I got quite friendly with the teachers and nurses and storekeepers there and occasionally I would go down to the Business Centre myself and have a few beers with them. I remember discussing politics with them and discovering that we were in broad agreement. Majority rule was on the way, but the transition needed to be handled carefully.

Life in the tribal reserve was grindingly hard. The rains never seemed to come. Maize withered in the fields; they replanted and it withered again. The truth was, it was a marginal area, not really suited to cultivation. Most of the families survived on the money sent back to them by breadwinners working in town. Few could afford cars, I encountered just the odd jalopy held together by wire and optimism. Bicycles or feet were the main form of transport, or buses. There were two bus services, the Ncenga Ncenga Bus Service or the smaller Super Godlwayo.

When you encountered one of these buses you were best advised to pull over. Their forty seats usually carried twice that number of passengers, their roof racks were piled implausibly high with bundles of clothes, bicycles, chickens in wooden coops, hobbled goats, building materials, and occasionally an extra passenger or two. Because their nearside suspension was invariably gone, they bore down on you diagonally like a crab. The front of the bus stuck out into the middle of the road, menacing oncoming traffic, while the rear overhung the edge of the road, threatening to sideswipe unsuspecting pedestrians.

I drove all over the district, even to villages far from the road which had never been visited by a white man before, talking to kraal heads and trying to get a feel for the place. Often we would camp overnight away from base, Moses, a constable and I. Moses would set up the tents and make a fire, and we would sit around it on logs under the cavernous star-filled sky, chatting.

They weren't used to having actual conversations with POs, and they clearly felt uncomfortable to start with. Most of the constables were Matabele and I used to quiz them about their customs and culture.

'What about your name, Constable Ndlovu,' I asked on my first camp, 'that means elephant, doesn't it?'

'Yes, I am Constable Elephant,' he smiled. 'Most of the Matabele constables have the surnames of animals. These animals are our totems.'

'What about Constable Nkala?'

'Buffalo,' said Ndlovu.

'Sergeant Ncube?'

'Baboon.'

'Constable Shumba?'

'Lion.'

'Sergeant Major Khumalo?'

'Fish.'

'Sergeant Ngwenya?'

'Crocodile.'

'Christ, I'm surrounded by a menagerie of constables,' I laughed.

'And the thing is,' continued Ndlovu, 'you are not allowed to eat the animal of your totem, or this will be like eating yourself. It is a very bad thing.'

'What about you, Moses,' I asked, as he stirred the *sadza* into a thick porridge over the fire, 'What's your totem, then?'

'Me? My totem? I am Moyo. It means heart. I am Moyo because I have big heart.' And with that he beat his narrow chest with his fist, and dissolved into a phlegmy coughing fit.

I learnt as much as I could about local politesse, and did my best to observe it. I tried not to rush people to whom time was unimportant, even though I fairly danced with impatience. I tried to remember to show respect to age, even when the old one was dressed in rags and appeared to have no status. I never walked on to the area of beaten earth around a cluster of huts, for this was as bad as barging into someone's house unannounced. I avoided direct eye contact with young girls, I drove sick people to the clinic, I helped deliver babies, I gave lifts to people whenever I had room in the vehicle, I shot rabid dogs for them, I even slowed down when I passed people on the road, so as not to shower them in dust. And I didn't see another white man for weeks on end. I was, to use PO Moffat's phrase, 'a regular fucking *kaffir*-lover'.

There was another thing Inspector Buxton had asked me to do once I had found my bearings. 'See if you can find out what Chief Maduna is up to,' he had said to me in my original briefing. 'Now there's a cheeky *munt*, if ever I saw one. Gwanda's pushing for us to lift him.' Gwanda was the headquarters of Matabeleland South district.

I'd read the Special Branch file on Chief Vezi Maduna Mafu. He was a well-known nationalist who had been charged under the Law and Order (Maintenance) Act as long ago as 1960, for illegal political activity.

I had expected him to live in grand quarters with dozens of retainers, but when I finally went to visit the chief at his kraal near Avoca, I found that he lived in a tiny three-roomed brick house with a tin roof. I stood at the edge of his kraal leaning against my Land Rover, and after a few minutes he emerged to see me. He was younger than I expected, in his early forties, with deep-set eyes and a shaved ebony head which gleamed in the sun. He wore a threadbare navy blazer, with tarnished brass buttons and leather loafers with holes where the decorative tassels had once been.

Maduna invited me on to his little verandah and gave me a

warm Coke to drink, but his hospitality did not extend to conversation. I made a desultory attempt to talk politics, but he wasn't going for it, and I didn't blame him, really. In front of us, on the edge of his kraal under a cluster of mopani trees, was a huge concrete grave, not much smaller than his house.

'Who's buried there?' I enquired.

'It is my father. Would you like to visit him?'

We walked over to the grave. Scratched into the cement were the words, 'Chief S. D. Maduna. Died 1969.' There was no birth date. We stood silently in the heat while small whirlwinds picked up the dust and spiralled it across the parched bush.

Eventually the chief spoke. 'My father's father was the famous Chief Maduna Mafu. You have heard of him, of course? He is in all the history books.'

'No, I'm sorry, I am from Manicaland, I haven't heard about your grandfather,' I said.

'Ah, well, Chief Maduna Mafu, my grandfather, was one of King Lobengula's senior commanders in the Matabele rebellion. He led his warriors against the whites in the Filabusi area, and he won important victories here. He was much feared by the *mukiwa*.'

I did know that Filabusi had been one of the main battle-grounds of the 1896 rebellion. And PO Moffat had briefly shown me the memorial to thirty-five whites killed in the fighting.

'Eventually, when they were defeated, he was arrested and taken to Bulawayo,' continued the chief. 'Then he managed to escape from there into the mountains. But the police were harassing his family after that so finally he gave himself up and was put on trial in a court of law. The only Queen's witness was a white prospector who said he had seen my grandfather killing the whites. But on his way to court on horseback to give evidence against my grandfather, this *mukiwa* was struck by lightning and killed. So the case fell down and my grandfather was freed.'

Maduna smiled at the thought of this. It was the first time I had seen him smile, and it changed his looks entirely. He bared wide white teeth and his deep-set eyes disappeared into little slits.

'Do you think it was an accident, the death of this witness?' I asked.

This time Maduna gave a full toothy grin. 'No, that is not what my people believe.'

That night, on my verandah at Avoca base, I wrote up my account of meeting Chief Maduna. *The Maduna chieftainship has been fighting white rule for four generations*, I observed. *The present chief sees this war as simply round two of the 1896 rebellion*. I rated the chances of his co-operating with the authorities at nil. I rather admired him.

I concluded: *I do not think that this is a man who will be in any way intimidated by the prospect of prison, but, on the whole, his continued presence among his people is probably a stabilizing influence. If he is detained, it could well radicalize what has been, up until now, a fairly quiet area.*

Until now, it was true, the area had been rather quiet. There had been evidence of a few guerrilla incursions, but these had simply been groups passing through. In Filabusi we were faced with a very complicated situation. We were on the boundary between two tribes and two provinces. At the northern end of Godlwayo reserve was a long line of mountains called the Doro range. On the other side of it lived Shona people, in the Midlands province. Over there guerrillas from the Shona army, the Zimbabwe African National Liberation Army, ZANLA, were active.

The Matabele had a guerrilla army of their own, with a name every bit as portentous, the Zimbabwe People's Revolutionary Army, ZIPRA. Although both were ostensibly fighting for the same thing, the overthrow of the white government, they were traditional foes, at odds with each other. So far ZIPRA guerrillas had not yet infiltrated Filabusi in any numbers, and ZANLA guerrillas had stayed on the other side of the Doro range.

All that changed one weekend.

I had been back in Filabusi village, resupplying, and drinking too much with the crazed old prospectors at the gloomy Fred Mine bar. In the mail waiting for me at the mess was a letter of acceptance from Cambridge. There was going to be a life outside for me, after all.

On Monday morning I drove back down to Avoca to find all the Special Branch detectives gathered at the base.

'There have been some incidents,' said a grim-faced Detective Sergeant Ngwenya. He was wearing his standard plainclothes uniform of long trousers, a checked jacket which concealed a pistol in a shoulder holster, and a wide-brimmed felt hat with a leopard-skin hatband. He kept his hat on though we were indoors. He never took the thing off.

'Three kraals by the Doro mountains have been visited by *magandanga* from ZANLA,' he said. That's what the black policemen called guerrillas down here in Matabeleland: *Gandanga*, which meant murderer. Ngwenya had with him a scared young boy from one of the villages who had walked some fifteen miles to make the report. The guerrillas, he said, had conducted a *pungwe*, an all-night meeting at which people were politicized. So we went out to investigate.

The first village we came to looked normal enough as we drove up. A few goats, some scrawny chickens pecked at rubbish, bright washing fluttered on a line. We were armed but not expecting trouble, since the young boy said the guerrillas were long gone, back over the Doro mountains. We called out a greeting, but the village seemed deserted. I walked around a hut and saw an old woman in a red dress, sitting against the wall, her knees drawn up against her chest, her head resting on her knees. When I called to her she didn't reply. I touched her gently on the shoulder, to wake her. Still no reply. Then I realized her dress had not originally been red, it was soaked in blood. I lifted her head. Her throat had been cut. Two others had been similarly dispatched. The rest had run away.

From then on, there were lots of incidents like that. And worse. Incidents that I try not to remember. Women impaled on stakes. Whole families burned to death inside their own huts, their hands tied behind their backs with wire. People accused of being 'sell-outs', killed 'to make an example'. As I moved around afterwards, opening up Sudden Death Dockets with no hope of ever solving these crimes, I began to feel weary and depressed. I began to feel my youth ebbing away. It was ludicrous the way we continued to act as if this was routine police work and not really a war. I never seemed to be able to prevent any of these incidents. I was always too late, intruding on people's grief with my little buff 'scenes of crime' manila folders and my Sudden Death Dockets, asking a lot of silly questions, the second name of the deceased, their *situpa* numbers. I grew to hate those buff manila folders. The very sight of them meant death.

The large-scale operational map on the station wall at Filabusi began to fill up with so-called 'incidents'. Different coloured pins for a sighting, a murder, a contact, tracks. We put up posters in the stores and schools and cattle-dips across the reserves, offering rewards for information. *Make money! Look for these!* said the posters. Underneath were photos of land mines, Kalashnikov AK 47 rifles, Chinese stick grenades, and rocket launchers. *Also,* said the poster, *you will be paid at least $1000 for information leading to the death or capture of a terrorist.* A thousand dollars was about five years' wages to an average African man here.

I changed out of my police uniform and into my camouflage battledress. The only things that distinguished me from the army now were my one-bar PO's shoulder flashes and the lion's paw badge of the Police Anti-Terrorist Unit on my sleeve. PATU was a strange hybrid of regulars, national servicemen and reservists. We usually operated in 'sticks' of six, one black and five whites. Some of the city sticks were jokes, and were good only for roadblocks or guard duty. But the ones we had were made up of Matabeleland ranchers and their black cattle-men, and they were bloody good soldiers. But there was little for them to do. The attacks were hit and run, the guerrillas in and out in a single night.

Sometimes we got close. One day we followed fresh tracks into a rocky outcrop, until we came upon what we were sure was a buried arms cache. I tried to remember the lectures in Depot about booby traps. I checked for wires. I brushed ahead with a branch for anti-personnel mines. Then, very carefully, I smoothed away the leaves and debris which had been put over the cache. Using all the care of an archaeologist, I slowly scooped up the final layer of soil with my bare hands. Finally I broke through and my hands plunged into a vile mound of runny, mustard-coloured shit.

As the situation was deteriorating so rapidly, I was sent to Gwanda for a combat refresher course under a tough Support Unit instructor, an old Afrikaner who was a Reserve inspector. We fired off thousands of rounds, and carried out an exercise called 'jungle path', which we did over and over again. It involved running through a section of bush, shooting at targets which popped up unexpectedly on either side. They only stayed up for a few seconds and then went down again, so we had to carry our rifles at the ready and shoot immediately. Jungle path was designed to reduce our reaction times in the event of a close-quarters contact. The average contact, we were told by our instructor, took place with the sides being less than a hundred yards apart, so our ability to shoot quickly and accur-ately at surprise targets was essential.

In an ambush, said the instructor, our best and often only

hope of survival was to head straight for the source of attack.

'Remember, at the point of ambush, the enemy have all the advantages. You are in a killing ground of their choosing, if you turn and run you will be doing exactly what they expect and they will pick you off like so many guinea fowl at a hunt. What they don't expect is for you to go straight for the source of fire. Very, very few terrs will be well enough trained to hold their ground if you go for them. They'll cut and run, and then you'll have seized back the advantage.'

Naturally, heading for the source of fire goes against all your instincts. So we had to do it again and again, firing and screaming as we went, until it overrode our natural reaction to run from the killing ground. Then, to make it more realistic, we had to do it all over again while marksmen shot around us.

At the end of the course, I was asked to stay on in Gwanda as the prime minister, Ian Smith, was paying an official visit and extra manpower was needed to look after his security. I installed myself in the Gwanda mess and had my dress uniform shipped up from Filabusi. Moses had packed it carefully in my holdall, with some spare razor blades and my mail.

I was in charge of the prime minister's security at the District Commissioner's VIP guest house, where he would be for part of the morning. We had searched the place thoroughly the day before with an inspector from the Close Security Unit and then established a secure cordon around it.

I returned on the morning of the big man's arrival, did a cursory check and settled down to wait, relaxing with a soft drink and the papers. I hadn't read a paper in ages. I knew vaguely that the latest round of talks between Ian Smith and Matabele nationalist Joshua Nkomo (the leader of ZAPU and commander-in-chief of its military wing, ZIPRA) had recently collapsed, and that both Smith and General Peter Walls, the commander of Combined Operations, had warned of an upsurge in terrorist infiltration into the country.

I unfolded the paper and scanned down the headlines. La

Bohème, one of the Salisbury nightclubs that we had frequented during training, had been attacked by guerrillas. They had lobbed a grenade inside, but luckily no one had been hurt. The windows were blown out and, according to the report, the only other damage was sustained by a car parked outside which belonged to Zillah, La Bohème's resident stripper.

I picked up another paper and looked at the banner headline, 'NATIONAL SERVICE TO INCREASE.' I whizzed down through the text with a feeling of panic rising in my chest. National service, Ian Smith had just announced, was going up from a year to eighteen months because of the severe shortage of manpower. Well, there went Cambridge. My acceptance was for that year only. I'd have to apply all over again for the following year, if I survived till then. The piece went on to say that the government was seriously considering making national service indefinite until the security situation improved. Christ, I might never get out. I felt a surge of fury at it all.

I went into the hall and sat on the sofa to wait for Ian Smith. There on the wall was a signed photograph of him. The face was impassive, half of it refashioned in plastic after his Spitfire accident in the Second World War. The eyes bore down on me, the thin mouth pursed in dour disapproval. I got up and paced the floorboards, but the eyes seemed to follow me, in the way that they do. The bastard, this was all his fault. My life was going to be totally screwed up because he didn't have the imagination or leadership to sue for peace.

There was a flurry of activity outside. Car doors slamming, footsteps on flagstones. A worried constable stuck his face round the door. 'PM is here. PM is here,' he warned.

I smoothed down my uniform, and the entourage swept in. Smith looked taller than I expected, he was thin and gaunt. His aide, a slight blond man in a dark suit, scuttled behind him, clutching a clipboard and reading aloud from it the timetable. He returned a minute later. 'The prime minister is going to wash and freshen up, and go over his speech here for an hour or so, then he'll leave for lunch,' he said. 'I'll be next door.' And he left, closing the front door behind him.

After a few minutes the toilet flushed and the plumbing wheezed and Ian Smith emerged from the bathroom in his shirt-sleeves. He sat down at the dining-room table directly opposite me through the open door and began to look over some documents. A waiter appeared with some tea but Smith waved him away. He looked immensely tired. He rested his head in his hands for a few moments, then began flicking impatiently through the pages of the speech.

So this was the man – good ol' Smithy – followed blindly by white Rhodesians even though he had no bloody idea where to lead us. This was our icon. Then, completely unbidden, the thought popped into my mind that I could easily shoot him. My pistol was in my holster, its bullets snugly spring-loaded into their magazine. He was about twenty-five feet away from me; it would be perfectly easy.

I tried to imagine the consequences: the whole history of Rhodesia would be changed; the war would be bound to end sooner with Smith gone. I wondered what would happen to me. It was unlikely that the black constable outside the door, one of mine from Filabusi, would shoot me. I'd be arrested, tried for murder and hanged, like members of the Crocodile Gang, going to the gallows as some sort of liberation hero. Or I'd be declared criminally insane, like the parliamentary messenger 'Blackie' Tsafenadas, who had assassinated the South African prime minister Hendrik Verwoerd ten years before.

Smith looked up from his papers and for a moment our eyes met across the room. His looked tired and hopeless. They seemed to be begging me to go ahead and do it, to give him an honourable way out of this fiasco.

Just then the door flew open and his aide arrived with the Close Security inspector. I realized I was standing with one hand on my holster and the other tightly clutching the rolled-up newspaper, which I was slapping against my leg. The inspector looked at me oddly. 'Are you all right, PO?' he enquired.

'Yes, sir,' I answered. 'Why?'

'You look, well, angry.'

'No, sir. I'm fine,' I said, and I turned down the steps and walked quickly away over the flagstoned path and back to the war.

Fourteen

In my absence, orders had been received to raid Chief Maduna's kraal to search for subversive literature or any other evidence of illegal political activity. I tried to counsel against it, but it was no use. Inspector Buxton came down into the TTL himself, a rare event, to oversee the search. We arrived at the chief's kraal in two Land-Rovers and drove right up through the yard to the house. Inspector Buxton and the Special Branch constables leapt out and rushed the front and back doors of the tiny building to prevent Chief Maduna from destroying evidence. Then we set about picking through the frugal pieces of his life.

Maduna stood in the corner of the main room, straight-backed and angry, while the search progressed. We turned over this thin, lumpy mattress, we explored the pockets of the few clothes hanging in his old cupboard. We emptied the little pantry dresser and peered into the tins of tea and sugar we found there. Then, to my dismay, the chief himself was spread-eagled and searched.

I watched it all with growing unease, going through the motions of searching, myself. I flipped through his few books in a desultory way, and there in the middle of his Bible I found a double page of the banned ZAPU newsletter. I looked up from the Bible and saw that Maduna was watching me closely. This was exactly the sort of thing we had been looking for.

'Find anything?' asked Buxton, looking at the Bible.

'No, sir. Nothing here,' I said, and replaced the book.

Inspector Buxton was clearly irritated that he'd come all this way down to the reserve, through the dust and heat, only to return empty-handed. He turned to Maduna. 'You know we have evidence that you've been communicating with the leaders of banned organizations outside the country?'

Maduna shrugged. 'Then you should charge me.'

Inspector Buxton walked briskly from the little house without farewell. 'We'll be back,' he warned.

And indeed we were. Two weeks later. This time Special Branch had a witness who'd attended an illegal meeting addressed by Chief Maduna. At that time you required a permit to hold a meeting of more than a dozen people. According to our witness, the chief's political meetings were bigger than that.

Again Inspector Buxton attended in person. Maduna was sitting in his sagging armchair on his verandah, and Buxton drove right up beside him. He leant out of the vehicle window and said, 'Chief Maduna, you are under arrest in terms of section twelve, subsection four, of the Law and Order Maintenance Act, chapter sixty-five.' He handed him a warrant through the window. 'Get your things. You may be away a long time.'

The chief got up wearily from his chair and went into his room to collect his belongings. I got out of the second Land Rover and followed him in. He was carefully folding shabby pairs of underpants into a small brown cardboard suitcase, like the ones children take to school for the day.

'I'm sorry about this, Chief Maduna,' I said.

'And so you should be,' he replied, 'I have done nothing wrong.' He put a toothbrush and a bar of soap and a face cloth into his suitcase and put on his threadbare navy blazer, with the buttons of tarnished brass. It was clearly his best jacket.

'There's nothing I could do,' I protested as he moved to the other room. From his small desk he selected a Bible, a Croxley writing pad and a biro pen, and put them into his suitcase too. He squashed the lid down with some difficulty and clipped it shut. As we walked from the house he looked me in the eyes for the first time.

'I hope you are ashamed of yourself,' he said. And I was.

Chief Maduna was held in solitary confinement for two months, then tried for the illegal meetings. He got himself a clever white lawyer from Bulawayo and was acquitted because the meetings had been deliberately limited to groups of only eleven people at a time. But it didn't do him much good. They detained him anyway, under the emergency regulations, the government's great legal catch-all. He sat out the rest of the war in Wha Wha, a detention camp near Fort Victoria.

Looking back on it now, being in Wha Wha probably saved Chief Maduna's life.

Attitudes hardened pretty quickly after that. The compliant old headman who was elevated to the position of acting chief in Maduna's absence was ignored by his people, his authority dismissed. And people started acting differently towards me, too. The teachers and shopkeepers didn't care to chat any more. They looked down at the floor when they saw me coming, as if they didn't know me. And the kids who constantly played football under the tree outside the Jabulani Cycle Repair shop in Avoca no longer welcomed me to join in. And one day they just disappeared. A whole class of fifteen-year-olds, more than forty of them. Sergeant Ngwenya informed me that they had been recruited by the terrorists, to join ZIPRA, the Matabele army. Moses stopped going into Avoca for his nightly drink. It was too dangerous, he grumbled. At night the Special Branch constables now came and slept at the base, too, and we mounted a permanent guard.

When PO Moffat came down to Avoca one day in pursuit

of some stock theft suspects, he was shocked at the change. 'Bloody hell, these *munts* won't even talk to me any more,' he complained in the vehicle as we drove back to Filabusi together. 'All my sources have dried up.'

'Didn't you show them who was boss, then?' I said sarcastically, clenching my fist.

'Yeah, well it's your job to kick arse down here,' he replied. He looked at his watch. 'Christ, can't this thing go any faster?' It was late Friday afternoon and we were both anxious to get back before dark. We were now stuck behind a cart pulled by two little donkeys. It was a modest wooden platform set on the cannibalized wheels and back axle of some old car. The Africans called them scotch carts, and this one was loaded down with plump hessian sacks of maize meal, on its way back from the grinding mill. On top of the bags sat a little boy of about nine or ten. He was flicking his little twine whip at the donkeys but they could go no faster than a dainty trot.

The road had narrowed to a single track with a steep bank on either side and there was no way I could get our vehicle past. We had slowed to a crawl, but I could see that up ahead, in about five hundred yards, the road widened again, and I'd be able to get by.

'Hoot!' said PO Moffat. 'Hoot at the fucker. We haven't got all day!' He lurched over to my side and punched the horn. The little boy looked round in alarm and whipped his donkeys frantically. PO Moffat climbed up on the seat and put his head through the command hatch.

'Hey you, it's the police!' he shouted. 'Out of the way! We're in a big hurry. Go on, move over!' As he lowered himself back through the hatch, three things happened at once. The windscreen became opaque and I could no longer see through it, the steering wheel turned violently in my hands as though it suddenly had a will of its own, and my ears popped painfully. Then there was an enormous noise and I noticed chunks of flesh and fur and white powder splattered over the windscreen.

I tried the wipers but they didn't work. We seemed to have stopped, and the vehicle was pointing into the bank.

I got down from the Land Rover and my head cleared. A huge cloud of dust hung over us and birds were screeching in alarm. The scotch cart no longer existed – it had hit a land mine. A pinkish goo, a mixture of maize meal and blood, covered the banks on either side of the track and the front of the Land-Rover. The little boy was dead, bits of him were scattered about, mixed up with bits of donkey. One donkey had disintegrated. The other donkey's back legs had been blown off but it was still vainly trying to get up, hee-hawing hideously. I took out my pistol and shot it in the head, and the birds all started screeching again at the noise.

PO Moffat staggered out of his side and surveyed the gruesome scene. 'Jesus!' he breathed. 'Just as well you didn't overtake.'

We swapped all our vehicles for mine-protected ones, after that. I was sorry to see my old Land Rover go. Its departure seemed to represent the end of any hope of peace, and the final gearing up for civil war. My father was on the team that designed the new mine-protected vehicles. The Land Rovers had a half-inch steel floor and huge metal rollbars over the cab. Instead of the old police grey, they were painted olive green or camouflaged. There were all sorts of other designs, too, given animal names by their inventors: Kudus, Leopards, Pumas, Crocodiles and Rhinos, ever more thick-skinned. They had various different features, all designed to protect you from land mine and ambush: vee-shaped metal floors to deflect the blast, armoured glass, little slit gun ports and special wheels that sheared off when a mine exploded under them, to dissipate the blast.

For some reason, training I suppose, or my father's exhortations, I was fastidious about vehicle safety. My father said that as long as you followed the rules, they could almost guarantee you wouldn't be killed. Rifles had to be firmly clipped into the rack, no loose objects left lying around the cab, a 30 m.p.h. speed limit, and safety harnesses strapped on at all times. In the Black Museum at Morris Depot we'd been shown photographs of the lasting impression simple bric-à-brac lying around in the cab when you hit a mine could leave on you. In each picture there was a dead or horribly injured person, with the culprit carefully labelled: *Figure A – a couple of small bolts. Figure B – an empty Coke bottle. Figure C – a sidearm.*

The real nightmare was when the terrs boosted the land mine with extra explosives or piggybacked one mine on top of another. Jesus, that was a real bang. Or worse, when they laid an ambush at the land-mine site, so you staggered out of your vehicle, disorientated and in a state of shock, straight into the killing field.

But when I was eventually blown up, with Sergeant Ngwenya, we were lucky. The mine was an ordinary, unboosted one, and it was detonated by a back wheel. The vehicle shot forward and sat back heavily at an angle, the bonnet and cab pointing upwards to the sky. I was just relieved that neither of us was seriously injured – only ringing ears, superficial shrapnel cuts, bruised bums and aching shoulders from hitting the safety belts. But Ngwenya flew into a rage because his beloved felt hat with the leopard-skin band was in tatters and his sunglasses were shattered. It had happened just outside a kraal and soon a large crowd of Africans had gathered to gawp.

I think it was the humiliation of the whole situation that really got to Ngwenya. He climbed down from the vehicle, beating his battered hat against his thigh to get the dust off, and started to rail against the crowd.

'You knew that bloody thing was here. It is just outside your kraal. You must have known. And yet no one reports it. Well, that's *it* now. I've had enough. We try to protect you against the *magandanga*, but you won't help us to help you. Next time they attack you. Next time they rape your wives and daughters, and kidnap your children to carry their things. Next time they torture you. Next time they steal your food or kill your goats or cows. Next time they do these things. Don't come running to us. Why should we risk our lives to help you? Pah!' And he limped off to sit on a tree stump and sulk while we waited for back-up.

The crowd had listened in silence to his outburst, and now they resumed a low murmuring among themselves. I sat, leaning back against the bank, with my rifle across my knees. I think I must have been in a mild state of shock. I seemed to have lost all sense of time. In my head I was composing another letter to the Ministry of Manpower requesting my release from national service, to go to university. It was part of a long and futile correspondence, in which a clerk in the ministry kept telling me that they couldn't make exceptions or everyone else would want release too.

Eventually an old woman broke through the ranks of the onlookers, carrying a gourd of water. She approached me, sank to her knees, and laid the gourd at my feet. I washed my hands and my face, and thanked her. A little later a young girl arrived with a mug of what turned out to be sweet, lukewarm tea. She took a second mug to Ngwenya but he waved her away angrily.

The radio crackled into life to report that my requested assistance was on its way. It arrived an hour later, a PATU stick with PO Moffat at its head, a great roly-poly figure, in camouflage himself now. They herded all the residents of the kraal into a truck, to take them away for questioning.

'What's the point?' I said to PO Moffat. 'I've already asked them. They say they saw nothing, that the mine must have been laid at night. We'll never get anything out of them.'

'Well, we can't just let them get away with it,' he said. 'We've got to be seen to be acting firmly. We could charge them with failing to report terrorists. Leave them in cells for a bit, to stew.'

'We'll never get it to stick,' I said. 'And anyway, if they really were assisting the terrs, why would the terrs lay the mine right at their front door, where it makes them the obvious suspects?'

'The problem around here,' said Moffat bitterly, 'is that the civvies are more scared of the terrs than they are of us. And whichever side scares them most is the side they'll obey. They disobey the terrs, what happens? They get their throats cut or their lips hacked off with pliers, or their family are grilled to a crisp over a fire. They disobey us, and what do we do? Ooh' – he gave a fey flick of the wrist – 'we get weally cwoss and fweaten to charge them and sent them to pwison for a few months, *if* we can convict them. Well, who the fuck would *you* obey? Until we change that balance of fear, we'll never win this bloody war.'

'You know as well as I do, we'll never *win* this war. The most we can manage is a holding operation while the politicos hammer out an agreement,' I said. I didn't know why I was getting the ear-bashing. I'd just been blown up, for Christ's sake. Anyway I'd heard all this before. But PO Moffat was on a roll.

'You know what your problem is?' he asked rhetorically. 'Your problem is, you're too soft, with all your hearts and minds shit. Get real, half these peasants haven't got fucking minds, they just want a quiet life. Like they said in Vietnam, "Get them by their balls and their hearts and minds'll follow." Well that's what I say too.'

Sure, I thought, you and every other amateur strategist. Come to the TTL once every few months and already an expert.

As I hobbled off to the front vehicle, I caught sight of the old lady who had brought me the water gourd. She was angrily remonstrating with a policeman who was prodding her in the bum with his rifle barrel to get her up into the truck. She looked at me and held her palms up in a gesture of appeal, but I just walked away.

Back in Filabusi Inspector Buxton asked me to write an assessment of the security situation for him to incorporate in his monthly report to Gwanda. I sat at my old Triumph typewriter, ripping out version after version, trying to work out what I really thought about it all. The irritating thing was that PO Moffat was half right. The civilians *were* more afraid of the guerrillas than of us. But more crucially, I thought, they had no faith in our ability to protect them. The fact was that the guerrillas operating there were still men from the alien ranks of the Shona army, ZANLA. If we could act efficiently on information received to hit them, and make sure that the civilians weren't punished in the aftermath, there was no reason why we couldn't wrest back control of the area. But what we needed was a much bigger reaction force based down there. I couldn't be everywhere with a few PATU sticks, the area was just too vast.

The problem is, I wrote, *that normally we sit back and wait until local white ranchers start being attacked, before we act. By then it is almost invariably too late, because the guerrillas only start attacking white districts when they have already successfully infiltrated the adjacent black district, from where they can launch attacks and where they can confidently hide out afterwards.*

I was getting quite steamed up, and went on.

If we have a racial attitude to the war, only bothering to protect white farms and mines, then we must not be surprised that black areas slip out of our control so quickly and easily. Blacks there, even those who do not voluntarily support terrorists, believe that we have no commitment to protecting them. They see little option but to co-operate with terrorists. And in this assessment, it seems to me, they are absolutely right.

I typed all this out, backed up by figures and intelligence summaries, diagrams and annotated maps of infiltration routes. And I ended with a final recommendation that, in Filabusi at least, because of the complex trans-tribal nature of the war, we stood a realistic chance of turning things around. What I wanted was a company of black troops, either from Police Support Unit or from the Rhodesian African Rifles.

Inspector Buxton called me into his office the day after I'd put my report on his desk. He leant back in his chair and tapped the report with his ruler. 'This stuff,' he said. 'Do you believe it, or are you just trying to impress us?'

'No, sir, I think it's true. In spite of the Maduna episode, I think we *can* claw this place back.'

'I tell you what I'm going to do,' said Buxton. 'I'm not going to incorporate this in my report, I'm going to send it to Joint Operational Command in Gwanda, just as it is, under your name. OK?'

'Yes, sir. Thank you, sir,' I said, and left the room.

Initially, they gave me more PATU sticks. They were a mix of black constables and reservists, who'd been given extra combat training and volunteered for PATU duties because they got danger money on top of their regular salaries. We had more vehicles and radios and a choice of weapons. Some preferred to use Israeli-made Uzi sub-machine guns instead of the bulky FNs. One or two even preferred pump-action shotguns. At Avoca base, I organized the men into sticks, each stick with a local ground-coverage member, and I briefed them as they sat under the big fever tree where I had once held tribal mediations.

'These people are ready to help us if we can show that we are strong enough to protect them and to destroy or chase away the enemy. We have to show these people that we are their friends. Powerful friends who can guarantee their safety.'

The sticks set off into their assigned sectors, each in radio contact, and I kept a stick of the most combat-experienced men back in Avoca, to use as a reaction force. Some sticks went around the kraals tirelessly explaining the 'new deal', as we began to call it. Others established covert OPs, Observation Points, on hilltops, from which they clandestinely observed life in the Tribal Trust Land below.

For weeks nothing happened. No information was forth-coming, but no civilians were killed either.

I used my time waiting at Avoca to read and reread a new intelligence manual entitled *ZANLA and ZIPRA Tactics and Modus Operandi*. It was classified as 'Secret' and had been given to me by o/c Special Branch in Gwanda. It began with a verse from the Chinese strategist Sun Tzu entitled *All Warfare is Based on Deception*. The manual, 150 closely typed pages, was a meticulously detailed description of guerrilla organiza-tion, tactics and bushcraft distilled from the debriefing of hundreds of captured guerrillas. It made the CTs (which was army-speak for Communist Terrorists, inherited from Vietnam) sound cunning and resourceful and well trained. Much of it made depressing reading. For example, it revealed that 99 per cent of OPs were spotted within hours. *Mujibas* were every-where, apparently, and usually knew the exact location and movement of security forces.

For the first time, in this manual I saw the phrase 'liberated areas' used, even if in inverted commas, to describe areas in which guerrillas had more or less complete control, areas which the security forces had to treat as enemy territory. In public, the government continued to insist that there were no 'liberated areas' at all. They dismissed the possibility with derision.

The tone of the manual was serious and matter-of-fact, but some of it made amusing reading. In a section headed *Dress and Clothing*, the manual included some useful pointers on the guerrilla fashion preferences.

   e. *Some CTs wear socks in cold weather.*
   f. *Women's clothing is worn after contacts and even wigs.*
   g. *Suits are worn by some commanders.*

It went on to inform me that '*berets of various colours are very popular – one pink beret has even been seen*'.

And in another incident:

One call-sign was ambushed by a group of CTs wearing long white gowns. It was assessed that these CTs were disturbed while taking part in some kind of religious meeting.

Again on the subject of cross-dressing guerrillas, it said,

Occasionally, CTs dress up as women so as to afford themselves greater freedom of movement. One point to note here is that African women always carry suitcases etc. on their heads, whereas pseudo-women will more than likely carry suitcases in hand.

'CTs *will never eat the following types of foods,*' said the manual mysteriously:

a. *Groundnuts,*
b. *The lower legs, head, lungs or intestines of any animal,*
c. *Okra,*
e. *Barbel (Catfish),*
f. *Snakes, especially python.*

There was also a section on *pungwes*, the night-time propaganda meetings held by the guerrillas. The manual helpfully included the words of some of their favourite revolutionary songs.

Pamberi ne Chimurenga (Forward with the revolution)
Pasi ne Smith (Down with Smith)
ne Zvimba wasungata zwake (And the dogs who follow him)
A luta continua (The war continues)

Another was entitled *Kunyengere Mabhunu* – Persuading the

Boers. (*Mabhunu* was now used as a derogatory word for all whites.) It was a round, and went simply like this:

Persuading, persuading the Boers,
Persuading, persuading the Boers,
We are tired of persuading the Boers.

Then, just as Gwanda was on the point of wrapping up the operation because the manpower was needed elsewhere, an OP reported that a young boy had climbed up to their supposedly hidden position to tell them that a group of about nine guerrillas had come over the Doro mountains to their kraal the night before. They had killed two people in his kraal, he said, 'as a punishment', and then they had left, taking two youths and three girls with them, heading north-east.

I pored over the map as we drove towards the area. We dumped the vehicles with guards a good distance back, and cut across the spoor line on foot behind the sighting, to pick up tracks. They were plain to see, and still fresh. Without the men I'd detailed to guard the vehicles we were down to seven, but it never occurred to me that we might be out-gunned. We jogged along behind the tracker, breathing hard.

I didn't really have any profound thoughts about death; I didn't even consider it. I was just relieved that, after all the waiting, something was happening at last. We moved steadily through the bush for several hours, saying little. We hadn't eaten and were utterly fatigued. My sweat-sodden clothes stuck to my body and my hands were slippery on my rifle. Our initial state of alertness slowly eroded into a numbed endurance.

Finally, as the daylight drained away and it became obvious that the chase was futile, we began to think about stopping for the night. We emerged into a clearing that looked like a suitable place to camp down, and wriggled out of our packs. I walked a little away from the patrol, leant my rifle against a tree and unbuttoned my flies to take a piss. As the flow started, I looked around idly. We had lost the terrs now, so we might as well relax. I thought about what we would eat. I had only emergency rations with me – *biltong* and dried apricots, water and some sachets of instant coffee and sugar.

I was still in full flow when I heard a twig snap over at the other side of the clearing, one of my men going for a piss, probably. I looked over and there in the half-light, about a hundred yards away, I saw a man in a dark trench coat, with a baseball cap on his head and an AK rifle slung from his shoulder. I could see him quite clearly; I even noticed that his rifle butt had a red bandanna tied around it. For a second everything was frozen. then he pulled the AK off his shoulder and screamed '*Mabhunu! Mabhunu!*' Other terrs appeared from the bush around him. They just seemed to rise up from where they'd been resting, ethereal figures in a dream. The sentry was shooting wildly at me now, holding his AK low, at his hip. I remember thinking dispassionately, he should shoot from the shoulder, really. He'll never hit anything spraying like that.

Bullets were ricocheting through the trees, making a high-pitched zinging sound.

I don't actually recall finishing my piss or picking up my rifle, but I was on the ground firing too. The sentry had disappeared into the bush and I was aiming at the vague shapes in front of me. The air was full of noise and cordite and the sounds of men crashing through the undergrowth. I remember my hands trembling as I fumbled to change my magazine. We skirmished forward in silence, firing in short bursts as we advanced. I couldn't see what we were firing at now, even the shapes had gone, so I aimed at the sounds. The terrs had 'bomb-shelled' – scattered in every direction to meet up much later at a pre-arranged rendezvous. I looked around and did a quick head count. No one was hurt – on either side, apparently. Incredibly, hundreds of rounds fired from such a short distance, and yet there were no casualties. We followed up briefly but it was dark now and the advantage was all theirs, so I took my men back to the clearing, pausing to fasten my flies on the way.

It was only then, on our way back, that a constable stumbled on a body lying at the base of a tree, and called me over. The body was on its back, its mouth gaping open, blood bubbling down its chin. It was a man of about thirty-five, and he had taken several rounds in the side of his chest. He was dressed in a dark, double-breasted polyester suit with wide lapels and a steel fob watch in its top pocket. On his feet he wore shiny black plastic shoes, with holes in the soles padded with newspaper, and he had on a pair of women's butterfly-winged sunglasses. He still had a Tokarev pistol grasped in his hand and an AK strapped across his back with a plaited bark strap.

I stooped to go through his pockets. He had a pouch of marijuana, twenty-five dollars and a scruffy school exercise book. On the inside cover in a neat, childish hand, was written: *Property of comrade commander Fearless, Zimbabwe African National Liberation Army – ZANLA.* In the book were several crude maps of the area, and some of the neighbouring white ranching district.

Suddenly there was a movement several hundred yards away in the undergrowth. Everyone wheeled around and one of the constables shouted a challenge. A tremulous female voice shouted back, 'Don't shoot! Don't shoot! We are innocents,' and three girls emerged slowly from the bush. They were dishevelled and had twigs and leaves in their hair, and their arms and faces were covered with scratches.

The constable talked with them for a few minutes. 'These were the ones who were abducted by this one,' he said, and prodded the dead guerrilla with his boot. The eldest of the three girls walked over to the corpse, hawked fruitily and spat at him. It was a good shot and the gob splattered onto his forehead.

She looked up at me. 'He killed our brother,' she said, and gave him a tremendous kick in the ribs.

We radioed in to report the contact and settled down at the battle site for the night. The next morning we discovered that almost the entire group had dropped their weapons and kit as they ran. In the vicinity around the contact we picked up five AK rifles, several belts of machine-gun bullets, two land mines and a box of spare ammo. The dead man was later confirmed as a known section leader from Belingwe, 'Fearless' Magamba, someone they'd been after for ages over there.

PO Moffat was at Avoca when we finally got back the next day. He was quite envious.

'Were you scared, then?' he asked me, after I'd described the contact.

'Scared?' I considered the question for a moment. 'I don't know, really. I was trying to take a piss at the time. There wasn't long enough to be scared.'

'Lucky you didn't get your cock shot off,' he laughed. I laughed too, but suddenly I did feel scared. Scared and tired, but it wouldn't do to tell PO Moffat. He might think me soft. I walked off on my own down to the dam and watched the cows drinking at the water's edge, their bells tinkling gently as they drank. It was a comforting sound, and I savoured it for a moment. Then the image of comrade 'Fearless' Magamba came to mind again, lying on his back with blood bubbling down his chin and newspaper stuffed into his old shoes.

I wondered which one of us had actually killed him.

Fifteen

There were several more contacts after that, and a number of captures. And suddenly information began flowing again. On the strength of the level of contacts, a company of Rhodesian African Rifles arrived to replace the PATU sections. Well, it was supposed to be a company, but on the way in some of them were diverted over to Tuli, with their white officer. Only three platoons arrived at Avoca under a fierce-looking black sergeant major. In fact they all looked pretty fierce.

They arrived in a long convoy of Mercedes Unimogs and snub-nosed Bedford RL trucks and Land Rovers, bristling with weapons and radio antennae. Most of the soldiers had olive-green netting scarves tied around their heads as bandannas, and they were wreathed in belts of ammunition; the riflemen carried spare belts for the machine gunners. Many of the rifle-men had rifle grenades attached to the muzzles of their weapons, great explosive pods called Zulus.

As soon as the convoy pulled up, the sergeants barked out a string of orders and the men set to work revamping the security at Avoca. They dug mortar emplacements with interconnecting trenches. They set up sandbagged machine-gun posts at the perimeter, scooped out new pit latrines at the back, rigged up a radio mast and sent out patrols to recce the surroundings for several miles around.

Sergeant Major Gondo, the man in charge, was very tall and very solid, and very black, almost indigo in fact. He was surprisingly old, about forty-five, and he was clearly rather sceptical about taking orders from me. It fact the chain of command was rather ambiguous, as we were from different units. Like the BSAP, the Rhodesian African Rifles was an *askari* regiment – black men with white officers. Technically, I was being seconded to them as an advisor. But I outranked Sergeant Major Gondo.

At sunset, he called the men together for a muster parade and they worked out sentry duties. Then they fell out and began preparing supper. I invited Gondo to set up his camp bed on the verandah, where I was billeted, and he nodded curtly at the hospitality. Moses seemed a bit surly at the idea of extending his services to include Gondo, so I took him round the back and had a few sharp words with him.

'What's the problem, Moses? Why don't you want to serve Gondo as well as me?'

Moses looked down at his feet and said nothing.

'Do you want more money because it's going to be more work for you? Is that it, huh?'

Moses shook his head. 'No. I am not worried about the work.'

'Well what the hell is it, Moses?'

Still he said nothing.

'Oh for God's sake, Moses, how can I sort this out if you won't tell me what's wrong?'

'It is . . . It is . . .' Moses looked uncomfortable, and his voice trailed off.

'Go on, it is what?'

'It is because I am used to working for a European. I am not used to working for a black man.'

'Oh come on, Moses. I don't believe I'm hearing this. Why don't you want to work for a black man?' I asked.

'Yes, sah. Only, that he will think he is better than me.'

I didn't have time to argue, so I promised to supplement Moses's pay, and left it at that. Back on the verandah, Gondo had rolled out the map on the table and was studying it under the light of the Tilly lamp. I pulled up a chair next to him, and began to brief him on the infiltration routes, contact patterns, land-mine sites and all the other minutiae of our little war here. I talked for an hour without interruption. Gondo listened intently, and from time to time he grunted in agreement. At the end I looked up and asked Gondo if he had any questions. His stern expression seemed to have softened somewhat.

'No, no questions at the moment,' he said. 'You seem to know a lot about the area' – he paused – 'for a white man.' And his broad indigo face split into a wide, gap-toothed grin.

The next morning the men paraded at dawn, and Gondo briefed them. I stayed on the verandah during the briefing, and when it was over, Gondo came up the steps and asked me if I would come down to inspect the men. As we walked back down, they came to attention and he saluted. They had a different salute to us – in their salute they thumped their hearts with their right fists. Gondo introduced me to them as Lieutenant Godwin, the new *inkosi*, which was actually the Matabele word for master. I stood them at ease and gave them a few words of introduction.

It was a curious thing about the RAR, they were almost all recruited from a small area around Gutu, near Fort Victoria, and they were almost all Karanga, the most martial of the Shona sub-tribes. The *askaris* themselves were different to my police constables and sergeants – less chatty, and less educated, used to operating in groups, not individually.

They were fastidious about their weapons and equipment. Each man had his particular role: there were medics, cooks, driver/mechanics, radio operators, mortar crews, machine gunners, armourers, explosive experts, trackers and storemen – to handle logistics. Their discipline was absolute. In the entire time I was with them I never heard a man question an order once. By contrast, the constables were constantly quibbling with their sergeants and even backchatted me occasionally.

I learned a lot about guerrilla warfare from the RAR. Above

all I learned that the motto for military success in most situations is not so much 'he who dares wins' as 'he who waits wins'. Gondo's *askaris* had enormous patience, far more than my policemen. I remember sitting up in an OP with a stick of RAR men, doing nothing, lying completely quiet for days. When I was ready to go completely out of my mind with boredom and suggested we pack it in, the young corporal explained to me that we had to wait, because he felt sure that the kraal under observation was feeding terrs. There'd been no hint of this, as far as I could discern.

'No, sah, there is something wrong down there. Sure, sure,' said the corporal. 'Nine people are living there but they are cooking food enough for many more. And when the girls take the pots for washing up there is still food inside the pots; you can see by the way they carry them that they are still heavy with food. Also the girls stay in the fields too long. Is not necessary at this time of year.' He went on, cataloguing all the reasons why this kraal was acting suspiciously.

'How can you tell all this?' I asked admiringly.

'Well, sah, you forget, I am from a kraal just like this one. I know their life. It is the same like my life. So I can tell when something is wrong there.'

I think I realized then how white soldiers could never win a war in Africa because of our obsession with kill-ratios and fire forces and all the rest of it. Basically we were fighting blind, absolutely blind. I knew miles more than a town white and yet even with my rural background I could never hope to pick up all the subtleties that were so obvious to this corporal.

It turned out that I wasn't the only person seconded to the company. The other person was a Bushman tracker, Chipikiri. He was a quite extraordinary man who was originally from Namibia (then still called South West Africa), from the nomadic people they called the Khoi. He was well under five feet, with the build of a slight twelve-year-old, and a mischievous sense of humour to go with it. Chipikiri was his nickname and meant a small hard nail. He had a crinkly, round caramel face with slanted oriental eyes and no teeth to speak of. He always went barefoot, and he refused to wear a proper uniform but wore instead a mixture of civilian clothes and other bits and pieces cadged off other soldiers. Chipikiri also refused to carry a firearm. He was afraid of firearms, he said. He didn't like the loud noise. Instead he carried a clutch of traditional stabbing and throwing spears.

For all his many eccentricities, Chipikiri was a truly gifted tracker. He was so good he could follow tracks over a sheer granite *dwala*. He found clues in everything: the time it took for a blade of grass to spring back into place, or for termites to rebuilt their mounds, broken cobwebs, the alarm calls of various birds. He could age a patch of piss on the ground by the state of the crust that had formed on the soil. He could work out the time from how far the shadows had moved off resting positions, which were always in the shade. He could gauge the age of tracks by the amount of leaves on them, taking into account wind conditions. He could even smell humans, and he had an impressively acute sense of hearing.

Chipikiri was also well versed in the cunning arts of anti-tracking used by our quarry. They would walk along rivers, or along busy paths. They would walk backwards or on their toes or heels, tie rags around their feet, or even crawl sometimes, to leave behind confusing tracks. They would carry changes of footwear and change their boots along the way, or simply take their boots off and go barefoot. They would deliberately go ahead of a herd of cattle, or instruct herd boys to drive the cattle along behind them, to obliterate their tracks. Chipikiri knew all these tricks, and took great delight in the chase.

I went on several uneventful patrols with Chipikiri, and he would always explain to me what he was doing. The pattern of each patrol was the same. The soldiers would start off weighed down with supplies in their narrow-profile, compartmentalized, army-issue backpacks. Chipikiri on the other hand, had a cavernous Second World War rucksack made of mouldy canvas and leather, and it would begin the patrol virtually empty. But he was an inveterate scrounger and at the end of the patrol, when the soldiers' packs were almost empty, Chipikiri's rucksack would be bulging with supplies he had bummed off them.

On my third patrol with Chipikiri, we ended up following fairly old tracks, more for intelligence, to establish where the guerillas were going, rather than with any expectation of finding them. But you never knew for sure with tracks. You could be following day-old tracks, but your quarry might have decided to doss down for the day, and you could stumble into them at any moment. So it paid never to treat old tracks too complacently.

We were moving through fairly open bush in a wide arrowhead formation, with Chipikiri a little ahead of me at the apex of the arrow. Next to me was the radio operator and, in a line sloping backwards on either side, machine gunners and riflemen. We'd been going along all morning without much sense of urgency or anticipation. Tonight would be our last night out, I remember thinking. Tomorrow morning we would rendezvous with the trucks by the Insiza bridge and go back to Avoca base.

In front of me, I noticed Chipikiri lowering himself face down on to the ground, in a little hollow. I signalled the men to halt, and they took cover. I waited for several minutes, thinking that Chipikiri must be making a particularly fastidious examination of some bit of bird shit or other. But he didn't appear to be moving. Finally I leopard-crawled up to him on my elbows.

'Chipikiri!' I hissed. 'What the fuck are you doing?'

'I am ducking bullets,' he mumbled into the ground.

'There aren't any bullets,' I pointed out.

'No, but there soon will be,' he replied.

I looked up and there, in the distance at the base of a long incline, was the group we had been tracking.

It wasn't a particularly successful contact, a running, rolling action. We wounded several, we could tell by the blood spoor, but then the light gave out. At one point they fired a couple of rocket-propelled grenades at us. One fell way short, and the other whizzed over our heads and air-burst behind us. I pulled the men back to the top of the slope, and as we got there Chipikiri was hopping around, chattering excitedly in sharp musical bursts of his native tongue, Khoi.

'What's wrong?' I asked.

What was wrong, it transpired, was that the second RPG had air-burst over Chipikiri's position, and he had collected some shrapnel in the bum. He was most indignant and it took some time before we were able to persuade him to drop his trousers so the medic could clean up the wound. It wasn't much really. The medic tweezered a few bits of metal out of his buttocks, cleaned up the wound and dressed it. The men were suppressing their mirth with great difficulty and Chipikiri was in a real sulk at the indignity of it all.

When we got back to base Chipikiri came over to me and demanded a weapon. In the end we chose him a .410 shotgun. We cut the barrel down into a whippet, and gave it to Chipikiri to test-fire. I showed him how to pull the butt into his shoulder, but he was lethal – every time he fired it, he would shriek and let it go, just as he yanked the trigger. The shot could go anywhere. After several rounds Chipikiri announced that he'd now had enough practice. He borrowed an old belt from some-one, which he used as a strap, and from then on he wore the whippet across his back. But I never saw him use it.

The war was entering an entirely new phase. So much was going on all over the place that it was difficult to keep up. It had become a three-way conflict, with units of the Matabele ZIPRA guerrillas entering the fray for the first time. They were better trained and better armed, and the *askaris* had a grudging respect for them as adversaries. But the ZIPRA guerrillas mixed less with the locals and we didn't see that much of them.

Up in the ops tent at Avoca there was now a big blackboard on which the kill-ratio was chalked up. The score of the war was listed in columns:

> Total: *Terrs killed by SF [us]*
> Total: *Terrs killed by each other*
>   *(Sub-total: ZIPRA killed by ZANLA)*
>   *(Sub-total: ZANLA killed by ZIPRA)*
> Total: *SF losses*

Some of the men bet on the scores. The point of honour was to keep the *Terrs killed by SF* higher than the *Terrs killed by each other*. But frequently they killed more of each other than we killed of them. I got the distinct feeling that the whole thing was spinning into anarchy.

For the first time, the war was spreading out of tribal areas into the ranching district. And as soon as white farmers started being killed, Gwanda HQ suddenly started jumping around. After all, these were Ian Smith's electors.

When Doug Hammond's ranch was attacked they even offered to helicopter us in, but it was quicker to go by vehicle. I took all the men available, about eleven, and we drove up through Godlwayo, across the main tar road, to Piccadilly Ranch. It was an unusual attack in that it had been launched early in the morning. We were first on the scene, debussing and approaching cautiously on foot, in case the road leading to the homestead had been land-mined to sabotage any follow-up, a common tactic. The first thing I noticed was an Alsatian dog lying heavily on the lawn. It didn't move as we arrived. One of the medics went over to it and pulled its lips back from its teeth. Its mouth was frothing.

'Poisoned meat,' he said.

I deployed men in defensive positions around the perimeter of the garden and then climbed up the steps to the house. It was a long, low building of whitewashed stone with a green corrugated iron roof. We moved warily inside. The house was very still. The first thing we came across was the cook, dressed in his uniform of white trousers, tennis shoes and apron. He was lying dead across the kitchen doorway, his intestines oozing out of a gaping hole in his stomach. At the end of the passage the door to the master bedroom was standing ajar. I nudged it open with the end of my rifle barrel.

Old man Hammond hadn't even made it out of bed. He was lying sprawled across the bedclothes. I assumed it was him. To be honest there wasn't much of him left, he'd been shot so many times. They must have emptied several magazines into him. I looked around at his bedroom. On his bedside table was an alarm clock, a novel – *The Day of the Jackal*, by Frederick Forsyth – a Supersonic radio, a glass of water, Alka-Seltzer tablets, a pack of Kingsgate cigarettes, a half-finished cup of cold tea, and the beginnings of a shopping list in an open notebook: *detergent, potatoes, bread, Harpic*. A wicker dog basket stood in the corner, worn slippers on the floor.

On the white wall above the bed hung a photo of the whole family together, grinning cheesily into the sun against a spray of lurid bougainvillaea. But the photograph and the wall behind it were speckled with blood and bits of Hammond's brain. Jesus, I thought, what a way to end your life.

We followed up the tracks at speed. Chipikiri had the scent in his nostrils. From time to time he stopped and cocked his head to one side, like a terrier on the trail. 'It is the same one who killed the army family,' he said, looking at the tracks, 'the feet are the same.'

A few days earlier the family of a serving black soldier had been murdered in their kraal a few miles north, a mother, grandparents and two small children herded into a thatched hut which was then set alight. I was still shaken at the memory of having to sift through the charred bones, trying to count the dead.

The tracks led into a small kraal at the edge of the TTL. We fanned out in open formation and walked slowly up to it. There was a radio on the ground playing loud *simanje-manje* music, like the music played by the band at Mangula compound. The kraal was empty but for one person, a youth of about sixteen. He was wearing denim dungarees and a T-shirt, and his hair was gelled into frizzed tendrils, the latest style. When he first saw us he made a move as if to run, but thought better of it. Now he was lounging back in his deckchair trimming his fingernails with a clipper. *Clip . . . Clip . . . Clip . . .*

I went over to him and said: 'How long have you been sitting here?'

'Me?' he asked.

'Yes you, who the fuck else is here?'

'Me. I have been here all day. Since this morning.'

Chipikiri was walking around the kraal in ever wider circles. He drew me over to one side, out of earshot of the youth. 'It is no good,' he said, 'they have swept the tracks with branches and then driven cattle over them. Now we cannot see which way they left after this.'

'Were they definitely here?' I asked him.

'Oh yes. For sure.'

'How long ago?'

He dropped to his knees and examined some tracks, then he lay right down on his front and put his temple to the ground, squinting at the profile of the tracks.

'At the longest, they were here four hours ago. But maybe just two hours.'

We had maybe four more hours until dark, then we would lose them for sure. I went back to the youth. He was still in the deckchair, but now he had progressed to his toenails. He was hunched over using the file attachment to scrape out dirt underneath them. *Scrape . . . Scrape . . . Scrape . . .*

I was beginning to lose it. My jaws had started to clench and unclench on their own. They did that sometimes when I was brewing up a rage.

'So you've been here all morning. At least, what, five or six hours?'

He grunted in agreement without looking up from his toes. I looked around the kraal. The soldiers, standing, squatting, sitting, waiting patiently for me to get directions from this boy, directions to those who had killed at least seven civilians. And a dog. My face was growing hot. Time was short.

'I'm going to ask you nicely, just once, for some help. I don't want any bullshit, OK?'

The youth shrugged, noncommittally.

'Now we know, we *absolutely* know for sure, that this morning a group of *wa-gandanga* terrorists, guerrillas, freedom fighters, comrades – whatever the fuck you want to call them – came through this kraal. There were eleven of them. We know this exactly, because that man,' I pointed to Chipikiri, who was now seated on a log scrabbling about in his vast rucksack, 'that man is the best tracker in the whole of Africa, probably in the whole fucking world, and he has seen their tracks right here, right up to your chair in fact. Now, it's very simple. All I want to know from you is which way they went, because *someone* has wiped away their tracks with branches. If you tell me, then we will go away and not bother you any more. Do you understand?'

He shrugged again. 'I saw nothing. No one was here.'

Then he smiled. He *smiled*. A condescending, smirky smile. Something inside me just snapped and I grabbed him by the bib of his dungarees, lifted him out of his deckchair, clear off the ground, and slammed his body up against the wall of the hut. I could hear the breath wheeze out of him. I twisted the dungaree straps in my fist so that they were tight around his neck, and with my other hand I unholstered my pistol and pushed the barrel against his gullet.

'I am going to give you one more chance, fuckhead, and then I am going to shoot you. Don't worry, I'm not going to kill you. First I am going to shoot one foot and then the other, and then I am going to shoot each leg, and before each shot you will have a chance to tell me what I want. It is entirely up to you.'

I loosened my grip fractionally on his neck to allow him to talk. His eyes were wide now, the whites showing all the way around in panic.

'Please, I don't know,' he gasped.

I tightened my grip again and brought the pistol down to my side and fired a round into the ground between his legs. The noise shattered the quiet of the kraal, chickens squawked away in fright and several of the soldiers leapt up in surprise and cocked their rifles.

The youth was wailing in terror now, and I saw that he had pissed himself, a large damp patch had appeared around the crotch of the dungarees. I pushed him back against the wall, and put my face close up against his. 'I-am-not-fucking-around. Do-you-understand.'

Then I felt a restraining hand on my shoulder. It was the corporal. 'Sah, I think he wants to tell you now.' The corporal was looking at me strangely.

I turned back to the youth. He was in tears and he was trying to speak. I loosened my grip, and he began giving us detailed directions. Chipikiri was at my elbow, listening intently and nodding. I let go of the youth and he collapsed in a heap against the wall, sobbing. I was trembling myself, and I walked over to one of the huts and breathed deeply to calm down. In the window of the hut I momentarily caught sight of the reflection of a face. It was greased black and green with camouflage cream. It was a terrifying face, coursed through with anger and despair. It was the face of someone who would kill an unarmed civilian for withholding information. It was my face.

I was aware of the corporal by my side. 'We go now, sah? We have good directions. We take that little *mujiba* with us, in case he lied, and then we let him go when we confirm tracks, OK?'

'OK,' I said wearily and made my way back. The men were buckling on their webbing, getting ready to leave. The youth had changed out of his soiled clothes into a new outfit. I went over to him, and he instinctively cowered.

'I'm sorry,' I mumbled. 'It's just that we're in a big hurry. OK?'

He looked at me sceptically. Then he shook his head slightly, refusing to grant me absolution.

We followed the tracks for the next few hours. It was a group of eleven. They knew we were on to them and they pulled every trick in the book. They doubled back, they clambered over boulders, but they stayed together. Then as the pace began to tell, they slowed. Chipikiri said we were close, very close. I changed the men from single file to extended line formation. Chipikiri was certain now that we were within half a mile. Within half a mile of the men who had burnt a family, spread Hammond's brains across his bedroom wall, disembowelled his cook and poisoned his dog. I'd never been in this position before, where I could anticipate a contact. I found myself humming a tune, the same tune, again and again under my breath. I couldn't identify it, and it was beginning to irritate me.

Suddenly my right machine gunner chattered into action with his MAG, and then everyone was firing. I was humming louder now, and at last I recognized the tune. It was my old school song, *Ex Fide Fiducia*. I found myself singing it as we skirmished forward into the long shadows of the Matabeleland afternoon:

Peter Godwin

Great Saint George our patron hear us,
In the conflict be thou nigh,
Help us in our daily battle,
Where each one must live or die.

Sixteen

Slowly all other life faded. The potent images of war crowded out the memories of my life before this, of my very identity. I had become a soldier, a technician of war. My correspondence with the Department of Manpower had trailed off in the face of their refusals to consider my release. This was all there was now. Sergeant Major Gondo and his men, and our grim little struggle. Gondo and I had become firm friends. He and his men had decided that I was good for the unit because, though several men had been lightly wounded, they had suffered no fatalities under my command.

Gondo and I would sit in the operations tent, planning patrols and ambushes and OPs, and chatting. Outside, the men on standby played volleyball or endlessly prepared their kit. They would sit in groups quietly taping their magazines together – side by side, but reversed, so that as soon as one mag was empty you could unclip it and flip it round to insert the fresh one. It was quicker than fiddling around in your webbing for your next magazine. They were very particular about the sequence of bullets in the mags, alternating incendiary, tracer, straight, in particular ratios, each type colour-coded just behind the bullet head. And a ballistite bullet first up, for those who fitted rifle grenades.

Some soldiers also carried garotte wire on their belts, or traditional *knobkerries*, which were part of the regimental crest, or *pangas* with curved blades like Gurkha *kukries*. They were intensely superstitious and, as well as their various weapons, they carried lucky charms and twists of herbal *muti* and they wore special elephant-hair bracelets and leather necklaces.

While we sat in the ops tent, I tried to chat to Gondo about politics, but he became distinctly uneasy.

'I am professional soldier,' he said, 'it is my job. I leave politics to others, to the politicians.'

'But don't you sympathize a little bit with the aim of the terrs, to get black rule?' I probed.

'These people are just communists,' he spat, 'they are being used by the Russians. They are just greedy for power. These *magandanga*, they are not fit to rule this country. They kill old men. Women even. You see what they do. They are cowards. I don't want to be ruled by them.'

Gondo was happier to talk about religion. Though he was nominally a Christian, he was in fact a firm believer in traditional ancestor worship.

'Our spirits are more useful than God,' he maintained. 'We can consult them whenever we like, for advice, through the spirit medium. But the Christian God has no tongue. He never speaks at all. His wishes can only be divined through the Bible.'

I had noticed that Gondo would chose older, married men to serve on the reaction stick – one of the most dangerous duties. Personnel was his exclusive domain, but one day I challenged him on this tendency.

'Why don't you choose some single men without dependents to do fire-force duties,' I suggested, 'so if they're killed at least there won't be a widowed wife and orphaned children?'

'See, that is why it is better to leave these things to me,' he chastised. 'If a man, an adult man, dies before fathering a child, his spirit may be unclean, because he has no one to make the rituals. They cannot be done by his parents because they can only do it for their children, not for grown-ups.'

I tried to remember the explanation of Shona religion given to me by Father Kennedy the Carmelite all those years ago. Food was put at the graveside each day, he had said, until the *makonye*, the maggot grubs, appeared, and only then did the lost spirit find its way out of the forest.

Not long after our conversation about Gondo's choice of men for fire force, there was great excitement on mail day because one of the young riflemen had received a letter from his wife to say she had given birth to their first baby, a son.

'I will call him Godwin,' he said to me, 'Godwin Mhlangu. Yes, it is a good name.'

He showed me a photo of his wife, a very young girl, about sixteen. Her hair was intricately braided along her scalp and she was wearing a powder-blue cardigan, smiling shyly and holding a tiny baby in a long white dress and a woollen bobble hat.

'Now I am not afraid to die,' he said, 'I have got a son to follow me.'

'Godwin is usually a surname,' I pointed out. 'Maybe you would prefer Peter as a first name.'

'No, Godwin is better,' he insisted. 'God-win. *God*-win. God-*win*. It is a strong name.' And he danced off to share the happy news with his mates, singing, 'God-win Mhlangu, God-win Mhlangu.'

Qualified now as a father, Mhlangu was put on the fire-force rota by Sergeant Major Gondo. It wasn't that dangerous, actually. Most of the men preferred it to normal patrolling, when boredom tempted you to relax just as danger might strike. At least with fire force you were expecting trouble and you were ready for it. Mostly, there wasn't much to do, though. The patrols could generally look after themselves and anyway it took too long to reach them. We didn't have helicopters yet, that came later. Then we still deployed by vehicle.

Sometimes Gondo went with them, sometimes I did. This time I did. We'd had a report of terrs at a kraal quite close by. The report was six hours old, so there wasn't much danger of a contact. We travelled in four vehicles, down over the Insiza river and up again towards the watershed. The men were in good spirits – it was the end of the month and they'd just been paid. Several of them, including Mhlangu, were due home leave.

When we reached the kraal it turned out that the report was incorrect, they hadn't seen terrs at all. Such confusion was pretty common. The men searched the huts, looked around for signs of tracks, but there was nothing. It was getting late so we climbed back into the trucks and headed for home. I was sitting up front in the lead vehicle and behind me the men had started to sing one of their hunting songs. It was similar to the Shangaan hunting songs that the beaters sang in Silverstream on their way to a forest fire, and it was strangely comforting.

Then the singing stopped and I heard men shouting. I turned round to see what was going on. I remember noticing sparks flying around in the back and thinking it was cigarette ash caught in the wind. Just behind me, one of the soldiers began firing. I saw his tracer rounds arcing off into the bush, and I realized we were being ambushed, and that the sparks were bullets ricocheting around the back.

When you're caught like that in an ambush, you can't stop and debus because you're in the killing ground. You return fire and drive out of it if you can, then regroup and pursue. We hurtled through the ambush, and behind me I saw that the other three trucks were all still coming.

At the top of the rise we stopped. In the truck behind mine the medics were stooped over a figure. I don't know why, but I knew it was Mhlangu even before I got there. He had taken two shots to the chest and was breathing raggedly and unevenly. He had lost a lot of blood and the medics had set up a drip and were dressing the wound. I called for the radio operator and asked for a helicopter casevac from Gwanda. But it was already dark, and the dispatcher sounded unenthusiastic.

The medics were chattering urgently to each other, trying to decide what else they could do. They were losing him. Mhlangu opened his eyes, blinked rapidly several times, and then a distracted look crossed his face. He inhaled raggedly again and, with a resigned sigh, he died. Just like that. His body trembled briefly and then he was still. Singing a Karanga hunting song one minute, dead the next.

His eyes stayed open. Open yet dead. Eyes that once mirrored the soul now reduced to glazed orbs which held no clues. Hesitantly I moved closer to shut them. I'd seen my mother do this but I'd never done it before myself. I drew my hands gently over the lids to shut them but they sprang open again, staring at me in baleful reproach.

I got up from the body and walked away to be alone, to collect myself. But the radio operator came after me holding out the handset.

'Seven zero alpha,' he indicated. 'They want to check we still need casevac.'

I took the proffered instrument and spoke briefly to Gwanda HQ.

'Negative. That's a negative,' I replied. 'It's no longer necessary.'

'Roger that. Over,' said the air dispatcher, the irritation showing in his voice even through its metallic static. He clearly thought that we'd exaggerated the injury, and that we'd now realized it wasn't life-threatening after all.

I took up the handset again and spoke tersely into it.

'Please amend our sitrep from "one injured" to read "one dead". Repeat "one dead", over.'

After a pause the radio crackled into life again.

'Roger, copied. One dead,' said the thin metallic voice. Then it softened slightly. 'Bad luck, over.'

As I gave back the handset, I realized that I was crying. Great tears of frustration coursing down my cheeks, sliding over the grease of my camouflage cream and splattering on to the dust at my feet. The radio op looked at me, confused. He was about to try to console me, but thought better of it. The gulf of command and culture was too wide, even at a moment like this. Instead he simply took the handset, stood briefly to attention, arms stiffened at his sides, swivelled smartly on his heels and marched away. And I was left alone.

It was clearly my fault. The whole thing. I should have spaced the convoy out more. I should have checked the information more thoroughly. I should have waited until the following morning.

Back at Avoca the next day, they brought me a cardboard box with Mhlangu's personal effects, to be sent home to his family. There wasn't much inside the box, really. Toiletries, a Shona novel, some money and volume one of a correspondence course on bookkeeping. He had been hoping to get a job as a clerk on a mine, he'd told me. And to wear a tie to work.

From his combat jacket they had retrieved a photo of his new baby. The photo was discoloured from his blood and the edge of it had been shot away. I turned it over and on the back in carefully looped joined-up writing he'd written his son's name, 'Godwin Mhlangu', and underlined it twice with a ruler.

Shortly after Mhlangu's death, I took a weekend's leave to try to forget it all. In a year, it was the only leave I ever took, because I was trying to get through my service days as quickly as possible. I spent the night at Filabusi, drinking with PO Moffat at the Fred Mine bar, which had grown even gloomier. PO Moffat was a changed man. Gone was the confident, tough-talking get-them-by-the-balls strategist. He seemed quieter and distracted. After a few Lions, he began to tell me about a three-week PATU call-up he had just completed across in op Repulse.

'You know, over there they've shoved all the *munts* into Protected Villages, to cut them off from the terrs. It's on that Mao Tse-tung principle, you know, the people are the water and the terrs are the fish or whatever. And there's a six-to-six curfew. All the *munts* must be back in the PVs by six. So anyway, I was out with this army stick, right, and it was about quarter to six. We were just having a smoke at the side of the road and this old *munt* comes cycling slowly by. He even greets us and everything. He says, "Afternoon, *baas*," and lifts his little hat off while the bike wobbles along. So the sergeant looks at him, and he says to his corporal, "How far d'ya reckon it is to the PV from here?" And the corporal says, "About five miles?" So the sergeant rests his rifle on the side of the vehicle and takes a bead on this old *munt* as he cycles away, and fucking shoots him. Dead.'

PO Moffat took a long draught of his beer. 'So I say, "What the fuck did you do that for?" And he says "C'mon, he'd never have made it to the PV by six. He was a curfew breaker." And then the sergeant wanders over to the bike and calmly checks out the contents of the basket strapped to the rack, and he finds an orange there and he peels it and starts to eat it. And he says, "Anyone want a piece?" '

PO Moffat wiped his eyes angrily with the back of his hand and ordered another round. 'I mean, "Anyone want a piece?" for fuck's sake!'

'Did you report him?' I asked.

'Nah. What's the point. He sitrep'd the dead *munt* as a curfew breaker and he had five of his guys to back him up.'

I left early the next day for Bulawayo. It was a crisp blue morning and I was back in civilian clothes for the first time in months. But I found the city confusing and overwhelming. I was mesmerized by the women. Women just walking along the wide pavements, tottering on their cork-platform shoes, sashaying their hips, women drinking iced coffee in cafés, flicking their fringes and clinking their bangles. I had forgotten how to talk to them, though. I was pursuing a grey-eyed vicar's daughter who I had met before and with whom I'd corresponded. But I wasn't much good at socializing any more. Eventually she complained that I always looked worried, cross even. That I frowned a lot. It was hard to have a good time around me, she said.

I came back from my weekend in a foul mood to find that, in Filabusi at least, we had now comprehensively lost the war. All our civilian co-operation had evaporated because of one incident that weekend. A patrol from the all-white Rhodesian Light Infantry, the RLI, had got permission to continue a hot-pursuit action, following up a contact with a big group of guerrillas on the other side of the Doro range. They didn't have a decent tracker and so they just went from kraal to kraal, beating people up and burning huts, trying to find out which way the guerrillas had gone. And most of the people really had no idea. They would probably have said if they knew, because these guerrillas were Shonas from ZANLA.

The RLI had left a trail of devastation behind them and wrecked the tacit agreement that we had going with the locals. Sergeant Major Gondo gave me an account of it all. I'd never seen him so angry. We went out to survey some of the destroyed kraals. And amidst the smouldering ruins of their huts I tried to apologize to the people, to promise them compensation. But they were sullen and furious. We hadn't kept our promises. They wouldn't trust us again and I didn't blame them.

On the way back to Avoca we bumped into the offending unit, about twenty men from the RLI. They were leaning against their vehicles smoking and eating and laughing with each other.

'Hey, howzit,' said the RLI sergeant. He was wearing *veld-skoens* without socks, black shorts and an olive-green sleeveless T-shirt which had the words *RLI – THE INCREDIBLES* emblazoned in black across the chest. Around his neck, a cluster of dog tags and a bottle opener clanged noisily against each other.

'You're "incredible" all right – incredibly fucking stupid,' I said, and his face darkened with anger.

'What's your fucking case?' he demanded.

'You come in here, with no intelligence at all, and just go around kicking heads and burning houses,' I shouted. 'Why the fuck didn't you come through us? These people on this side of the mountains don't even support ZANLA, you idiot. But they sure as hell will now. Thanks to you morons.'

We were fronting up to each other now, and there was going to be a fight. Behind him, his men had drawn close in a threatening semicircle. They were jeering and shouting abuse at me. Then we heard the sound of a machine gun being cocked and everyone froze. On the vehicle above me Sergeant Major Gondo was hunched over the cab-mounted Browning machine gun. 'I think you stop now, sergeant,' he said to my RLI adversary, 'you have made enough trouble already. You go home now.'

I climbed back into my vehicle and drove away, and above me Gondo kept the machine gun trained on them the whole time until we were out of sight.

I did my best to repair the damage done by the RLI's scorched-earth foray. We made our trucks available to carry thatching grass for the rebuilding of the huts, and transported wood-chopping parties to the mountains to cut down trees for their walls. From time to time I checked up on the long line of kraals that had been burnt to see how the rebuilding was going. Slowly the new huts took shape out of the ruins of the old. The conical thatched roofs went up and the walls were plastered with mud. And when the mud dried, they decorated the walls with traditional Ndebele patterns, bright geometric patterns, zigzags and circles and squares.

At one of the rebuilt kraals I visited I noticed some writing amidst the decorative patterns painted on a hut wall. I walked nearer and saw, written in uncertain letters, the words: *Hate us and see if we mind*. I looked at it again. The words had a profound effect on me. They seemed to be an audacious challenge. *Hate us and see if we mind*. Maybe these people had conquered hatred, maybe they were immune to it.

I walked over to the hut. There was a young woman sitting

on a rough wooden bench against the wall, knitting. At her feet a pile of scrawny beige puppies were playing, chasing each others' tails and yelping. I pointed at the motto on the wall. 'What's that mean?' I asked her.

She looked up at the wall, and smiled sweetly at me. 'Hate us and see if we mind."

'Why?' I asked.

'Hate us and see,' she said, 'we won't mind.'

'Do you think we hate you?' I asked.

She shrugged. 'We don't mind any more,' she said, and went back to her knitting.

The truth was we could expect very little help from the local people. Until now they had been pretty friendly towards us, respectful and generally polite. Now they were hostile and uncooperative once more. And the flow of information dried up again.

The soldiers' attitude changed too. They began to treat the locals like enemies. It came to my attention that our patrols were now routinely picking up civilians from the roadside and making them sit in the lead vehicle, as insurance, so that if they hit a mine or an ambush, the civilian would get it too. The practice troubled me, and I finally tackled Gondo about it.

'Did you know that the drivers collect hostages from the roadside to take on their patrols?' I asked him.

He thought for a minute, and then he looked up from his maps. 'Yes, I knew this one,' he said quietly.

'Do you think it's right?'

'I don't know if it's all right,' he shrugged, 'I only know it can work. Sometimes, these civilians will bang on the roof to stop the truck because they know there is a land mine there. It is the best mine detector we have got. It saves soldiers' lives.'

So I let it ride. I convinced myself that this wasn't really hostage taking but intelligence gathering, with a little extra motivation.

'Anyway,' said Gondo, 'lots of people do it. There is one

white officer of ours who has welded a tractor seat to the
bonnet of his truck, and he makes the local headman sit in it
when he drives around. He has never hit a land mine yet.' He
went back to his maps.

But of course the locals didn't always know where the land
mines were. Neither the driver nor the passengers of the Ngenga
Ngenga bus knew that a mine had been laid under the edge of
a culvert near Vocola. I can't remember how many people died
in that explosion. Bits of their bodies were lodged up in the
surrounding mopani trees. The crows and vultures feasted on
them for weeks afterwards.

Still, the practice of hostage taking spread, I discovered. Now
the soldiers were penning people within a ring of claymores at
night. It was a common tactic, when a patrol based up in the
bush at night, for them to lay claymores around the perimeter
of the camp. Claymores were curved explosive discs connected
together by electrical wire. The wires would be fed out to a
sentry in the middle. If the position was ambushed, the sentry
detonated the claymores and each one sprayed a lethal arc of
metal shrapnel into the bush in front. It was said that, if correctly positioned, they would kill anyone within fifty yards.

I had always been a bit nervous about claymores. I worried
about them being set off accidentally, or being detonated by a
nervous sentry and killing other soldiers or friendly civilians.
And I had read somewhere that in Vietnam the guerrillas would
creep up to American patrols dossed down for the night and
quietly turn the claymores around so that they faced in towards
the sleeping GIs. Then the guerrillas would retreat, and fire off
a few rounds so that the Americans, believing themselves to be
under attack, would detonate the claymores in on themselves.

Now my soldiers, when they based up in the bush at night,
were just assuming that their position had been compromised.
They would collect a group of locals and pen them within an
inward facing circle of claymores. They would tell the locals
that if there was an ambush that night, the claymores would

be detonated. I tried to ban this practice, but I knew it continued out there in the bush at night, when they were on their own, though the threat was never put into action while I was there.

Matabele guerrillas from ZIPRA had started to infiltrate in a big way now. And as well as battling with their enemies from the rival ZANLA, they had time over for us. Their tactics were different from ZANLA, however: they were better trained and most had been through conventional infantry courses. It was a bit of a shock for us, really. We were used to spending most of our time trying to hunt down guerrillas; we felt pretty confident that once we found them we could outfight them.

Not long after the RLI fiasco we finally caught up with a new ZIPRA unit that we'd heard had just moved into the area. We had expected them and had quite good intelligence about them; I even knew some of their names.

Chipikiri outdid himself tracking that day. He correctly anticipated their tricks and took short cuts to save time. Finally he came to a place under some trees where they had rested – two hours before, he reckoned. He was down on his hands and knees again and he came up frowning. 'This group,' he indicated the tracks of the ten we'd been following, 'have now been joined by another group,' and he started counting on his fingers. 'Now there are more than fifty.'

Fifty? Jesus! We were, as usual, two sticks, twelve in all. I pondered what to do.

'Do you think some might be civilians or *mujibas*?' I asked Chipikiri.

'No, they are all men, and they are wearing boots and carrying heavy things.'

It was mid-afternoon. I got on the radio and arranged for a stop line to be deployed ahead of us to cut off the terrs. But it would take the soldiers several hours to get into place. While I was still considering my options, something whistled overhead and exploded. *They* were initiating the contact. This was pretty unusual. We skirmished forward and I shouted a command to the gunner at left point to wheel around in a flanking move. As I did so, I heard four sharp blasts of a whistle, as the guerrilla commander also moved his men to a new position. We had a text-book battle, skirmishing from hill to hill, flanking round, pulling back, and I kept hearing his whistle blasts counteracting our tactics.

Finally we grew short of ammunition and pulled back as night fell. One of our men was slightly injured, but for the most part we had been more than five hundred yards apart. We were exhausted and the soldiers were quite shaken.

'Those ones,' said my corporal, 'I think those ones have been to battle school also,' and he shook his head in admiration. It was the first time that terrs had not fled from us.

Back at Avoca, I recounted the incident to Gondo. 'I don't know, the terrs are getting better trained and better armed and they're coming in bigger numbers and we have almost no information from the people,' I confided. 'I think we may have lost this area now – for good.'

'I know,' he said, 'but we must hold the line while they negotiate. That's what you always told me.'

It was some months after Ian Smith's famous surrender speech, where he acknowledged the inevitability of handing Rhodesia over to black rule, and I was sitting at the verandah table teaching Gondo to do sitreps and general admin. It had recently been announced that, for the first time, blacks could become officers and he needed to learn how to do all this if he was to get commissioned.

'By the way,' said Gondo, 'there's a radio message for you from Dispol Gwanda.' Dispol Gwanda was the police district HQ. Gondo handed me a radio message sheet, folded in half.

'Why don't you open it?' he suggested.

I flipped it open. It was two lines long: *Your release now approved by Comops. Report to Bulawayo HQ and return all kit and equipment. Good luck.* I looked up and Gondo was grinning at me from the other side of the table. 'So finally you get away,' he said.

I felt a huge relief and at the same time, guilt at going.

That night Gondo and I were eating supper on the verandah, with Moses smashing things down from time to time, when the radio operator came running up the steps. 'Sah, sah, your father is on the radio.'

'My *father*? Are you sure?'

'Yes, sah, sure, sure,' he said. 'He is calling from Alpha Base, in op Hurricane. He has patched through.'

Though my father was now well into his fifties he was still eligible for call-up and he was usually deployed to relay stations because of his radio expertise. I jogged over to the radio tent and transmitted our call sign. And back came my father's faint voice against a background of ocean waves. He sounded hundreds of miles away. He was hundreds of miles away.

'How are you, Pete? Over,' he asked.

'I'm fine, Dad. I've got my release, over.'

'Yes, I know, a Ministry of Manpower letter arrived for you here, and we opened it. We've spoken to Cambridge, and they've kept your place open, copied?'

'Copied. That's great news.'

'And we've booked you on Sunday night's flight, via Joburg. Copied.'

'Roger, copied.' I couldn't believe I was actually going to get away.

'I'll be back by the weekend so I'll see you at home, over.'

'See you then, Dad, over.'

'See you then, Pete. Over.' And his voice was replaced by the sound of the sea again.

It took me several days to wind things up and hand over to Gondo. The unit was getting ready to move on anyway. One of the last things I did was to write a recommendation that he be commissioned.

On a Thursday morning, early, they all paraded and I said goodbye. Gondo made a very brief speech, just saying they'd enjoyed working with me and that they all wished me luck at university. Then he presented me with a gift. It was a beautifully soft *kaross*, a quilt made of thirty-six rock-dassie pelts, superbly cured. All along one end the dassie pelts had been left intact to include the eye sockets, and along the other end protruded the tails.

'We know it is very cold in England,' said Gondo, 'and that there is even snow there, so we have made you this very warm blanket so you don't freeze at night. *Endai zvakanaka* – Go well.'

I left later that morning. Gondo saw me to my Land Rover. We stood there in the dappled shade of the fever tree, while arund us the soldiers tooled up for another patrol, stripping down their rifles and cleaning them, loading their magazines, sorting through ration packs. It was an awkward farewell, really. First he saluted, the RAR fist-on-heart salute. Then we shook hands the Shona way, reversing the grip with each shake. And then we clumsily hugged each other. Moses had loaded his kitbag and pots and pans into the back and was sitting up front now, waiting for me.

'Bye, then,' I said weakly and got into the vehicle. Gondo held up his palm in a static wave, like a Red Indian.

'*Sarai zvenu!* – Stay well,' I called over to the men. They all waved and some lifted their rifles above their heads in a weary victory salute. I put the Land Rover into gear and drove away from the war.

On Thursday night I stayed at Filabusi and they had a farewell bash for me at the mess. Everyone got very drunk and I think I made a rather bad, slurred speech. Then they presented me with a silver tankard, just like the one Form Three had given me at St George's. The tankard was inscribed: *Peter, Best wishes for the future, Member-in-charge and staff, BSAP Filabusi.* I have it still, although the silver plating has tarnished, a bit like the buttons on chief Maduna's jacket.

Friday I spent in Bulawayo returning kit and completing paperwork. I had to sign a document accepting that I would be called up to serve when I returned. I spent Friday night in a bare barracks at Stops Camp in Bulawayo, and early the next morning I took a police truck to Salisbury. I arrived late on Saturday afternoon, completely exhausted. I talked briefly to my parents and then went for a rest. I woke up on Sunday afternoon, shortly before we had to set off for the airport. My mother had packed all the civilian clothes I owned in our best suitcase. But there weren't very many, I had been in uniform of one sort or another almost all my life. The few civilian clothes I had were flimsy and tropical, nothing warm. On top of the clothes she had carefully laid the folded *kaross*.

I flew first to Johannesburg on an Air Rhodesia flight. Because of sanctions no international airlines flew into Salisbury. I sat at a window seat, craning down at the land far away below, until it looked like the Ordnance Survey maps by which I'd navigated through the war. And as we got higher and higher into the ragged edges of cloud the land below seemed unreal, a patchwork of beige and ochre and khaki. It was hard to believe that down there, 20,000 feet below, in that delicate patchwork landscape, people were laying ambushes, detonating land mines, tracking each other through the bush and shooting one another. It all seemed monumentally pointless, from up there.

I felt a wave of relief that I was still alive, that I hadn't been killed in this stupid little war, that I was going to be allowed to live to be an adult after all.

In Joburg I changed flights onto South African Airways and after a half-bottle of Cape chardonnay, I soon fell asleep. And in my sleep I dreamt troublesome dreams. Not dreams of violence and danger, those came later, but dreams of the villages that had been burnt. And in these dreams the woman knitting with the yelping puppies at her bare feet was sitting on her bench against her burning hut. On the wall of the burning hut was written the motto *Hate us and see if we mind.* She looked up from her knitting and smiled. The youth with the dungarees and the shiny gelled hair was with her, hunched over his feet again, studiously clipping his toenails. He looked up at me and said: *Hate us and see if we mind,* and he smiled too. And in the dream I tried to shout out, 'But I don't hate you – I don't hate anyone . . .', but my mouth wouldn't make the words. So I tried again, but a group of little children had surrounded me and they chanted: '*Mukiwa! Mukiwa! Mukiwa!*' in shrill, piping voices which drowned me out. And the woman kept on knitting and the youth kept on clipping and the puppies kept on yelping, and no one could hear me at all.

Seventeen

After just over a year away, I returned to Rhodesia in 1978. My elder sister, Jain, was killed on 22 April of that year. She was twenty-seven years old and about to be married. She died together with her fiancé, Neville Williams, and their best man to be, Mark Ewing. The sole survivor was Mark's fox terrier.

It was early evening and they were driving back to Shamva, a town in the North East, when the car ran into an army ambush. Jain and Mark were killed instantly. Neville lived a short time. He was put on a drip by an army medic and driven to Salisbury, to the main casualty department at Andrew Fleming hospital. But he was dead on arrival. Friends of Jain's in Shamva phoned ahead to casualty to warn the sister-in-charge to make sure my mother was not on duty.

The evening the news was broken, my father had just arrived home from military call-up, and my little sister, Georgina, had just come out of hospital after having her tonsils removed. The next day they drove out to the ambush site with the local police. The car had already been removed and there was nothing much to see there. My mother picked some long pink tasselled grass which she later pressed between the pages of her diary and, as they were leaving, she found one of Jain's sandals on the verge. It had a tiny spot of blood on it. The other sandal was at the police station, and Georgina put them on, even though they were too big, and she wore them constantly for six months until they fell apart.

At the police station some members of the army stick responsible were in custody, and the police presented the man in charge to my parents. My father shook his hand and mumbled something about forgiveness, but my mother refused to shake hands. They drove back from Shamva to Salisbury through Enterprise late that afternoon despite being warned that this was 'Apache country' completely infiltrated by guerrillas. They no longer cared.

My father subsequently sought legal advice about taking action against the army, but he was warned that he would simply be blocked by the Victims of Terrorism (Compensation) Act, an omnipotent piece of legislation by which the security forces could not be held responsible for any harm done or law broken in the course of their duties. The Act only applied if the duties were being carried out in good faith. But it was the security forces themselves who decided if their actions were bona fide. A subsequent inquest recorded a verdict of accidental death.

I was in the middle of university exams when my father called to tell me the terrible news. I made arrangements to return as soon as possible and just before I left I received a long letter from my father, written immediately after Jain's death. His usually firm sloping handwriting was shaky and inconsistent.

'Georgina says the last time she saw her, Jain said that everything was going so well, she thought something terrible must happen soon,' he wrote. 'Jain was absolutely at her peak – in love, just completed furnishing their cottage, happy as can be – and then this. It is the worst experience any of us have ever had, and we just can't realize what has happened.'

From time to time in the letter, the tense slipped. He wrote that he had visited the cottage. 'Jain has just about finished furnishing it. In the last few weeks she had bought a three-piece suite and a fridge-freezer; she just about spent all her money on it. I took some photographs before anything had been touched.'

The photos were enclosed with the letter. They were in black and white, it was almost impossible to get colour film by then, and they reminded me of scene-of-crime photographs, forensically cataloguing the contents of their cottage. The sitting room with its new suite, newspapers casually thrown down on the sofa, and through the open door the new fridge-freezer in the kitchen. Georgina told me later that they had found a beef casserole still bubbling away slowly in the oven, on low heat. In another shot, the hi-fi, with a record out that she would never play now, and the sewing machine, with some cloth there ready to be made up. The bedroom with mosquito spray on the bedside table and a Supersonic radio, just like the one at the bedside of Doug Hammond, the murdered rancher. In fact the photos reminded me of that day at Hammond's ranch house, stumbling upon the intimate mundanities of an interrupted life.

They cremated my sister and her fiancé together at Warren Hills, just outside Salisbury, on the Bulawayo road. Her body was in a white coffin, with an arrangement of blue orchids set on the lid, like a bridal bouquet. And at the end of the service Georgina placed a small bridesmaid's posy on the coffin. Among the hymns my mother had included *Abide with Me*, which Jain and I used to sing on our way across the Hunyani bridge, because we were sure the bridge was land-mined. We would roll down the windows and bellow:

> *Abide with me, fast falls the eventide;*
> *The darkness deepens, Lord, with me abide!*
> *When other helpers fail, and comforts flee,*
> *Help of the helpless, O abide with me.*

The theory was that if you were killed with *Abide with Me* on your lips, you wouldn't have to queue for heaven. Jain hated queues.

After the funeral my mother was distraught. All her sanguine medical savoir-faire, her experience of twenty-five years of dealing with illness and death, deserted her. When a bundle of Jain's clothes came back from Doves Morgan, the undertakers, she made a bonfire and burnt them in the garden. And she became obsessed with tracking down Jain's wristwatch and her topaz ring, which had gone missing at the death scene. Georgina, who was just eleven, didn't seem to be able to take it in. She knew that Jain had gone but I suspect that she thought Jain would eventually come back. Jain was sixteen years older than Georgina, and had been like a second mother to her.

I felt guilty at Jain's death almost immediately. I knew my parents had tried to prepare themselves for the possibility that something might happen to me. Although I never worried them with the details of my wartime experiences, they knew that there had been some hairy times. But Jain was always the homemaker, keeper of the family flame, she would be our anchor when I went away to foreign places and my parents grew older. And now she was gone without farewells.

I had never seen my parents like this, so vulnerable, exposed and hopeless. They seemed suddenly old now, leaving robust middle age behind. My father's hair, still thick and wavy, seemed to fade straight to white. The red in my mother's hair, still waist length, was riven through with the grey of grief.

I tried hard to comfort them, observing my duties as the eldest child now, but the truth was we had always been rather reserved with one another, and we almost never made physical contact. We didn't really hug or kiss in greeting or anything like that. But we talked and talked and talked after Jain's death. My mother spent her time answering letters of condolence, and she read the Bible and Kahlil Gibran and just about anyone else who purveyed the idea of an afterlife.

My father was back at work the day after the funeral but at night, when he returned, he just sat in his chair, not reading whatever he was reading. He set about gathering up all the photos of Jain and placing them meticulously in several albums, to make up a history of her life: the little baby left behind in Kensington, when her parents first came out to Africa. the girl with pigtails and a felt hat on her first day at a new junior school, on horseback at a gymkhana, birthday parties at Silverstream, posing with me at the top of Spitzkop mountain, holding a baby Georgina on her hip, in the chorus of Iolanthe at Marymount in Umtali, graduating from Teachers' Training College in Bulawayo. And my father framed the batiks she had made, and the pictures she had painted, and he hung them on the sitting-room wall, moving aside the grand gilt-framed oil of our ancestor on horseback to make room for them.

In all of my attempts as a self-appointed cheerleader of emotional recovery I postponed my own grieving, thinking to come back to it when the immediate tasks of family survival had been achieved. But it didn't work like that, I discovered. Grief was not an emotion that broached delay. And in time the relief that grieving eventually brings was replaced by the labyrinth of guilt. In the back of my mind, unbidden, was the absurd notion that had I been killed at war, Jain would have been spared. That fate had required a sacrifice from us. I had been kept alive, so now she had to pay the price. It was a notion that persisted for years afterwards. And for years, whenever I was in danger of enjoying myself, I felt guilty at doing so, and pulled back. Survival was just about acceptable but happiness seemed inappropriate.

A few days after entering the country, I had received my callup papers from the Ministry of Manpower. I phoned and explained that I had only returned for a matter of weeks because of my sister's death, and would soon be going back to university. I added that as she had been killed by the army, I was particularly disinclined to return to uniform under the circumstances. But none of it made any difference and I was ordered to report for service immediately or go to jail. They reminded me of the document that I had signed on my release. Apparently it said that I had to go back into the security forces whenever, and as soon as, I returned. I couldn't believe it, that they were this desperate for manpower. So with a heavy heart I opened my black tin trunk and broke out my combat gear.

There had been a compromise hammered out over my posting. I pointed out that if they put me straight back in the field, I would need refresher training, and by the time I'd done that, it would be time for me to go back to university. So they posted me to the police ballistics unit, based in Salisbury, where I could at least be near to my parents. Ballistics was situated in the armoury on the edge of Morris Depot, where I had trained. I had been there once before, to the Black Museum – the gory gallery of different ways to die violently.

I can't remember much about my four months' service there. I was still numb from the loss of Jain. I remember we spent most of our time cross-matching bullets from battle scenes and working out where particular guerrilla groups were heading, what their patterns of movement were. We also fitted various anti-ambush devices to vehicles. And it was while testing one of these devices that I was most nearly killed.

This particular device consisted of AK rifles fitted to an armoured Land Rover, two weapons facing either side. They were operated remotely by the driver, who pressed two red buttons on the dashboard, one for the left guns and one for the right. The buttons connected to a starter solenoid which pulled a wire which pulled the trigger. It was pretty basic really. The whole idea was that when you were ambushed, you needed to make some response immediately. If you could fire off a couple of magazines in the right general direction, this was often enough to convince the guerrillas not to hang around. We fitted remote-controlled grenade launchers too, on the same principle, three on each side at different gradients so that they would remotely lob grenades to different distances.

One day we were down at the range test-firing one of these remote-firing AK systems. We had parked the vehicle with its right-hand side facing the butts, and the African armourer got in to test fire the right-hand guns, so I could sight them correctly. I stood on the left side, away from the line of fire, and gave him the all clear. When he hit the right-hand button, the left guns fired and bullets flew all around me. I could actually feel the air blowing around my head, the bullets were so close. Behind me the bullets had ripped into the side of the range shed, forming two neat clusters, one on either side of me.

From the armoury I used to watch the new recruits, square-bashing, and running and wrestling with the obstacle course. I could hear the instructors bellowing at them. And I saw Pops Crabb bullying them into conformity and using all the same purple phrases of abuse. But I didn't go over and talk to Pops. I had nothing to say to him, really, nothing at all. The recruits he was yelling at now looked so young, and so fresh-faced, just as we had once looked. And although I wasn't yet twenty, I felt very old looking at them. Very old indeed, and tired.

In the evenings I went home to my parents and tried to fill the space, chatting brightly about my experiences at Cambridge. And at night I lay on my bed, miserable and confused and guilty, until I drifted off into a troubled sleep.

Quite often the phone would ring during the weekend or in the middle of the night and it would be the casualty department needing my mother to attend an emergency. My mother would pull on her white coat, and put her hair up in a bun and knock quietly on my door. I would be dressed already, and I would put the pistol in my shoulder holster under my shirt and drive my mother to the hospital. Even the drive into town could be dangerous now as there had been attacks right up to the suburbs.

In a sleepy daze we would drive down the Enterprise road,

past Nazareth House, where the old priest had taught me about *King Lear*, past the old British Governor's red-brick house, now used as a civil service training centre, past the Central Prison with its looming white guard towers, and down Rhodes Avenue to the hospital.

When we got there injured soldiers would arrive by helicopter on the landing-pad, if it was still light, or after dark in army ambulances, or just in the back of armoured trucks; young men swathed in bloody bandages, drips dangling above them, groaning in pain or knocked out by morphine. Sometimes they would be dead on arrival. DOA. Like my sister's fiancé, Neville. The tough white nurses, some themselves so young, paled with the waste of it all. My mother would bristle with efficiency. I think it was only immersed in such pressure that she could really forget.

After it was all over, I would drive my mother back home. She would make a pot of tea and we would sit at the table in the garden and wait for the sun to come up, because neither of us would sleep now. We talked about how bad things had got and what would happen next. An unnatural quietness encompassed the city, only broken by the lonely sound of dogs barking across the suburbs. The night was so still it felt like the whole country was holding its breath. The soldiers in their ambushes and OPs, the Africans cooped up now in what were officially called Protected Villages, but which they called concentration camps, the white farmers in their fortresses, the guerrillas preparing stealthy attacks or hurrying away after them.

The situation had deteriorated quite sharply in my absence. There had been a so-called 'internal settlement' between Ian Smith and some of the black nationalist leaders, but Robert Mugabe and Joshua Nkomo has stayed out and the war had only intensified. The main 'internal leader', the great black hope, was Bishop Muzorewa, a diminutive man that not even the whites took seriously. Even while they tried to build him up, they tore him down.

We talked, my mother and I, about people we knew who had been killed, and there seemed to be more and more of them. Eventually the dawn would come and save us with its birdsong and its vivid palate of streaked oranges and reds, to remind us that Africa was still a place of beauty after all.

From time to time I went out to the operational areas, to collect ballistics evidence. Mostly I went to Operation Hurricane, north-east of Salisbury. Once I ran into a platoon of RAR at a fire-force base near Mount Darwin, and I wondered whether Sergeant Major Gondo or anyone else I knew might be among them. In the beginning, Gondo had written to me quite often at Cambridge. Short, painfully formal letters about operations, complete with little diagrams of contacts and ambushes. He would seek my advice on battle plans and tactics. In one letter he told me that he had been invited to apply for a commission, but after thinking about it for a long time he had decided not to go for it. It was the paperwork, he said, he would never be good enough at the paperwork.

Eventually the letters tailed off. The last thing I got from him was a Christmas card. It was an official RAR card with a picture of the regimental mascot, a white billy goat wearing a green coat which bore the unit's emblem, crossed *knobkerries*.

But the RAR soldiers at the Mount Darwin fire-force base were from a different battalion and they didn't know Gondo. They seemed younger and listless and taciturn. As I left they asked me to give a young boy a lift to my next stop along the way. The boy, about fifteen, climbed into the back, next to the spare tyre and the shovel and wheel jack. After a few miles he began frantically banging on the roof. I pulled over to find out what the problem was.

He was in tears. 'Please, sah,' he sobbed, 'I will tell you what you want. There is no need to kill me. I will say everything I know.'

'What's the matter with you, boy? Why are you crying?' I asked.

'You think I am *mujiba*, sah, that I have the information. Please, sah, don't kill me. I am still too young.'

I was incredulous. 'Why do you think I'm going to kill you, for God's sake?'

'Because I have seen your shovel here. You are going to drive me into the bush and make me dig my own grave, and then you will shoot me and put me inside there. And there will be no one to see. No one to witness. I have heard about this. Please don't do it to me, I pray you.'

I wondered just how terrible the war had become since I had been away, and I longed to be gone from this place, gone far away across the sea.

After four months I was finally allowed to leave, to go back to university. I went up to Warren Hills to see my sister's grave one last time before I left. Jain and Neville and Mark were buried next to one another in the crematorium park. Their ashes were built into one of the low granite walls that curve gently through the park. Each one had a little brass plaque with a simple inscription. Behind the wall was a flowerbed dense with canna and azaleas and frangipani shrubs. The air was heady with jasmine and honeysuckle. Above the graves, callused old msasa trees creaked and sighed and groaned in the chill winter breeze. Black-eyed bulbuls, their feathers puffed up against the cold, hopped and chirruped on the branches.

A very old black man in faded green overalls and a floppy hat was tending the garden with a rake. He hobbled by, and as he passed me he tugged his floppy hat in greeting and said, 'Sorry, *baas*, for your loss. But I will take good care of your ancestors' graves.' He stood there for a while and I suppose he was angling for a tip, but I was too self-absorbed to notice.

When I got home, I took off my uniform with relief, and resolved never to come back to Rhodesia. And I never did.

Book Three

Book Three

Eighteen

When I did return three years later, it was to another country, Zimbabwe – 'house of stone'. It had a 'former terrorist', Robert Mugabe, as prime minister and cabinet ministers who called each other comrade. The leader of the Crocodile Gang, Willie Ndangana, who had murdered oom Piet Oberholzer, was now Deputy Minister of Paramilitary Affairs, whatever that meant. Other names had been changed too, by order of a special Place Names Commission. Salisbury was now Harare, after the black chief whose land it was originally, and most of the old white pioneer street names had gone, dispensed instead to black politicians. There was said to be a Robert Mugabe Avenue in every town in the land. There appeared to be two in Umtali, which had been renamed Mutare. The commission, in its search for nominal purity, said that this had been its original Shona name, corrupted by the settlers. Rhodes's and Founders' weekend, a public holiday in honour of Cecil Rhodes and the other white pioneers, was renamed Heroes' and Ancestors'. Some whites had nicknamed it Gooks' and Spooks'.

The civil service, the army and police had been rapidly Africanized. The Rhodesia Broadcasting Corporation was now the Zimbabwe Broadcasting Corporation, and it had gone from being the publicity arm of Ian Smith's Rhodesian Front to being the enthusiastic trumpeters for ZANU(PF) the new ruling party. The symbol of the ruling party, the crowing cockerel, the *jongwe*, was everywhere.

For most of the white community it was a pretty distressing

time. A time when old value systems had been up-ended and old devils had suddenly become gods; when witch doctors became traditional healers and formed their own trade union; when servants insisted on being called domestic workers, joined the Party, acquired a surname and demanded the minimum wage. When you could be prosecuted for calling a black adult 'boy' and thrown in jail if you breathed the word *kaffir*.

It was all too distressing for many, who poured over the border to South Africa seeking sanctuary from change. From 300,000 at its peak, the white population was now down to about 150,000 and falling. Some of those who left the country for a new life could not afford to take their elderly relatives with them. They were left behind with the promise that they would be collected as soon as their families had become established. But many of these old whites remained unclaimed, languishing in Nazareth House and other old-age homes, marooned by the great tide of history, waiting to die – bewildered.

White society was seriously wounded. Peace had achieved something fifteen years of war could not. It had robbed us of our identity. All around me, as I watched, white society shrivelled and changed. In search of a divine reassurance, whites flocked in great numbers to the new evangelical churches which had sprung up across the suburbs, peddling the sedative of certainty in an uncertain world.

Slowly the whites were undergoing a metamorphosis from settler to expatriate. The traditional 'Rhodie' shrank back into a *laager* of home and video, *braaivleis* and sports club, muttering privately about how the blacks were ruining God's own country. The place was turning into a banana republic, they complained. The new president, the ceremonial head of state, was even *called* Banana, the Reverend Canaan Banana. The new Zimbabwe flag they disparaged as a garish beach-chair cover, made worse by the presence, at one end, of the sinister red star of communism. Even the fact that we no longer had to go to war was a transient relief – many became nostalgic for it, the camaraderie of it all, the sense of purpose, now lost.

But not all were whinging Rhodies. There were thousands, whites and blacks, who came back from abroad to take part in the bold new experiment, to help create a multiracial society that would be the envy of Africa. They called us 'returnees' and we believed in the government's policy of reconciliation – between races and between tribes.

I revelled in that brief and liberating period of social anarchy that marked the change between societies. I loved the bizarre mix of people. The Scandinavian sandal brigade and the Third World groupies, the sudden flood of communist diplomats: shifty Balkans, hard-drinking Russians and bearded Cubans, the censoriously sincere aid workers, the *jeunese dorée* from Western ambassadorial nurseries, the con men and shysters who called themselves international businessmen. The cultural boycott was over, so we no longer had to get by on Jimmy Edwards and the theatrical cast-offs. Now Bob Marley performed at our independence celebrations and UB40, Paul Simon and Michael Jackson played Harare.

I had come back to do my field research for an Oxford doctorate on the Rhodesian war, which I'd embarked on after my law degree at Cambridge, unwilling to plunge back into the war itself. My choice of thesis was impelled mostly by personal curiosity. I wanted to unravel something I'd been too close to at the time to comprehend fully, and in doing so I hoped to put to rest some of the demons that still raged in my head. I began trawling the library of the Ministry of Information and going to see all manner of security-force commanders, my old bosses, collecting secret documents and conspiracy theories, and listening to them shuffle the blame on to each other.

But as my research grant dwindled, I realized I had to find a job to subsidize myself while I tried to complete the doctorate.

So I put on a suit and tie and went to work at a prominent legal firm, Scanlen and Holderness, in their smart air-conditioned offices at the top of a new Harare 'skyscraper'. It had panoramic views out over the fountains and jacaranda trees and the flower-sellers on Cecil Square, where the British flag was first hoisted in 1890 to mark the occupation of Mashonaland by white settlers. The park was now called African Unity Square, but from my vantage point high above it, I could see that the paths had been laid down in the pattern of a Union Jack.

At Scanlen and Holderness I had an office all to myself and, for the first and only time in my life, a personal secretary. I was finally doing a job my father could respect – I was a lawyer. Although it was only a stopgap job, it was a pleasant enough existence. At lunch I strolled down past the Shona sculpture hawkers to one of the outdoor cafés that lined the First Street pedestrian mall, and friends passed by and stopped for coffee and exchanged gossip and invited me to parties. In the evenings I got in my ancient Renault 4, the car in which I had first learnt to drive all those years ago in Mangula, the one with the gear stick that came out of the dashboard, and drove back to the cottage I shared with my girlfriend.

I tried to write up my research. But mostly I went out to parties, attended embassy soirées, gorged myself at *braaivleis* out on the farms, or played tennis and squash. My life was filled with the tinkling of ice in tall drinks, the pat of tennis ball over net, waking up to the cat on the pillow and fresh orange juice in the morning. I spent time with my parents like I'd never really done before. I swam in their pool with its rock waterfall designed by my father, surrounded by beds of cannas, and bougainvillaea and a special grand cactus, of which my mother was particularly proud, a euphorbia called Queen of the Night that only flowered after dark. The restaurants were cheap, and the beer was cold and plentiful, sanctions were over, petrol rationing had finally been lifted, and no one was shooting at us. For the first time we were enjoying the country without a conscience. We were no longer in charge and, frankly, it was a relief.

Slowly the rest of the world seemed to fade away and feel foreign again. The sun warmed my bones and melted my marrow to honey and the ambition oozed out of me on to the fresh breeze that blew down from the Domboshawa Hills and rustled the ivy at my window.

But although we were enjoying a peaceful post-colonial life in Harare, tensions were growing down in Matabeleland, which was deep in drought again. The Matabeles were grumbling that they were being starved of drought relief and government development funds. Finally, in early 1982, less than two years after independence, the thin membrane of the tribal alliance ripped apart, just as the white doom-sayers had eagerly warned it would. The prime minister denounced the Matabele leader, Joshua Nkomo, as 'a cobra in the house' and fired him from the cabinet. Shortly afterwards he fled to England in fear of his life.

Senior Matabele officers, former members of the Matabele guerrilla army, ZIPRA, were arrested on suspicion of planning a *coup d'état*, and a wave of disenchantment swept through the ranks of the former Matabele guerrillas. They claimed they were being discriminated against in the new Zimbabwe National Army, and four thousand of them deserted, many with their weapons.

There was news of sporadic attacks in Matabeleland by rogue guerrillas, and a truckload of them drove past the prime minister's residence next to St George's and sprayed it with gunfire. The local papers began to call them 'dissidents', and the early optimism of independence finally dissolved.

The tempo of violence picked up throughout that year. Six foreign tourists on an Africa overland expedition were kidnapped as they drove down the main road from Victoria Falls to Bulawayo. And, in the most audacious attack so far, thirteen aircraft, half of the air force's fighter planes, were blown up at

Thornhill air base outside Gweru in the Midlands. The prime minister was said to have turned pale with rage. South African saboteurs with 'inside help' were suspected, and six white air force officers, including the force's two most senior men, were arrested.

Down in Matabeleland the cattle ranches and isolated mines were becoming the new targets of the 'dissident' Matabele deserters, just like they had been in the Rhodesian war.

It was against this background that our firm agreed to represent the seven Matabele commanders accused of plotting a *coup*. Their arrest had followed the discovery of several huge arms caches at various sites where Matabele guerrillas were waiting to be demobilized or integrated into the new National Army. One of them was near Filabusi, where I had been stationed in the war. The caches were stuffed with rifles, bazookas, grenades, anti-aircraft missiles, land mines, machine guns and ammunition – the contents of fifty railway wagons – quite enough to start a conventional war, never mind a guerrilla one. The seven now faced the death sentence for high treason, and alternative charges of illegal possession of arms of war. After only a few months at my new job, I was asked to clear my desk and assist in the trial.

The accused were being held inside Chikurubi Maximum Security prison, out on the eastern edge of town. Chikurubi was a large modern hexagonal fortress of raw, unpainted concrete, built by the Rhodesians for the most dangerous Category 'A' prisoners. It loomed improbably from a copse of eucalyptus trees, amidst manicured tobacco beds and maize fields and hothouse flowers. I drove out with my boss to interview our clients for what was to become a marathon case. Our briefcases were checked for weapons and then a warder escorted us into the bowels of the building, clanging through several layers of gates and doors and finally into a little visitors' cubicle. However hot it was outside, within it was always chill. Not even the African heat, it seemed, could penetrate Chikurubi's thick concrete crust.

Behind the iron grille sat two of our clients, wearing prison uniform, khaki shirt with baggy khaki shorts, just like the old murderers who used to weed the lawns at Morris Depot and watch while we bayoneted their straw effigies of guerrillas. The first was General Lookout Masuku, the former Commander of ZIPRA and, until his arrest, the Deputy Commander of the new Zimbabwe National Army. 'Lookout' was his *nom de guerre*, or *chimurenga* name. When they returned from the war, many of the guerrillas had kept on their *chimurenga* names as badges of honour. 'Lookout' was pretty benign compared to some. The Minister of Women's Affairs was a formidable lady who still went by the name of comrade Spillblood.

I was slightly nervous of meeting Lookout Masuku. This was a man doused with infamy by white Rhodesia, the military head of an organization that during the war had shot down two civilian airliners as they took off from Kariba and later murdered the crash survivors. I peered through the grille at him. He was an elderly man with grizzled hair, very affable and genial as it turned out, but rather forgetful of any detail.

On the bench with Lookout Masuku sat Dumiso Dabengwa, considered by most to be the real Matabele leader. He was a much younger man, in his early forties, heavy set with a neatly cropped beard and an unblinking gaze, direct and disconcerting. Dabengwa had been the head of ZIPRA's intelligence, and during the war we called him the Black Russian, because he had trained in Moscow and was said to be a devout Marxist. He was an austere man, quietly spoken and reserved but sharply attentive.

Preparing for the treason trial soon took up my entire professional life, trying to unravel all the complexities of the returning guerrillas – the process of integrating the three armies, none of which considered themselves defeated on the battlefield. That Dabengwa's men had cached weapons was beyond doubt, everyone was still holding back weapons in those politically volatile days, using them as an insurance policy in case things went wrong. But our defence was that Dabengwa and Masuku, far from plotting to bring Mugabe down, were regarded as 'sell-outs' by many of their more radical rank and file for agreeing to join the government of national unity. In fact they had done their best to promote reconciliation between the two tribes.

In the months leading up to the trial, I travelled the ten miles out to Chikurubi prison on an almost daily basis, armed with bulging lever-arch files. I would talk to the accused, going over their statements, getting their assistance in tracking down defence witnesses. In the long process I got to know my clients quite well. And slowly we opened up to one another, chatting about their wartime experiences.

Mostly they had been outside the country, at base camps in Zambia or training in Russia or Cuba. But several of the younger ones, in their thirties, had been on active operations inside the country. Slowly I probed for more detail, I was fascinated to hear what it had really been like for them. These were the first ex-guerrillas I'd really spoken to at any length. Their war sounded a lot more social than mine, they seemed to have spent most of their time holding political gatherings that turned into parties. By the end, they said, they could move around freely without worrying about 'the enemy'. They always referred to the old security forces as that – 'the enemy' – and whenever they did it made me feel uneasy.

At first they didn't press me on what I'd done during the war, but one day one of the young commanders mentioned that he had carried out 'some missions' around Filabusi.

'When were you there?' I asked.

''76, '77, around then.'

'I was there then too,' I blurted out.

He pulled his head back and surveyed me closely. 'With RAR?'

'Yup, and the Police Anti-Terrorist Unit,' I said.

'Based at Filabusi?'

'Uhuh. Godlwayo and Silalabuhwe, mostly.' I was beginning to get a bit apprehensive about all this, and I steered the conversation safely back to high treason.

The next day the young commander asked me more about my wartime experiences, and I found myself describing to him the last contact, the one where the guerrilla commander had blown his whistle to counteract my tactics, the one where we had been forced to pull back because we were running low on ammunition, where my corporal had shaken his head in admiration and said, 'Those ones, I think they have been to battle school too.'

The commander looked at me and said, 'That was my section. I was the one. I was the one blowing the whistle,' and he grinned broadly, and lifted his palm for a high five. I lifted my palm too and slapped it against his, and only the metal grille prevented our hands from touching.

'You were quite all right too,' he said sportingly. 'Quite all right indeed.'

Later, as the warder let me out with a jangle of keys and banging of bolts, I wondered what had happened to us all. Five years ago we had been shooting at each other. Now Zimbabwe was liberated, he was in prison for high treason, wearing bandit khaki, and I was defending him. I felt like I'd returned to an old play but none of us were playing the same parts any more, we'd all been confusingly recast.

When I met the commander alone again, I waited until we had finished our legal business and as I gathered up my notes to leave I turned to him. 'You know, I'm sorry. About the war and everything.'

He looked puzzled. 'The war?'

'Yes, the liberation war. I'm sorry that we fought one another, that we were enemies. I—'

But he cut me short. 'Oh, that war,' he said dismissively.

'Well we were soldiers, you and I. We were soldiers together. Just on different sides.'

With that we parted and my little pre-rehearsed speech on how I'd ended up in the war and all my excuses and caveats, how young I'd been, and how I'd never supported the Rhodesian Front and Ian Smith, remained unsaid.

Finally the trial date arrived. I was wearing my new pinstriped suit, made to measure by the Indian tailor at Saville's, 'Outfitters to the Modern Gent'. Inside, the court was heaving. As well as a crush of supporters there were dozens of journalists from all over the world. The treason trial had all the elements of a political thriller, and it was being widely touted that its outcome would determine the young country's future.

The seven accused were all attired in sober dark suits, looking more like accountants than Marxist guerrillas. They were too many for the dock, so the court orderly escorted them up into the old wooden jury box. Jury trial had been dispensed with twenty years before, and the judge sat instead with two lay assessors. In another remarkable loop of history, the judge presiding was Hilary Squires, Ian Smith's former Minister of Law and Order, and the man who had been the officiating VIP at my passing-out parade at Morris Depot six years before.

I looked at Judge Squires now, above us on his wood and green-leather throne, kitted out in his red robes and greyish wig and I remembered marching past him that day, SO Crabb saluting and shouting: 'Eyiss, *right*!' as we snapped our heads round to look at him in his dark suit and homburg hat. I remembered his speech as we stood to attention, about how we were joining the finest counter-insurgency force in the world and how we were winning the war.

The rest of the cast gathered within the high ceilings and wood-panelled walls of the colonial courtroom that day was just as strange. The investigating officer was a senior white detective from the old Rhodesian Special Branch who had a quiff of Brylcreemed hair and long sideburns, like a country and western singer. The Attorney General, a punctilious Indian, had been ordered to prosecute the case in person. Our main defence advocate was the impressively named Adrian de Bourbon, tall, rotund, florid and every bit as flamboyant as his name suggested. Supporting him was Bryant Elliott, the earnest Scottish partner from Scanlen and Holderness who had handled the case from the outset, and myself, resplendent in my new Saville's made-to-measure suit.

The witnesses were former guerrillas, Marxists and Maoists and nationalists from both tribes, and former Rhodesian soldiers now integrated into the new National Army or recently retired from the fray. There were police informants, intelligence officers from the Central Intelligence Organization, the CIO. There were agents and double agents, some that were so devious that I still have no idea who they were really working for.

There was also the enticing spectre of comrade Max, a KGB agent who was based in Zambia and was impossible to subpoena. He formed the subject of a letter from Dabengwa to the KGB, and this was the state's prize piece of evidence. The letter had been intercepted by government intelligence agents and its veracity was beyond doubt. It was addressed to 'The honourable Chairman, KGB, Moscow' and signed by Dabengwa.

The letter dealt mostly with a request to leave in place the KGB's advisor, 'comrade Max', to counter the activities of western agents in Zimbabwe. President Mugabe, said the letter, was turning out to be 'more reactionary and pro-western' than his brief predecessor, Bishop Muzorewa. Crucially for our defence, however, the writer of the letter, one of Dabengwa's assistants, had shown the sense to include the rider: 'As far as political power in Zimbabwe is concerned, we consider this an internal affair for the people of Zimbabwe to decide.'

The legal precedents bandied about the courtroom were just as cosmopolitan as the cast. They were plucked from the time of Oliver Cromwell and the English Civil War, from the Anglo-Boer War in South Africa, and from the trials of Afrikaners who sympathized with the Nazis during the Second World War.

Events outside the court made our job even harder. The dissidents who had kidnapped the foreign tourists issued a demand that Dabengwa, Masuku and the others be released immediately, conclusive proof, in the government's eyes, that the accused were guilty as charged.

Meanwhile dissidents continued their attacks on white ranchers in Matabeleland. While the trial was in progress two more white families were killed by dissidents down there. First there was the Stratfords: Tania, twelve, and Candy, fifteen, and their grandparents. Newspaper reports told how they were made to kneel, their hands were tied behind their backs and then they were shot. A few weeks later, a white senator, Paul Savage, his daughter and her friend were also executed on their knees.

The army stepped up its operations in the South and the pressure for a conviction of our clients, accused of being the dissidents' leaders, grew fevered. Now whites too were baying for their blood.

Each day, against this backdrop of a steadily worsening security situation in the South, the seven accused would arrive from Chikurubi, caged in a prison truck flanked by a heavily armed escort. The truck would turn into the yard of the High Court in the Vincent Building, now renamed Mapondera after a chief prominent in the Shona rebellion. Outside, a crowd of several hundred supporters would whistle and ululate. And in the afternoon when the truck began its journey back to prison they were there again, dancing and cheering. When the truck had passed through, they scurried away in different directions, fearful of being followed by security agents of the CIO.

At lunch we consulted with the men in the holding cells below the court. Above, a deceptive peace reigned behind the distant shield of traffic noise. Flies buzzed against the panes in the quiet corridors and the court orderlies played draughts with bottle tops on a home-made board, slapping the tops down as they made their moves.

Finally, after twenty-eight days of dense legal argument and fifty-five witnesses, Judge Squires delivered his three-hour judgement. All seven accused were innocent of treason, he said, and only one, Misheck Velapi, a junior ZAPU official, he found guilty of possessing arms of war and sentenced to three years. As Velapi was led down to begin his sentence, he turned to the packed courtroom and gave a clenched-fist salute. He shouted, '*Zee!*' – the ZIPRA war cry.

'*Zee!*' the crowd roared back and the sound swelled to fill the courtroom and render Judge Squires's gavel inaudible.

'Stand firm against the forces of negation!' Velapi shouted, and then he was gone, bundled away by the prison officers into the holding cells below, his curiously stilted Marxist exhortation hanging in the courtroom.

For the rest there was jubilation. The court was still in uproar, Dabengwa gestured like a winning boxer and a huge cheer went up from the packed public gallery. Judge Squires banged his gavel irritably, but to no effect. He declared the accused free men, and they stepped down from their wooden pen. Dabengwa hugged his wife and shook our hands formally. I couldn't quite believe we'd done it. Adrian de Bourbon beamed with pride. Bryant Elliott allowed himself a brief, self-deprecating grin. The prosecution team scurried out of court looking grim – the result was a major embarrassment to the government. The trial had departed from its scripted outcome.

Dabengwa and the other five were taken down to the cells beneath the court to sign their liberty documents. Outside, the police were having trouble holding back the throng of jubilant supporters who were blocking Samora Machel Avenue as they waited to welcome the ZIPRA men to freedom. But the men failed to emerge. We went down to find out what the delay was, just in time to see them being led into the courtyard and hastily shoved into the prison trucks and driven away, back to

Chikurubi prison. A police officer confirmed that they had been redetained under the Emergency Regulations, the draconian set of laws inherited from Ian Smith. This had always been our second greatest fear, after a conviction, and it was not unexpected.

Upstairs we explained to their families that the men would not be coming home after all. And then we had to go outside and tell the throng of supporters and waiting journalists that our clients – though declared innocent – were prisoners once more. That in the new Zimbabwe, just as in the old Rhodesia, innocence was no guarantee of freedom.

The seven men were to spend another four years of their lives languishing in Chikurubi, despite various appeals. General Masuku never saw freedom properly again. He became ill there and was only allowed out to die.

As for me, I'd had enough of the law, African-style, after that. It was little better than window-dressing. The trial had gone ahead with all the legal trappings, but once the state had lost, they simply resorted to their all-powerful armoury of emergency regulations to rule by decree. All we were doing was helping to camouflage the reality of it. I felt it was pointless to go on, and I resigned from Scanlen and Holderness. My brief legal career was at an end.

I went back to writing my thesis, and in between time I took up freelance journalism to earn a living. I'd already done bits for the *Economist* and the odd travel piece for *The Sunday Times*. Now I began stringing for other publications and for radio stations and wire services. Though not the big story it had been during the war, it was still quite a lively beat. We covered the African staples of wildlife, conservation and drought, and also the volatile political situation. The redistribution of farmland from whites to blacks and the continuing tensions in Matabeleland, though after a tough 'pacification' campaign by the army it had got quieter down there and the army had cut back its presence.

We also covered a series of cases in which whites fell foul of a government running scared from South African destabilization tactics. Chikurubi was filling up with troublesome whites: intelligence officers, an MP, an ex-general, several farmers and even a dentist who had advocated the secession of Matabeleland. Bishop Muzorewa was also detained briefly on suspicion of subversion. They all joined Dabengwa and company in prison. The government's official policy of postwar reconciliation between the races and tribes was becoming pretty threadbare.

In the same court where we had defended Dabengwa and his men, I now reported on the trial of the air force officers accused of blowing up their own fighter planes. They told how they had been denied access to lawyers, how they were put in leg irons, handcuffed and hooded and then beaten with metal pipes, how they had wires attached to their feet and backs and were tortured with electric shocks.

One officer recounted how he was made to kneel, and informed that he was to be shot 'for attempting to escape'. He told the court, 'I just knelt there waiting to die.'

Another could take no more and he barricaded himself inside his cell with his bedstead. Then he removed the glass from his spectacles, broke it on the floor and slashed his wrists. As he bled to death, he was anxious that his suicide not be construed as an admission of guilt, so he wrote on the wall in his own blood, the words 'the CIO torture prisoners with batteries'. But his blood drained into the cell of a neighbouring prisoner who alerted the guards. The fire brigade cut their way into his cell and rescued him.

In the front row in court, so recently occupied by the wives of the ZIPRA treason trialists, the air force wives now sat in their high-necked frocks and colour-co-ordinated shoes, listening to it all, ashen-faced. And a tremor went right through white society with each new revelation, and more of those who could prepared to emigrate. In the end the 'air force six' were acquitted too, and by a black judge, much to government disgust. They too were redetained and sent back to rejoin Dabengwa and his men at Chikurubi. But British diplomatic pressure soon secured their expulsion from the country.

At the request of *The Sunday Times* I accompanied the first two officers to London on their 'Flight to Freedom'. Once on board, they told me they couldn't speak to the press at all for fear of jeopardizing the release of their colleagues still in Chikurubi. As Air Zimbabwe flight RH 124 reached its cruising height, somewhere over the Zambezi, the voice of the white pilot, crackled over the loudspeakers giving us our flight details and asking us to 'bid a special welcome to two celebrities on board'. He named the two air force men and wished them a pleasant flight to the UK. Short of material, I used the announcement in my report and a week later the pilot was fired by Air Zimbabwe for gross misconduct because of it.

But despite all these experiences, I tried my best to remain optimistic. I thought it would all settle down soon. I thought this was just a temporary stage the country was going through, a relatively mild backlash, all things considered. No one was ever unpleasant to me. I had lots of black friends and neighbours, all of whom were at pains to encourage us to stay on, and ordinary, working-class blacks seemed particularly anxious that we remained.

Then one day an old lady came to Newsfile, the offices I shared with half a dozen other correspondents. She waited patiently in the reception, sitting quietly on the bench, knitting, while the telex chattered incessantly, spewing out its journalistic junk food. She was wearing the candy-striped pinafore of a hospital cleaner and a lurid *dhuku* around her head. She had insisted to Winston, the telex operator, that she did not want to disturb me.

I sat next door in my little office, unaware of her presence, trying to write a feature about witch doctors, traditional healers, to feed the foreign papers' appetite for the African cliché. I was having difficulty with the intro and I stared dreamily out of the window across Kenneth Kaunda (formerly Railway) Avenue at the trains shunting back and forth in the sidings by the station. Finally, I emerged from my little office to get a sandwich for lunch. The old lady rose to her feet to greet me.

'I have been told,' she said without preamble, 'that you can help. That you will tell the truth.'

Behind me, old Winston the telex operator smirked loudly. He had a rather low opinion of foreign correspondents.

'I has started again – the killing in Matabeleland. This time it is in the south.' She fiddled self-consciously with her knitting. 'In my home area many people are already dead. Some from my own family. You must write about this thing in your newspapers, otherwise it will never stop until all of us are killed.'

With that she put her knitting inside her carrier bag and walked out of the door.

I ran out after her. 'Hang on a minute, who are you? Who sent you?'

But she continued clattering down the stairs. 'It doesn't matter who I am. Just go down there and see, please,' she shouted up, and then she was gone.

Nineteen

From the moment I stepped off the Air Zimbabwe Viscount at Bulawayo airport it was clear that things were different down here. This was occupied territory. There seemed to be an unspoken conspiracy between white and Matabele, a silent alliance of losers. Here the Shona triumphalism of Harare was absent. The smiling girl with the brittle blonde hair at the Echo car kiosk cheerfully hired me a veteran Datsun. It was canary yellow with bald tyres. I drove to the Holiday Inn, a low modern structure next to the racecourse on the outskirts of Bulawayo. As soon as I'd checked in, I made for St Paul's, a Catholic secondary school out in a black township, or, as they had now been renamed, 'high density' suburbs. St Paul's was run by Father Hebron Wilson, a Coloured priest. Fate had played a cruel genetic trick on Father Hebron. He was the product of two minorities – half white, half Matabele.

I had spoken to Hebron on the telephone, but always in the riddles and cryptic codes of those who know that they are not alone on the line. Now, free of the restraints of the hidden listener, he still spoke in a quiet, kindly voice, but it was flecked with rage. His anger was the more impressive because it was clearly so out of character. The government, he said, had just launched a concerted offensive against the 'dissidents'. Troops had sealed off the whole of southern Matabeleland, imposed a dusk-to-dawn curfew, closed all stores and shops, banned all private traffic and civilians from the area and vowed to flush out the dissidents once and for all. The soldiers were torturing and killing civilians, he said.

St Paul's had been turned into an impromptu refugee camp. Its classrooms now doubled as dormitories, filled with boys who had been smuggled out by their families to escape the purges in southern Matabeleland. I spent the day talking to eyewitnesses. By the end of it, I had a notebook full of the most harrowing stories. Of summary executions, of rape, of mass arrests. One phrase that was repeated throughout the day began to haunt me: *Gukurahundi*. Invariably the perpetrators of whatever violence was being complained of were from *Gukurahundi*. The word literally means 'the first rains of the wet season', that much-awaited downpour which washes away all the accumulated dust and debris of the preceding year. *Gukurahundi* was also the unofficial name of the army's new Fifth Brigade. It was to be the force that would purge society of all the unacceptable debris of history.

Fifth Brigade was trained in conditions of great secrecy by a contingent of North Korean military advisors up at Nyanga, near Umtali in the eastern highlands. No one ever saw the North Koreans. But to the whites they were the new bogeymen, rather like the Cubans had been during the guerrilla war.

There was only one tangible sign of the North Korean presence. At the edge of Harare, on the top of Warren Hills, above the cemetery where my sister's remains are buried, they had built a huge bronze frieze commemorating the liberation struggle. It was like a grisly cartoon strip crowded with images of the war, caricatures of cruelty. The centrepiece was a white policeman encouraging the German shepherd on the end of his leash to sink its teeth into the forearm of a cowering black woman with a baby on her back. But in the first version of the tableau submitted by the Koreans there was something wrong with the faces of the black guerrilla heroes. They all had oriental features.

The North Koreans had also tried to create Fifth Brigade in

their own image, training them in the ways of absolute obedience and conformity that accorded with their own absolute dictatorship. The only time that soldiers from the new brigade had been seen in public was at an independence celebration at Rufaro stadium, Harare's main football venue, where they put on a display of martial arts and marched in a North Korean goosestep style – not like the rest of the army, which still marched like the British. Now the Fifth Brigade had been let off their leashes in southern Matabeleland.

I interviewed the young Matabele refugees at St Paul's with all the pedantry of an ex-lawyer. Places, names, times, descriptions. I probed for inconsistencies and exaggerations. In my heart of hearts, I think I was hoping that the whole thing was a fantastic construct of the politically dispossessed, the ethnically antagonistic. I made no allowances for the fact that many of these boys had recently seen family members killed and had narrowly escaped death themselves. And they seemed to expect no sympathy. They told their tales in quiet, controlled voices, dealing patiently with my many interruptions. The more I heard from the young Matabele refugees, the more horrified I became. By the end of the day, my doubts had been swept away by an awful certainty.

The stories I heard that day, sitting at the wooden school desks at St Paul's, had a pattern to them. These were no random acts of violence, these were not soldiers roaming out of control. This was worse. It was calculated and methodical. In almost all instances the boys told me that soldiers arrived armed with a list of names. Those on the list were taken first – they were almost invariably office-bearers of ZAPU. Then the soldiers rounded up any men of military age and took them away. If co-operation was not forthcoming, and often even if it was, some were shot there and then, and the villagers were forced to dig communal graves for them.

Father Hebron had been keeping a list of those who had been killed so far, names given to him by the boys who had turned up at St Paul's. He retrieved the list from its hiding place behind the cistern in the lavatory and showed it to me. It was a ledger, the kind normally used for cash entries. It had 629 entries so far, each with date, place and witnesses and even, in some cases, the registration numbers of military vehicles present at the scene.

But the worry for him, and now me, was that if any of the names were made public, the witnesses would not survive for long. So how to publicize the massacres without setting off new ones? We talked long into the night, and eventually we decided that the only way would be for me to get into the killing fields myself. Our problem was that the whole area had been declared off limits to non-residents and cordoned off by the army. Even the locals were under dusk-to-dawn curfew.

I drove back to the Holiday Inn, exhausted. We'd discussed various possibilities, from sneaking in on foot to stowing away on a delivery truck. None seemed practical. All were dangerous. That night I fell asleep having more or less decided that I would cobble together a report based on what I'd heard from outside.

At six-thirty the next morning, the ringing of the bedside phone wrenched me from sleep. It was Hebron Wilson, sounding alert and long up. He'd already said Mass and taken an early morning geography class.

'We must speak,' he said. 'I've had an idea.' And then the phone went dead.

As I drove through Bulawayo's wide streets back to St Paul's, everything seemed so normal. It was rush hour, which in Bulawayo lasts about twenty minutes. White commuters were driving in from their garden suburbs to their jobs in the city centre. They sat at traffic lights in their pick-up trucks, their little Japanese saloon cars and their stately old Mercedes diesels. Secretaries and shop assistants, schoolteachers and bank clerks. The *Bulawayo Chronicle* that I bought from the hawker at the lights headlined a speech by the prime minister congratulating Iran on its national day.

Past the city centre, with its mixture of graceful old colonial buildings and half-hearted high-rises, the black townships began. Long queues of blacks waited patiently for Bulawayo United buses to take them to work out at the industrial sites. The electrified treble of *simanje-manje* music blared from shops and market stalls. *Mealie* cobs were roasting on open braziers along the roadside. There were no soldiers in evidence, just a few police constables hitchhiking to work. The only patrol I saw was a long line of Lyons Maid ice cream vendors, in their red and white uniforms topped with little air force-style caps, cycling into town from the depot on their ice cream tricycles. The normality of it all sowed new doubts in me. Maybe the whole Fifth Brigade thing was being vastly exaggerated. Maybe Hebron was just being hysterical.

I found him in the refectory drinking tea with three black nuns. Sisters Constance, Charity and Eunice made a high-spirited posse who laughed a lot and teased Father Hebron unmercifully. The nuns were about to make a routine trip to Minda mission, deep inside the prohibited area, and Hebron thought I might be able to sneak in with them. We had long discussions about who I would be. Eventually we agreed that I was to be a monk. Brother Peter, they christened me, and after a short search, they found me an old dog collar. There was much hilarity as they danced around me fixing it in place. The whole venture was assuming the atmosphere of a picnic.

But before we left, I sat down with Hebron to work out a plan. We talked for an hour, poring over an Ordnance Survey map of the area and his ledger of names. Although the refugees at St Paul's could furnish detailed accounts of their own particular experiences, none had much of an idea what was happening overall. Many of the villages where killings had taken place were now deserted and most people, they had warned, would be far too scared to talk to me.

The main danger I faced, as Hebron kept reminding me, was that if caught inside the prohibited zone, I could be killed and my death blamed on 'bandits'. But the way those Matabele boys told their terrible stories to me, clearly believing that I would now *do* something about it, convinced me that I really had no choice but to go in.

After bidding our farewells, the nuns and I clambered into their old Peugeot estate. The back was riding low on its axle, weighed down by half a dozen pedal-powered Singer sewing machines that were destined for Minda mission. Sister Constance was at the wheel. She was a truly awful driver who appeared to have no sense of distance at all. She sat hunched over the wheel and peered through her butterfly-rimmed spectacles with a perplexed expression. She drove very slowly and very dangerously, with almost no regard for oncoming traffic. I had soon entirely forgotten about the dangers of what we were setting out to do.

Just before the Matopos Hills came into view we hit our first roadblock. There was no warning sign, just two staggered lines of metal spikes across the road. A couple of green canvas tents were pitched to one side, and next to them was a sandbagged machine-gun post. Sister Constance stalled the Peugeot to a halt a couple of yards short of the spikes. For several minutes nothing happened, and then a tent flap opened and two soldiers emerged. They wore the red berets of the Fifth Brigade. Not perched on their heads, in the normal military style, but pulled down over their ears. So *this* was *Gukurahundi*. I'd never seen them up close before. There was a powerful mystique surrounding the men of the Fifth Brigade: they possessed the swaggering confidence of those who believe that they are the chosen ones, that they can go that bit further.

We sat in the car, all four of us beaming foolishly until our faces ached. But the soldiers didn't speak. Not even a cursory greeting. In my experience, even the bad guys in Africa tend to be polite, but apparently not these ones. The corporal had swollen red eyes, eyes that you instinctively knew could not be reasoned with. His colleague wore a pair of sunglasses at a lopsided slant across his face. The sunglasses had only one lens, and from the other, empty frame a single disconcerting eye regarded us with frank hostility. My neck was sweating under the unfamiliar itch of the dog collar.

The corporal jabbed his finger towards the back of the car, and Sister Constance got out to open the back door. She chattered away to him brightly in English, about the drought, about where we were going, what we were doing. But the corporal ignored her. He ordered her to empty the car, and I got out to help Constance lug the Singer sewing machines on to the tarmac. The corporal watched us impassively, and when we'd unloaded everything he grunted and dismissed us with a toss of his head.

'God bless you, my son,' I found myself saying, absurdly, and I made a little sign of the cross at him. He looked annoyed, and stalked off to join his men, who were now lounged out on the grass verge, listening to a transistor radio and drinking Chibuku beer out of waxed cartons. It was a little before ten in the morning.

We reloaded the Singers, Sister Constance crunched the Peugeot into gear and we juddered off on our way. On our right were the Matopos Hills, outcrops of great granite boulders, which have a commanding view over the vast rolling territory of southern Matabeleland. As all white children were taught in school, it was here, on the highest of these granite domes, that Cecil Rhodes asked to be buried. He called it World's View, and he used to escape here, to contemplate his imperial vision. After his death his body was brought here by train from Cape Town. His grave was cut into the rock, and his coffin covered by a simple brass plaque. Surrounding it are free-standing boulders that Miss Gloyne, my Melsetter schoolteacher, told us were symbolic guardian angels.

The Matabele called this hill *Malindidzimu* – place of spirits – and buried their kings nearby. Once World's View was a tourist attraction – patriotic whites drove out from Bulawayo at the weekend to clamber up the rock, and to *braai* their sausages in the little picnic area below. During the war it became too dangerous. Now it was cut off by the army cordon.

We had left the white farming areas, now renamed 'Commercial Farming Areas', behind us, and entered the Communal Area, what used to be the Tribal Trust Lands. The names might have changed, but not much else. The elephant grass on either side of the narrow tar road was a crispy dry khaki from the drought. The herds of goats and cattle that would normally be grazing along the way were absent. So were the people. For ten miles we saw no one. The emptiness was eerie.

Then we came across an old man in gumboots and ragged blue overalls plodding along behind a small herd of emaciated cattle. He kept walking with his eyes downcast, even after we had stopped the car to talk to him. Finally, when he realized we were not soldiers, he halted. His name was Samuel, he said, and today was a very sad day. He was taking his gaunt animals to the nearby town of Kezi to sell them for slaughter. He was doing this with heavy heart, for to sell your cattle went against all local tradition in this pastoral society where wealth, prestige and social status all depend on cattle ownership. But he had no choice.

'The grass should be almost waist high at this time of year,' he said, 'but as you can see there is only sand here.' He kicked disconsolately at the dust with the toe of his gumboot. 'My maize crop has failed again,' he sighed, 'so my cattle must go.'

Samuel pointed his walking stick along the Matopos range to a prominent dome-shaped granite hill glistening in the sun. It was *Injelele* mountain he told me, where the Matabele people gather annually to pray for rain. Led by their spirit medium they brewed traditional beer and sacrificed cattle there as an offering to the ancestral spirits. But the army and the curfew had kept the worshippers away this year. Only a token delegation had managed to reach the mountain top. And, he said ominously, some of them never made it home. Samuel blamed the government for the broken pilgrimage and for the failure of the rains that, he believed, inevitably followed. While we talked, his cows stood patiently together on the roadside. There was nothing worth grazing. As we left, he reluctantly prodded them towards the Kezi slaughterhouse.

After another five miles of emptiness we approached a little settlement straddling the road – a few stores and houses, a bus stop, an old hand-operated paraffin pump and a herd of donkeys milling about in the middle of the road. From the far side of the village we heard the high-pitched whine of armoured personnel carriers. As they crested the hill and came into view I saw that they were two Crocodiles, vehicles that my father had helped to design in the war. They were basically Isuzu trucks, but they had been encased in a jacket of steel, with narrow gun ports along the sides and only a small square of armoured glass for the driver to peer through.

The Crocodiles came careering down the hill into the village and kept up their speed despite the obvious obstruction ahead. We watched, amazed, as the trucks smashed straight through the herd of donkeys. Several of the beasts were tossed up in the air and fell heavily on the roadside, bloodied and bone-shattered. The herdsman looked after the departing Crocodiles in horror, too shocked even to attempt token remonstration with the troops. The entire incident had taken less than thirty seconds, and then the Crocodiles were whining off around the bend and out of sight.

One donkey was dead, another three were badly injured, lying in pools of dark arterial blood. They twitched and kicked and tried to get up, but their legs were broken and their bodies rent with deep gashes. The dazed villagers gathered around the carnage, assessing the animals' wounds. Finally the herdsman took out a *panga* and slashed the throats of the three prone donkeys. With a few last spasms they were dead. The mood in the village was sullen and hate-filled.

The nuns and I commiserated with the locals on the verandah

of the shuttered store. I fell into conversation with a middle-aged man who had with him three young girls, all tearful and dishevelled. He told me that they were his daughters and that a few hours earlier soldiers had raped them at gunpoint. As Sister Constance and Sister Eunice ministered to them, a thin young man tapped me on the forearm.

'I am Bongali Dube,' he announced, 'I wish to show you something.' And with that he led off up a rough track behind the village. For fifteen minutes we clambered up the hill in silence. When we emerged from the undergrowth near the summit, Bongali stopped and pointed out a pile of charred bones. 'This is my father,' he told me matter-of-factly, as though he were introducing me to a living man.

'The soldiers gathered all the people of the area together for a compulsory rally,' he continued in a quiet, impassive monotone. 'They made us shout government slogans, and they beat many people with rifle butts, screaming at us the whole time: "Where are the dissidents?" The officer then addressed us through a loudhailer. He told us that all stores would stay closed and no food deliveries would be allowed into the curfew area. He said: "First you will eat your chickens, then your goats, then your cattle, then your donkeys. Then you will eat your children, and finally you will eat the dissidents."

'After the officer had finished speaking, the soldiers selected three men at random, including my father, and took them behind the hill. We heard three shots, and then the soldiers returned alone. They warned us not to report the matter or to collect the bodies for burial. They were left there for three weeks and their remains were eaten by dogs.' Bongali placed some stones on top of his father's bones and we made our way back down to the village.

The nuns and I continued our drive in silence. The tar road ended, and we closed our windows against the thick dust of the dirt road. Several more convoys of Crocodiles passed us. One convoy was escorting four cattle trucks carrying civilians who stood packed together up against the railings. As they hurtled past us I saw that their faces and hair were ochre from the swirling dust. When I wondered aloud where they were being taken, Sister Constance gave a shrug of ignorance.

'Maybe prison?' suggested Sister Eunice helpfully from the back seat. And then silence descended once more in the Peugeot as it rattled and clattered over the corrugations towards Minda mission.

The sun was high in the sky by the time we reached the whitewashed stones that marked the mission's driveway. Ahead of us was a granite church and a collection of red-roofed buildings that made up the mission school. There were no pupils about. In fact the mission seemed deserted. We all got out of the car and stretched our limbs after the long drive. Still no one came out to greet us. Then I noticed a pair of eyes peeping at us over a windowsill. When I looked back the eyes quickly bobbed down again. Several minutes later people began emerging cautiously from various buildings, calling to each other that it was safe to come out. Soon a small crowd of workers and staff had gathered to welcome the nuns and gawp at me. Feeling suddenly self-conscious, I removed my dog collar and put it in my bag.

Down the steps from the church limped a small white man with rimless glasses. The crowd opened to let him through. His clothes belied his profession: open-toed sandals over white socks, baggy polyester trousers, a short-sleeved white shirt with a string vest showing through underneath, and a plastic zip-up document case under his arm. He had to be a Catholic priest. This was Father Gabriel, a Franciscan from Austria. After greeting the nuns warmly he enquired of me. When I introduced myself, telling him my real identity, his curiosity quickly turned to annoyance and he hustled me up the stairs into his house.

Father Gabriel's initial irritation turned out to be largely protective. Hundreds of his parishioners had disappeared over the last few weeks and he was in a state of high anxiety. The army had visited his mission the day before, warning him not to interfere in any way with their 'operations'.

'If they find a journalist here, there'll be terrible trouble,' he worried aloud. 'These are not like the other soldiers. These ones can do anything they want.'

Fragment by fragment Father Gabriel eventually got the story out. When the soldiers had first arrived at Minda, they had confined him to his house. They had herded the staff and pupils on to the football field and harangued them for hours. The children and teachers were made to shout the rallying cries of the ruling party.

'*Viva* ZANU PF!' called out a soldier, and the staff and pupils had to roar back, '*Viva*!'

'*Viva* Fifth Brigade!'

'*Viva*!'

And so the approved list went on. Then came the roll call of villains, preceded in each case by the phrase '*pasi ne*', which in Shona means 'down with'.

'*Pasi ne* dissidents!'

'*Pasi*!'

'*Pasi ne* ZAPU!'

'*Pasi*!'

It went on and on for hours, in the blazing sun, until the children were quite hoarse from shouting. Several fainted in the heat, and the teachers protested that the children needed a break and some water to drink. Incensed at this insolence, the soldiers hauled the teachers to the front. They spread-eagled them in turn, up against the side of a Crocodile, and beat them across their backs with wooden staves, in front of the assembled children. The children wept quietly. After each teacher was beaten, they collapsed on to the ground, and another one was pulled roughly into position. Men and women teachers were beaten alike. And through it all the rally cries had to continue, said Father Gabriel. Finally, the soldiers loaded several of the teachers and many of the older boys into the waiting cattle trucks. Then they switched their attention to the small mission hospital.

Out of his window Father Gabriel saw the matron remonstrating with the soldiers as they ordered her patients into the cattle trucks. The matron pointed out that some could barely walk and many needed regular medication. The soldiers ignored her and she kept up a steady stream of objections, getting more and more agitated the less notice they took of her. Finally, said Father Gabriel, she made the mistake of pulling at the sergeant's sleeve to get his attention. Almost casually, he swung round and struck her a blow to the side of her head with his rifle butt. Gabriel heard the crack from the other side of the mission. The matron slid to the ground unconscious. Two other soldiers heaved her inert figure into the truck like a sack of *mealie* meal, and her stunned patients climbed in after her. The tailgates of the trucks were clamped up, and they were driven off in the direction of Kezi.

The following Sunday, the mission church was crowded with worshippers, drawn to God in time of crisis. Father Gabriel preached what was for him a particularly rousing sermon. He couldn't bring himself even to utter the word 'forgiveness'. Now was not the time to be asking these people to forgive their enemies, he told me. Instead he concentrated on the theme of divine justice and the ultimate punishment of evildoers. As he was getting into his stride, punching the air in his enthusiasm for the many and terrible ways that God would find to pay back the soldiers, the church doors swung open and in they walked.

'Out, out, everybody out!' ordered their sergeant.

The congregation looked uncertainly at Father Gabriel, still at his pulpit.

'This is the house of God,' he said, drawing himself to his full height above the lectern. 'Do not dishonour it by bringing your weapons of death in here.'

'Everyone out!' repeated the sergeant, and for a minute military and ecclesiastical authority hung in the balance. Then with a flick of his hand, the sergeant cocked his rifle. The metallic *clack*, as a bullet lodged in the chamber, sent a tremor through the congregation, and several people, mostly old ladies, eased themselves out of the packed pews and scurried away. But the bulk of the congregation remained. The sergeant walked slowly up the aisle, the fall of his heavy boots ringing out on the flagstone floor. He held his rifle almost casually in one hand, the butt resting in the crook of his arm, the barrel pointing up at the ceiling, his index finger along the side of the trigger guard. When he reached the altar, he swung around to face the congregation.

'Last warning!' he hissed.

Next to him, Father Gabriel suddenly raised his hymn book.

'Everybody stand,' he said. 'Hymn number one.' The elderly organist peered over his reading glasses in mild surprise, paged deftly back through his music, and struck up his opening chords. He began to sing in a tremulous voice:

Abide with me, fast falls the eventide;

By the second line, the congregation had joined in:

The darkness deepens, Lord, with me abide!
When other helpers fail, and comforts flee,
Help of the helpless, O abide with me.

It was after the last 'abide', Father Gabriel recalled, that the sergeant's shots exploded through the church. There were only two shots, and they went up into the ceiling, bringing down a shower of plaster. The screaming congregation swarmed for the door. And within a minute the church was empty but for Father Gabriel, the organist and the soldiers.

'I think my God is stronger than yours,' chuckled the

sergeant, patting his rifle, and he strode out with his men behind him.

I began to commiserate with the padre, but he brushed my sympathy aside.

'That,' he said, exasperated, 'that was nothing!' He reached for my map, and muttered to himself for a few minutes as he familiarized himself with it. 'Here,' he said finally, jabbing his finger at the map, 'Belaghwe. That's where the soldiers are camped; that's where the detention centre is. My parishioners tell me that terrible things are happening there.'

He ran his hands through his pewter-grey hair. 'I just don't know what to do,' he admitted. 'I have got messages out to the Bishop in Bulawayo, but he tells me he is speaking directly to the prime minister and I am to do nothing more.'

Father Gabriel was exhausted. He removed his glasses, rubbed his eyes wearily with his knuckles and sighed heavily.

'I am not a young man, you know,' he said. 'I have lived through the Second World War in Austria and I have seen the terrible things the Gestapo could do. But let me tell you something, the Gestapo couldn't teach these Fifth Brigade fellows a damn thing.'

Twenty

It was getting late when we emerged from the church at Minda mission. Outside on the verandah a large group of people had gathered. Most of them had been beaten at the hands of the soldiers. They had swollen eyes, broken noses, split lips, teeth missing, great bruises on their arms and legs and angry welts across their backs. All of them wished to show me where they'd been beaten, and even the women pulled up the backs of their blouses to display their wounds. Some had sustained their injuries during the events at the mission, others had been beaten at their homes in the countryside nearby and had come to the mission hoping for protection. Some had seen relatives taken away. Some told stories similar to Bongali Dube's, of people being shot dead 'as an example'.

I was on to my second notebook, but many of the details I was collecting could not be used without compromising the identities of the witnesses and placing them in further danger. I needed to get closer to Belaghwe, at least to see the place and be able to describe it. I would need a guide. I explained this to the group of refugees and they discussed my request among themselves for a few minutes. I could understand enough Ndebele to follow their discussion. Naturally enough, it revolved around the danger of being caught nosing around the area gathering information. Finally, from the back of the crowd a middle-aged man who'd been listening intently to the conversation with his head inclined to one side held up his hand.

'Let me do it,' he said, getting to his feet and shuffling slowly to the front. He was a very tall man in a suit and thick rubber sandals made from the outer treads of an old car tyre. His suit was well cut in the same delicate pinstripe as my Saville's suit, but it had ragged holes at each elbow and knee. The turn-ups of his trousers ended a good six inches above his tyre sandals.

We had only about an hour of light left at most, so without further discussion we got into the Peugeot and drove back on to the Kezi road, which led past Belaghwe, about five miles away. I had agreed to come back later to collect the nuns, and as I steered the car with one hand, I fixed my dog collar back on with the other.

My guide's name was Phineas and he ran a small trading store close to Belaghwe. Like all the stores in the curfew area it had been closed for several weeks, but because it was across the road from the army camp, the soldiers frequently came over for soft drinks and cigarettes. A few of them paid for their purchases, but mostly they ran up tabs which he knew, and they knew, would never be settled. But at least they left him alone.

We turned off the Kezi road before the army camp and followed a scotch-cart track up on to the side of a hill that overlooked it. Belaghwe is at the foot of a typical Matopos granite mountain, after which it takes its name. From the main road all that was visible of the camp was a water tank on an elevated platform and few outbuildings that used to be a Roads Maintenance Depot. From up here you could make out rows of green canvas tents, an aerial mast and armoured Crocodiles parked in lines. Behind that, glinting in the dying sun, we could just make out rolls of razor wire. The wire was laid out to enclose large rectangular pens.

'Those,' said Phineas, 'are where they keep the prisoners.'

It was now after six o'clock – curfew time. From now until six the next morning, southern Matabeleland became a 'free-fire zone'. Any civilians who moved more than fifty yards from their houses would be regarded as 'bandits' and shot on sight. Any non-military traffic would be treated as hostile and would be fired upon. Phineas and I decided it was safest to leave the car where it was, on the scotch-cart track. We put a few branches over the side facing the road so it wouldn't reflect the sun in the morning. Then, as quietly as we could, we walked the half mile down to Phineas's house.

'At the beginning of the curfew there were too many patrols at night,' said Phineas, using the word 'too' to mean 'very', as it invariably does in African English. 'They would shoot anything at all which moved. Anything at all. Even cows or even dogs. They also shot people who went outside for toilet.'

Phineas's short history of the soldiers' curfew enforcement tactics wasn't exactly comforting me.

'But now there are not so many patrols,' he continued, smiling at my nervousness, 'so maybe we can be lucky.'

Half an hour later we reached a small clearing in which there were a number of thatched mud huts. This was Phineas's home. His large wife came swooping out of the low door of one of the huts and immediately began scolding him for being out after curfew time. Phineas grinned sheepishly at me.

'I think even the Fifth Brigade are afraid of this one,' he said, introducing me. She gave me a brisk once-over, taking in the dog collar. I was the first white man ever to set foot in their village, Phineas had said. His wife immediately set about issuing instructions to unseen people inside the various huts, and soon the smell of cooking was emerging from the kitchen hut, as smoke filtered up through its thatch. Another fire was burning on the area of beaten earth between the huts. Here we sat cross-legged, Phineas and I, on rush mats.

A shy young girl – his daughter, he told me – appeared from the gloom to present me with a bowl of water, a cracked bar of soap and a little threadbare square of towel to wash for supper.

'And how old are you?' I asked in the slightly patronizing tone adults use when trying to befriend children.

'My name is Elizabeth and I have ten years of age,' she replied, as though she had learnt the phrase off by heart.

'And where do you go to school, Elizabeth?' I continued.

'I used to go to Minda school, but that was before the *sojas* came. Now we cannot go to school any more. So I am staying at home and I helping my mother to dig in the fields.' She collected the bowl and disappeared into the gloom once more.

Supper was *sadza* and relish and goat's meat. Another seven children joined us, ranging in ages from three to sixteen. They ate in silence, casting furtive looks at me, while Phineas told me more about the siege. During the meal I noticed that food was being taken into one of the sleeping huts by Phineas's wife, and I heard the murmur of voices from within. When we had eaten, Phineas rose and beckoned me to follow him to the hut. I stooped under the thatched eaves and inside was a young man lying on a rush mat, swaddled in a cheap grey horse blanket. A small kerosene lamp burnt dimly at his side. Phineas's wife hovered in attendance.

'This is my nephew, Luke,' Phineas introduced. 'He has come from Belaghwe.'

'Good evening, Father,' said Luke, as he struggled to sit up against the wall.

'No, he is not really a priest,' said Phineas in Ndebele. 'He has come from the BBC World Service.' I had told Phineas that I worked for *The Sunday Times* of London, but he, like most Africans, equated a foreign correspondent with the World Service, their main source of information.

Luke corrected himself.

'Oh I am sorry. Good evening – sah.' He nodded formally.

I reached down to shake his hand, but stopped when I noticed it was bound in a tight mitten of sheeting. Luke followed my eyes to his hand, and from under the blanket produced his left hand identically bound.

'The *sojas*, they broke my wrists,' he said. 'And not only my wrists.'

Phineas's wife pulled aside the blanket from Luke's legs. Both his feet were wrapped in bandages of sheet, too.

'My ankles, also,' said Luke, shaking his head in apparent amazement at his fractures. 'But I am quite lucky,' he continued. 'Many people are dying in Belaghwe. The *sojas* are killing them during interrogation.' Luke recounted his tale in a quiet voice. There were, he said, hundreds and sometimes thousands of detainees in Belaghwe at any one time. He called Belaghwe *Bulala lapa*, which in Ndebele means 'the place of killing'. Hundreds had died there, he estimated, and started reciting the names of those he could remember. I laboriously noted them down in my book. I could check them later against Father Hebron's list hidden behind the cistern in Bulawayo. Women were raped there and killed too.

Electric-shock torture, said Luke, was a favourite of 'the CIOs', the men of the Central Intelligence Organization. After half an hour Luke's face was turning grey with pain, and Phineas's wife declared, 'Enough, the boy must sleep now.'

Luke thanked me. 'You are very kind, sah, to come from far away to help us.'

I felt a surge of inadequacy.

Phineas ushered me into another hut where there was another young man. He had sneaked across from a nearby village to tell me more about Belaghwe. And after him another and another. These were all people – neighbours, friends and relatives – that Phineas had managed to spring through his acquaintance with the soldiers who patronized the store.

That night was a procession of witnesses. I didn't sleep at all. As fatigue overwhelmed my sense of perspective, the individual cases crowded in on me in such profusion that they began to merge.

The breaking of wrists and ankles was very common in Belaghwe. To some of the soldiers it was a game, a competition. They broke the joints by jumping on them with their heavy boots. This was sometimes carried out during bone-breaking speed trials, on which the men would take wagers. Mostly it was part of the ritual of interrogation. Before they even began to question you, they would break one wrist. If you didn't yield any information about dissidents, they broke an ankle, then the other wrist, then the other ankle.

Inevitably, most people were gabbling away with all sorts of made-up confessions, implicating people they knew in fictitious events. Anything to prevent that brown boot from crashing down again. Acting on the 'confessions', the soldiers would go off and collect a fresh batch of victims and so the cycle would continue.

Many of those interrogated did not survive. If they became too ill or were picked out, for reasons unknown to their fellow detainees, they were taken down to the firing range and shot against the butts. Other detainees were made to pile the bodies in a heap within a canvas screen behind the range.

But one question no one seemed able to answer for sure was what happened to the dead. They confirmed that few were being buried at Belaghwe. All that they could say for sure was that the bodies were loaded on to trucks at night and driven away. Most of the trucks would return after about half an hour, without the bodies. So the main dumping ground had to be somewhere within a few miles of Belaghwe. But where?

Three in the morning found me sitting alone outside by the fire, studying my Ordnance Survey map. Outside, the cicadas kept up a steady chirping. A soft breeze rustled the parched undergrowth and carried with it, up from Belaghwe, the throbbing of a diesel generator. Eventually Phineas came out to join me. Very deliberately he made a cigarette, rolling the tobacco in an old piece of newspaper. With a flourish he twisted it, lit it from the fire and inhaled deeply. He blew a stream of smoke out through his nostrils and mouth and only then did he speak.

'What are you looking for?' he asked.

'I'm just wondering where they take the bodies,' I mused.

'I know where the dead people go,' said Phineas, flicking his ash into the fire. 'They are taken to Antelope.'

Of course. I'd been staring at the answer all along. Little red crenellations on my map that marked small mine workings. This area was part of the same gold rush as Filabusi. Almost a hundred years earlier, white men had trekked up from the South Africa in response to reports that there was a gold reef here that would dwarf even the giant gold seam of the Witwatersrand, west of Johannesburg. But like that in Filabusi the gold rush here had proved largely illusory and there were small abandoned mine shafts scattered across the Kezi district. Antelope was simply the closest disused mine shaft to Belaghwe, less than five miles from the camp itself.

Shortly before dawn Phineas and I walked back up the hill to check on the car. From the track we looked down on Belaghwe again: the generator throbbing away all night, powered flood lights that shone down on the holding pens.

'I need to see Antelope,' I told Phineas.

He shook his head vigorously.

'Ah, ah, ah. It's too dangerous there. It is very close to the main road, and if they see you there – big trouble.' He drew his forefinger across his throat.

Back at his house we breakfasted on hot sweet tea and cold *sadza*. From the camp below we heard the ragged bugle notes of a wildly off-key reveille. The prisoners would be standing to attention there as the Zimbabwe flag was raised. Those of them that could stand.

Phineas had decided that although he would not accompany me to Antelope, he would at least furnish me with some advice. He gave me precise directions and told me what he could about the movement of local military traffic. There was a heavy spurt of traffic to and from the camp between six and eight, as trucks went out to collect the night patrols and deploy the day ones. Then there was usually a lull until late morning.

At about eight-thirty we brushed aside the branches from

the Peugeot and I turned it around with some difficulty on the narrow track. Phineas's whole family had turned out to say goodbye. It was quite a crowd. Phineas made a little farewell speech.

'I hope you can put our problems on the World Service,' he said, 'otherwise our future will run out. Surely, surely.' It must have been the longest speech his family had ever heard him make in English and the children all cheered and patted the car as it rolled by. I could hear Phineas's wife roundly chiding them for their noise as I drove slowly away.

Antelope mine was only 500 yards from the main road between Kezi and the small village of Antelope itself. To reach it you turned off through a dilapidated gate. On the fence next to the gate was a small sign: *Antelope Mine, part of the Attica Mine Group, Lonrho.* Beneath that was a skull and crossbones bearing a warning in Shona, Ndebele and English: *Beware – mine shafts – area liable to subsidence. Strictly out of bounds. All trespassers will be prosecuted.*

I left the Peugeot idling in full view of the main road and leapt out to open the gate. It consisted of about ten strands of thick-gauge wire strung tautly between six vertical poles, the last of which was firmly held to the gatepost at top and bottom, in two bands of iron. The bloody thing wouldn't budge. I struggled and heaved at it, cutting my fingers in my growing panic. Then, faintly at first, but quite distinctly, I heard the sound of a truck approaching. I gave one last desperate heave, and the pole leapt free. Without bothering to move the gate aside, I jumped back into the car, threw it into gear and drove over the prone gate down the small road, pulling off sharply behind a clutch of mopani trees. I watched through the foliage as a convoy of four Crocodiles drove past on the main road. So much for Phineas's military traffic predictions, I thought.

I wondered whether anyone would notice from the main

road that the gate was lying open. Was it worth the risk of walking back to close it? Probably. I ran back and propped it closed. Satisfying myself that the car was not easily visible from the road, I walked on towards the mine itself. The workings had long been abandoned, when the modest gold seam ran out. On the left as I approached was an old shaft cordoned off with a rusty barbed wire fence, its entrance overgrown and undisturbed.

A hundred yards away was a second shaft. The soft surface soil around the entrance of this shaft was criss-crossed by heavy tyre tracks. From the pattern, it looked like the trucks had reversed up to the shaft and then driven off again. The entrance to the shaft was about three yards by five yards and it plunged vertically down, the yellow rock face disappearing into the darkness below.

I leant over and peered down the shaft. It was too dark to see anything but a putrefying stench billowed up at me. It was the unmistakable stink of rotting human, indelibly marked on my olfactory memory by the postmortems of my childhood. This must be the nightly destination of the Belaghwe body run. Around the shaft were telltale signs of an army presence – empty ration packs, some brass cartridge cases, ubiquitous Chibuku beer cartons. I made my way back on foot to open the gate. Then I got back into the car and drove out on to the main road, leaving the Antelope gate open behind me.

A few hundred yards away, across the main road, was a small village, and on impulse I pulled off the road and parked the car behind the huts. There was no one to be seen. I shouted a greeting, but just like at Minda the day before, no one replied. I banged on the ill-fitting wooden door of the biggest hut, and after a moment it scraped open and the worried face of an old man appeared around it.

I didn't even ask the names of the people in that village opposite Antelope mine. It was safer not to know. Neither did I conceal my true identity. I simply said I was a reporter investigating a story about bodies from Belaghwe being dumped down Antelope Mine. I proffered a grubby business card. The old man looked at it for a second, then said he couldn't read. But he emerged from the shadows, and agreed that the story about Antelope was indeed true. Almost every night the trucks came with bodies, he said. It had been like that for weeks now.

'Often they put a small bomb in afterwards and we can hear explosion.' He went to another hut and returned with a young boy of about ten. 'This one has seen them,' said the old man.

The young boy had been searching for a lost cow and, caught by the new curfew, he settled down to sleep in the brush near the mine shaft.

He looked down at the ground and said in a singsong little voice, 'The trucks came about ten o'clock in the night. The soldiers opened the canvas at the back and took the dead persons and threw them down the hole, one by one.'

'How many bodies?' I enquired.

'About ten dead persons, I think. Then the soldiers drove away.'

Early the next morning, overcome by curiosity, he had risked a peek down the 'hole' and was horrified to see one of the bodies, that of a young man, snagged on an iron girder at the side of the shaft about twenty feet down. When he returned for another peek a few weeks later, the body had gone.

We had been talking for more than ten minutes, and I needed to get out of there before I landed them in trouble. I called for silence and we listened intently to ensure no traffic was imminent. Then I hopped into the car and drove quickly back on to the main road and made towards Minda. In my rear view mirror I could see the villagers brushing away my tyre tracks with branches, just like guerrilla sympathizers had done in the war to prevent us following tracks. Only now it was my tracks that were being swept away.

At Minda I had intended to collect the nuns and drive back

the way we had come, to Bulawayo. But when I reached the mission, Father Gabriel came dashing down the stairs.

'Quickly, quickly,' he urged, 'park the car out of sight around the back.' I pulled into an old shed as indicated and mission workers promptly began moving sacks in there to conceal it.

Gabriel came rushing around.

'You must get the hell out, you are in big danger. The soldiers *and* the CIO have been asking about you by *name*. They know you are inside the curfew area. They know the description of the car. You must leave the mission immediately. You can take the old Mazda pick-up. Leave it at St Paul's with Hebron Wilson if you get through.'

'What about the nuns?' I asked.

'The nuns will go back to Bulawayo later,' said Gabriel. 'It's too dangerous for them to be with you.' He looked at my dog collar disapprovingly. 'And they also know you are dressed as a priest.'

I took the dog collar off and handed it to him.

'They said that if I saw you I should tell you that when they find you they will kill you,' he said quietly.

The best hope I had of getting out was to take the most unexpected route. According to my calculations that would be northeast towards Gwanda, the opposite way to Bulawayo. Gabriel agreed, and I bade farewell to him and the nuns, apologizing to them for having hijacked their car. Constance had a rosary in her hand, and was working the beads through her fingers.

'I will say the rosary until you get out safely,' she called out as I set off.

I drove for two hours along atrocious roads, doubling back on myself to avoid the main routes through the Communal Area. Twice disaster loomed. First I got the pick-up truck stuck in the fine dust, but some unquestioning young boys appeared from nowhere and heaved it out. Later, I rounded a bend and there was a convoy of Crocodiles coming in the other direction. I sank down in my seat and pulled a sun hat low over my eyes. Between the hat brim and my sunglasses, I might have passed as black. Luckily the battered old pick-up truck was a commonplace vehicle in rural Zimbabwe.

At last the pick-up rattled over a cattle grid, and with a sag of relief I realized I was out of the curfew area and on to commercial farming land. I thanked Sister Constance aloud, and relaxed my sweaty grip on the steering wheel.

Then, the most appalling sight ahead: a soldier was standing in the road waving me down. From 500 yards away I could already see his scarlet Fifth Brigade beret. In the few seconds that remained to me I considered my options: I could turn around and head back at full speed. I could dump the pick-up and run for it (most of these soldiers weren't terribly fit, and it would be ages before they could summon up air support.) Or I could put my foot down and drive straight through – if they didn't hit me with their first burst of fire, I might be faster than their vehicles. It would take them some time to radio through for roadblocks ahead, and they couldn't cover all the options. I might be able to lose them down some back road, dump the pick-up and escape on foot.

As my options flashed before me, so did the variables. How big was the roadblock ahead? Was it a proper one with a stop group another fifty yards after the initial soldier, or was it a complacent, sloppy one that I could get away from? How many of them were there? What weapons did they have? Did their radio work? The Zimbabwe National Army were not good at radios. Had this particular patrol been alerted about me?

In the midst of all this I kept getting flash frames of the worst – images of myself dead at the side of the road with the back of my skull punched out by a high-velocity bullet. Or slumped over the steering wheel with the front of my skull crunched hideously against the dashboard. Or worse: captured. I saw myself being taunted by the grinning soldiers as they subjected me to all the things my notebook was full of – attaching electrodes to *my* balls, smashing *my* wrists and ankles, hurling *my* broken body down Antelope Mine. All those cases that I'd been assiduously noting became real and personal again, not just some tide of generic suffering. And in those last few moments I decided: I would run the bastard over and go straight through their fucking roadblock. I floored the accelerator and whooped exultantly. Here goes. But something was wrong. My mind grasped at the possibilities as the old pick-up cranked up to full speed.

He didn't have a weapon.

That was it.

Fifth Brigade never moved without weapons, especially not down here in enemy territory. But this soldier was clearly empty-handed, and his movements were slightly tentative, not quite commanding enough. I lifted my foot slightly on the accelerator. He looked as though he was *smiling*. That did it. I slammed on the brakes and brought the vehicle to a halt in a cloud of dust, just past the soldier.

'Good afternoon to you,' he said at the window, still smiling. I noticed a 2nd lieutenant's pip on his epaulettes. 'I am looking for a lift to Gwanda.'

'Of . . . of course,' I stuttered in disbelief. 'Jump in.'

He collected his backpack from the side of the road and threw it on to the back seat, joining me up front.

'Thanks a lot,' he said as we drove off. 'Where are you coming from?'

'I'm a farmer,' I mumbled. 'Just been checking on my lands.'

We chatted about the drought, how many cattle I owned, how many he owned back home in Sipolilo. Slowly I got over the shock of our meeting. I wondered what awfulness this rather engaging young man had witnessed or even ordered. After some more safe pleasantries, I began complimenting him on the army's record in Matabeleland.

'It's a fine job you blokes are doing down here,' I said.

369

'Thanking you,' he grinned happily. 'We came here to protect the white farmers like you from the dissidents.' He paused to look out of the window at some civilians sitting by the roadside. 'These Matabele people, they too cheeky. They don't like the Shona, and they don't like the *mukiwa* either. But now we are teaching them not to be so cheeky.'

I nodded in agreement. He offered me a cigarette and we drove on in companionable silence.

Ten miles before Gwanda we hit a real roadblock, with spikes, a stop group hunched over a machine gun, tents bristling with radio antennae. The soldier in charge was a Fifth Brigade sergeant. He snapped a salute as soon as he saw the lieutenant, then I heard him say in Shona that they were looking for a young white man who was helping the dissidents. The suspect might be dressed as a priest, and was last seen in a blue Peugeot estate. They were under strict orders to stop any white man, to check IDs and question them. My lieutenant tried to brush him aside but the sergeant was insistent. It was Code Red, he said.

'Just a minute, you wait here for me,' said the lieutenant, unnecessarily, and got out of the pick-up. He walked with the sergeant over to the tent and they disappeared inside.

I was left looking bleakly ahead at the two soldiers manning a heavy machine gun on a bipod. As they were required to do in a Code Red, one was clutching the twin handles of the gun, training the barrel straight at me. The other was holding a belt of bullets that fed into the breech. They stared balefully back at me, looking as though they were itching to put their hardware to good use. For the second time that day, I wondered dully what would happen to me.

After a few minutes, the lieutenant strode back from the tent and got back into the cab beside me.

'OK, let's go,' he said.

Outside the sergeant saluted again, the spikes were dragged aside and I drove through.

The lieutenant shook his head. 'That one, he tried to say you

are a journalist spy,' he laughed, 'that you help the dissidents.'
He pulled out his packet of cigarettes and offered me one. 'But
I tell him that you are a farmer and I know you from long
back. I tell him that we are old friends.'

Twenty-One

Back in Bulawayo, I wrote up the story in a daze. *The Sunday Times* published it under the headline *Mass Murder in Matabeleland: The Evidence*. We tried to dilute my exposure by adding extra bylines and fudging the dateline, but it did little to divert the government's fury when the story broke. The next week I wrote a follow-up piece. And to my surprise I learnt that the editor of our main rival paper, the *Observer*, had arrived in Matabeleland. The *Observer* was then still owned by Lonrho, which also had major investments in Zimbabwe. Senior Zimbabwean ministers had apparently approached Lonrho's head, Tiny Rowland, and appealed to him to rubbish my story, so he had sent in his biggest gun – the editor, no less.

But the plan backfired. The *Observer*'s editor, Donald Trelford, realized that things *were* in fact terribly amiss in Southern Matabeleland, and wrote an article which backed me up and invoked his owner's wrath. But after a day in Matabeleland, Trelford had returned to England and, inevitably, I was blamed for the *Observer* story too. Tiny Rowland himself issued a statement saying that his editor had been misled by me. He derided me as '*The Sunday Times*' most junior reporter', which, at the time, was probably true.

When *The Sunday Times* ran my third story the following week, the government realized that foreign press interest in Matabeleland wasn't going away. They announced that they would arrange a media facility trip to the area to show that my allegations were nonsense. I stayed on in Bulawayo, nervous and uncertain, trying to monitor the situation within the curfew zone.

The staff at the hotel, mostly Matabeles from the affected area, had heard about the news reports. The switchboard operator relayed my phone conversations to them, and the telex operator distributed samizdat versions of the stories I'd filed. As I waited for my world to fall in around me, waiters and cleaners would shake my hand surreptitiously in the corridor, or slip me unordered second helpings of food. The chef came out of his kitchen one night, a great fat mound of a man in a tall white hat, and under the guise of asking how the food was, he sidled up to my table, looked slyly around and said: 'It is a good thing you do, we thank you.' And I felt absurdly pleased.

Other foreign correspondents arrived from Harare for the facility trip, bearing frightening tales of just how angry the cabinet was and passing on various rumours about what would happen to me: I would be banned, detained, expelled, killed. I phoned my parents to apologize for the fuss and to make sure they weren't being hassled in any way.

'Well, well, you certainly seem to have caused some ripples,' said my father sardonically, and then indicated that their phone was probably not now a good one on which to have any private conversation.

The facility itself was a fiasco. Fifty-five reporters all piled into a bus accompanied by an army escort of Crocodiles with cab-mounted machine guns, headed by the army commander comrade General Rex Nhongo. 'Nhongo' meant goat in Shona and it was his *chimurenga* name. He was the husband of comrade Spillblood Nhongo, Minister of Women's Affairs. As a guerrilla, the general was famous for leading the Altena Farm attack just before Christmas 1972, which had begun the war.

Not to be outdone, the chief of police, Commissioner Nguruve, was also there. 'Nguruve' was Shona for wild pig, and it was his real name. He didn't have a *chimurenga* name as he'd been on the wrong side in the war. He'd served as a sergeant in the old BSAP, though he didn't like to be reminded of it.

In preparation for this operation, Comrade General Nhongo had brought along a good supply of Johnny Walker Red Label whisky, which he drank out of a plastic beaker throughout the day. The main function of his aide-de-camp was to keep it topped up. I realized that it was largely up to me to produce witnesses to atrocities, but I was terribly worried that anyone I led the group to would be harassed, or worse, after we had gone. In the three weeks since my first story, I'd had reports that Fifth Brigade had launched something called Operation Clean-up. They had been busy moving the injured out of local hospitals and into army hospitals outside the area, and a special task force called the Green Group had combed the area, disinterring mass graves and moving bodies. Belaghwe and other detention camps had been emptied for our inspection.

I went up to St Paul's and talked to the latest arrivals. One refugee said the army was warning all people not to talk to journalists. 'They say, "Remember, if you complain to the journalists we will know who you are, and we will still be here after they have gone," ' he told me.

Several white CIO officers had toured the area posing as sympathetic journalists, to test the threats. If people talked freely to them, they were arrested and taken away.

'Now,' said the refugee, 'the people are much too scared to talk to anyone. They will tell you nothing.'

At the initial briefing before the trip, I asked the general if he would mind signing 'immunity from prosecution' forms guaranteeing that witnesses who spoke to us would not be detained or prosecuted or harmed in any way. I'd had such forms drawn up by a local lawyer. But this request only provoked him further. He angrily pushed the forms away, and when I tried to insist he threatened to tear them up.

On that first day of the trip, our bus got stuck in a river bed and then our army escort lost its way. Thirteen hours later, the tired and hungry journalists finally arrived back in Bulawayo, in mutinous form.

On the morning of the second day, the general called us together for a briefing. 'This morning,' he announced, 'your Peter Godwin will lead the convoy since he is the one accusing my army of atrocities.' He looked at me and bared his teeth in a dangerous smile. 'You will go ahead in a car, by yourself. You show us about these things you have been saying, OK?' And then he added, 'Be careful of land mines.' And he laughed. So now I was to be used as a hostage mine detector, I thought bitterly, just like *my* soldiers had once used local civilians in Filabusi, during the war.

We had been asked to supply the army with a list of the locations we wished to visit. But I was in a panic about compromising ordinary villagers, who would be far too frightened to talk, and whose lives would be at risk if they did. I would be endangering them even by putting them on such a list. As well as the journalists, now in cars, our party still included dozens of soldiers and CIO officers.

I discussed the quandary with the other journalists and we decided to concentrate on mission hospitals and schools, where the staff would be relatively safe. We wrote out a list of eight locations and handed it over. The closest was Matopos mission hospital. As we set off, with me in front, I noticed that a CIO contingent had already gone ahead of us, no doubt to soften up our reception at the various locations on the list.

When we arrived, the nurse in charge looked cowed. She stood with her hands clasped, her eyes downcast, speaking in a soft monotone. But, to her great credit she told us that she had treated thirty women for serious injuries inflicted by the army.

'How do you know it's the army?' shouted the local journalists from the *Herald*. 'It must be the dissidents.'

'We know it's the army,' insisted the nurse, quietly, 'because they have army vehicles and radios and army uniforms and they speak Shona. They are the ones from Five Brigade, the ones with the red hats. We know who they are. I can show them to you if you want.'

But patients at the hospital denied having seen anything, and my heart sank. The CIO cameramen were filming everyone we talked to and their photographers took mug shots of them all and wrote down their names and *situpa* numbers and addresses. But as we were leaving one of those who'd 'seen nothing', tugged at the sleeve of a correspondent. 'I'm sorry,' he whispered, 'so many terrible things have happened here, but we cannot talk to you. We are being watched.'

Next we tried a mission run by Americans. They had to talk, surely? Dr Devee Boyd came swishing through in his white coat to be confronted by our 150-strong party. He consulted his admissions ledger and announced that his hospital had treated over 125 cases of serious assault and twenty-five rapes by soldiers since the army offensive began.

'I have written to the prime minister every week since the offensive began, begging him to stop it,' he said, 'but I have heard nothing.'

The comrade general was starting to get seriously cross. As the journalists milled around, getting back into their convoy of cars, he came up to me and said: 'We know all about you, you were a Selous Scout in the war.' (The Selous Scouts were a Rhodesian unit which operated behind the lines disguised as guerrillas. They had a reputation for ferocity and 'dirty tricks'.)

I noticed that the general's hands were trembling. On his hip he had a holster and from it he now eased a Russian Tokarev pistol. It was rather a beautiful weapon, I noticed, its handle inlaid with mother-of-pearl.

He slapped the pistol irritably against his palm. 'You, you . . .' he spluttered for words, 'you swine!' he said at last. 'You *bloody* swine!'

He raised the pistol and pointed it at my chest. 'I am going to kill you,' he announced.

I remember thinking, oh well, this is the way it happens. In front of the entire press corps. At least there'll be no doubt who did it.

I glanced at his young ADC, who was hovering at his elbow, looking anxiously at the general's gun. I folded my arms and said nothing. Of course it was a bluff. Surely? I looked at the general sceptically.

'Really. I will, you know. I'll shoot you,' he said. 'And *then* you'll be sorry.'

'Drink, General?' invited his ADC, and produced the some-what depleted bottle of Johnny Walker. The general fumbled around for his tumbler and I slipped away.

'Damn!' breathed a voice next to me. It was Alexander Joe, AJ, the Associated Press wire photographer. 'I thought I'd have an exclusive: *GENERAL SHOOTS HACK*.'

I laughed nervously. 'Do you really think he'd have done it? In front of all these people?'

'Well, the day's not over yet,' said AJ hopefully, loading more film. 'I'll just stick close to you, if you don't mind . . .'

I got back into my car. We were setting off now for Minda mission. I had talked to Father Gabriel on the phone and he'd promised to try and find some witnesses who were not afraid to talk. He could offer them some sort of protection inside his mission. But we'd been cut off in the middle of our conversation and we hadn't spoken since. I had no idea if he'd managed to find anyone.

As I started up the engine the passenger door opened and in stepped the senior government press spokesman, John Tsimba, a man who I'd been fairly friendly with before this Matabele-land episode.

'Can I have a lift with the mine detector?' he asked good-naturedly, and we drove off, billowing through the dust of Matabeleland towards Minda mission. For a while he was silent and pensive, and then he sighed. 'I just wanted to say that I didn't know anything about what was going on down here.

And I'm sure the prime minister was ignorant of it too. I think it was just a case of the army getting a bit, a bit . . . how can I say, a bit overenthusiastic.'

I shook my head. 'The really depressing thing, John,' I started, 'is that this isn't an army out of control. Uh uh. This is a well-trained army with a proper command structure, following orders. They're doing this because they've been ordered to do it from higher up. How much higher up, I don't know.'

'Well *I* didn't know about it,' he insisted, and we lapsed back into silence.

At Minda mission Father Gabriel had gathered together some witnesses. They stood in a sad little group surrounded by the mass of soldiers and spies and journalists. They looked terrified. One of them, the leader, started trying to tell a story about how the army had arrived at their village nearby and executed six people, but he was being jostled and heckled. He was an elderly man, stooped and grizzled and rheumy-eyed, but strong of voice still. 'I will take you to where this thing happened,' he offered. 'It is nearby.'

Without further formality, I bundled him into my car and we drove off, followed by angry soldiers and local journalists.

The old man directed me to a ragged little village several miles away. Only two huts were still standing, the charred outlines of the other five were still clearly visible, their blackened rims etched into the ground. When we arrived he disappeared into his hut, while I waited outside for the storm to arrive. In the distance I could see the Crocodiles charging down the road, followed by the convoy of cars. A huge plume of dust marked their progress and obscured the late-afternoon sun.

The old man ducked out of his hut. He had changed his clothes. Now he wore the regalia of a sub-chief, a long red cloak, a white pith helmet and, on a chain around his scrawny neck, a crescent-shaped copper disk bearing the government coat of arms. The outfit seemed to imbue him with a new confidence and authority.

Everyone was milling around in confusion and without any further prompting he took charge of the event. 'My name,' he announced in a new, surprisingly sonorous voice, 'is Chief Baywayi.' He looked around at the journalists poised with pens at pads. 'Baywayi,' he repeated, and he spelt it out. 'B-A-Y-W-A-Y-I. I am the senior headman for this whole part.' He cast his arm around in a wide arc. 'The soldiers from the Fifth Brigade came here at night and took six people, including my sons, and they just shot them. Then they made us dig a grave here.'

He walked over to the side of his kraal and stood at the edge of a patch of freshly turned earth. He began to speak again but the journalists from the *Herald*, the CIO men and some of the soldiers started jeering and booing and shouting him down. And I heard some of them threatening him in Shona, warning that they would 'get him' later, that he would 'suffer'.

Baywayi lifted his hands for silence and, miraculously, the hubbub died down. 'These people—' He indicated those who had been threatening him. 'These people say bad things will happen to me if I speak to you.' He paused dramatically for a moment. 'But I am an old man now and my sons have been taken away from me, so it does not matter any more.'

He adjusted his sub-chief's badge and continued. 'Three weeks ago the Fifth Brigade came back and they made us dig up the grave. They poured paraffin on the bodies of our people and then they burnt them. Then they loaded the remains in their truck and took them away.'

The jeering and shouted had started again, and this time the foreign correspondents were remonstrating with the local ones, trying to shut them up and give the old man a chance to speak. Above the angry argument Baywayi's voice rang out like an officiating cleric at Mass. 'I must speak the truth and shame the devil,' he concluded.

Behind him the huge shimmering yoke of a harvest sun was nudging the horizon.

Another witness, a shrunken old man leaning heavily on a walking stick, stepped forward. He turned to his audience of reporters and soldiers and CIO men. 'My name is Alfred Mvuli and in there,' he said, pointing his stick at the grave, 'they put my brother, Solomon. The soldiers shot him for no reason. They put the gun at his head, and just shot him. Even though he had done nothing wrong.'

From behind the crowd, the voice of Police Commissioner Nguruve interrupted him. 'You are a dissident supporter!' All the soldiers and policemen and local reporters jeered angrily again.

Alfred Mvuli surveyed the incensed group around him. 'I know I have crucified myself with my statements,' he said quietly. Then he replaced his ragged hat and strode away into the gathering gloom without looking back.

John Tsimba, my friend from the ministry, called for our attention. He wanted to wrap up the day's events. 'So, you have found no mass graves, no killings today,' he concluded. He had clearly made a rapid recovery from his car confessional. 'If from now on you people write stories about genocide we can only interpret that as meaning you have a personal vendetta against the people of Zimbabwe.'

I noticed that he was actually standing on the grave of Baywayi's sons as he delivered his warning. Behind him the general joined in. 'Yes, you have been writing nonsense!' he shouted, and then he jabbed his finger at me. 'Bloody lies.'

I suppose I knew I was finished after that. In spite of the fact that Church and human rights bodies backed me up and called for an inquiry. At a press conference the next morning, the Secretary of Information announced darkly that they had a large dossier on my military background. I had been, he announced, a serving member of the Selous Scouts, the most notorious of all Rhodesian combat units.

Back in Harare the next day, I went home to my parents' house. I suddenly felt deeply weary. Zimbabwe would never be quite the same again for me. Not after what had gone on in Matabeleland. I recounted it all to my parents, over tea, sitting at their round metal table in the garden, with the swimming-pool waterfall splashing behind us and the loeries washing and preening in the water. It all seemed so far away.

'I wonder what'll happen next?' said my father when I had finished my story.

We soon found out. That week the *Herald* ran an editorial about Matabeleland which ended by asking its readers '*whether this country should allow some people, who are only able to walk the streets of Harare today instead of being in prison because of the policy of reconciliation, to continue smearing the name of Zimbabwe in London*'?

Several journalists rang me up, asking me to comment on a threat clearly aimed at me. I said nothing.

The following week another editorial, headed *Crush Them*, went further: '*We would not like to believe that the apparent relaxation of operations in Matabeleland has anything to do with the current foreign press campaign, some of it written by Zimbabweans who deserved the hangman's rope for their war crimes.*'

The temperature was being turned up deliberately. Campaigns like this were run by the *Herald* to soften up opinion before the fall. Journalists, friends of mine, kept calling to see if I was still at large. AJ rang frequently. 'Just a checking call,' he would say brightly, 'to make sure you haven't been lifted yet.' Everyone clearly expected it. Even me.

The next day I drove into town to do some shopping and check my mail at Newsfile. I parked the car in the Meikles car park and as I walked through town I realized that someone was following me. I doubled back on myself and walked right round the block, but he was still there, a small black man in his thirties. He wasn't making any particular attempt to conceal himself. I went up into Newsfile, and he stayed downstairs. Half an hour later when I came down, he was still there, leaning against the wall, smoking a cigarette. I walked slowly back to the car park and he followed me all the way. And when I got into my car, he rapped on the passenger window and indicated for me to open the door. As he climbed in I noticed that he was sweating copiously and appeared to be even more nervous than I was.

'What do you want?' I demanded aggressively.

'Drive. Just drive around. I want to talk to you. But it is dangerous for me.'

So I drove out of the car park, down Second Street, past the Passport Office with its permanent queue of passport applicants, and left down Samora Machel Avenue.

'I am on the arrest detail to pick you up,' said my companion. 'We will do it tomorrow night, very late. You will be taken to Chikurubi prison.'

I had turned now and was driving back along Baker Avenue, past the South African Trade Mission, which served as their embassy, where another queue of blacks, this one lining up for South African visas, stretched right around the block.

'You will be detained in Chikurubi,' he continued, 'indefinitely. It will be announced that you are an agent spying against Zimbabwe.' He pointed up at the flag fluttering over the South African Trade Mission. 'That you are working for Pretoria.'

I wasn't really surprised at this news. I was surprised only at being given such explicit advance warning.

'You must get out,' he warned. 'Now. Today. Once you are in Chikurubi, you will be locked inside there for years.'

We were back in the centre of town, and I stopped at a red light on Kenneth Kaunda Avenue. 'That is my advice,' he said and opened the door to leave.

'Wait.' I said. 'Why are you telling me this?'

He closed the door and leant in at the window. 'I may have a Shona surname, but my mother's family is from Matabeleland.

Many of my people have been killed there.' And he walked quickly away, disappearing into the crowds of lunch-time shoppers.

I drove out along Enterprise Road one last time to my parents' house in Chisipite to explain to them that I was going to get out for a few weeks while this all died down. Then, just in case, I told them about the warning. 'Maybe it's true. Maybe not,' I said. 'I need a few weeks away from this anyway, then I'll come back.'

I had packed a small bag and my father drove me to the airport. My mother was needed back at the hospital. There were no transcontinental flights that night so I was booked on a plane to Botswana. The airport terminal was almost empty. I checked in and we went upstairs to the bar on the verandah overlooking the runway. Nobody took any notice of us, a young man in khaki chinos and a blue shirt and an old man with a flourish of white hair in a beige safari suit. We sat there nursing our beers in the warm evening until the flight was called.

'See you soon. I'm sure it'll all blow over soon enough and you'll be back,' said my father, but he sounded unconvinced and unconvincing. I put out my hand to shake his but instead he enveloped me awkwardly in a brief hug, something he'd not done before. Then I walked away across the parquet tiles, under the advertisements for game parks and banks, car hire and city hotels, out across the tarmac to the Air Botswana jet.

As we gained height and the city's lights fell far below us, I had the strongest surge of *déjà vu*. Once again I was leaving a war behind in a rush. Once again, as we left the earthly bonds far below, the conflicts and passions down there seemed so pointless, more so with every foot we climbed into the cold thin air. Our route to Gaborone took us directly over Matabeleland. I peered out of my porthole into the dark void beneath. Here there were few lights, just the orange glow of bushfires.

I was feeling lonely and sorry for myself, leaving behind girlfriend, family and friends. Then I thought of Alfred Mvuli, with his gnarled walking stick and his patched hat, and wondered if he would in fact be 'crucified' as he had foretold. I wondered what would become of Chief Baywayi, or Bongali Dube who had shown me the bones of his father, or Phineas my guide who had cheerfully risked his family and himself to help me. They couldn't catch the next plane out of the country. They were stuck with it. This was their life, there was no way out for them.

It didn't blow over and I was wasn't back soon. The next morning, before dawn, as I had been warned, the police arrived at my parents' home asking for me. Finding me gone, they searched the house. They confiscated some hunting rifles from the gun cabinet, including the Brno .22 I had been given for my fourteenth birthday, the one with the intricately carved stock and the shiny smooth steel bolt. They left a seizure certificate stating that I was considered a person unfit to be in possession of firearms.

In parliament, a few days later, the Minister of Home Affairs made a statement about Matabeleland, while introducing a motion to extend the state of emergency. Reports of widespread atrocities by Zimbabwean security forces against civilians there were the result of an orchestrated propaganda campaign by the British press, he said. He condemned what he called 'the James Bond-like exploits of Mr Godwin, who came here to represent the London *Sunday Times*'. And then he revealed some dramatic news to the hushed House. 'In fact we know that Peter Godwin was a secret agent.'

The minister went on to deny that the army had done anything wrong in Matabeleland. And nothing, he said, nothing at all had been proved against them.

He concluded: 'Peter Godwin realized he had been exposed

and discredited and quickly dropped his contacts and left the country, never to return, and his services are now on offer to the South Africans.'

Shortly afterwards I was declared an enemy of the state, *persona non grata* in my own home.

Twenty-Two

I tried hard to forget about Africa after that. I tried to dismiss it from my head as a brutal, violent place. A place of death. And when people asked me what nationality I was, I replied, 'English, of course.' And if my accent betrayed me, I might concede vaguely, 'I did spend a bit of time in Africa, as a boy.'

The Sunday Times appointed me East Europe correspondent, and I trawled around Poland, Czechoslovakia, Romania, Bulgaria and Hungary, becoming increasingly depressed at the greyness of the oppression there. After a couple of years they posted me to South Africa, where the black townships were now in flames on a daily basis.

It was from my base in Johannesburg that I ventured back to report on Mozambique, the first time I'd been back there since my childhood.

Mozambique had been battered by two decades of war and famine by then. It was said to be the poorest country in the world. The black Marxist government was bogged down in a struggle against a new generation of rebel guerrillas, who were supported by white South Africa.

It was being widely reported by other papers that the Mozambique rebels had bases in neighbouring Malawi, but no one had any proof. Malawi, under its ancient dictator Dr Hastings Banda, normally had a blanket ban on foreign journalists. So I took advantage of a royal tour of the country by the Prince of

Wales to slip in as part of the official press entourage. I soon split off from the official group and made south for the Mozambique border.

For a day and a half I drove along the border speaking to locals and missionaries. Finally, in the middle of the second day, I stopped at a trading store right on the border. The store's interior was almost black after the bright sun outside. I asked the storekeeper if he ever saw rebels on this side of the border. My eyes got used to the darkness just in time to see his wide white smile disappear. From the furthest corner I heard the sound of metallic chinking.

'Who wants to know?' asked a deep voice.

In the corner were six men swathed in bandoliers of ammunition, with dull brown grenades dangling from their webbing. Kalashnikov rifles were propped against the wall and a rocket launcher was laid across the cement table. The men had been drinking Cokes through straws. Five of them remained bent over the Cokes, their lips still pursed around their straws, as they regarded me with deep suspicion.

'You coming with us,' said the sixth, 'back to our base.'

And with that the slurping ceased and they all got up to leave, their ironmongery clanking.

We walked south through thick scrub, the rebels clearly feeling in no danger. Unfortunately for me, the one English-speaker in the patrol veered off to some other destination and I was left with five heavily armed guerrillas and no way to communicate. They were led by a thuggish sergeant who, despite the intense heat, wore a fleece-lined Russian aviator's hat with furry earflaps that dangled down to his shoulders like spaniel's ears, completely undermining his efforts to appear warlike. They had no rank badges but you could tell he was in charge because he was the only one with boots. His boots obviously hurt him terribly, and he limped along with the laces untied and the tongues pulled forward on to the toecaps.

At every rebel encampment we passed, I sensed the story of

my 'capture' being notched up. I had been armed. I had resisted. I was a spy. The more *dagga* they smoked the more I became a Special Forces legend and, by implication, the more heroic they were to have overcome me. Sometimes the retelling of the story of my dangerous disarmament was accompanied by a few cuffs or the odd kick – nothing too violent, but I started to worry that the red-eyed sergeant in particular might up and shoot me, as a blurry hallucinogenic party trick to impress his comrades in arms.

On the second day we finally reached their base. I was fed a plate of *sadza*, allowed to wipe down with a wet cloth and, finally, presented to the camp commander. He was a small man in olive fatigues and a pair of flipflops. He sat at a scarred Formica table, manoeuvring a matchstick around his mouth and taking the occasional sip of Mateus Rosé from a bottle by his side. First he listened impassively to a long and, as usual, wildly embellished report of my capture by Sergeant Dopehead. When this was finally over, his dinner arrived, borne with great ceremony by a batman with a small threadbare towel over his arm, mâitre d'hôtel-style. I was bid wait while the commander spooned up his plateful of *sadza*.

Until now I had not understood any of the languages they were speaking, a mixture of northern Mozambican and Malawian dialects interspersed with phrases of pidgin Portuguese. But now I distinctly heard the commander give orders to his batman in *chiNdau*. I listened a little longer to be sure, and then I tentatively greeted the commander in what I could remember of *chiNdau*.

He was amazed.

'Where did you learn to speak this language?' he asked. I told him I had lived in the Chimanimanis, on the Rhodesian side, as a boy.

'What is your name, your family name?' he asked.

'Godwin.'

'Godwin,' he said thoughtfully, turning the name over. 'Was your mother the doctor on that side?'

'Yes,' I said. 'She was the GMO for the whole of Melsetter district.'

He smiled and shook his head, and put his hand out for an African 'low-five' handshake.

'She was the one who vaccinated me when I was a child,' he said. He pulled up his sleeve to show me a small vaccination scar on his shoulder.

He told his men what had transpired and they all started talking in animated fashion.

'Did you ever go with your mother to help her?' asked the commander suddenly.

'Uh huh,' I nodded, 'I sometimes helped with vaccinations. The polio ones for the children. The ones in the sugar lumps.'

'Yes,' he said, 'you gave me the sugar medicine too. I remember now. We put out our tongues and you came down the row with a tray of lumps and put one on each tongue.'

He finally relinquished my hand.

'And look now,' he said, brandishing his fist. 'I grew up strong.'

In the space of a few minutes I had been elevated from hostage spy to honoured guest. I was poured a beaker of the wine, handed a pre-lit cigarette, and ushered to a log seat at the commander's right-hand side. My capturing sergeant had meanwhile melted away.

The commander raised his beaker to propose a toast.

'A *luta continua!* – The struggle goes on!' he shouted, and downed his wine.

'*Até a vitoria final!* – Until final victory!' his ragged men bellowed back. And having no drinks to toast, they raised imaginary glasses. I sipped mine as required, only to find that it contained tepid cherry cola. The commander had been drinking cherry cola secretly decanted into his Mateus Rosé bottle. It seemed an appropriately ludicrous icon to recall the largely imaginary grandeur of the old Portuguese days.

The following day I was returned to the Malawian border. No tortuous trudging this time. This time I bounced along on the back of a Suzuki trial bike, the most sophisticated transport the rebels possessed. At the border they ceremoniously handed back the items they had 'confiscated' from me, my watch, my water bottle, my sunglasses and my camera. Even my notebook and biro.

Before they left, they insisted on a formal group photograph of all of us. The storekeeper took the shot, after brief instruction. We make an odd company, four rebels and me. The sergeant is still wearing his furry flying hat. And his arm is draped over my shoulder in an act of possessive camaraderie.

Later I went into Mozambique officially, for the first time in nearly twenty years. I was staggered by the change. Beira itself was a town under siege, difficult to recognize as the town we had holidayed in all those years ago. Most of the graceful avenues of flamboyant trees had been hacked down for firewood. The luxury seaside villas were ruined, cannibalized for building materials. There was almost no traffic, except for the odd army truck belching black exhaust and a lone tank that clattered uncertainly down the esplanade, running over a traffic sign on its way.

The *nova praia* was festooned with shipwrecks, rusty hulks lying on their sides at the water's edge just down from the centre of town. No one could tell me how they got there. In the town centre itself groups of amputees, war-wounded mostly, scuffed along the dusty pavements on crutches, or propelled themselves towards me on little home-made carts. They plucked at my sleeve and asked for money. At the cinema a handwritten hoarding advertised that the film *Ninja Taramatau* was showing. It had a childish drawing of a tortoise throwing a karate punch. Patrons were stepping gingerly over a dozen or more people huddled up asleep on the pavement outside.

The municipal market, a bustling fruit and vegetable emporium as I remembered it, seemed to have nothing for sale. Nothing at all. I trawled up and down the empty stalls, watched solemnly by idle traders, until finally I came to one stall with a single coconut proudly displayed. I picked it up and felt its weight in my hand and enquired of the price. But I didn't have the heart to buy it, to leave the market utterly without purpose.

The shop windows were also empty and so, for the most part, were the shelves inside. The only thing for sale was toilet paper, rolls and rolls of coarse, abrasive, beige toilet paper.

It seemed impossible to find anywhere to stay. The Estoril Hotel was choked with *dislocados*, refugees fleeing the war. I stopped outside and stared up at it. A young black woman with a baby on her arm beckoned to me from her vantage point at a smashed second-floor window. I walked over and stood beneath her expectantly. She smiled beatifically at me and called down in perfect English, 'Fuck off home, white man. Fuck off back to the Transvaal.' A ragged cheer went up from the refugees at the other windows.

The Grand Hotel, designed to be the plushest hotel in the country, was similarly ravaged and long since closed to paying guests. Its exterior was smoke-stained and several substantial fig trees had taken root in its balconies. In the marbled entrance hall, women were pounding *manioc* with mortar and pestle.

All 405 rooms were full, the self-appointed *chefe da guarda*, the chief guard, told me, beating back inquisitive *piccanins* with a length of plaited electric flex. There was no electricity or water, but still it was a desirable place to live and was occupied by policemen, teachers and harbour officials.

The lift shafts were clogged with rubbish so we took the solid teak stairway that swept up in an elegant curve from the reception. As we made our way up, buckets of slop were emptied out of windows above into the street outside. I felt as though we were in some medieval street scene. I followed the *chefe da guarda* down the long unlit corridor, walking gingerly to avoid the malodorous coiled turds that waited there in the darkness to be squelched upon, and gagging on the stench. He was reminiscing all the way.

'I was a valet here in the old days. The Grand Hotel was so beautiful, once you had stepped inside you couldn't bear to leave. Ahh . . . the guests would dance all night. We even had the president of Portugal staying here, Admiral Americo Thomaz. And I *myself* attended upon him.'

We emerged from the stinking corridor, blinking in the soggy heat outside, and I asked for directions to Mrs Trinidade's zoo. 'It is closed, I think,' warned the *chefe da guarda* as he told me how to get there.

I was looking forward to seeing Mrs Trinidade. In a horribly altered town she would be a vaguely familiar figure. But the figure escorted to me by the little children playing at the entrance of the zoo was wrong. Instead of the big bustling matron with hammy arms, this was a little taut twig of a woman.

'What happened to the old Mrs Trinidade?' I asked.

'Mrs Trinidade, she was my stepmother. She died. And my father was killed by robbers,' she said. 'The rest of the family has gone away. They went to Australia. They left me behind. But I am hoping to go too. One day.'

Around her the zoo looked abandoned, its fenced enclosures collapsed and overgrown.

'What happened to the zoo?' I enquired.

'We had no money for food,' said the young Mrs Trinidade, 'and the animals starved to death.'

She set off on a strange retrospective tour anyway. A tour of an imaginary zoo. 'It was really beautiful. Parrots, python, lions, leopards, tigers, turtles, crocodiles, flamingos, and chimpanzees – you know, special monkeys without tails.' She counted off the menagerie on her fingers.

'And here, here in this pen there were the vervet monkeys, *many* of them,' she announced proudly, and then her voice dropped. 'But the soldiers from the barracks next door, they liked to tease them. They gave them batteries from the radio, and the monkeys they were so hungry, they tried to eat them and they were poisoned from the acid inside, and they died.'

We walked over to another ruined enclosure. Inside were the remnants of a broken tank.

'This is where the crocodiles lived,' continued Mrs Trinidade junior, 'they had a really hard time. People used to throw rocks at them. One even lost an eye when someone hit it with an iron bar. At the end we had no food for them, so I said to the children: "If you want to see the crocodiles you must bring cats and dogs for them to eat." And that's how we fed them.'

We stood together staring at the memory of it.

'They were very fussy eaters, those crocodiles,' mused Mrs Trinidade. 'They would only eat the animals if they were still alive.'

'What? You fed live cats and dogs to the crocodiles?'

'*Fresco. Fresco.* The crocodiles would only eat fresh meat. It had to be still alive. They wouldn't eat it if it was already dead. They would just leave it to rot.'

I felt impelled by a ghoulish curiosity to know how you actually fed live pets to crocodiles.

'You just throw the dog or the cat over the fence into the cage,' she said.

'And what happens?'

'Nothing happens, the crocodiles just kill them.'

'But don't the dogs or cats try to fight back, or ... or to escape?' I pressed.

'They wouldn't fight, they were scared of the crocodiles. But they would try to jump up and escape, but the fence was too high. The crocodiles would just come over and bite them and eat them.' She made a snapping motion with her bony hand.

'Isn't that cruel,' I asked weakly, 'to feed live pets to crocodiles?'

'Hmm.' Mrs Trinidade thought for a second, and then she laughed, a dry, unattractive cackle. 'Yes,' she said, and we made our way over to the lions' cages. These were substantial concrete pens with a front wall of bars. On the step outside sat a woman in a bright wraparound cloth. She was carefully arranging wild flowers in a chipped teapot vase.

'The lions lived in here. But they starved to death as well and now these people live in the cages instead,' said Mrs Trindade in a matter-of-fact way.

I introduced myself to Theresa Diaz, the flower arranger, who was resident in the lion's den. She smiled prettily and curtseyed.

'Um, do you live here?' I asked, gesturing at the bars behind her.

'Yes,' she sighed, 'since we ran away from the war.'

'I used to come to the zoo when I was a boy,' I said. 'I remember when a lion used to live in there.'

'So do I,' she replied, 'I used to visit the zoo also when I was a child.'

'Did you ever imagine that you might end up living in the cage one day?' I asked, and immediately regretted it. She laughed self-consciously and looked down at her bare feet.

'Would you like to see inside?' she said suddenly, and stooped through the cage door. It was meticulously tidy inside: a sagging bed with crocheted cover, a wooden box as a bedside table and a thin cardboard suitcase filled with neatly folded clothes. Theresa was positioning the teapot of flowers on the bedside box.

'I live here with my four children, and my husband who was wounded in the war,' she said.

They had tried to weave strips of cardboard through the bars to give them some privacy. I noticed that the roof had bars too, making the room open to the rain.

'How long have you lived here?' I enquired.

'More than two years.' She fiddled with the flowers some more. 'But as soon as I can, I'm going to build my own house. A nice house with a bathroom. I don't want to die here in a cage. I want to die in my own house.'

We stooped back out of the cage into the sunlight.

'It's good of Mrs Trindade to let you stay here,' I said, 'You've made it very comfortable.'

'Oh, but we pay rent, you know,' said Theresa.

'Well, they can't live here for free,' said Mrs Trinidade crossly. 'They must pay something.'

As we left the cage I noticed some of Theresa's children playing happily nearby with their pet guinea pigs.

'Nice guinea pigs,' I said, patting one on the head.

'Yes, they are very nice,' agreed Theresa. 'They taste just like chicken.'

Lorenco Marques, now called Maputo, was said to be better off than Beira. But it was still in a sad condition. In this city of high-rises with no working lifts, sporadic electricity, unmaintained roads, broken windows, and fetid garbage heaps, the Polana Hotel was said to be an island of luxury to which only hard currency could earn you access.

From the outside the hotel looked largely unchanged. Its façade was overdue for a paint but the same avenue of palm trees still curved round to the same portico. The entrance hall still gleamed with burnished wood. And the complicated prewar lift, with its exposed cables and cage, was still in operation.

The wall of the lobby lounge was now dominated by a vast bas-relief of southern Africa, a postmodern collage of scrap metal. But something was wrong with the shape of the continent; white-ruled South Africa had been excised. Africa came to a premature end after Mozambique and the Indian Ocean lapped in place of the last 1500 miles of land. It was the ultimate in politically correct sculptures.

My room was unchanged. Completely unchanged. Nothing had been replaced. The towel that had once been deep and fluffy was thin and holed, the monogram now just a faint impression. I went downstairs for dinner. The splendour of the dining room was as it had been, the chandeliers still twinkling thanks to the hotel's back-up generator which chugged noisily outside the french doors.

Many of the staff were now elderly and stooped, the same ones who had been there when I was a boy. They were still in the same linen suits, but the cloth was threadbare, the Gandhi collars worn through, and the gold braid on the epaulettes was frazzled and dull. They scuffed around in ancient white tennis shoes with their toes poking through the ends, and served a thin soup so diluted that its original flavour was undetectable, and minute portions of boiled rice with tinned vegetables imported from China. And notwithstanding the lobby sculpture, they served South African Castle beer in cans, at an extortionate price.

At the table next to me a group of Soviet pilots wearing olive jumpsuits got noisily drunk on South African cane spirit. They proposed toast after toast, downing each in one gulp. The Soviet pilots were here to help the government forces keep the guerrillas at bay, the ones by whom I'd been briefly kidnapped. I had seen the Soviet Hind helicopter gunships and MiG fighters lined up on the apron of Maputo airport, awaiting their next sortie.

On my other side I listened as a table of white South African businessmen complained loudly, about the food, the price of the drinks, the noise of the generator. Eventually the duty manager was summoned to placate them. He listened politely, and when their noisy barracking became too much, he finally held up his hands, palms forward.

'Gentlemen, gentlemen,' he said. 'Allow me to give you some advice from the distinguished writer H. G. Wells: "In the country of the blind, the one-eyed man is king." ' And he turned on his heel and strode briskly from the room.

I got up before dawn the next morning, after a fretful night when the heat and the broken air-conditioner conspired to deny me sleep. Dawn blushed across the sky as I walked out along the clifftop, on the edge of the hotel grounds overlooking the sea. Then a great molten, tangerine sun finally eased above the Indian Ocean.

Below me the waves were obstinately hurling themselves against the rocks, churning and roiling and frothing, pulling back and hurling themselves at the rocks once more, in the relentless ritual of coastal combat.

I thought of Malcolm Muggeridge and his futile suicide attempt in the sea below, and of Bartholomew Diaz, first chancing upon these shores, and of the Portuguese conscripts disembarking for a lost war, the last unwilling champions of a European nation in decline, defeated by Africa. And a verse of their homesick *fado* came back to me from across the years:

> *Look gentlemen,*
> *At this Lisbon of days gone by*
> *Of the Crusades, the Esperas,*
> *And of the Royal Bullfights;*
> *Of the Festas, of age-old Processions,*
> *Of street-cries in the morning*
> *That are no more.*

The sun was already hot by the time I got back to the Polana Hotel. Around the pool the Russian pilots of the helicopter gunships and the MiG fighters had exchanged their flying suits for minute swimming briefs. They were cavorting with squealing bikini-clad *mestiza* hookers to the tinny music that crackled out over the Tannoy.

Back in South Africa, I got the chance to visit Great-Aunt Diana's grave for the first time since her funeral. I was sent by my newspaper to Bloemfontein to interview the barefoot marathon runner Zola Budd. When I had finished, I made a call to Harare, 1000 miles away. Over a crackling line my father gave me the details of Diana's grave. She'd been cremated and her ashes were stashed in Bloemfontein's main crematorium, a landscaped garden on the eastern edge of town.

I arrived late and the African night-watchman was just locking the gate for the night. After a blazing day it was going to be a cold highveld night and the watchman already had on his woollen balaclava and a thick green government jersey with leather elbow patches. He pointed with his *knobkerrie* to the notice showing the visiting times. I'd missed them by over two hours. Sighing, and with little hope of success, I explained that I'd come all the way from Zimbabwe to pay my respects at my ancestor's grave and would be so disappointed to leave without seeing it. He listened and then without demur he unlocked the gate and let me in.

The Bloemfontein crematorium was organized vaguely in date-of-death order, with the memorial plaques set into long granite walls. The night-watchman and I separated and trailed up and down different walls looking for the remains of Diana Rose. We searched for half an hour as the sun set over the Free State plateau. It was the night-watchman who finally found it, with a triumphant cry.

It was almost completely dark now, and he shone his torch on the plaque for me to see.

Diana Muriel Rose,
born 15/10/1887,
died 30/5/1968.

I pulled half-heartedly at a few weeds which had insinuated themselves between the edge of the brass plaque and the granite wall, and gave the plaque a futile rub with the sleeve of my jacket. What had begun as an outing motivated by little more than mild anthropological curiosity had suddenly changed. As I knelt at the wall, my throat tightened and my eyes pricked with tears for the first time in years. Small, self-conscious tears at first. But then wracking gushes of repressed weariness and self-pity. At the impermanence of my family in Africa. At our silly misguided attempts to fashion the continent to our alien ways.

Images of turn-of-the-century white southern Africa tripped through my head. Diana in her hoop-skirted finery, revolving a frothy parasol. Diana in leather helmet and Biggles goggles, gunning her motorcycle round a corner in a shower of dust. Diana the loser in love, ending her years as a music teacher trying to teach fat-fingered farmers' daughters to play the piano, her vain attempts to impose brittle English values on the *veld*. Her whole life seemed as out of place as a bone china teacup at a beer drink; her bright English social set destined to be wiped from this austere fortress of Afrikanerdom.

I got up and angrily wiped away the tears with the back of my hand and turned to find the night-watchman standing behind me, torch still held aloft all this time. His head was inclined, and one hand cupped the top of his *knobkerrie*. Together we walked back to the gate in silence. The wind was picking up now and from a distance it carried the swell of martial chants from the black township. And behind the chants, the insistent throb of the African drums. Closer, in a white suburb, the giant screen of the drive-in cinema was flickering into action with the Saturday evening movie.

Twenty-Three

In all the years that I was exiled from Zimbabwe, my father had written regularly to me, his sure sloping hand now restored, telling me what was happening back home and including bunches of newspaper clippings. Fifth Brigade had pulled out of Matabeleland, leaving the people there stunned and cowed. Church groups and human rights lawyers estimated that up to 7000 civilians had been killed and thousands more injured during the campaign. The government set up a commission of enquiry to take evidence of atrocities and promised to make its report public. But it never did.

Finally my father wrote to me in Johannesburg with the news that my old client Dumiso Dabengwa had been released from prison and appointed Deputy Minister of Home Affairs in a new government of national unity, the two tribes having finally realized that they had to learn to live together. Discreet enquiries were made on my behalf and we were told that there would be no objection to my return, so long as I didn't do any reporting and stayed away from the old killing fields of southern Matabeleland. So it was that I did eventually go back to visit Zimbabwe, to reclaim my past.

The British Airways Boeing 747 taxied up to the terminal building on a crisp December morning and it looked just as it had when I left it. They used to joke that on arrival the stewardess would announce 'Welcome to Salisbury, where local time is

1950.' And it still looked like a monument to the fifties. My father met me at the arrivals hall. He was standing under the Standard Bank sign, a big map of the country with a winking light for every branch of the bank. He was in his beige safari suit and his *veldskoens*.

We loaded my case into his old Peugeot and drove into town. Freedom monument was still there, a great arch straddling Airport Road with a huge concrete V-sign thrust up into the sky. V for victory. But some whites said it was a two fingers, a 'fuck-you' sign. Then there was a clutch of signs from Rotary and Round Table and the Lions Club, welcoming us to Harare, 'Garden City', and telling us at which hotels we might attend their weekly get-togethers.

Further in on Airport Road, Cranborne barracks, home to the RLI, 'The Incredibles' of old, now had a large sign saying it was home to a unit called One Commando Battalion. In a patch of wasteground after the barracks a group of Apostolics in their red robes, their *gammonts*, were gathered in a wide circle, praying.

Town itself was bigger, taller. The tower block which contained Scanlen and Holderness was now dwarfed by other blocks rising out of the canopy of jacaranda and flamboyant trees. There were more cars on the streets, but the taxis were still the same fleet of ancient Renault 4s, so old and battered now that some of them were said to have done a million kilometres. My father told me that the people from Renault had come out from France to make a film about them, they were so impressed.

It was the last day of term for the government senior schools and the city centre was full of black children in blazers and ties and matching straw boaters struggling with tin trunks, their mothers at the opposite ends. Their surnames were stencilled on the trunks, just like ours had been. Not Van Reenens and Paphoses and Badenhorsts, but Moyos and Shoniwas and Sitholes. The revolution might have come but they didn't want to change everything at all, they just wanted a part of it.

We drove out the other side of the city along Enterprise Road, past central prison and Nazareth House to Chisipite. Many of the big suburban houses had enormous satellite dishes planted in their gardens now, so that their owners could stop watching the comrades on ZTV news, and watch instead wrestling and golf and weather reports from the other side of the world.

When we got home, my mother and the maid, Mavis, and the dogs were all there to meet me. The house was unchanged, Jain's framed batiks still had pride of place on the sitting-room wall. There was a Christmas tree standing in the corner with a pile of presents at its foot. Several of them were for me, one was a small packet with small printed writing on it, 'To *baas* Peter from Mavis.'

'It's a doily,' said my mother. 'She's been crocheting it ever since she heard you were coming home.'

On the beaten-copper cowling of the fireplace my parents had stuck their Christmas cards in rows. Most of them bore pictures of snowmen and mistletoe, robin redbreasts and reindeer, all the exotic Christmas icons of another world. We sat and had tea at the little round metal table by the swimming pool, and it was just like the old days. Across the road on the playing fields of Oriel Boys' High School, which was almost entirely black now, the school band was playing 'Colonel Bogey' on marimbas.

The next day I went first to see Dumiso Dabengwa, to thank him for letting me back in. His office was on the top floor of the Earl Grey building. It had now been renamed Mukwati, after another leader of the 1896 rebellion, but the entrance was still dominated by a huge stone frieze of the white pioneers, their wagons drawn into a defensive *laager*, fending off marauding natives.

It was the first time I'd seen Dabengwa since he'd been loaded into the prison truck and taken back to Chikurubi after the treason trial. He was heavier now, still softly spoken and authoritative at the same time.

It was an awkward meeting, really. I suppose I was a reminder of a time he'd rather forget, now that he was back on board the government. I asked him about his time in jail. Conditions were bad at the beginning, he said, but then the new Justice Minister came to visit them and they complained to him.

'The minister called the prison superintendent,' said Dabengwa, 'and he told the superintendent: "We were all inside Ian Smith's jails and the conditions there were much better than those here now. Remember it's thanks to these people that you now have stars on your shoulders. These men are the best commanders we have – they have done nothing wrong – they are only here in prison because we fear them." '

Dabengwa leant back in his executive chair and grinned. From then, he said, conditions improved. 'We were allowed family visits, almost every other day, and they could send us food. We were even given a fridge.'

We chatted about his family and the drought in Matabeleland, and as he was describing how parched Bulawayo was, he walked over to the window. We looked down together at the well-watered lawns and avenues of Harare, and he told me how he had launched his own personal scheme to pipe water 200 miles from the great Zambezi river to Bulawayo 'before the city dies of thirst'.

As he spoke, the skies over Harare opened in a downpour. He gazed enviously at the rain and shook his head at the unfairness of it all. Then he caught sight of the clock on the cathedral tower and snapped out of his reverie. 'I'm running late,' he announced and our little chat was over.

In view of the downpour, Dabengwa offered me a lift in his ministerial car to the car park a few blocks away. The chauffeur drew smoothly away from Mukwati building, the bodyguard cued up Dire Straits on the tape, and we drove off through the wet Harare streets to the sound of 'Sultans of Swing'.

I found myself curiously detached from Harare this time. The landmarks of my past were still there, the police training base at Morris Depot, the High Court, and there, rising out of the botanical gardens, the granite turret of St George's College. As I went up the drive I felt that same old sickly feeling of apprehension in the pit of my stomach.

Term had finished and there was no one around so I wandered through the buildings and came eventually to the little chapel of remembrance, just off the main refectory. I looked around at the stained glass and the wooden boards carved with the names of those alumni killed in the two world wars: twenty-six killed in the First World War and another fifty-six in the Second. Then I noticed a new board. It was a list of boys killed in our civil war. The board was headed simply '1974–79' and there were twenty-eight names on it. Almost all were boys from my time, boys I could remember well. Good friends, prefects, team-mates, juniors. I knelt down at a pew and said a prayer for all the lost talent, the wasted lives – reduced now to a list of names in the school chapel.

As I drove back to my parents' house it occurred to me that I really didn't know many people in Harare any more; I felt like a stranger here now. As I thought about it, I realized that, even after all these years, home was probably still Melsetter, and I suddenly felt an overwhelming urge to go back there. I hadn't been back since I had left at the age of fifteen, and now it seemed to represent my whole childhood. So after New Year I set off for the eastern highlands.

After a 300-mile journey I felt once again that familiar excitement as I caught my first glimpse of the glittering quartz of the Chimanimani Mountains rising above me. Melsetter wasn't Melsetter any more, of course, the village had now been given the name of the mountain range above it, Chimanimani.

At first sight, it looked much the same. The hotel, and the low red-roofed colonial offices of the District Commissioner at the top end of the village square. But something was different about the village square: the pioneer monument had gone from the middle of it. The big old granite ox wagon standing high on its flagstone plinth. I walked over to where it had been. The only clue to its existence was a rough concrete base among a spray of yellow wild flowers.

My mother's old clinic had been replaced by a district hospital now, down the hill. The clinic looked abandoned. Even the purple-headed lizards had gone away. The *rondavel* walls were chipped and crumbling. Creepers and weeds had started to grow from them. The sheet-iron roof was working loose; it flapped and banged as the breeze tugged at it. And the grass of the waiting area, which was usually flattened by a hundred patients, where Mr Arrowhead had sat quietly waiting his turn, the grass was high and thick now.

St George's-in-the-mountains, the tiny stone church copied from one in Cornwall, was still there. Inside, it was dusty and airless. Spiders had colonized one corner, their webs shimmering in the multicoloured light that poured down through the stained-glass window – the window that had been salvaged from a church in the East End of London, destroyed in the Blitz during the Second World War. I turned the pages of the wooden baptism record hinged to the wall, and there was my little sister's name, Georgina Caroline Godwin. I remembered walking down in crocodile file from school to attend the service.

Up the hill my old school was now fronted by a board announcing: *Chimanimani Government School*. It looked much as I'd remembered it. One or two new low buildings, the car park tarred, electricity installed. Sitting on the verandah of Mr Simpson's green clapboard bungalow was the new headmaster, an African. He welcomed me with great ceremony and called the school together to meet that rarest of species, a visiting white old boy. Where once there had been seventy white faces, there were now 300 black ones, singing out their greeting in unison.

The headmaster took me on a tour of the premises. The narrow iron beds were still there but the grenade screens had gone from the dormitory windows. Through a classroom window I saw that insects were still being pinned to boards and paper chains were still in fashion. The pool, though, was filled with green slime.

'We have no money to keep it up,' complained the headmaster. 'I managed with donations and collections to buy chlorine for a year, but then I had to give up.' He looked embarrassed.

Later he took me into the school office and dug out the large leather-bound school register. He paged back through the decades until he found the year 1962. He ran his finger down the column of names until he at last found mine.

'You see,' he said proudly, 'we still try to keep up the old standards.'

I looked through the phone book for names I recognized but there was not much continuity to be found here. The war had purged Melsetter of settlers. There had been more than three hundred white farmers here once. Now there remained only three. One of those who had remained was Lord Plunket. In some ways the Plunkets didn't count because they spent as much time in England as out here. I remembered them from when I was little. We used to laugh because their entry in the phone book said 'Plunket, The Lord', like he was The Lord God or something. Jain and I used to strut around saluting each other and saying in very plummy voices, 'Plunket, The Lord. Plunket, The Lord.' At the time my father had explained to us that 'The Lord', was in fact the correct title for an Irish Lord, but it made no difference to our antics.

The Plunkets had caused a great stir by bringing a black man to the hotel to a meeting of the Capricorn Society, which was a society for the advancement of multiracialism. Even though the black man was the only man there wearing a jacket and tie, he hadn't been allowed in the bar for a drink. The manager had said it was against the law. I remember some of the grown-ups muttering darkly that Plunket, The Lord, was a communist, and I smiled at the memory of it now, as I drove out to visit them at the foothills of the Chimanimanis.

We sat in the sitting room drinking locally grown tea and being periodically buffeted by a pair of boisterous Labradors. On the drinks cabinet was a cluster of photographs of various royal occasions. Lord Plunket was, I remembered, the Queen Mother's godson. Over tea the Plunkets recounted Melsetter's misfortunes. The district, with its long border with a hostile Mozambique, had been devastated. One in every six white male adults had been killed. Nearly every farm had been attacked, most of them on numerous occasions. The hotel had been taken over by the forestry companies to use as a safe base for estate workers. No tourists came near the place. The only way in or out was to join the armed convoys, which went thrice weekly to Umtali. But even with military escorts these convoys were often ambushed.

'Oh, it was terrible. Just terrible,' sighed Lady Plunket. But through it all they refused to take security precautions. They hoped that their liberal reputation and openness would be their best defence.

'Our neighbours, the Symes, they were persuaded to put up a security fence, and shortly afterwards they were murdered, shot dead at their dinner table over supper. Another farmer, nearby, he was found shot dead, with his severed genitals stuffed into his mouth.' She shuddered at the memory of it. 'More tea?'

In time, the Plunkets had eventually been attacked. Twice, in fact. But on both occasions they were out of the country. On the first occasion the guerrillas simply departed on hearing that the Plunkets were in Scotland. Then some time later a group of seventy guerrillas turned up saying that the previous group hadn't done their duty. They piled all the furniture in the middle of the sitting room and set fire to it. Then they stumbled on the Plunket's wine cellar, and apparently proceeded to get roaring drunk on Plunket, The Lord's finest claret.

The Plunkets had a screen on which Lady Plunket had pasted a collage of pictures of the Queen's coronation. And before they went, the guerrillas left a memento on it. They daubed the message: *DOWN WITH LORDS AND LADIES! AND DOWN WITH YOUR QUEEN!* Then they made off with the blankets, the curtains and, what clearly irritated Lady Plunket most of all, they stole a set of Wedgwood plates.

'They were a limited edition,' she recalled wistfully, 'beautifully decorated around the rims with pictures of African wildlife, painted by the wife of the warden of Kruger National Park in South Africa.'

After the attack, the guerrillas had retired to the forest and hidden in trenches for a while. I tried to imagine this group of seventy armed insurgents lying under the pines in the damp soil, glugging Lord Plunket's vintage claret and eating off Lady Plunket's limited edition Wedgwood, and I suppressed an unkind smile.

'When we got back I found out who was responsible, who did it,' said Lady Plunket. 'The leader was a fellow by the name of Washington Matikiti, and he came from Mutambara mission. *Matikiti* means pumpkin, apparently. I was going to go over there and post reward notices for the Wedgwood, offering to buy the plates back, but I was persuaded that this was not a wise course of action. They're irreplaceable, completely irreplaceable, you know.'

Lord Plunket retired to his office, the top floor of a charming folly he'd built himself. It was a square tower with stunning views out over the mountains. Lady Plunket and I took the Labradors for a walk. She wanted to show me her 'indigenous garden'.

'It's about sixty acres which I call the wild garden. Nothing exotic is allowed here at all, only local plants.'

From time to time on our walk she would dart off the path to wrench out an offending wattle sapling or some other banned exotic species. And as we walked through the wild garden I was struck by the irony of it all. Here were the Plunkets, a pretty exotic species themselves, who had always returned to Britain for more than half of every year. Yet hundreds of the real settlers, the roots-down settlers, had fled. And the Plunkets were virtually the only ones to survive, the only ones to live on here in one of the most beautiful corners of Africa. Come to think of it, they had only survived the war at all because on both the occasions their farm was attacked they were absent in Britain. Yet they were now better adjusted to the new realities of Africa than most. And they were still here, in the phone book. Plunket, The Lord. Still here after all of us had gone away.

I went back up Orange Grove Road to the village, and took a late-afternoon stroll around the grassy square. The air was sharp and pure, slightly chilled from its journey up over the mountains. The orchestra of the African night was striking up, the screeching and hooting and chirping and rustling of a thousand night birds and insects.

I found myself eventually back at the site of the demolished pioneer memorial. From the Plunkets I had got the story of what had happened to it. Shortly after independence, members of the youth league of the new ruling party, ZANU, had marched on it, armed with picks and sledgehammers and smashed it down. When the manager of the hotel, a white man, tried to intervene, they beat him up.

'Actually,' Lady Plunket had said, 'I thought the pioneer memorial rather ugly myself.'

Back at the hotel I dined on Mulligatawny soup, grilled trout, local cheeses and coffee. I was served by Herman the waiter, with trembling hands. He said he could remember me from when I was ' still a small one'. Herman still wore his maroon fez pulled down over his ears like a balaclava. It no longer sported a black tassel, just an empty hole from which the tassel had once protruded and swung briskly with his stride.

In the morning I went to the cemetery, the old white cemetery, for in the old days death was no bar to segregation. It was much fuller than I remembered, and most of the new entries dated from the late seventies when the war was at its peak here. The Symes, who had been gunned down as they ate their supper, they were here. And Ron Barton, the Silverstream chemist who had been so angry with me for shooting a rare eagle. He was a casualty of war too.

Up on the hill overlooking the cemetery, I saw a new cemetery, overgrown and neglected. It had a faded sign at the gate: *Heroes' Acre*. This was where guerrillas who died in the war had been buried. I pushed through the waist-high grass and there, stacked steeply up the hill, were several dozen graves. No one had been here for months, years perhaps. The graves had rough cement headstones without crosses, without names even. On one of them I noticed a rotting plank. I turned it over, and there amidst the termites and the red ants were carved the words: *UNKNOWN COMRADE*.

Even in death, the black guerrillas were neighbours of those they had fought and killed and those they had been killed by. The Symes and the Ron Bartons next to the unknown comrades. All buried in this hill at the entrance to Chimanimani. I looked up and noticed the school, peeping out from between the gum-trees across the valley. And I realized that the cemeteries, both of them, were actually on the side of Green Mount, the hill I had gazed across at when I was a boy. The hill I had thought was just the sort of hill upon which Christ would have been crucified. *A green hill far away, outside the city wall, where our dear Lord was crucified, he died to save us all.*

I left Chimanimani and set off up the valley, past *tokalosh* corner, where I muttered our old prayer, and up over Skyline Junction, to Silverstream. It looked small and tumbledown and I couldn't bear to stop, so I just kept on going, up over the Italian prisoners-of-war road to the Chipinga turn-off. The Willemses' house, the one built in the shape of an ox wagon as an eccentric homage to the pioneers, that was still there.

At the bottom of the Willemses' drive stood Moodie's Rest, where Thomas Moodie, leader of the Gazaland pioneers, was buried, that was still there too, untouched by mobs with picks and hammers. There inside its little enclosure was a stark iron cross marking Moodie's grave. The inscription said: *For Queen and Empire. T. Moodie. Pioneer. 1893.* Underneath was a quote from the book of Timothy: *I have fought the good fight, I have finished the course.*

When I got back to the car there was a middle-aged black man standing there, asking for a lift back up to Chimanimani. We drove along in silence for a while and then I said, 'Do you live in Chimanimani, then?'

'Yes, sah, I am a forester, I am working at Charleswood,' he said.

'Tell me something, you know the old pioneer memorial in the middle of the village square—'

'Oh yes,' he interrupted, 'it was the one broken down by the party youth league.'

'Yes, well, why do you think that one was broken down and this one here, Moodie's Rest, which is much bigger, is allowed to stand?'

'Oh that is easy,' he laughed. 'The statue in Chimanimani, it had no dead people underneath, so it can be broken, but this one here, there is dead *mukiwa* buried there, so we cannot break it, otherwise their spirits will become angry and take revenge.'

He thought for a minute, looking out the window at the rolling, fertile countryside going by. 'If you want your monuments to be safe here,' he advised, 'you should always build them on the graves of your ancestors, then we will never touch them.'

I dropped him off at Skyline Junction and headed back towards Umtali, past the seminary, past Sir Hugo's old farm, past the spot where oom Piet was murdered, over the Umvumvumvu river, past Mutambara where Washington Matikiti, the Pumpkin guerrilla leader, had taken Lady Plunket's best Wedgwood china. Finally I stopped and looked for the last time back over the Chimanimanis. At the roadside a couple of oxen were ploughing up the rich red earth, a black man in blue overalls and an old felt hat steering the plough. When he got near me, he stopped and greeted me in Shona. I told him that I used to live here and that I was back to visit for the first time in many years.

'This land, I think it used to belong to Mr Heynes,' I said.

'That's right,' he said. 'Now it is all resettlement area here for black farmers.' We chatted for a while about land shortage and rain shortage and fertilizer shortage and money shortage.

'Have you always been a farmer?' I asked him.

'Yes, except for the war years.'

'What did you do in the war?'

He smiled. 'I was guerrilla, a freedom fighter.'

'Really?' I said, 'How interesting. Where did you, um, operate?'

'Around here,' he said, 'in Melsetter, Cashel, Chipinga, all over. They called me Weekend Moto Moto. That was my *chimurenga* name.'

Moto meant fire.

'Why "Weekend"?' I said.

'Because I always used to do attacks on the weekend when the Europeans were trying relax,' he grinned.

'Was it hard for you in the war?' I asked.

'Ah, yes. Too, too hard. I was even shot by soldiers from the helicopter.' He shrugged his shoulders out of his old overall and there diagonally across his back was a series of round scars. 'Five bullets,' he said proudly, 'but still I didn't die. I am too strong for that.'

His son arrived to take over the ploughing and I gave Weekend a lift back to his kraal nearby. I dropped him off at his front gate, which was in fact a very old car door, on which he had painted in white the motto: *Your hands are your best friend.*

He stood there at the old car door, waving me goodbye, wide straight-armed waves. I watched him in my rear-view mirror and he was still there, Weekend Moto Moto, waving hard, when I finally crested the hill and disappeared from sight.

When I got back to Harare, I did something I ought to have done at the outset – I visited my sister's grave out at Warren Hills. The cemetery was nearly surrounded now by a huge new African township called Warren Park which threatened to overtake it. On the hill overlooking the cemetery was Heroes' Acre with its fierce frieze. By the roadside at the entrance to the cemetery an impromptu market had grown up, stalls selling mangos and oranges, souvenirs and groundnuts. The cemetery itself still seemed fairly orderly and once again I traversed the walls looking for Jain's plaque. The old msasa trees still groaned in the wind but now they had been colonized by an aggressive troupe of vervet monkeys, which barked and chattered whenever you passed beneath them. As I tried to find the grave, I noticed that there were now only blank squares of concrete in place of many of the brass plaques. Maybe the ashes had been removed by relatives, I thought.

Finally I saw the old gardener and I recognized him as the one I had failed to tip all those years ago. He was still wearing his faded green overall and he still had his floppy hat. I told him I was having trouble finding a grave and, after hearing the date of death, he led me across the cemetery. As we walked I asked him what had happened to all the missing plaques.

'They are being stolen,' he said. 'The *tsotsis* come from the township and break them off. Then they take them home and melt them down and sell them. It is brass you know. Worth much money.'

When we got there, I was relieved to find that Jain's plaque and those of her two companions, Neville and Mark, were all still in place. And this time I made sure to tip the gardener.

I had one last place to visit before I was ready to leave: back to Filabusi to make my peace with Chief Maduna. My part in his arrest was something that troubled me most about my war. His look of sorrowful reproach still came clearly back to me across the years. It had shamed me then, and now I wanted to apologize to him – admittedly more for my own benefit than his.

Maduna wasn't on the phone so I made arrangements with the District Administrator, who sent one of his messengers to tell the chief to expect a visitor. On this rather tentative arrangement I flew to Bulawayo and drove down to Avoca. The remains of the base were still there, great red earth ramparts and sandbags and empty machine-gun posts. Next to it, cut off by the defences, the fever tree and the little dam, almost empty now with the drought.

Chief Maduna's kraal looked just the same, although a big new house was under construction behind the little three-roomed one. Maduna also looked the same, he still had his navy blazer with the tarnished brass buttons. He clearly didn't recognize me – it was all such a long time ago. And I was tempted to leave it at that. He was obviously thriving now, he was a member of the National Assembly, and he sat on a special committee looking at the future of land reform.

'When I came back to Godlwayo, in 1980, at independence, ten cows were slaughtered in my honour here,' he said proudly. 'Ten voluntary, *donated* cows, to celebrate my return.'

Maduna handed me a two-page typed document, dog-eared and much folded and refolded. It was entitled *The Political History of My Life – Chief Vezi Maduna Mafu*, and it contained a chronology of his political fortunes: arrests, years spent in detention, and then his various posts after independence. He reeled off all the prisons he had been in, 'Filabusi, Gwanda, Colleen Bawn, Wha Wha, Ross Camp, Khami, Zvishavane . . .' He smiled and his eyes twinkled as he recalled them – this was his nationalist pedigree after all, a matter of considerable pride.

After a while he turned to me and asked, 'How do you know this place so well?'

'I used to be here, in the war,' I said. 'I was in the police during my national service here.'

A look of recognition swept over his face. 'You were with the member-in-charge when they arrested me!' he said.

I nodded.

'Hah! He gave a delighted laugh and clapped me on the shoulder. 'Hah!' he laughed again, and shook my hand.

Here we were sitting up on his little verandah drinking warm Cokes again, after all these years, reminiscing about the area, about the war.

'Let us go and see the Business Centre,' he said. 'It has grown much since your time.' So I drove him down the road to Avoca. It had grown slightly since my day, a few more stores, a co-operative bakery. As we walked through, everyone bowed their heads and solemnly greeted the chief. I had been asking about the war so Maduna took me to Jabulani Cycle Repair shop, and introduced me to the owner. 'This one remembers it, he stayed throughout.'

The old man behind the counter nodded. Hanging above him from the ceiling were dozens of cycle parts.

'Oh yes, terrible things happened, many people died on all sides,' he said. 'And land mines, ah, ah, ah. There were many land mines. The Ngenga Ngenga bus was blown up and many people were killed and injured. You can still see them around here in wheelchairs and on crutches, those that lost their legs.'

A young girl returned with Cokes for us. When she got to the door she went down on her knees. She lowered her head and, with her eyes downcast, she crawled across the floor to the chief, proffering a bottle.

'We had many soldiers here,' Mr Jubulani, the cycle repairman continued, 'from the Police Ground Coverage, from the Police Anti-Terrorist Unit, from the Rhodesian African Rifles, even from the Rhodesian Light Infantry . . . they were terrible. And later they came with helicopters too, shooting with machine guns from the sky, *daka-daka-daka-daka* . . .' He made as if to spray the store with an imaginary machine gun.

Maduna and I made our way back to his kraal. All around us the maize was withering in the fields – once again Godlwayo was in the grip of a terrible drought. It was a stunningly hot day, that heat that I remembered so well, the heat that radiates up off the ground at you, as well as down from the sun. The little eddies of dust twirled up around us as the wind tugged irritably at the ground.

When we got back to the kraal, Maduna turned to me and said, 'Would you like to see the graves of my parents?' We went over to the great concrete graves and he told me the story of his grandfather, Lobengula's general, all over again. How he was a great warrior during the Matabele rebellion, and how the white witness at his trial had been struck dead by lightning before he could give his evidence, evidence that would certainly have sent the old chief to the gallows.

A group of elderly men approached, took their hats off and greeted the chief, and he spoke to them for a few minutes. 'These are my rain pilgrims, the interceders,' he told me. 'They have just come back from Injelele Mountain in the Matopos, where they have been making the annual sacrifice to the rain spirit.'

'And do they say it will rain?' I asked him.

'Yes. They say now is the time.'

We made our farewells and I drove away, up through the parched reserve, north-west towards the distant tar road. And as I drove the sky darkened. On the grey horizon ahead a rainstorm was approaching. It looked like Maduna's rain interceders were right.

I finally reached the tar road and turned left towards Bulawayo, and as I picked up speed I suddenly recognized where I was. If I remembered correctly, you turned right off the main road on to the Epoch Mine road, and left down a short track to the Filabusi memorial, the monument erected to the memory of the white troopers killed by Maduna's grandfather and his warriors. There was no longer a signpost, but this was definitely the place. I turned off and drove slowly down the Epoch Mine road. But the bush was much thicker than I remembered and I couldn't find the memorial. After five miles I turned the car around and drove slowly back towards the main road.

It was getting late now and I would have to return to Bulawayo without seeing the memorial. I stopped the car and walked a little way into the bush to take a piss and, as I did, I noticed that I was at the foot of a small pyramid-shaped hill that seemed familiar. I followed the contour of the hill down and there in front of me, completely overgrown and invisible from the mine road, I saw the Filabusi memorial. I was actually standing just a few yards from it.

Clearly no one had visited it for years. I pulled aside the

creepers and the saplings and pushed my way into the little enclosure. The fifteen-foot granite obelisk glowed pinkly like Cotswold stone in the late-afternoon sun. On the four faces of the obelisk were inscribed the thirty-five names of the troopers killed by Maduna's grandfather. Above the names there was no patriotic message, simply the words *In Memoriam 1896*. The base was garlanded with a faintly Art-Deco border of abstract hieroglyphic motifs. To the side was a little brass plaque, greenly corroded with neglect, which proclaimed that the monument had been erected by the Rhodesian Memorial Fund.

The wind was freshening in advance of the approaching storm, and the bush rustled and creaked around me. In the distance baboon barked to each other. The rain was upon us now, fat individual drops splattering down. You could smell the dust as they hit the ground. I was soon soaked and it felt glorious. I busied myself removing the vines from the monument as best I could, and trampling down the bush at its foot. As I cleared the list of names I noticed that, a hundred years on, the memorial was still unfinished. Two of the troopers, Johnston and Koch, were without Christian names. There was just a gap where their Christian names should have been. Imagine that, fighting and falling for Queen and country, and then no one can even remember your bloody name.

As I turned to leave, a tremendous shaft of lightning forked violently down into the pyramid hill above me. The air crackled with static and a great wall of thunder shook the bush. I gasped with the surprise of it, and wondered briefly whether Chief Maduna's ancestral spirits were going to strike down another white man before he could bear witness.